# Something TO Think About

## Motivational & Inspirational Anecdotes

# Something TO Think About

Over **1200** entertaining **stories**,
captivating **quotes**, and
memorable **humor** alphabetized
and indexed for easy use.

# Raymond McHenry

## FOREWORD BY ZIG ZIGLER

### HENDRICKSON
#### PUBLISHERS

# *Dedication*

This book is dedicated to the
three greatest blessings
this side of heaven:
My wife, Michelle
My daughter, Meagan
My son, Myles

# TABLE OF CONTENTS

# FOREWORD

*Something to Think About* is a book which offers something for everybody. Those who are discouraged will find examples, illustrations, and stories that will give them encouragement. For those who are without hope, there are countless examples of people whose circumstances were probably worse than theirs and they will figure "if they can, I can, too." For a curious person who wants to know a lot about a lot, here's a virtual encyclopedia of information that will fill the bill. For those who enjoy a good smile or a soft chuckle, there's something here. For those who are story-tellers in life or in the ministry, here is an invaluable resource.

I personally found it fascinating to discover this much information in one publication. When you consider over 1,200 examples, illustrations, and stories, you're talking about an abundance of usable information. Pastors, preachers, Sunday school teachers, speakers, program chairs, masters of ceremonies and people of this ilk will acquire much information from this book. More important, here's a book that will motivate and inspire anyone who reads it.

The neat thing about *Something to Think About* is the fact that its organizational structure will enable you to quickly find just what you're looking for. The index is most useful and will cut down on your search and research time a great deal. It's a fascinating book with a bundle of valuable information.

Any pastor, regardless of church size, who doesn't take full advantage of this encyclopedia of information, is denying the congregation the benefits of an incredible amount of research and work done by someone else. I highly recommend it.

Zig Ziglar
Author, *Over the Top*

# ACKNOWLEDGMENTS

A book of this nature owes a tremendous debt to countless people. Space permits the recognition of but a few of these individuals.

My wife, Michelle, has been a key player in the production of not only this book, but the day-to-day management of the research service *In Other Words . . .* from which these illustrations originated.

My father-in-law, Loyd Fannin, has painstakingly read over each word to assist in the improvement of this manuscript.

My parents, Al and Martha McHenry, instilled within me a love for God and a desire to find spiritual meaning in the daily events of life.

Mr. Zig Ziglar has believed in me and graciously penned the foreword.

The subscribers of *In Other Words . . .* have made this whole endeavor possible.

Gulf Meadows Baptist Church (Houston, Texas) provided our family with ten and a half years of more love, joy, and patience than most pastors are fortunate enough to receive.

Westgate Memorial Baptist Church (Beaumont, Texas) has now embraced and affirmed this ministry of writing while showering our family with overwhelming love.

To all of these, and many more, thank you!

# INTRODUCTION

S everal years ago, the YMCA ran a billboard campaign to promote healthy child care. The ad contained a picture of a newborn baby with the caption, "If only they came with directions." Books can be like babies, and any volume that contains over twelve hundred stories definitely needs some directions. The following information contains "directions" that we hope will assist you in getting the most from this book. It contains five key sections:

1. Motivational Stories is the first section, comprised of 947 stories and quotes.

2. Motivational Humor makes up the second section. It includes 332 jokes and anecdotes.

3. Section three is the Source Index. This section lists the resources from which each illustration was written.

4. The fourth and vital part of this book is the Summary Index. It contains a one-sentence summary of every story, quote, and joke in the book. The Motivational Stories are summarized first; then Motivational Humor is summarized. In the Summary Index, each illustration is referred to by its alphabetical title, not by its numerical footnote.

5. The Master Index is the final section. It contains the alphabetical title of every illustration, plus several key words to assist in cross-referencing and locating information. Every illustration has been given a numerical footnote. The number following each key word is the corresponding numerical footnote.

We hope the information in this book meets the needs and desires that inspired you to make this purchase. May the pages which follow truly motivate you as you seek to reach your full potential for Christ.

Raymond & Michelle McHenry

To obtain more information about the quarterly resource from which these stories originated, write to:

*In Other Words . . .*
6130 Barrington
Beaumont, Texas 77706

# MOTIVATIONAL STORIES

**A Great Awakening** In 1934, Mordecai Ham preached in Charlotte, North Carolina, and a great awakening took place. A farmer was deeply concerned about the meetings, so he invited a group of his Christian friends to come spend a day in prayer at his farm. As they prayed, they felt compelled to ask God to raise up a man from their city to carry the gospel to the ends of the earth. Although they didn't see an immediate answer to their prayer, the great awakening had begun. The farmer's teenage son was converted during the crusade, and that boy has indeed carried the Gospel to the ends of the earth. His name is Billy Graham. Good thing that farmer took time to pray for revival![1]

**Abandonment** It is crudely called "granny-dumping." It refers to the practice of leaving elderly people at the doorsteps of hospitals and then quickly speeding off to leave the nurses and staff with the task of figuring out the person's identity, insurance coverage, and plans for the future. In 1991, newspapers picked up on the story of an eighty-two-year-old man named John Kingery who was dumped by his daughter at an Idaho racetrack. It sounded like a rare and unusual story, but Dr. Robert Anzinger, past president of the American College of Emergency Physicians, estimates that between 100,000 and 200,000 senior adults are dumped at hospitals each year. It looks like the abortion mindset may now have a counterpart for the end of life.[2]

**Abortion** After World War II there arose a great cry because the Allies never bombed the railroad tracks which led to Auschwitz. Although they knew hundreds of thousands of Jews and Slovaks were being transported along these tracks to death camps, the Allied forces never stopped the process with their bombs. The tracks which lead to our legalized abortion clinics are known to even the casual observer. Like the Allies of World War II, we have the power to stop the killing. The question is, will we? [3]

**Abortion** It seems that all of the people who favor abortion have already been born.[4]

**Abortion** Statistics reveal that 96 percent of the women who have had an abortion later say abortion is the taking of a human life.[5]

**Abortion** The Alan Guttmacher Institute (the research arm of Planned Parenthood) has quietly uncovered the fact that over 95 percent of the abortions in America are done for reasons of convenience, not because of incest, rape, physical abnormalities, or threatened health of the mother. C. Everett Koop, M.D., formerly the Surgeon General, states that during his more than thirty-five years of practicing medicine, "Never once did a case come across my practice where abortion was necessary to save a mother's life." In all the wars in which our country has participated, 1,160,722 Americans have been killed. Since the 1973 ruling on *Roe* v *Wade*, more than twenty-five times that number have been exterminated through abortion.[6]

**Abstinence** Abstinence is regaining ground, but there are many who still laugh at the concept. Those who are still snickering should read an important report from Atlanta. Marion Howard is a professor of obstetrics and gynecology at Emory University. Dr. Howard asked one thousand teenage girls in Atlanta what they wanted to learn in sex education. Eighty-four percent answered, "How to say no without hurting the other person's feelings." Some feel sex education only involves teaching kids how to have *safe* sex. Dr. Howard's report indicates a majority of teenage girls are interested in learning how to have *no* sex.[7]

**Abundant Life** Friedrich Nietzsche (1844–1900) was a German philosopher who said, "His disciples will have to look more saved if I am to believe in their Savior." [8]

**Abundant Living** "Enjoy life. This is not a dress rehearsal." This sign hangs in the office of Betty Blackerby, district manager of American Family Life Assurance Co. in Anderson, South Carolina. It is a great reminder that today is the best day to seize the moment and live life to the fullest. Opening Night isn't tomorrow; it's today![9]

**Acceptance** In 1984, Mark Lenzi had his whole life planned out for him. The sixteen-year-old from Virginia was supposed to become a college and Olympic wrestler, or so his dad thought. But after watching Greg Louganis dive in the 1984 Olympics, Lenzi decided he wanted to try diving for gold. His father thought it was a ridiculous idea. Mark was a very tough wrestler and his future success was on the mat, not in the pool. Mark disagreed and started to pursue diving. He and his dad feuded over the direction of his life. Finally, in 1986, Mark left home for nearly a month. Unacceptance existed on both sides. Eventually, the Lenzis worked it out. "I guess it goes to show that sometimes we parents who think we know what's best for our kids are sometimes very, very wrong," said Bill Lenzi. Mark also learned to accept his dad's viewpoint, and it showed as he continually waved and smiled to his parents during his performances on the three-meter springboard in Barcelona. Had the two men not been more understanding and accepting of each other, Mark may have never won the Olympic gold medal in Men's Diving.[10]

**Accidental Church** On January 28, 1992, Southern Baptist missionary Rob Moor and Tanzanian pastor Sostenes Karoli were involved in a head-on crash. Sixty miles from their homes in Bukoba, Tanzania, they crashed into a vehicle carrying five passengers. Although neither Moor or Karoli were seriously hurt, all five in the other car were injured. One passenger, whom they feared would die, was rushed to a hospital and received medical treatment that saved his life. Karoli and Moor led in prayer for all those in the accident and praised God that nobody died. The people who gathered at the scene were intrigued by what they saw, so the two men began passing out tracts and sharing their faith. Moor eventually caught a ride in to Bukoba, and Karoli waited two days for a truck to take both him and the wrecked car back home to Bukoba.

During that forty-eight-hour wait, Karoli was joined by two Baptist laymen and a fellow Tanzanian pastor who had learned of the accident. Together these men led fourteen people to Christ, and a new church was established within two weeks after the crash. The new church is named Kanisa la Ajali—Swahili for Accident Baptist Church. Given the chance, God can bring triumph out of tragedy.[11]

**Accomplishments** Helen Keller said, "I long to accomplish a great and noble task, but it is my chief duty to accomplish small tasks as if they were great and noble." It's easy to lose sight of the important duties in life when we are pursuing things that we think will make us important.[12]

**Accountability** George Bernard Shaw believed we should all be obliged to appear before a board every five years and justify our existence.[13]

**Achievement** The tombstone of Annie Armstrong appropriately summarizes her life. It simply reads, "She hath done what she could." That's a worthy goal for us all.[14]

**Acquisitions** William Randolph Hearst was a very wealthy newspaper publisher who had an incredible collection of art. The Hearst mansion in northern California is a testament to his insatiable desire for artistic treasures. On one occasion he learned of some artwork he was determined to obtain. He sent his agent abroad to search for the treasure. After months of investigating, the agent reported that the treasure had been found. To further sweeten the find, Hearst learned that the relic wouldn't cost him a dime. He already owned it. The rediscovered piece was in Hearst's warehouse with many other treasures that had likewise never been uncrated. The desire for acquiring more can sometimes blind us from what we already possess.[15]

**Acres of Diamonds** In the mid-1800s, Dr. Russell Conwell dedicated his life to the formation of a college for poor but deserving young people. Almost single-handedly he raised several million dollars, with which he established Temple University. In each of his more than six thousand fundraising lectures throughout the country, he told a true story that deeply affected his listeners. It was called "Acres of Diamonds." The plot starts with an African farmer who had heard tales of others making millions by discovering diamond mines. He was so excited about the possibilities which lay ahead that he sold his farm and used the money to traipse across the African continent in search of the valuable gems. Unfortunately for him, he never found his fortune and died a despondent and dejected man. Meanwhile, the man who purchased the farm from this wealth-seeking African discovered a beautiful rock while crossing one of the streams on his newly-acquired property. He placed it upon the fireplace mantel because of its curious beauty. Several weeks later a visitor noticed the rock and nearly fainted. The farmer thought it was just an impressive clump of crystal. As it turned out, it was one of the largest diamonds ever discovered and it came from a creek full of many more large and precious stones. Dr. Conwell concluded his story by stating that the farm turned out to be one of the most productive diamond mines on the entire African continent. We need not waste our lives looking elsewhere for "better opportunities." We already own the most valuable resources available, in that the Creator of diamonds has said he is polishing us into the image of Christ. (See Romans 8:29 and Philippians 1:6.)[16]

**Adversity** Biologists recognize a principle at work among plants and animals. This natural wonder is called "the adversity principle." As strange as it seems, habitual well-being is not advantageous to a species. An existence without challenge takes its toll on virtually every living thing. This may explain the astonishing results of a recent survey where 87 percent of the people surveyed said "a painful event (death, illness, breakup, divorce, etc.) caused them to find a more positive meaning in life." Jesus said, "'In the world you will have adversity, but be of good cheer, I have overcome the world'" (John 16:33). Ironically, adversity can be therapeutic.[17]

**Adversity** In 1987, Gary Richmond published a book titled *A View from the Zoo*. Illustrations from the animal world fill the pages with spiritual truths. The birth of a giraffe gives insight to life's trials and hardships. When a calf is born, he falls ten feet and lands on his back. The mother momentarily hovers over the newborn before kicking the baby head over heels. If the calf doesn't get up, he gets another good kick. She repeats this process to stimulate his efforts. Finally, when the little giraffe gets up on his wobbly legs, the mother kicks him off his feet again. To an outsider such behavior seems cruel. To the mother it is an expression of love. This first lesson in life helps the newborn quickly develop the skills needed to move rapidly with the herd when predators are near. Sometimes we feel as though God has no sooner gotten us on our feet when he turns around and knocks us down. The next time that happens, think about the newborn giraffe. God may simply be strengthening you for your own protection in the future.[18]

**Adversity** In 1993, Charles Colson received the Templeton Prize for Progress in Religion. The $1 million prize is the largest prize for achievement in any field. It is ranked higher than the Nobel prizes in such fields as science and literature, in the belief that religion is more important. Colson, having served seven months in prison for obstructing justice in the Watergate cover-up, was known as the scandal's "hatchet man." His conversion later led to the founding of Prison Fellowship in 1976. In response to this award, Colson said, "Out of tragedy and adversity come great blessings. I shudder to think of what I would have been if I had not gone to prison." Adversity can be God's refining fire.[19]

**Adversity** Norman Vincent Peale loved to talk about success. He was always learning from the successes of others. Dr. Peale once asked J. C. Penney, "In one sentence of as few words as possible, tell me the secret of your outstanding success in life, both as a businessman and an outstanding Christian." Without hesitation Penney replied, "Here's the answer in four words: 'Adversity and Jesus Christ.'" Penney then explained how his father, an impoverished preacher in the hills of Missouri, left a will that simply said, "I bequeath you some honest debts, manly character, and faith in the Lord Jesus Christ." Penney's world was filled with disappointments. Yet, he allowed Jesus Christ to use that adversity as an instrument for success. Adversity usually appears to be a threatening foe, but through Christ it can become an endowing friend.[20]

**Advertising Overload** On an average day in America, twenty-nine new products are introduced, each person is exposed to eighteen hundred commercial messages, and $700 million is spent on advertising. With such a barrage of messages bombarding American people, it is imperative that we make the gospel of Jesus Christ crystal clear. We don't want anybody to miss the most important message of all![21]

**Advertising** A study by the Centers for Disease Control found that teenage smokers prefer the most heavily-advertised brands of cigarettes. The three biggest advertisers, Marlboro, Newport and Camel, accounted for 80 percent of teen consumption. Despite the fact that 19.8 percent of all deaths in American men relate to smoking, the slick ads attract teenagers. The issue of smoking aside, this shows the persuasive might of ads. What a difference we could make in the lives of our youth if they saw more "living billboards" advertising the good news of Christ. Matthew 5:16 calls for greater publicity.[22]

**Advice** A collection of sayings to save for the right moment:
- Life is short. Eat dessert first.
- One today is worth two tomorrows.
- The easiest way to find an item you've lost is to buy a replacement.

- Never wrestle a pig. You both get dirty, and he enjoys it.
- Nostalgia is life in the past lane.
- Out of the mouths of babes come things parents never should have said.[23]

**Affairs** The grass on the other side of the fence may start off green, but it usually ends up brown. Seventy-five to 85 percent of all men who have had an affair end up staying with or returning to their wives. Of those who do divorce, only 15 percent marry the woman with whom they had the marriage-wrecking affair. Affairs are destructive and do not deliver what they seem to promise.[24]

**Affirmation** When dealing with people it is wise to remember the Triple A Principle. Everyone feels better and does better when you give Attention, Affirmation, and Appreciation. Triple A usually stands for good service, and that's exactly what you get when you treat people with affirming respect.[25]

**Aging** At age twenty-six, Pat Moore performed an unbelievable experiment. An industrial designer, Moore wanted a better understanding of senior adults, so for three years she frequently disguised herself as an eighty-five-year-old woman. From 1979 to 1981, she utilized the skills of a professional makeup artist and visited 116 cities throughout fourteen states and two Canadian provinces in her elderly persona. From her experience, Moore estimates that one of every 25 senior adults is abused, with most victims being 75 or older. She was impressed with the compassion and care she received from senior adults when she was in character, but she received harsh treatment from younger generations. Unfortunately, society has widely accepted a practice called "social dismissal" of the elderly, poignantly illustrated in what Moore classifies as "one of the most touching letters I've ever read." The letter came from a nurse who works in a geriatric ward at Ashludie Hospital in Yorkshire, England. This nurse found the following poem in the belongings of an elderly patient, who wrote it before she died:

What do you see, nurses, what do you see?
Are you thinking when you are looking at me
A crabby old woman, not very wise
Uncertain of habit, with faraway eyes
Who dribbles her food and makes no reply,
When you say in a loud voice, "I do wish you'd try";
Who seems not to notice the things that you do,
And forever is losing a stocking or shoe?
Who uninteresting or not, lets you do as you will
With bathing and feeding the long day to fill?
Is that what you're thinking, is that what you see?
Then open your eyes, nurse, you're not looking at me.
I'll tell you who I am as I sit here so still,
As I rise at your bidding, as I eat at your will;
I'm a small child of ten with a father and mother,
Brothers and sisters who love one another.
A young girl of sixteen with wings on her feet,
Dreaming that soon now a lover she'll meet.
A bride soon at twenty, my heart gives a leap,
Remembering the vows I promised to keep.
At twenty-five now I have young of my own
Who need me to build a secure, happy home.
A woman of thirty my young now grow fast,
Bound to each other with ties that should last.
At forty my young sons have grown and are gone,
But my man's beside me to see I don't mourn.
At fifty once more babies play at my knee,
Again we know children, my loved one and me.
Dark days are upon me, my husband is dead.
I look at the future—I shudder with dread.
For my young are all rearing young of their own,
And I think of the years and the love that I've known.
I'm an old woman now, and nature is cruel;
'Tis her jest to make old people look like a fool.
The body it crumbles, grace and vigor depart,

There is now a stone where I once had a heart.
But inside this old carcass a young girl still dwells,
And now and again my battered heart swells.
I remember the joys, I remember the pain,
And I'm loving and living life over again.
I think of the years all too few, gone too fast;
And accept the stark fact that nothing can last.
So open your eyes, nurses—open and see,
Not a crabby old woman. *Look closer at me!*[26]

**Aging** You know you're getting older when:
- most of your dreams are reruns
- you sit down in a rocking chair and you can't get it started
- your mind makes commitments your body can't keep
- the little gray-haired lady you help across the street is your wife
- everything hurts, and what doesn't hurt, doesn't work
- you sink your teeth into a juicy steak and they stay there
- you watch a pretty girl go by, and your pacemaker makes the garage door open.[27]

**Aging** Those who adhere to America's love of youth should not dismiss older folks too quickly, as these statistics indicate:
- People age sixty-five and older control about 80 percent of the wealth in America.
- By the year 2009, one out of three Americans will be over fifty. The percentage of senior citizens living at or under the poverty level has decreased from about 25 percent in the early 1970s to the current level of just about 12 percent.
- The fifty-plus age group represents 80 percent of all U.S. travel dollars.[27]

**AIDS** After Earvin "Magic" Johnson announced he had AIDS, the following statistics were released from a national survey. They reveal the way many Americans view AIDS. Three-fourths of those interviewed said they had not changed their sexual behavior for fear of AIDS. Forty-nine percent said the principle AIDS prevention message for young people should be education in safe sex. Forty-five percent felt abstinence is the message young people need. In response to Magic Johnson's situation, 51 percent said he "should have known better and is now paying the price," while 39 percent felt he "is an unfortunate victim of chance." [28]

**Alcohol** *An Effective Solvent* was written to describe the dramatic effects of alcohol: "Alcohol is a product of amazing versatility. It will remove stains from designer clothes. It will also remove clothes off your back. If by chance it is used in sufficient quantity, alcohol will remove furniture from the home, rugs from the floor, food from the table, lining from the stomach, vision from the eyes, and judgment from the mind. Alcohol will also remove good reputations, good jobs, good friends, happiness from children's hearts, sanity, freedom, spouses, relationships, man's ability to adjust and live with his fellow man and even life itself. As a remover of things, alcohol has no equal." [29]

**Alcohol** In our world of ever-increasing crime, you might be surprised to know the number one reason for arrests in the United States is "Driving Under the Influence." Each year more Americans are arrested for that reason than any other. Larceny and theft generated the second highest volume of arrests, while drug abuse violations came in third.[30]

**Alcoholic Learning Curve** College campuses are often known for the free-flowing beer. The average college student drinks 34 gallons of alcoholic beverages a year. A new report from Columbia University's Center on Addiction and Substance Abuse revealed two interesting trends: (1) freshmen consume the most alcohol per week, sophomores are next, juniors rank third, and seniors consume the least alcohol per week; (2) grade point averages showed the same hierarchy of ranking: A students drink the least, B students rank second, C students consume the second most alcohol per week, and D or F students down the most. Does this mean the more educated you become, the less you use alcohol? There appears to be a learning curve for alcohol consumption.[31]

**Ambition** In 1876, Dr. William Clark was invited to take up the position of Vice Principal at the newly established Sapporo Agricultural College (now part of Hokkaido University). He had faithfully served as President of Massachusetts Agricultural College and was well loved by the students. As he was about to ride off for his new place of service, he turned in his saddle and shouted, "Boys, be ambitious!" Jesus' words in Acts 1:8 sound very similar and are desperately needed in a time when America houses 170 million lost people.[32]

**Ambition** "Women who seek to be equal with men lack ambition." —*Timothy Leary* [33]

**American Men** The following indicators reveal some disheartening truths about American men:
- Percentage of births outside of marriage: 1960, 5.3%; 1970,10.7%; 1980, 18.4%; 1990, 28.0%
- Number of divorced males per 1,000 married males: 1960, 27.4; 1970, 33.3; 1980, 76.2; 1990, 112.5
- Number of prisoners per 1,000 males: 1960, 23.0; 1970, 19.1; 1980, 27.4; 1990, 57.4 [34]

**Anger** Although Alexander the Great conquered the known world, he couldn't conquer his own temper. On one occasion, Cletus, a childhood friend and a general in Alexander's army, became drunk and insulted the leader in front of his men. Alexander became enraged and hurled a spear at Cletus, intending merely to scare him. Instead, the spear killed Alexander's life-long friend. Remorse engulfed Alexander as he assessed the destruction of his uncontrollable anger. If we don't control our anger, it will control us! (See James 1:20.)[35]

**Anger** In 1870, B. H. Carroll, founder of Southwestern Seminary and a stalwart among Texas Baptists, began his pastorate at the First Baptist Church of Waco, Texas. During that time, Carroll told his visiting brother, J. M., about his concern regarding his sons' tendency to fight. The conversation was focused on Carroll's boys when the two older Carrolls boarded a street car. B. H. placed his ticket in the box, but it was immediately covered by another ticket. The driver then accused Carroll of not paying. An argument ensued, and the driver tried to flee from the car. The large pastor was a former Texas Ranger. He grabbed the driver and refused to let him go until he apologized. After the incident, the two Carroll brothers sat down. J. M. could hardly contain his laughter. B. H. Carroll then broke the awkward silence by confessing, "I think I can see where my boys got some of their fighting proclivities."[36]

**Anger** "It's wise to remember that anger is just one letter short of danger." —*Sam Ewing*[37]

**Anger** The Academy Award-winning movie *Forrest Gump* has been viewed by millions of Americans. Most people remember "life is like a box of choklits," but there is another line worth noting. This particular scene has one of the central characters, Jenny, returning to her old home after her father has died. The old farm house is dilapidated and abandoned. As she reflects on the sexual abuse that she endured as a child, she is overcome by rage and begins throwing rocks at the house. The photography is powerful as it shows her rapidly reaching for rocks and then violently throwing them at the house. Jenny finally falls to the ground in exhaustion and the scene closes with Forrest Gump sympathizing, "Sometimes there just aren't enough rocks." Many of us struggle with anger. It can stem from a variety of reasons, and some anger seems very justifiable. Yet, unresolved anger leaves us reaching and crying out for more rocks. The rage is never satisfied, and contentment is never found. Through the power of Christ we can find the strength to lay down rocks of anger rather than needing to reach for more.[38]

**Answered Prayer** During a morning worship service, Ellen noticed a nice looking man sitting by himself on the back pew. As a single woman she had a vested interest in meeting him. She approached him with an extended hand and said, "Hi. I'm Ellen." He took one look at her and bolted out the door without saying a word. The following Sunday he returned to church and made this apology: "My name is Bob Price, and I owe you an apology for my rude behavior last Sunday. You see, my deceased wife's name was Ellen, and I had been praying, 'Dear God, please send me another Ellen.' When you approached me and said, 'Hi. I'm Ellen,' I lost it." Bob and Ellen have now been married twelve years and are both very thankful for the way God answered Bob's prayer.[39]

**Anxiety** I enjoyed finding these salient comments on anxiety:
- Dr. Robert Eliot is a cardiologist from Nebraska. He has two rules for managing stress and worry: (1) Don't sweat the small stuff, and (2) It's all small stuff.
- Dr. Peter Marshall, the late Chaplain of the United States Senate, once opened the Senate with this prayer: "Help us to do our very best this day and be content with today's troubles, so that we shall not borrow the troubles of tomorrow. Save us from the sin of worrying, lest ulcers be the badge of our lack of faith."
- Dr. Billy Graham says, "Anxiety is the natural result when our hopes are centered on anything short of God and his will for us."
- Dr. Charles Mayo observes, "Worry affects the circulation, the heart, the glands, the whole nervous system. I have never known a man who died from overwork, but many who died from doubt."
- Oswald Chambers writes, "All worry is caused by calculating without God."[40]

**Apples of Gold** In a chapter on Misunderstanding, Charles Swindoll writes about a woman who committed suicide. She left an unfinished note that simply read, "They said . . ." She never completed her final thought, but whatever "they said" was painful enough for her to extinguish her own life. We say that "words can be deadly" and indeed, sometimes they are, literally. "A word aptly spoken is like apples of gold in settings of silver" (Prov. 25:11).[41]

**Aptitude vs. Attitude** Most people think top scholars have a leg up on life. A recent study shows otherwise. Karen Arnold, an assistant professor of education at Boston College, and Terry Denny, a professor emeritus at the University of Illinois, followed eighty-one valedictorians and salutatorians for ten years. They all graduated in 1981 from private and public schools in Illinois. To the surprise of these researchers, most of their scholars have achieved only average success in the real world. Three-fourths of this group went on to excel in college and earn academic honors, but few have risen above average success in the workplace. The success of ministry depends more on one's attitude than one's aptitude. It's easy to think God only uses the brilliant Christians who can teach the Bible or answer questions in Sunday School, but in reality, a willing heart is far more useful than a saturated mind.[42]

**Arguing** In a construction company there was a foreman who always worked hard and was very conscientious, but he never received a promotion. A younger employee noticed this apparent breach of justice after working under the man for several years. He bravely asked his foreman why management treated him so unfairly in the area of advancement. The wiser and more mature foreman explained, "Many years ago I had an argument with my supervisor . . . and I won." Winning an argument can have very grave consequences.[43]

**Armageddon** Most people think of Armageddon as a massive war where the forces of Satan unleash their fury against Christ. In reality, there is no war—only Christ destroying his enemies (Rev. 19:19–21). An illustration from boxing puts it in perspective. On April 6 and 7, 1893, the longest boxing match with gloves took place between Jack Burke and Andy Bowen. They fought for 7 hours 19 minutes (9:15 P.M. to 4:34 A.M.) in New Orleans. After the 110th round, the fight was ruled "no contest" when both fighters were unable to continue. The longest bare knuckle fight took place in Australia on December 3, 1855. James Kelly and Jack Smith beat on each other for 6 hours 15 minutes. Many think this is the picture of Armageddon. But it is more accurately portrayed by the following two fights. On September 23, 1946, the quickest knock-out ever was scored: Al Couture took down his opponent, Ralph Walton, in under eleven seconds. The shortest fight took place in Minnesota on November 4, 1947: Mike Collins floored Pat Brownson with the first punch and the contest was stopped, without a count, four seconds after the bell. The war of Armageddon will have a lot of pre-game hype, but it will be over before it begins.[44]

**Assumptions** Charles Swindoll tells of a woman forced to spend layover time in an airport. During the layover she became hungry. Knowing she would receive a full meal on the next flight, she bought a small package of cookies to tide her over. Sitting at a table in the snack bar area, she pulled out her newspaper. After a few minutes of reading, she heard the crinkling of plastic. She lowered her newspaper to find a stranger dressed in a fine suit eating the cookies. Aghast at what he was doing, she frowned at him and pulled the cookies to her side of the table. Minutes later he was at the cookies again. She repeated her silent assertiveness. Soon there was only one cookie left. As she glared at him, he broke the last cookie in half, slid her the remnant and walked off with the final cookie in his mouth. She fumed until her flight was called. At the ticket counter she reached in to her purse for the boarding pass and found the package of cookies she had purchased earlier—still unopened. Somewhere in that airport a businessman was telling his colleagues about the unusual woman who ate his cookies.[45]

**Atheistic Concession** Madalyn Murray O'Hair said in her latter years, "When I see the March for Jesus [which is only four years old] in Austin, Texas, and they have 20,000 out in the street; and when we met for our convention, we got 300 or 400 participants —you can't have that." The famous atheist went on to concede that she believes the window for atheism has closed.[46]

**Atonement** Capital punishment is a controversial issue. Both sides of the argument cry out with ever increasing fervor. Regardless of which view you hold, there is one common ground. When a convict is strapped to a gurney, an electric chair, or the porous gas chamber seat, everyone recognizes that a heinous crime has been committed. Capital punishment is never administered to marginal offenders of the law. The cross of Jesus Christ should stir the same emotions that are triggered by capital punishment. We should be reminded of the severity of our sin. Jesus didn't die because we were marginal offenders of God's law. He died because we have committed the most serious offense of all: rebellion against God. It's a crime worthy of death, but thankfully, Jesus took our place on the hill of execution.[47]

**Atonement** Dr. Claude Barlow was a medical missionary to Shaohsing, China, in the early part of this century. During his ministry there, a strange disease began killing people. He couldn't find a remedy. In search of a cure, he filled his notebook with observations of the peculiarities he had witnessed in hundreds of cases. Then, with a small vial of the germs, he sailed for the United States. Just before he arrived, he injected himself with the deadly disease and hurried to his alma mater, Johns Hopkins University Hospital. He had become very sick and now depended on his former professors to find a cure. They were able to save his life and send him back to China with a cure for this dreaded disease. In the process, a multitude of lives was spared. In the midst of our epidemic called sin, Jesus went to the cross and injected himself with our deadly disease. He then committed himself to the Father's care and returned on Easter morning with the cure. Praise God! Death is no longer our destiny.[48]

**Audio/Visual Faith** How many times has this same testimony been shared: "The Lord has given me such peace in knowing that I don't have to tell people about Christ. I can just be a witness with my life"? Dr. Rick Warren counters this argument with a call for all Christians to be audio/visual believers. Few people are interested in watching television when the audio or visual features are not working. Likewise, Christians need to give the both/and of the Gospel—a verbal witness that accompanies a Christian lifestyle.[49]

**Authority** Former British Prime Minister Margaret Thatcher said, "Being powerful is like being a lady—if you have to tell people you are, you aren't." If you have to tell people you are Christ-like, maybe you aren't as Christ-like as you think.[50]

**Authority** From *Proceedings,* the magazine of the Naval Institute, Stephen Covey captured a great truth about authority. While on maneuvers, a battleship lookout noted a light in the dark, foggy night. After noting the light's coordinates, the captain recognized his ship was on a collision course with the other vessel. The captain instructed, "Signal the ship: We are on a collision course, advise you change course 20 degrees." The return signal countered, "Advisable for you to change course 20 degrees." The captain signalled, "I'm a captain, change course 20 degrees." The response was, "I'm a seaman second class, you'd better change course 20 degrees." By this time the captain was furious. His signal curtly ordered, "I'm a battleship. Change course 20 degrees." The reply: "I'm a lighthouse. You make the call." God's authority is never changing, it's always constant. Whenever a change of course is required we must make the correction from our end.[51]

**Availability** Edward McCabe said, "The world is a better place as a result of Michelangelo not having said, 'I don't do ceilings.'"

The Church would be a better place if more members were willing to climb a few scaffolds.[52]

**Awesome Victory** Romans 8:37 speaks of our ability to "overwhelmingly conquer" as victorious Christians. A definition of "overwhelmingly" was provided on October 7, 1916, when Georgia Tech played Cumberland University in what is recorded as the highest-scoring football game in history. Georgia Tech set a record of thirty-two touchdowns while racking up 222 points. Cumberland never made a first down, much less a point. Such decisive victory awaits those who wait upon our victorious King.[53]

**Backdoor Reminder** The Southern Baptist Home Mission Board recently learned about a big problem with the back door. For every two churches started, another church reverts to mission status, disbands, leaves the denomination, or merges with another congregation. During the last nineteen years, Southern Baptists averaged 430 church starts annually. For the same period, 233 churches were lost each year. The report noted dwindling membership was the major reason for failure. Shutting the back door may be one of the best strategies for church growth.[54]

**Backsliding** The old hymn "Come, Thou Fount" was written by Robert Robinson when he was just twenty-three years old. The third verse contains a phrase, "Prone to wander, Lord I feel it, Prone to leave the God I love." Unfortunately, this phrase was prophetic for Robinson: in his later life, he lapsed into sin. While riding a stagecoach, Robinson heard a woman humming his hymn. She later engaged him in conversation and asked what he thought of the hymn. Overcome with emotion, he said, "Madam, I am the poor unhappy man who wrote that hymn many years ago, and I would give a thousand worlds, if I had them, to enjoy the feelings I had then." Since we are all "prone to wander" we need to hold each other up from the clutches of sin and the unhappiness of backsliding. (See Galatians 6:1–2.)[55]

**Bad Habits** "Bad habits are the unlocked door to failure." —*Og Mandino*[56]

**Baptism** The Trinity Baptist Church in Athens, Greece, has been a congregation made up of U.S. military families and a rather large group of internationals from all over the world. Many in this church have no church background. This became humorously evident when a couple requested that a fellow church member take pictures during a parent/child dedication service. The proud parents told her to focus the camera on the pulpit since they would be near the podium during that special portion of the service. She promised to do as they asked and pointed to the baptistry as she reiterated her intent to focus the camera on the "pool-pit." From this apparent miscommunication comes a clearly stated truth. Although the pulpit should never be taken lightly, sometimes it receives more attention than the baptistry. Long after the "pulpit" sermons have been forgotten, we will remember the mighty sermons preached by the new saints in the "pool-pit."[57]

**Baptisms** The world's population grows by eighty-five million each year (equal to the combined populations of London, Tokyo, Mexico City, New York, and Sao Paulo). "The harvest is still plentiful, and the workers are still few. Therefore beseech the Lord of the harvest to send out workers into his harvest" (Matt. 9:37–38).[58]

**Basketball with Purpose** On December 21, 1891, Dr. James Naismith invented basketball ". . . to lead other young men to Christ." According to sports historian Dr. Tony Ladd of Wheaton College and Naismith's grandson, also named James Naismith, the inventor had spiritual motives. Naismith was both a physician and an ordained minister. After joining the International YMCA Training School in Springfield, Massachusetts, he faced the age-old problem of bored young men in winter. The cold prevented activity outside, and there were only a limited number of things that could be done indoors. Naismith felt it was important to maintain the boys' interest because he thought exercise was a perfect way to keep young men fit *and* on the straight and narrow path. On that December day, Dr. Naismith received the inspiration for a game that almost became "boxball." The thirty-year-old minister asked the janitor to secure two boxes that could be used for goals. The janitor could only find a couple of peach baskets, so Naismith "improvised" and had him mount them on the gym railing which was ten feet high. Within an hour the good doctor had created thirteen rules and started the new game with a soccer ball. The game spread rapidly, and Naismith was content. James Naismith never patented the game or made any money from it. He simply relished the satisfaction of providing another vehicle to help "in training mind, body and soul for the good of God." [59]

**Behavioral Modification** Scientists studied a native tribe in South America whose people have been dying prematurely for generations. After thorough investigation, the cause of premature death was determined. The disease was transmitted by an insect that lived in the walls of their adobe homes. This new information presented several options. They could move to another area where such insects don't exist, tear down their homes and rebuild them, use insecticide to rid their homes of the bugs, or, continue as they have and die early. Surprisingly, these people have opted to remain as they are and do nothing about their problem. Many people behave similarly. To save themselves, they know what they must do; instead, they opt to remain unchanged. [60]

**Behavioral Modification** The Promise Keepers note the following in their Point-Man training: 10 percent of all people will change when they hear the truth, 10 percent will never change, and 80 percent will only change in the context of a relationship. [61]

**Bible** Kay Arthur is well known for her "precept upon precept" Bible study. She has been a part of a strong resurgence toward more in-depth studying of God's Word. This has been her positive response to a tragedy within her life. Her first husband attended a liberal seminary that denied the inspiration of God's Word. His confusion over this issue not only had an impact on their divorce, but eventually led to him hanging himself. Mrs. Arthur knew she needed a sure foundation for her life and turned to God and his Word for direction. Her emphasis on inductive Bible study has since led hundreds of thousands of other women to find divine guidance from the Bible. She has allowed God to confirm his promise from Romans 8:28.[62]

**Bible** Thomas Jefferson served as President of the Washington, D.C. school board during his tenure as President of the United States. One of his duties on the school board was to select the textbooks to be used by the students. He selected the Bible as the primary text with this rationale: "I have always said, and always will say, that the studious perusal of the sacred volume will make us better citizens."[63]

**Bible Reading** By his own admission, Terry Anderson had little use for the Bible before being taken hostage in Lebanon. During the Middle East correspondent's captivity of nearly seven years, he found a new appreciation for God's Word. Since his release on December 4, 1991, Anderson has been praising the Bible's power: "Constantly over the years of captivity (March 1985–December 1991) I found consolation and counsel in the Bible I was given. I read the Bible more than fifty times, cover to cover. It was an enormous help to me." The longest-held American hostage in Lebanon survived for biblically obvious reasons.[64]

**Bible Reading** Have you ever wondered how long it would take you to read the entire Bible? If you read it out loud at a pace that is easy to understand, you could travel from Genesis to Revelation in seventy-eight hours. Divide that out over the course of one year and you would discover that God's Word could be completed in 365 days by reading it just twelve minutes a day. As Christian

Johnson said, "A Bible that's falling apart probably belongs to someone who isn't."[65]

**Bible Shortage** The need for Bible funds is the highest unmet financial need of overseas missionaries.[66]

**Bible Study** Hudson Taylor (1832–1905), missionary to China, founded the interdenominational China Inland Mission in 1865. During his fortieth year of ministry, he was in the presence of a friend when he closed his Bible and said, "For the fortieth time I have finished reading the Bible." Taylor's tenacity to stay in the Bible explains why God used him in such a significant manner.[67]

**Biblical Apathy** Mahatma Gandhi spoke forcefully to Christians when he said, "You Christians have in your keeping a document with enough dynamite in it to blow the whole of civilization to bits, to turn society upside down, to bring peace to this war-torn world. But you read it as if it were just good literature, and nothing else."[68]

**Biblical Application** Sometimes the hardest thing to do with Scripture is apply it to your life. For many of us, it's easier to make the application for other people. One pastor became acutely aware of this when a church member consistently met him after the service and said, "You sure preached to them today." The pastor dreamed of someday hearing this woman take the message personally. He thought he had finally gotten his chance when one Sunday a severe storm prevented all but the pastor and this woman from showing up. After the message he knew she couldn't quote her standard remark. She didn't. She said, "Too bad they weren't all here, because . . . you sure preached to them today." The first priority of Bible study is personal application and transformation.[69]

**Biblical Authority** Voltaire, the French philosopher, did not accept the tenets of Christianity. Although he acknowledged the existence of a force greater than man, he didn't believe in the claims of Christ. Voltaire predicted Christianity would be swept from existence and pass into history within one hundred years of his lifetime. Voltaire died in 1778. Fifty years later, the Geneva Bible Society moved into his house and used his printing press to produce thousands of Bibles that were distributed worldwide.[70]

**Biblical Illiteracy** A pastor asked a class of Sunday School children, "Who broke down the wall of Jericho?" A boy answered, "Not me, sir!" The pastor was noticeably upset and turned to the Sunday School teacher, "Is this typical?" She replied, "Pastor, the boy is a trusted and honest child, and I really don't think he did it." Such a response sent the pastor straight to the Sunday School superintendent. After hearing the pastor's grievance, the superintendent consoled him by saying, "I've known the boy and his Sunday School teacher for a number of years and just can't picture either one of them doing such a terrible thing." In disbelief, the pastor sought out the Chairman of the Deacons. The wise deacon tried to smooth the waters with some of his conventional wisdom, "Pastor, let's not make a big issue of this. Let's just pay for the damages and charge it to our maintenance account." The Library of Congress recently conducted a survey which asked, "What book has most influenced your life?" The Bible landed in the number one position. Yet, during a typical week only 45 percent of American Christians read the Bible. Of the 45 percent, just 12 percent claim to read God's Word daily. Fifty-five percent don't even bother to open it once a week! With stats like these, the above story might be true.[71]

**Big Biblical Bang** NASA's Cosmic Background Explorer (COBE) satellite provided scientists with a wealth of information. On April 23, 1992, scientists reported on the satellite's $400 million mission to study the universe's origins. After more than 300 million measurements by COBE, the research scientists noted how closely their new discovery of the universe's creation compared with the biblical account. Harvard astronomer Owen Gingerish said, "Both the contemporary scientific account and the age-old biblical account assume a beginning, and its essential framework, of everything springing forth from that blinding flash, bears a striking resonance with those succinct words of Genesis 1:3: 'And God said, "Let there be light."'" Frederic Burnham, science historian and Director of The Trinity Institute in New York City, said many scientists would, at this time more than any time in the last one hundred years, consider the idea that God created the universe a respectable hypothesis. This discovery also supports the theory that up to 90 percent of the universe is made up of cohesive, invisible, dark matter that scientists haven't yet been able to identify. Again, the answer is in the Bible: Colossians 1:15–17 tells us that Jesus is the image of the "invisible" God and that through him all things were created and "in him all things hold together." [72]

**Big Fish Story** Jimmy Smith developed an interest in foreign missions while attending Houston Baptist University. After learning of his interest, two missionaries invited him to visit their work in Guatemala. Money was very tight so he and his wife knew the trip would be impossible unless God intervened. Several weeks later, Smith went fishing with a deacon in his church named Gene Alexander. They talked about an upcoming fishing tournament offering a $20,000 prize for catching a particular fish. Gene knew of Smith's desire to visit Guatemala and promised him $5,000 for the trip if he caught the fish. Upon learning of the prize fish, Mrs. Smith logged it in her prayer journal and began talking to God. Then on the day of the tournament, Gene reeled in the $20,000 fish as his first catch of the day. Officials speculated the odds of landing that fish as his first catch were 1 in 6.8 billion. Jimmy Smith and his wife made the trip and God confirmed his call on their lives. They later returned to Guatemala and served as foreign missionaries. Of course things like this have happened before. See Matthew 17:27 for the details. [73]

**Biggest Fears** A recent poll by *U.S. News & World Report* revealed some of America's biggest fears. "What is the biggest problem facing the country?" Forty percent said crime, violence, drugs, and guns. Fifteen percent noted the economy and unemployment. Seven percent cited moral and religious concerns. Five percent think it's education. Three percent believe health care. The magazine said, "Fear is never far away."[74]

**Biodegradability** Marilyn vos Savant is listed in the *Guinness Book of World Records* for having the highest IQ. Her intelligence is kept in perspective by a little motto she uses: "Remember, we're all biodegradable." When you're feeling irreplaceable, just think about the biodegradability factor.[75]

**Birthdays** Birthdays are nice, but too many of them will kill you![76]

**Bob** Bob was a salesman who became a Christian through the ministry of Doug. One day in discipleship, Doug taught Bob about prayer. At the close of their time together, Doug asked Bob what he felt impressed to pray for. Bob said Africa. Doug asked him to get more specific, so Bob named a particular country. Doug then took a unique approach to prayer. He told Bob to pray for that country every day during the coming month. If nothing significant happened, he would pay Bob $500. If something big occurred then Bob owed him $500. The bet was off if he didn't pray every day. Toward the end of the month, Bob was beginning to wonder if anything would happen. Then he was attending a dinner where he met a lady from "his" country. He lit up and asked her about her work. She was working in a medical center. Bob asked so many questions and was so enthused that the woman invited him to fly over and see their work. Bob took her up on the offer and flew over. He was saddened to see such limited facilities, so he flew back and wrote some pharmaceutical companies about their needs. He soon had over $1 million worth of donated supplies sent over. It was such a major contribution that Bob was invited back over to see the new supplies, and they paid for his airfare this time. Even the president of that country quickly struck up a friendship with Bob. The president invited Bob to his palace and showed him the capital. (Remember, Bob is just a quiet, unassuming insurance salesman.) While touring the capital Bob saw some prisoners. He asked the president why they were in prison. The president said they were political prisoners who disagreed with his philosophy of governing. Bob simply told him that wasn't a good idea. Not long after Bob returned to the U.S., he received a call from the State Department in the middle of the night. They verified who he was, whether or not he had seen some prisoners and spoken with that particular president. Bob affirmed their information. The representative then pressed Bob. "Those are political prisoners we have been working to free for a very long time. They have been freed. Bob, what did you say?" Bob said, "I told him it wasn't a good idea." Later, Bob was invited back by the president to evaluate his proposed selections for his cabinet. So what about Bob? More importantly, what about the God to whom Bob prayed? [77]

**Body of Death** Sin places a "body of death" upon us (Rom. 7:24). This term to which Paul alludes is descriptive of a horrible execution that was employed by the Romans. A cadaver would be fastened to the condemned person so that he could not be released from the corpse. Every move he made was accompanied by the deceased. The rotting flesh of this cadaver would spawn disease and infection upon the condemned individual. Eventually he would die a slow, painful, and emotionally horrifying death. Every person has been attached to the decaying carcass of sin (Rom. 3:23). Its end result is death (Rom. 6:23a), but God has provided an escape to everlasting life through his Son Jesus Christ (Rom. 6:23b).[78]

**Born Against** One layman noted the problem with some of his fellow church members who seemed "called" to oppose every aspect of the church. He said, "Some people are born again, and some are born against!"[79]

**Boundaries** Child psychologists discovered an interesting truth several years ago. Contemporary thought assumed that fences on playgrounds made the children feel restricted in their recreation. A consensus was then reached to remove the fences so children wouldn't feel confined. The opposite effect occurred. Researchers found that the children became more inhibited with their activities. They tended to huddle toward the middle of the playground and exhibited signs of insecurity. When the fences were replaced, the children played with greater enthusiasm and freedom. We all need boundaries—something to define the limits of safety and security. Existential thought suggests that boundaries restrict creativity, but as the children on the playground demonstrated, we need a clear understanding of what is safe and acceptable so our creativity can flourish.[80]

**Bowling Ball Booze** Some folks in Wisconsin have helped everyone see how ludicrous alcoholic-based entertainment can get. A recent fad up north involves drinking liquor out of bowling balls. You simply fill the thumb hole with your favorite drink, then raise the ball over your head and take a shot. Some more daring guzzlers load up all three holes of the bowling ball and go for broke. One can only imagine the added flavor a sweaty old bowling ball can add to the drinking experience. And some say abstinence is "crazy!"[81]

**Brevity of Life** Henry Kissinger became a household name during the Nixon administration. His brilliance was tapped by world leaders who readily recognized his genius. But, possibly, his wisest pearl did not come from politics. In a moment of contemplation he said, "What has most surprised me about life is how quickly it passes." Moses prayed, "Teach us to number our days aright" (Ps. 90:12).[82]

**Brotherly Love** A little six-year-old girl became deathly ill with a terrible disease. She needed a special blood transfusion, and her rare blood type further complicated the problem. The girl's nine-year-old brother qualified as a donor, but everyone was hesitant to ask him since he was so young. When the prospects of another donor dissolved, they talked with the boy about it. He didn't understand all of the dynamics, but he said, "Sure, I'll give my blood for my sister." When the transfusion began, he took the needle in his arm, closed his eyes and lay silently on the bed. After the transfusion was completed, the doctors thanked the boy for saving his sister's life. The brave brother began to quietly cry. He asked, "Doctor, when do I die?" The doctor understood the magnitude of what this boy had done and quickly reassured him that he would not die. He was amazed at the boy's courage and asked, "Why were you willing to risk your life for her?" The boy said, "Because she is my sister . . . and I love her." Jesus said, "Love one another, even as I have loved you" (John 14:34–35).[83]

**Bullet Hole Clothing** Frank Allgeyer makes his living selling "Drive-By Fashions." The forty-four-year-old resident of New Hampshire shoots holes into customers' clothing. The buyer can pick from a handgun, rifle, or machine gun, but Allgeyer says most customers prefer the "machine gun look." The state attorney general has complained that Allgeyer is profiting from gang violence. To this amateur clothing specialist, "It's just a fashion statement."[84]

**Bumper Stickers** Have you considered using bumper stickers to advertise your church? Professionals in the advertising industry say each bumper sticker is equivalent to over $300 of paid advertisement each month. I hate bumper stickers, but they could provide an economical method for attracting the lost.[85]

**Burning the Old Man** In Ecuador, the celebration of a new year has significance. During the week preceding January 1, people create and decorate scarecrow-like dummies. Then at midnight on

December 31, they take these dummies out and set them on fire. It's called "Burning the Old Man." This tradition gives the people a sense of new beginnings and represents the burning away of their sins and shortcomings. Many of these people have not experienced the dross-burning power of Jesus Christ, so they ignite these effigies in hopes of removing their sin. For Christians, the knowledge of Christ's redemption should cause us to confess our sins and "Burn the Old Man" every day.[86]

**Business Ethics** In an *Inc.* FaxPoll on ethics, respondents were asked, "Which of the following statements most closely approximates your view of ethics in business?" Fifty-two percent agreed with, "I play by the rules, but I'll bend them to my company's advantage whenever I can." Forty-six percent affirmed, "I tell the whole truth, all the time." Only 2 percent said, "All's fair in love and business, as long as you don't get caught." Among those under the age of thirty-five, 34 percent tell the truth all the time; for those over forty-five, it's 54 percent. Under age thirty-five, 62 percent bend the rules compared with 46 percent of those over forty-five. "Kings take pleasure in honest lips; they value a man who speaks the truth" (Proverbs 16:13).[87]

**Busyness** He hurried to an early grave, never to enjoy the time he saved.[88]

**Busyness** You know life is too busy when you succumb to utilizing the drive-through service of Matthew Cornish. Cornish is a mortician in Nassawadox, Virginia who recently opened his drive-through viewing window "for people who don't have the time or ability to bid farewells inside." Cornish continues, "People are too busy these days with work. This is just one way of making it easier for them." If Mr. Cornish is successful, we're too busy![89]

**Calling** His father was a successful barber, so everyone assumed young George would follow in the family trade. Unfortunately for his dad, George was more interested in music. Unfortunately for George, his dad thought musicians were nothing more than "vagabonds." At age seven, the Duke of Weissenfels accidentally heard George playing around on an organ. The Duke encouraged George's father to develop his son's obvious talent. Since a Duke's request was not to be taken lightly, George was given lessons while his father hoped the boy's love for music would pass. Mr. Handel was mistaken. His son's passion only grew, and he became the "Celebrated Saxon." George Friedrich Handel believed his music was a gift from God and composing was his calling. Handel enjoyed an easy and luxurious life until he made some bad business decisions and became the target of jealous less-talented musicians. His health was failing; his creditors threatened him with imprisonment. He almost gave up, yet from this valley of despair came his greatest work, *Messiah.* His health continued to decline over the remaining decade of his life. He suffered a fainting spell during a performance of *Messiah.* He went home to bed and never got up. The Lutheran saint expressed the wish that he might die on Good Friday "in the hope of rejoining the good God, my sweet Lord and Savior, on the day of his Resurrection." His wish was fulfilled in the early morning of Holy Saturday (April 14, 1759) when this man of calling met his Messiah face to face. When I hear the "Hallelujah Chorus," I'm thankful this would-be barber followed his calling from God.[90]

**Car Theft** It's a true story that sounds like something from Hollywood. A man by the name of Jones purchased his dream car on October 17, 1989. It was just what he wanted, a fancy red Porsche. He drove off the lot and headed straight to the third game of the World's Series at Candlestick Park. During that historic game, an incredible earthquake hit the city of San Francisco. The game was called off, and Mr. Jones returned to the parking lot. To his dismay, not only had an earthquake hit, but his car had been stolen, as well. The car remained missing for several days as the police were preoccupied with the devastation of the earthquake.

Finally the red Porsche was located. It was discovered under the collapsed Nimitz freeway. The thief died in the car he stole.[91]

**Carelessness** During Colonial days, Andrew Bradford had the contract for printing public materials in Pennsylvania. One day, the governor made an important address, and Bradford printed it in his usual careless manner. Another young printer saw an opportunity to capitalize on Bradford's shabby work. He reprinted the speech in elegant form, then mailed a copy with his compliments to the governor and each member of the assembly. The following year, Ben Franklin was rewarded for his conscientious work by receiving the contract for all of Pennsylvania's public printing. To maintain a "contract" of spiritual influence we must never become careless in the way we live out our Christianity in the church and in the community.[92]

**Change** Can you imagine church members protesting an invitation after an evangelistic sermon? They did in 1825. Not only did church members object to an invitation, but so did many of the ministers. A new evangelist named Charles Finney had come on to the religious scene in America and had become quite popular by 1825. He was reaching many Americans with the gospel by implementing what grumbling critics called New Measures. Among these intolerable changes were: praying for persons by name, having an invitation after the sermon, sharing the gospel by visiting in homes, allowing women to pray and testify, holding services on days other than the usual times for worship, and preaching in an informal manner that appealed to those who attended his outlandish new idea of holding Revival Services. Finney was perceived as a radical troublemaker in 1825, but his wrong approach brought many to Christ. Change is usually threatening, yet its results can often be tremendous.[93]

**Change** For many people, change never seems to happen quickly enough. A good word on managing change comes from Lyle Schaller in *The Best Is Yet to Come.* He says, "The most effective change is incremental, not catastrophic. We have six children and I've said to my wife many times, one of the smartest things she ever did was to bring them home one at a time. Therefore, my advice has always been to pastors, lay leaders, and congregations: one at a time."[94]

**Change** Marlene Wilson says, "The only people who like change are babies with bad diapers." Effective leadership recognizes the natural tendency to resist change and strives to make every transition as palatable as possible.[95]

**Change** "Of the twenty largest companies in the U.S. forty years ago, only two are still among the first twenty in size. Of the one hundred largest companies twenty-five years ago, almost half have disappeared or have declined substantially from their peak." Refusal to change spells decline![96]

**Child Abuse** Our nation cringed in horror when it learned Deborah Turner, age thirty-five, had hurled her sixteen-month-old son Tyler out the window of her sister's eighth floor apartment in Chicago. Ms. Turner became distraught on April 12, 1995 when her son would not stop crying. She then grabbed the toddler and threw him through a closed window to his death. Unfortunately, this is not an isolated incident. People fear for their children's safety from strangers, but a recent report from the U.S. Advisory Board on Child Abuse and Neglect revealed the stunning statistic that an estimated 2,000 children die each year at the hands of parents or caretakers. The 248-page report said neglect and child abuse kill more children under five years of age than do traffic accidents, drownings, or falls. In 1994, there were more than one million confirmed cases of child abuse or neglect in the United States. Congress enacted the Family Preservation and Support Services Program in 1993 that will funnel $900 million over five years to fight child abuse in our country.[97]

**Child Care** "Twenty-five percent of working parents with young children use day-care facilities, almost double that of a decade ago. . . . The typical American day-care worker makes $5.35 an hour. Small wonder that 40 percent of these caregivers leave their jobs in less than a year." [98]

**Child Rearing** The poet Coleridge was visited by a man who had a theory about raising children. He stated, "I believe children should be given a free rein to think and act and thus learn at an early age to make their own decisions. This is the only way they can grow into their full potential." Coleridge made no comment but simply led the man to his garden. "Come see my flower garden," he said. The opinionated visitor took one look at the overgrown garden and remarked, "Why, that's nothing but a yard full of weeds." The wise poet declared, "It used to be filled with roses, but this year I thought I'd let the garden grow as it willed without tending to it. This is the result." Children, like gardens, will not automatically flourish. They need daily attention and care. [99]

**Children** Jane Brooks has said, "Our children are like library books on loan with a due date that remains unknown." Make the most of every moment with your kids! [100]

**Choices** A Sunday School teacher told his class about the story of Lazarus and the Rich Man. He highlighted the plight of Lazarus and the blatant neglect of the Rich Man. One was privileged in this world, while the other found peace in heaven. After the teacher had shared these truths, he posed this question to his class, "Now, which would you rather be, boys, the Rich Man or Lazarus?" One guy raised his hand and replied, "I'd like to be the Rich Man while I'm living, and Lazarus when I die." We have to decide which kingdom we will join because God has not granted us the option of serving both kingdoms simultaneously. Commitment involves choosing to be faithful to one while forsaking the other. [101]

**Choices** Charles Allen tells the story of a wise man who always gave right answers to the difficult questions of life. One day a young and arrogant man sought to stump the older sage by concealing a live bird in his hands and asking, "Sir, is the bird in my hands alive or dead?" His plan of deception was simple. If the wise senior said it was dead, then he would open his hands and let the bird fly away. If he said it was alive, he would give his hands a quick squeeze and open them to reveal a dead bird. Surprisingly, though, the old man never looked at the younger man's hands. He looked deep into his eyes and quietly said, "My son, it is whatever you wish it to be." Dr. Allen then wrote, "So it is with each of us. The life we live is the one we wish to live—God's way, or some other way. The choice is in our own hands." [102]

**Christ-likeness** A silversmith doesn't need a fancy formula for calculating purity. He knows the silver is free of dross when he can see his reflection in the liquefied metal. When are we pure? When Christ looks at us and sees his reflection. (See Romans 8:29.)[103]

**Christian Activism** When Dr. Richard Halverson was the U.S. Senate chaplain, he spoke before a group of evangelicals who had expressed their anger about Congress' inactivity on the subject of school prayer. They were irritated that Congress had not acted with a strong initiative to restore prayer in schools. To these who were seeking greater initiative from the government, Dr. Halverson asked, "How many of you have prayed with your children this month, outside of church?" Nobody raised their hand. Spiritual initiative starts in the home, not on Capitol Hill.[104]

**Christian Living** A business man who was well known for his ruthless behavior once told Mark Twain, "Before I die I mean to make a pilgrimage to the Holy Land. I will climb Mount Sinai and read the Ten Commandments aloud at the top." Mark Twain said, "I have a better idea. You could stay in Boston and keep them."[105]

**Christian Unity** Madalyn Murray O'Hair was interviewed on Public Television. During the course of this interview it was noted that Ms. O'Hair seemed to have a lot of clout. The interviewer asked why she didn't organize the atheist movement better so as to be a stronger power. She responded with a telling answer: "Because every time a bunch of atheists get together, all they do is argue." Christian unity should always demonstrate regenerated believers working in cooperation and love to extend the gospel of Jesus Christ. Sometimes, though, churches sound more like Ms. O'Hair's camp of disagreeables.[106]

**Christianity** "Christianity is a come-and-go affair. We come up to the mountain, but we must go back down again. We come to worship, but we must go to serve." —*Zan Holmes*[107]

**Christianity** In 1991 actor Marlon Brando took the witness stand to plead leniency for his son, Christian, who was convicted of voluntary manslaughter. Brando refused to swear before God to tell the truth. He said, "I will not swear on God, because I do not believe in the conventional God . . . but I will swear on my children and my grandchildren." Unfortunately, such philosophy has not served the senior actor very well. His son Christian is serving a ten-year prison sentence and at age twenty-five, his daughter Cheyenne committed suicide in her home along the west coast of Tahiti. (Miss Brando had made three previous suicide attempts). She was discovered hanging in her bedroom on Easter, 1995. Christ arose on Easter so we could have life, but tragically, many never find such life. (See Matthew 7:13–14.)[108]

**Christianity** In 1992, Mississippi Governor Kirk Fordice truthfully declared, "The less we emphasize the Christian religion, the further we fall into the abyss of poor character and chaos." As might be expected, Governor Fordice received some heated reviews for his argument that America is a "Christian nation."[109]

**Christians** Bill Hybels, Senior Pastor of Willow Creek Community Church, has identified three types of Christians: Yawners, Maimers, and Killers. In the spiritual battle of light and darkness we are called to be soldiers of the Cross. Unfortunately, not all Christians can be classified as Killers. Some believers yawn at the tasks God has called us to perform in his Kingdom and can never be counted on to advance the cause of Christ. Other Christians periodically rise to the occasion if nothing more interesting catches their attention. As soldiers for God they maim the enemy every once in a while, but they seldom deliver a death blow. The final group, Killers, are the people by which you grow a strong and vital church. Their commitment is constant and zealous. They recognize the seriousness of the spiritual battle and are dedicated to being victorious for Christ and his Kingdom. Killers are few, but they can turn the tide in battle (just ask Gideon or Goliath). Greater attention should be given to this final group, even though they represent a small minority of the total church. A tiny group of Killers can help build a "killer" church. Likewise, each of us should evaluate which group best describes us and our level of commitment to God. Just because you may have been a Yawner or Maimer doesn't mean you can't change and become a Killer.[110]

**Christmas** Christmas was going to be different this year. The father called a family conference and challenged them to be more disciplined in the management of their time during the busy Christmas season and to curtail excessive spending on gifts. He talked about better relations between visiting relatives and a more congenial atmosphere around their home. He brought his speech to a crescendo with his final rally cry, "Let's make this the *best* Christmas EVER!" His little second-grade son countered the big motivational speech by noting, "But Dad, I don't see how we could ever improve on the first Christmas." We certainly can't improve on what happened that first Christmas, but we can improve on the way we celebrate it today.[111]

**Christmas** If our greatest need had been information, God would have sent us an educator. If our greatest need had been technology, God would have sent us a scientist. If our greatest need had been money, God would have sent us an economist. If our greatest need had been pleasure, God would have sent us an entertainer. But our greatest need was forgiveness, so God sent us a Savior.[112]

**Christmas** Luis Palau tells the story of a wealthy European family who decided to have their newborn baby baptized in their enormous mansion. Dozens of guests were invited to the event, and they all arrived in the latest of fashions. After depositing their elegant coats on a bed in an upstairs room, the guests were entertained like royalty. Soon the time came for the main purpose of the evening, the infant's baptism. When they asked for the child, no one seemed to know of his whereabouts. Panic ensued as they desperately searched for the baby. In a few minutes the child was found— buried underneath all of the coats, jackets, and furs. The very object of the day's celebration had been forgotten, neglected, and nearly smothered. May the overcoats of materialism, tradition, and schedules not smother the very reason for the Christmas season.[113]

**Christmas** The "hustle and bustle" of Christmas causes things to get crazy for a while. At some point during every Christmas season we all wish it wasn't as hectic so we could more fully enjoy the celebration. Those who imitate the American Indians that reside outside of Taos, New Mexico may find a more peaceful holiday. On their pueblo from December 15 to January 15, they observe "the time of being still." Peace and quiet are the reigning trademarks of these weeks. Although such an observance of Christmas may be a little too slow for your taste, it is a reminder that when we slow down we have a better chance of knowing God. "Be still, and know that I am God" (Psalm 46:10). Who knows? When you celebrate a more tranquil Christmas, you just might stumble upon a midnight clear, see some silent stars go by, observe the world in solemn stillness lay, and when the angels sing, you'll be there to hear them.[114]

**Christmas** We sing it every year during this special season: "Joy to the World." The inspiration for this hymn came to Isaac Watts from Psalm 98:4–9. Centuries later, we can read verse one, "Sing to the Lord a new song," and turn to the Seventh Day Adventists for additional inspiration. They altered this carol when they chose to focus on the Second Coming. They changed the lyrics to read, "Joy to the world, the Lord will come." As Christians at Christmas, we have two reasons to celebrate: "the Lord is come," and "the Lord will come."[115]

**Christmas Shopping** Lynne Hybels, the wife of renowned pastor Bill Hybels, tells of a touching scene she witnessed years ago. As a child she was very intrigued with a man in a discount store who was struggling with the purchase of a small and inexpensive figurine. His attire revealed much. He was an older man whose children were no doubt grown. The lines in his face and the worn clothes on his back told of a hard and bittersweet life. Yet everything about this man communicated the intensity of his love for the recipient of that gift. His gift would not compare with the countless other gifts purchased by those whose incomes afforded much more. The wrapping would probably be less than elaborate. It might be the only gift he could give her. But somehow his gift seemed more significant than any other. Since that time Mrs. Hybels has seen thirty years of Christmas shopping frenzies, but each year this anonymous shopper is the one who tugs at her heart and moistens her eyes. She says, "Sometimes the most beautiful love stories are etched on the faces of the lowly and shared by the humble." May such stories of intentional love define your Christmas season this year![116]

**Chump Change** Most everyone will remember the era of the Susan B. Anthony dollar. It lasted merely three years, for a very good reason. The coins looked too much like quarters, and people didn't like the confusion. In the public's mind a dollar needed to look like it was worth four quarters, not just twenty-five cents. The coin seemed like "chump change" so fell out of circulation and became a memory. Christians can learn a poignant lesson from the U.S. Treasury's error. The world expects believers to look like Christ, not a cheap imitation. People outside of the church see too many professing Christians who look more like "chump change" than the real thing. Live in such a way that others will easily recognize a significant difference.[117]

**Church** A church marquis deftly described the divine institution that God created for all people. It said, "Church: one place where you aren't too bad to come in, nor too good to stay out." God has designed his Church to be necessary for everyone.[118]

**Church** If absence makes the heart grow fonder, then some people must really love the church![119]

**Church** The great task of the Church is not only to get sinners into heaven, but also to get the saints out of bed. —*A. L. Todd*[120]

**Church Attendance** Call it a trump card if you must, but lawmakers in Virginia made a law in 1610 that prescribed the death penalty for people who failed to attend church three consecutive Sundays.[121]

**Church Attendance** Need to boost attendance? The following statistics reveal church is the safest place of all. Automobiles account for 20 percent of all fatal accidents, while 17 percent of fatalities occur at home. Fourteen percent happen to pedestrians on streets and sidewalks. Travel by air, rail, or water causes 16 percent of the deaths. Yet, of all reported deaths, only .001 percent occur in worship services.[122]

**Church Attendance** The following was reprinted from a Catholic bulletin as a sobering reminder to us all: "Don't wait until the hearse hauls you to church. If you do, you will go, regardless of the weather. There will be beautiful flowers there, but you won't enjoy them. The priest may say some good things about you, but you won't be able to hear them. There will be beautiful music, but you won't be enjoying it. There will be heartfelt prayers, but they will not touch your heart. There will be friends and relatives there, but you will not worship with them. You will go, no matter how many hypocrites are there. You will go, no matter how much you are needed at home. You won't be concerned about whether you're dressed right. After that final trip you will never have to decide whether to attend church or not. You'll never get another chance. Aren't you glad to be alive and well and have the choice of whether or not to go to church?"[123]

**Church Growth** "A mushroom grows up overnight, but it requires a decade to develop an oak." Dr. J. M. Price, the great Christian educator of countless Baptists, wrote these words in his classic little book *Jesus the Teacher*. He applied these words to the work of a minister and his ministry. The desire for explosive growth is ever before us, but it is the ministry of a mighty oak that we must strive to achieve. Mushrooms vanish quickly, but oak trees will speak to generations not yet born.[124]

**Church Growth** According to Dr. Bob Cox, dean of the Department of Education at the University of Texas at Tyler, churches are like most institutions or movements in that they generally digress through three stages. He says they begin as risk takers, then develop in to caretakers, and finally become undertakers. The early days are characterized by a willingness to try anything that might advance the cause. After a season of success there is a tendency to protect the fruit of earlier victories. This cautious mode leads toward decline and eventual death. It happens in businesses and churches, because growth requires a certain level of risk.[125]

**Church Growth** Dwight L. Moody once brought a pew full of boys and girls from the street to a church he anticipated joining.

The presence of Moody's guests so disturbed the aristocratic church that when he presented himself for membership, the church board suggested Moody take a month to pray about his desire to join their church. A month later Moody was asked by the board, "Did you follow our suggestions?" Moody affirmed he had. "And what did the Lord say?" Mr. Moody said, "He told me not to feel bad about it, because he has been trying to get into this church himself for the last twenty-five years!" Sometimes our churches don't grow because we extend a selective invitation.[126]

**Church Growth** "I am convinced that as we become so enamored with methodologies, models, and marketing strategies, we become almost carnal in our thinking about how the church grows." —*Ken Hemphill*[127]

**Church Growth** Surveys indicate newcomers must attend a church an average of 3.4 times before they will make a commitment either to trust Christ or join the church.[128]

**Church Membership** This could be a word of caution to those who place their eternal security in church membership rather than Jesus Christ. The late Corrie ten Boom, a survivor of the Holocaust, used to say, "A mouse in a cookie jar isn't a cookie."[129]

**Church Membership** When our church membership increases we need to evaluate whether or not the growth represents a sizable percentage of new Christians. In America, 80 percent of new members have come from another church. We need to monitor our fishing status because Jesus said, "'I will make you fishers of men,'" (Matt. 4:19) not traders of fish.[130]

**Church Purpose** Society addresses the Church as a non-profit organization. Peter Drucker disagrees with the connotation of such a description: "Non-profit is negative. One cannot define anything by what it is not. The product of a church is a changed life. Human-change institutions would be the right name." We must see ourselves as an institution of positive change rather than just a place where no profits are made.[131]

**Circumstances** "I am convinced that life is 10 percent what happens to me and 90 percent how I react to it." —*Charles Swindoll*[132]

**Circumstances** It wasn't your ideal wedding. When Victoria LeMelle and Roger Compton tied the knot on May 2, 1992, their wedding was well-planned, but they didn't count on the riots that broke out in South-Central Los Angeles. The bride's dress was stolen, the groom's tux was looted, and both the cameraman and the limo service canceled at the last minute. Only the caterer and flowers came through. Nonetheless, the couple went on with the ceremony in a sanctuary filled with the scent of flowers and smoke. The honeymoon was placed on hold because they couldn't get out of their riot-torn neighborhood in time to board their scheduled cruise. "I'm happy anyway," said the bride. "We just decided we weren't going to let a bunch of ignorant people get in our way. May 2 was our day, and nobody was going to stop us." Although riots aren't an everyday occurrence, there are plenty of adversities which bombard us each week. We must not allow "less than ideal" circumstances to rob us of our joy and purpose as God's children.[133]

**Circumstances** Many people speculate that they would be better off with a new spouse or a different set of circumstances. John Micofsky was confident his life would be greatly improved once he ridded himself of his wife. His dream came true on January 20, 1993 when his divorce from Maryann Kulpa was finalized. On January 21, she claimed the $10.2 million jackpot in the New Jersey Pick-6 Lottery. When the press asked about Micofsky's condition, attorney Thomas Kline spoke for his client by saying, "very upset, I think that's the word I would use." Sometimes changes don't produce the results we planned.[134]

**Clean Hands** Hospital-acquired infections are one of the leading causes of death in the United States. These infections are either the direct or indirect cause of 80,000 fatalities a year. As many as one third of these deaths could be prevented if health care workers strictly followed infection control procedures. Of those precautionary measures, "hand washing may be the single most important tool of infection prevention." Studies suggest that health care workers wash their hands less than half as often as they should. "Patients come into the hospitals to be made better, and they actually, in many cases, are made worse," said Dr. Robert Haley, director of epidemiology at the University of Texas Southwestern Medical School in Dallas. These hospital infections cost the hospitals themselves between four and four-and-a-half billion a year. The Church has frequently been compared to a hospital. Do we compare here? People are looking for a safe haven to find God but sometimes our churches send them home with a greater illness. This could be prevented if we would but heed the words of James 4:8, "Draw near to God, and he will draw near to you. Cleanse your hands, you sinners; and purify your hearts, you double-minded." Daily hand washing at the basin of God's Word will prevent us from spreading the deadly germs of sin.[135]

**Clear Conscience** John Wesley was working in his garden one day when a neighbor came by to visit. The neighbor attempted to jolt Wesley by asking, "What would you be doing now, John, if you knew for certain Jesus would return today?" Wesley jolted his neighbor instead by replying, "I would go right on doing what I'm doing." May we live in such a way that Christ could return at any time and we would be comfortable continuing the task at hand.[136]

**Clear Conscience** Legendary UCLA basketball coach John Wooden said, "There is no pillow as soft as a clear conscience." [137]

**Cohabitation** Some call it cohabitation, while others just say living together. Advocates of this set-up think it is wise to "test drive" the compatibility of a relationship before embarking on marriage. It is proposed as nothing more than a "trial run." "If magazine subscriptions come with trial periods, why shouldn't potential marriage relationships?" The logic can seem convincing to a couple not yet sure about marriage, but it just doesn't hold up to hard core facts. Jeffrey Larson recently completed his research on fifty years of data to arrive at the conclusion: "couples who live together before marriage have a 50 percent greater chance of divorce than those who don't." He went on to say, "Psychologically, marriage seems to be a significantly different type of relationship. Cohabitation is not a trial marriage." Nonetheless, the U.S. Census Bureau says 6,085,284 unmarried, opposite-sex partners live together.[138]

**Commercials** Researchers in San Diego monitored ninety-five hours of weekday afternoon and Saturday morning television shows targeted at children. The two-month study revealed children are exposed to twenty-one commercials an hour. Advertisers have secularized the concept of persistent and repetitive spiritual instruction as given in Deuteronomy 6:4–9. They are teaching our children to buy "when they sit in the house and when they walk by the way and when they lie down and when they rise up. And binding them as a sign on their hands and as frontals on their foreheads. And writing them on the doorposts of their houses and gates." Are we being as diligent and persistent with spiritual truth? Kids don't need twenty-one sermons an hour, but they could stand a few more commercials about the Lord from their parents.[139]

**Commitment** After Dallas won the Super Bowl in 1993, coach Jimmy Johnson said, "I played for a national championship team, I coached a national championship team, and I coached a Super Bowl team. There's a common thread in all three: quality people who are committed to do their best." Coach Johnson's observation should be heeded in the Church as well. God has gifted and empowered each of us to be "quality people." The question is, "Are we committed to do our best?"[140]

**Commitment** In Salt Lake City, in the downtown mall, between Radio Shack and B. Dalton Books, there is a unique shop: a Mormon missionary supply store. It provides young missionaries with everything they need to prepare for a mission to another country. They have T-shirts with the designated country's flag, brochures, books that give tips for packing, and just about anything else. Although you probably won't find a store like this in your mall, it is a vivid reminder of how committed Mormons can be to the cause of propagating their beliefs. If people can be that committed to the teachings of Joseph Smith, shouldn't we be more committed to the teachings of Jesus Christ?[141]

**Commitment** President Kennedy learned something about commitment from Frank O'Connor, an Irish writer. The Irishman told of his childhood days when he and his friends would wander through the countryside of their homeland. When they would come to an orchard with a wall too high to climb over, they would toss their hats over the wall so they would have no choice but to figure out a way to get over. Kennedy tossed the hat of America over the wall when he challenged us to land a man on the moon. Christians need to likewise toss their hats over more walls and look to God for help in overcoming seemingly impossible tasks.[142]

**Commitments** "When you say yes to one thing, that means you say no to something else. You can't do everything. —*Pam Tillis*[143]

**Committees** Ross Perot suggests, "If you see a snake, just kill it. Don't appoint a committee on snakes."[144]

**Common Sense** When *USA Weekend* asked celebrities what they wanted for Christmas, Bill Moyers gave an insightful response. After wishing for more time with his grandchildren, Moyers hoped "for a sudden epidemic of common sense to break out among the politicians, pundits and talk show hosts who shape the national debate." Common sense comes from God (1 Cor. 1:18ff).[145]

**Communication** During a recent survey, 100 divorce lawyers were asked the question, "What is the major cause of divorce in American marriages?" All 100 lawyers agreed that a breakdown in marital communication was the leading cause of divorce. Every meaningful relationship requires significant communication.[146]

**Communication** Matthew, three-year-old son of Stuart Cooke, was eating an apple in the back seat of the car when he asked, "Daddy, why is my apple turning brown?" Matthew's daddy explained, "Because after you ate the skin off, the meat of the apple came into contact with the air, which caused it to oxidize, thus changing its molecular structure and turning it into a different color." There was a long silence. Then Matthew asked, "Daddy, are you talking to me?" We may have the "correct" answers for people asking about spiritual truth, but such truth is only of value when it is understandable to them.[147]

**Communication** "Never be afraid to state the obvious. It is what most people have forgotten." —*William H. Ralston*[148]

**Communication** "Research has shown that our words account for only 7 percent of everything we communicate to others." For this reason, Peter Drucker's counsel is very significant: "The most important thing in communication is to hear what isn't being said."[149]

**Communication** The Ten Commandments contain 297 words. Psalm 23 involves 118 words. And the Lord's Prayer required just 56 words. Yet, the Department of Agriculture needed 15,629 to discuss the pricing of cabbage. Don't let the message of Christ get lost in unnecessary verbiage.[150]

**Communication** There are two kinds of people who don't say much: those who are quiet and those who talk a lot.[151]

**Communism** Before the fall of Communism, Dan Rather once interviewed Billy Graham about the state of religion in Russia. He asked Dr. Graham what he thought about the Communists' success of obliterating religion in their land. The evangelist corrected Mr. Rather, saying, "They haven't obliterated it, they've just oppressed it." Dr. Graham was right. Now religion is starting to obliterate Communism.[152]

**Comparing** "Comparison is the favorite indoor sport of Christians." —*Howard Hendricks*[153]

**Compassion** Drs. Hillel Finestone and David Conter of the University of Western Ontario think medical doctors should take acting classes so they can at least pretend they are concerned about their patients. These two doctors are not being facetious. They have written their thoughts for the medical community to seriously consider. "We do not put forward the idea cynically," they said. These physicians feel "acting classes should be required in medical school so doctors can learn just when to provide a perfectly timed compassionate look, or a touch on the hand." An accompanying commentary from Great Britain by Dr. Chris McManus of St. Mary's Hospital Medical School in London said, "Acting may ultimately save doctors who are at risk of professional burnout." Authentic compassion requires authentic concern.[154]

**Compassion** Park York has known the agony of seeing his wife suffer with Alzheimer's disease. It first began with an occasional incoherent or irrelevant question but digressed to round-the-clock perpetual care. As she declined from 125 pounds to 86, he continuously ministered to her needs. His daily routine consisted of feeding, bathing, diapering, changing beds, cleaning house, fixing meals, dressing and undressing her, and whatever else became necessary to care for his wife. Sometimes she would mumble a word or two but never a sentence. Then one Friday morning she seemed to step outside of her illness and asked a question with perfect

enunciation, "Do you want me?" These softly spoken words greatly impacted Mr. York. He cried out, "Of course I want you,
Flossie," as he hugged and kissed her. Mrs. York returned to her
state of oblivion just as quickly as she had momentarily escaped,
but her four brief words would never be forgotten. People every-
where are asking the same question this dear woman posed, "Do
you want me?" May we all respond with the same compassion Mr.
York provided for his wife.[155]

**Compassion** Stephen Covey tells of an unusual experience on
the New York subway. While people were sitting quietly in the car,
a man entered with his noisy and rambunctious children. The man
sat down and closed his eyes as though he was oblivious to his
rowdy children. The once quiet subway car was now a disturbing
place of chaos. The children's inappropriate behavior was obvious
to everyone except their father. Finally, Covey confronted the man
about his children. The man opened his eyes and evaluated the situation as if he were unaware of all that had transpired: "Oh, you're
right. I guess I should do something about it. We just came from
the hospital, where their mother died about an hour ago. I don't
know what to think, and I guess they don't know how to handle it
either." Compassion starts when we begin to understand the hurts
of others.[156]

**Compassion** The USS *Vincennes* made a terrible mistake on July
3, 1988. On that summer day our Navy cruiser shot down an
Iranian airliner with 290 passengers on board. The captain mistakenly thought they were under attack by an F-14 Iranian fighter. There were no survivors. When President Reagan sought to pay
compensation to the victim's families, public opinion revealed that
most Americans opposed his actions. The cruel treatment of
American hostages was still fresh in many minds. In response to
reporter's hounding questions that such payment would send the
wrong message, the President replied, "I don't ever find compassion a bad precedent."[157]

**Complaints** It's on the records. A lady actually complained to the government that the extra hour of sunlight during Daylight Savings Time was burning up her lawn. Most complainers are confused about the "facts." [158]

**Compliments** A young man in London wanted to be a writer, but the cards seemed stacked against him. He had only four years of school, and his father was in jail because he couldn't pay his debts. Just to survive the pain of hunger, he got a job pasting labels on bottles in a rat-infested warehouse. He slept in an attic with two other boys from the slums. With such little confidence in himself and in his ability to write, he secretly slipped out in the middle of the night to mail his first manuscript so nobody would laugh at his dream. That manuscript, along with countless others, was rejected. Finally, one story was accepted. He wasn't paid anything but the editor praised him for his writing. That one little compliment caused him to wander aimlessly through the streets with tears rolling down his cheeks. The compliment inspired him to continue and improve. It also led to a brilliant career for Charles Dickens. If we weren't so stingy with compliments, we might see a lot more people blossom like Dickens. [159]

**Compromise** The Boy Scouts were under fire in California during 1992. The Berkeley, California, schools closed their doors to the Boy Scouts because of the Boy Scouts' refusal to admit homosexuals and atheists. In Santa Ana, California, a judge ordered Cub Scout Pack 519 to readmit atheistic twins, Michael and William Randall. The two boys were ousted from the Pack for their refusal to say the word "God" during recitation of the Cub Scout Promise. And in San Francisco, the United Way withdrew its $849,000 annual funding of six local Boy Scout councils because of homosexual exclusion. The policy of Boy Scouts of America excludes all homosexual youth and adults because "they make bad role models." In response to all of this, Blake Lewis, national spokesperson for the Boy Scouts, said, "Mainstream American families want these values for their young people." Blake went on to say there is no chance the group will change its policy even if financial support is withdrawn. He summarized, "Our values are not for sale!" May the standard of such stalwart conviction permeate our churches as well.[160]

**Con"fax"ion** At Italy's annual church fair in 1993, certain vendors promoted a high-tech confessional by which a parishioner could fax in confessions. The $3,850 – $8,500 setup is targeted for busy people who can't swing the time to stop by a church. This new confession box received sharp reviews from the Reverend Giancarlo Santi, president of the Commission for Sacred Art in the diocese of Milan. He said the new invention had "turned the confessional into a space-age telephone booth." Traditional Catholic teaching holds that the sacrament of confession requires the presence of the priest and the person confessing.[161]

**Conflict Resolution** "Hot heads and cold hearts never solved anything." —*Billy Graham*[162]

**Conflict Resolution** In 1993, a fifty-six-year-old man (whose name was not released) in Quebec became very distraught with Attorney General Gil Remillard's handling of his case. The man was allegedly injured in a fire years ago and had been unsuccessfully trying to receive compensation for it. In protest against Quebec's attorney general, this man cut off his own finger with an ax and mailed it to Remillard. He was charged for uttering threats against the attorney general but didn't receive any charges for mailing in his finger. There is a way which seems right to a man, but in the end, it's about as useless as cutting off your finger (Prov. 14:12—loosely).[163]

**Conformity** A farmer once went to the county fair with a pumpkin that was the exact size and shape of a two-gallon jug. His pumpkin won the blue ribbon. When someone asked how he got a pumpkin to look like that, he said, "It was easy. As soon as it started to grow, I stuck it inside a two-gallon jug." Paul exhorts us to not be conformed to this world (Rom. 12:2). If we don't heed his advice, we will soon find ourselves pressed into the mold of this world.[164]

**Conscience** From the wisdom of Bil Keane's *Family Circus* comes a little jewel that helps define conscience. While the two little brothers were contemplating a deed that didn't seem right, the older brother felt the prick of his conscience and said, "Conscience is like Mommy tellin' you not to do somethin' but she isn't there."[165]

**Conscience** When asked to define conscience, one six-year-old boy wasn't quite sure what it was but thought it had something to do with feeling bad when you kick girls.[166]

**Consistency** In 1991, *The New England Journal of Medicine* published a study on dieting conducted by Dr. Kelly D. Brownell at Yale University. This research was based on thirty-two years of follow-up study on 5,127 men and women. Dr. Brownell and his associates discovered it is more hazardous to yo-yo diet than to stay consistently overweight. The study found that the risk of dying from heart disease is about 70 percent higher in those with fluctuating weight than in those whose weight stays reasonably the same. Spiritual inconsistency is equally destructive. A consistent diet of worship, Bible study, prayer, evangelism, fellowship, and prayer is far healthier than an occasional revival feast.[167]

**Constitution** John Adams wrote, "Our constitution was made only for a moral and religious people. It is wholly inadequate for the government of any other." Our rejection of his thoughts can be summarized by these truths:

- In public schools you may distribute condoms to twelve-year-olds without parental consent, but you may not give them a Bible under any circumstances.

- At school you may attack individuals with racially-motivated hate language, but you may not pray God's blessing over them.
- You may not display a cross on public property, unless it's on fire, in which case the First Amendment protects your action.
- In most states a minor may abort an unborn child without her parent's consent, yet she can't go on a field trip to the zoo without parental permission.
- In America, arguments are waged against the use of dogs for medical research but in favor of the right to abort babies for the same purpose.[168]

**Convenience** In 1992, Southwestern Bell Telephone Company started a new program called Call Completion. It is now a standard part of the phone company's daily operation. If you call directory assistance for a phone number, they offer to complete the call for you by dialing the number and charging you thirty cents. Obviously, you can hang up and make the call yourself and save the three dimes. Nonetheless, nearly 8 percent of their customers use the service and generate an extra $2 million annually for the phone company. "Customer Convenience" is the buzz-phrase of the 1990s, and it's no exception in the church. Significant numbers of people prefer to pay someone else to do what God has equipped them to do.[169]

**Conviction** "Standing in the middle of the road is very dangerous; you get knocked down by the traffic from both sides." —*Margaret Thatcher*[170]

**Cooperation** Cooperation in the church is imperative. We must all work together, just as the members of our physical bodies must cooperate with one another. Just to keep your balance while standing still, you need to work about three hundred muscles. If that much effort is needed to stay idle, how much more cooperation is needed to move forward![171]

**Cooperation** Southwestern Baptist Theological Seminary in Fort Worth, Texas is the largest seminary in the world. In 1930, things were much different. They had to cut faculty salaries by 10 percent in May of that year. Music teachers were given no salary; instead, they were asked to charge students for music lessons as their compensation. Eventually, no salaries could be paid, and faculty members accepted donations of food from local Texas churches. In September of 1930, Dr. L. R. Scarborough, the seminary's president, brought the following emotional report to the Southern Baptist Convention Executive Committee: "Brethren, we are through at Southwestern. For two years we haven't paid faculty salaries. We have nothing with which to meet expenses. Our percentage of the allocation will not see us through another year. Here is my resignation and I turn over to you the seminary property. You'll have to sell it to pay our debts, and Southwestern will go out of existence." After a few moments of stunned silence, Dr. Sampey, president of Southern Seminary, said, "I may lose my job for what I am about to say. Southern Seminary has some income from endowments on which we can live. I move that Southern Seminary's apportionment be cut and the difference given to Southwestern." Through unselfish cooperation, a financial disaster was converted into a mighty force for dispensing the gospel throughout our world.[172]

**Corporate Purpose** "To glorify God by being a faithful steward of all that is entrusted to us. To have a positive influence on all who come in contact with Chick-Fil-A." It's hardly a purpose statement you would expect to see in corporate America, but it's what you see displayed prominently in front of the Chick-Fil-A headquarters in Atlanta, Georgia. It's the philosophy by which the founder, Truett Cathy, lives. No wonder they are closed on Sundays but still outsell competitors who stay open seven days a week.[173]

**Cosmetic Surgery** Americans are spending over $1 billion a year on cosmetic surgery. Cosmetic operations have risen 60 percent in the last decade, and the number of plastic surgeons has quadrupled since 1965. In 1 Samuel 16:7 we are reminded that "Man looks at the outward appearance, but the Lord looks at the heart." [174]

**Courage** Gail Devers has been one of the fastest women in the world. In 1992, she covered 100 meters in 10.82 seconds to win the Olympic gold medal for the 100 meter dash. Just a year earlier she could barely walk. After a disappointing performance in the 1988 Olympics she began to experience declining health. By 1990 she was in terrible condition and finally pursued medical help. The diagnosis was Graves' disease, and radiation began in the early months of 1991. Devers received too much radiation and experienced alarming side effects. The pain became so intense that she returned to the doctors. The doctors then realized the situation of over-radiation and modified the treatment. They noted Devers would have required the amputation of her feet, had she walked on them two more days. Her condition was regulated by March of 1991, and she returned to the track. Less than eighteen months later she was in the Barcelona Olympic track stadium praying, "God, help me run the race of my life." Her prayer was answered. "If you have a problem and you are about to give up," Devers said, "think of me. Last year, I couldn't walk. Now, I've got a gold medal for running. The last three years of my life have definitely been a miracle." Strength is drawn from the knowledge that others have suffered and overcome. (See 1 Peter 5:9.) [175]

**Covetousness** If the grass looks greener on the other side of the fence, it may mean they take better care of their grass. [176]

**Covetousness** In his short story "The Window," author G. W. Target tells of two seriously-ill men who occupied the same hospital room. The man by the window was propped up for an hour each day to drain fluid from his lungs. The other man spent his entire time on his back. The two men enjoyed each other's company and talked for hours about all different types of subjects. During the hour that one man sat up in his bed, he would describe all of the things he saw to his bedfast roommate. Each day great detail would be given to the activities going on outside. He described the park with its lovely lake and grand old trees. He would tell of children playing and lovers walking through the park outside their window. One day, a beautiful parade went by. Even though he couldn't hear the music, the man on his back could see it all in his mind as his roommate gave exquisite details. But it seemed unfair. Although he enjoyed listening to his friend describe the sights, he began to crave the view himself. His desire for the bed by the window grew into a consuming thought. It even kept him awake at night. Then, in the darkness of one sleepless night, his roommate began to cough. He was choking on the fluid in his lungs, and desperately groping for the button to call for help. The covetous roommate could have pushed his own button to summon a nurse, but instead, he watched the old man die. The following morning the nurse discovered the man's death. The standard procedure was carried out, and the body was removed. The surviving man then asked to switch beds so he could see out the window. At last, he would have what he felt he deserved. Painfully and slowly he struggled to prop himself up for his first look at the park. To his chagrin, the window looked out to a blank wall. Fulfillment in life is never achieved with the venom of covetousness.[177]

**Creation** Sir Isaac Newton had a perfectly scaled-down replica of the then known solar system built for his studies. A large golden ball represented the sun at the center, and the known planets revolved around it through a series of cogs, belts, and rods. It was an incredible machine. One day while Newton was studying his model, an agnostic friend stopped by for a visit. The man marveled at the machinery and asked, "Who made this exquisite thing?" Without looking up, Newton replied, "Nobody." "Nobody?" his friend asked. "That's right," said Newton, "all of these balls and cogs and belts and gears just happened to come together, and wonder of wonders, by chance they began revolving in their set orbits with perfect timing." The message was clear.[178]

**Creativity** Although the scoreboard is the primary focus of the NCAA "Final Four" Championship, in 1991 a group of investors had their eyes on the floor. After the title game was played on April 1, 1991 in Indianapolis, a group from Iowa Sports Marketing Inc. used their creativity to make Wall Street cringe with envy. They plopped down $65,000 in an investment that gave them an 850 percent return in less than a week. That's $548,900 to be exact. By purchasing the basketball floor on which the Final Four Tournament was played, the folks from Iowa gained the rights to do whatever they wanted to with the wooden court. Most companies would take the $65,000 court and seek to find users that would eventually help them recover their costs. These guys did the exact opposite. They cut up this brand new basketball court into 22,000 little pieces. To some it seemed like quite a waste; only three basketball games had been played on it. To the Hawkeyes, those little $6\frac{1}{2}$ inch x 5 inch pieces of floor represented a great investment. You see, they sold all 22,000 pieces of that basketball court for souvenirs at $24.95 a pop. Their creativity turned $65,000 into $548,900 in less than a week.[179]

**Credit Cards** Before you whip out that plastic, remember, most people don't handle these little debt detonators very well. The fact is, nearly 75 percent of Americans who use credit cards make only the minimum payment each month. At that rate (minimum payments) you could spend the next thirty years paying back a $3,000 credit card debt and give the financial institution $8,000 worth of interest. It's the principle of compound interest in reverse.[180]

**Critical Thinking** A little boy put together a detailed story to explain why he was home much later than expected. He told of being chased by a tiger on his way home from playing with friends. He chronicled the event by saying he finally fended off the tiger by taking a stick and hitting the tiger in the nose. He then hid in the bushes so the tiger couldn't find him. His mother obviously didn't buy the story, so the little guy shouted, "If you don't believe me, look at the evidence." He pulled out a stick and said, "This is the stick I used to hit the tiger." Sometimes we are guilty of using lame logic to defend our behavior or beliefs.[181]

**Criticism** God calls us to get in the game; not to keep score.[182]

**Criticism** Harrison's Postulate states, "For every action, there is an equal and opposite criticism." [183]

**Criticism** A practicing lawyer loved to attack his opponents through scathing letters printed in newspapers. In 1842, he ridiculed the wrong man. James Shields did not take kindly to the anonymous writer who lampooned him in the *Springfield Journal.* Mr. Shields tracked down the attorney who had publicly embarrassed him and challenged him to a duel. The man was a writer, not a fighter, but he could not get out of the duel without losing his honor. He was given the choice of weapons and chose swords in hopes of using his long arms to his advantage. He trained with a West Point graduate as he prepared to fight to the death. On the appointed day he met Mr. Shields on a sandbar in the Mississippi River. At the last minute their seconds intervened and convinced the men to stop the duel. The lawyer returned to his practice as a changed man. Never again did he openly criticize anyone. In fact, years later when he heard his wife criticize the southern people of the Civil War, President Abraham Lincoln said, "Don't criticize them; they are just what we would be under similar circumstances." Do you have a critical spirit? Lincoln did, but he changed. Make the change today so you, like Lincoln, can be known more for your tolerance than your criticism.[184]

**Criticism** Whether or not you like Jay Leno, Johnny Carson, or *The Tonight Show,* an interesting lesson can be found from NBC's late night studio. When Leno became the new host of *The Tonight Show,* he took some real heat. Critics unfavorably compared him to his predecessor, Johnny Carson. From all of the criticism you would have thought he was in big trouble, but he never got too worried. In fact, he kept a stack of unpleasant reviews on his desk for inspiration. One critic said, "Too many soft questions." Another one read, "He's being too nice." These unkind words didn't bother Leno, though, because they were written in 1962 and were directed at Jack Paar's replacement, "an awkward nobody named Johnny Carson." Few people succeed without criticism.[185]

**Critics** When Robert Fulton first introduced his new invention the steamboat, plenty of critics crowded on the river bank. These critics yelled, "It'll never start, it'll never start." Fulton proved them wrong. After a lot of clanking and groaning, it started moving down the river. The critics were momentarily quiet. Then they rallied and hollered, "It'll never stop, it'll never stop!" Never strive to please the critics, because you never will.[186]

**Cross** Camp Smith is the military installation that overlooks Pearl Harbor. During World War II, many survivors looked to a large white cross that stood on the crest in front of Camp Smith's hospital. During the war, that cross served as a visual reminder of the hope to be found in Jesus Christ. This cross was lighted at night and could be seen for many miles. In due time, the cross became offensive and was removed. A flagpole was put in its place and only a small piece of the cross ended up in a lobby display case. The history of Camp Smith points to another piece of history found in 1 Corinthians 1:18–25. The cross of Jesus Christ makes no sense to those who refuse to accept the one who hung upon it, but to those who believe, it is a sign of eternal hope.[187]

**Cross** On May 12, 1993 two slivers of an olive tree, said to have come from the cross on which Jesus was crucified, were sold for more than $18,000 in a crowded Paris auction. The bidding started at $1,858 and was completed just ninety seconds later when a woman in the front row offered $18,587. Accompanying the two slivers of wood were two certificates from the Vatican that apparently authenticated the wood back in 1855. This woman is not much different than many of us. We are willing to pay a high price for pieces of the cross, but we tend to balk at the thought of doing what Jesus commanded—carry the cross.[188]

**Cross** There is a nomadic people in the Sahara Desert known as the Tuareg. The Tuareg cross is their symbol. It is not a typical looking cross, because it is diamond-shaped with four projections coming from each point. It is not a Christian symbol because these people are Muslim. Strangely, though, historians and anthropologists are unsure of its origin and why it is so important to the Tuareg people. Simply stated, its meaning has been lost. Today, the beautiful symmetry and design of crosses in jewelry and art can cause the meaning of the cross to be skewed. May we as Christians make certain the cross never loses its true and eternal meaning.[189]

**Crucifixion** During the summer of 1984, John and Lauretta Reynolds were in Rome touring St. Peter's Basilica. As they viewed the immortal Pieta, where Mary holds the body of her crucified son, the reverent hush was interrupted by the voice of a troubled little girl. She, too, saw the famous sculpture, but was bothered by what she saw. Turning to her mother, the child asked, "What in the world have they done to Jesus?" The lady quickly tried to hush her young daughter but to no avail. She repeated the question with even more fervor, "But Mommy, what in the world have they done to Jesus?" Suddenly, the work of Michelangelo was no longer just a piece of art, but an indictment to the stark reality of how the world has indeed treated Christ.[190]

**Cynicism** A cynic is a person who knows the cost of everything, and the value of nothing.[191]

**Danger** "I believe the world is in a more dangerous situation now than before World War I or World War II." —*Billy Graham*[192]

**Day Care** Understandably, some families must utilize the services of a day care center, but many Americans use such centers merely to increase their buying power by putting both parents in the workforce. A comprehensive study of American families discovered that "even among dual-wage earning couples, nine out of every ten believe that children are better off being raised with a mother at home rather than in a day care setting."[193]

**Daytime TV** Johnny Carson, former host of *The Tonight Show*, expressed the sentiments of many when he said, "Daytime TV has become just one big gab bag of dysfunctional people talking to dysfunctional hosts about their miserable lives."[194]

**Dead or Alive** Madiha el-Sayed had a unique problem. In 1992, the forty-year-old housemaid was trying to prove she was alive. The *Salem Express* ferry sank on December 14, 1991 and she was listed as one of the 464 who drowned. Although her baggage was loaded on to the fateful ship, she was detained and did not board the voyage across the Red Sea. As far as the government was concerned, el-Sayed died in the tragedy and was later buried. Unfortunately, another body was buried as hers, so the Egyptian government refused to cooperate with her insistence that a mistake had been made. Consequently, she was unable to care for her three children and return to her job in Saudi Arabia. Her family was delighted to see her return on another ferry a few days after the incident, but the government was not so enthusiastic. She said, "The law does not believe that I am alive." Would you have similar problems if you had to prove your faith? James said, "Faith without works is dead." Do your works indicate your faith is alive?[195]

**Death** Dr. A. H. Strong told the story of two martyrs who were about to be burned. Both of these men had disabilities, as one was blind and the other was crippled. On their way to the stake of fire, one said, "Courage, brother! This fire will cure us both!" The refining fires of a believer's death will purge away all pain and sorrow.[196]

**Death** In 1992, the National Center for Health Statistics released the following list as the ten leading causes of death in the U.S.:
1. Heart disease: 737,867
2. Cancer: 496,152
3. Stroke: 145,551
4. Accidents (auto, air, etc.): 95,028
5. Chronic lung disease: 84,344
6. Pneumonia and influenza: 76,550
7. Diabetes: 46,833
8. Suicide: 30,232
9. Liver disease and cirrhosis: 26,694
10. Homicides and legal interventions: 22,909

It seems significant that many Americans are fearful of being murdered, yet more people are murdered by themselves than someone else. Giving people a reason to live is a mandate of the Church.[197]

**Death to Life** On January 26, 1994, Frederic Green was found stiff and cold on his bedroom floor. A neighbor contacted the police after noticing nearly two weeks of mail and newspapers piling up at the eighty-two-year-old man's door. Officers broke into the house in San Leandro, California, and discovered Green. The report noted, "He did not appear to be breathing, his flesh felt hard and chilled, and the stench of decay permeated the house." Protocol for such events required a coroner's office technician to gather evidence and take photographs. Lt. Dennis Glover told the *Oakland Tribune*, "As the technician's camera flashed, there was a very soft gasp." Green was revived and immediately rushed to the hospital, where he was treated for a number of problems and doctors believed he suffered a stroke. This Associated Press release reminds us of a spiritual truth. Satan has deemed us dead and gone with no hope for life. Yet one flash from the Light of the World can bring about new life and the experience of being born again.[198]

**Debt** In the world there are three categories of people: the haves, the have-nots, and the have-not-paid-for-what-they-haves. This third category could be represented by a man who told his wife they were going to start living within their income even if they had to borrow money to do it.[199]

**Debt** "The average American family spends more than $2,000 a year on interest payments alone." —*Larry Burkett*[200]

**Deception of Sin** Years ago, Paul Harvey described how an Eskimo kills a wolf. He first coats his knife with animal blood then allows it to freeze. He later adds another layer of blood and lets it freeze. This process is repeated until the knife is completely concealed by the frozen blood. The Arctic hunter then fixes his knife to the ground with the blade facing up. The unsuspecting wolf senses the blood and begins to lick the frozen blood. His appetite for more blood increases with each lick. He begins to lick more vigorously and unknowingly starts slicing his own tongue on the razor sharp knife. The wolf then continues to satiate his thirst for blood with his own warm blood. His perpetual desire will not be satisfied until death overtakes him. Sin is packaged in an attractive manner but always contains the blade of destruction.[201]

**Deception** When Italy's mandatory use of seat belts went into effect on April 27, 1989, enterprising Claudio Ciaravolo cashed in. Dr. Ciaravolo, a psychiatrist in Naples, invented a "security shirt." It consists of a white T-shirt with a diagonal black stripe designed to deceive the police into believing the motorist is buckled up.[202]

**Decisions** Do you ever feel like your way is best, even though nobody else seems to agree? In 1784, Benjamin Franklin wrote his daughter and expressed his unhappiness over the choice of an eagle as the symbol of America. He felt it was a mistake to not select his preference, the turkey. Although we would like to think we're always right, sometimes we're not![203]

**Decisions** "Even the right decision is the wrong decision if it is made too late." —*Lee Iacocca*[204]

**Dependability** Some fatherly advice came to Bob Hendricks years ago when his dad, Howard, told him, "Be so dependable that if you say you will be somewhere and don't show up, they send flowers." Lax dependability characterizes many believers today. Whether it's a promise for a favor or a commitment to perform a task, "let your yes mean yes . . ." (Matt. 5:37).[205]

**Depression** The average thirty-year-old American male is ten times more likely to be depressed than his father and twenty times more likely to be depressed than his grandfather. At any given time in America, there are between fifteen and twenty million people suffering from depression. Fifteen percent of these depressed individuals will commit suicide.[206]

**Depression** When asked what someone should do when feeling on the verge of a nervous breakdown, Dr. Karl Menninger responded, "Lock your house, go across the railroad tracks, find someone in need, and do something for him." Christians who feel they "aren't being fed" need to heed the good doctor's word. In ministry to others, we find the satisfaction Jesus spoke of at Jacob's Well: "My food is to do the will of him who sent me, and to accomplish his work" (John 4:34).[207]

**Determination** Michael Jordan is known as one of the best basketball players of all time, but it wasn't always that way. During Jordan's sophomore year (1978–79) at Laney High School in Wilmington, North Carolina, he didn't make the varsity team. Leroy Smith (who never made it to the NBA) beat out Michael Jordan for the only sophomore spot on the varsity squad. Jordan settled for Junior Varsity. "He didn't sulk or threaten to quit. He just started working harder and improving his game," said his high school coach, Fred Lynch. "If anything, it made him more determined."

Of course, we shouldn't fault Lynch (assistant coach during Jordan's days)—Leroy was 6'7" and Michael was just 5'10"![208]

**Dieting** How many Americans are currently on a diet? Fifty million, or 27 percent of all adults. This does not include all of the extra participants who temporarily start a post-holidays diet.[209]

**Dieting Jewelry** Yasuo Tomoyuki is an expert acupuncturist from Osaka, Japan who has invented jewelry for dieters. His 18-karat gold earrings sit on pressure points of the ear which he claims help suppress hunger. These little jewels cost a mere $338 a pair. (Maybe they work because after buying them, you can't afford to eat!) [210]

**Difference Maker** After an ocean-churning storm, thousands of starfish were washed ashore. A little boy was walking along the beach and throwing these marooned fish back into the water. A more sophisticated man was watching the small savior and felt it was his duty to point out the futility of such an endeavor. He called this boy's attention to the thousands of starfish that lined the beach. He commended the little guy for his compassion but quickly noted, "What you're doing is great, but frankly, it's not going to make much of a difference." The little sage picked up another starfish and said, "Maybe not," as he threw it back into the surf, "but it sure made a difference for that one." The difference one person can make often seems minuscule in comparison with the need at hand, but what you're doing may make a big difference in the life and eternity of one person.[211]

**Direction** The late Supreme Court Justice Oliver Wendell Holmes was on a train when the conductor came through collecting tickets. Holmes was unable to locate his ticket and became rather distraught. The conductor tried to console him by saying, "Mr. Holmes, don't worry. When you find your ticket, just mail it in. We trust you." The Justice responded in continued frustration,

"My dear man, that's not my problem. I need my ticket to tell me where I'm going." Like Mr. Holmes, we all need to know where we're going.[212]

**Discipleship** In 1933, Waskom Pickett published his book *Christian Mass Movements in India.* Some of the material in this book included research on 3,947 individuals who had become Christians. Each person was placed in one of four groups to indicate their motives for coming to Christ. People who came for "spiritual" reasons comprised Group 1. Groups 2–4 were made up of people who came for non-spiritual reasons (social status, peer pressure, or family tradition). All four groups were given strong discipleship after baptism and were monitored by Dr. Pickett. He discovered that those who came to Christ for non-spiritual reasons ended up becoming very committed believers. Over 70 percent became regular church attenders, at least 90 percent became financial contributors, and more than 93 percent were free from all signs of idolatry. If such results happen with less than pure motives, how much more could be accomplished if we actively and consistently train and disciple the "pure in heart!" This may reduce the fear of those "would-be-evangelists" who think their inadequacies will cause them to say something that will eternally destroy a lost person's opportunity for salvation.[213]

**Discipleship** In Dr. James Dobson's newsletter for September 1991, he told of his aborted trip to the Soviet Union in August of that same year. While being forced to cancel his trip and stay in London during the Soviet coup, he was able to speak with Soviet dissident, Irina Ratushinskaya, who had spent four years in labor camps as punishment for her Christian activities. President Reagan heard of her plight and put pressure on Gorbachev to release her during their meeting in Reykjavik. She now lives with her husband in London and longs for the day she can return to her native land. After being raised in an atheist's home she found an old Slavic Bible when she was twenty-three. She taught herself to read it and discovered a personal relationship with Christ. Her faith was discovered by the KGB, who infiltrated the Russian Orthodox Church as phony priests, and she was sent to a labor camp. She refused to deny the Lord, so they tortured her. A tooth was drilled without anesthetic to test her tolerance for pain. She was placed in an unheated room at fifty degrees for five months and given only a cotton gown. She sat on the cold floor and was fed every other day. This immovable woman said, "Following Christ is not a very pragmatic thing to do. It doesn't bring you very many benefits in the Soviet Union."[214]

**Discipleship** "Jesus, like any good fisherman, first catches his fish; then he cleans them." —*Mark Potter*[215]

**Discipleship** On December 19, 1991, St. Louis Police Chief Clarence Harmon gave a speech to bank executives at the Equality Savings and Loan Association. In the conference room he explained what he was doing to make the city safer. His talk was interrupted by an employee, who burst into the meeting to notify them that the bank had been robbed. Initially, everyone thought it was a joke. It wasn't. A robber made off with $1,000 while those who could have stopped him were busy in a meeting about crime prevention. Discipleship can easily digress to the same type of folly if we are not diligent to practice what we learn. Too often the Church has been holed up in a meeting while Satan is out holding up the world.[216]

**Discipleship** The United States Department of Labor recently came out with the following statistics. Eighty-three percent of Americans must be shown a project and then be supervised. Fourteen percent must be shown a project and then left unsupervised. Three percent can figure out what to do without instruction or supervision. This indicates that disciples are made 97 percent of the time, yet we often expect them to develop on their own. Jesus said, *"Make* disciples" (Matt. 28:19).[217]

**Discipleship** When Luis Gonzales played outfield for the Houston Astros, he told the press about his personal motto: "Go hard or go home!" Jesus said something similar when he addressed the issue of discipleship while talking to the rich young ruler in Luke 18:22–25. The call is clear: "Go hard or go home!" [218]

**Discipline** Children need two pats on the back. One high enough to encourage them when they do right, and one low enough to discourage them when they do wrong. Effective discipline requires knowing which end of the child to pat. [219]

**Disobedience** In the Houston, Texas, zoo you might find an unusual phenomenon. Although you pay to see and learn about animals, the alligator exhibit can tell you much more about people. In every other cage you don't find a large display of scattered coins. You see normal habitat, as you might expect, without a spattering of loose change. So why is there frequently money in with the alligators? Is it because there's water, and people seem enamored with throwing pocket change into water? There are other exhibits with plenty of water, but they don't have all the nickels, dimes, and quarters. The reason for this abundance of money stems from a sign by the alligators. As you read to learn more about these interesting creatures, the zoological society presents a reminder *not* to throw money into the water, as it only takes one coin, digested by an alligator, to kill the huge reptile. To the chagrin of the zoo staff, coins are often thrown all around the alligators. Whether it's coins in the alligator pit or just one tree in a garden called Eden, sinful man has a tough time obeying the rules. [220]

**Disposition** "I might have entered the ministry if certain clergymen I knew had not looked and acted so much like undertakers."
—*Oliver Wendell Holmes* [221]

**Distractions** When Deion Sanders played for the Atlanta Falcons, he once benched himself for a couple of plays during a regular season game because his earring fell out. Once he took care of the jewelry, he went back in the game. Distractions can come in all shapes and sizes.[222]

**Divine Protection** One night while John Paton was a missionary in the New Hebrides Islands, his mission station was surrounded by hostile natives. They were intent on killing the Patons and burning the station. Paton and his wife prayed through the night in hopes that God would deliver them. When daylight came the natives were gone. A year later when the tribal chief was converted to Christ, Paton asked him why they did not attack. The chief was surprised by Paton's question. He asked, "Who were all those men with you?" Although Paton knew of no other men, the chief said he was afraid to attack because he had seen hundreds of big men in shining garments who circled the mission station with their swords drawn. God's presence is real, whether or not we see it.[223]

**Divine Retraction** The following retraction had to be printed in the *Milton-Freewater Valley Herald*: "The title of a First Christian Church program in last week's paper should have been recorded as 'Our God Reigns.' It was inaccurately recorded as 'Our God Resigns.'" Thankfully we serve a God who has not given up on his sin-stained world, but has chosen instead to reign as the Lord of Lords and King of Kings.[224]

**Divorce** Statistics prove that children are the big losers in divorce. Penelope Stokes tells of a heartbreaking true story about one such child. Misty's parents divorced when she was four, and her dad moved away. The following summer she went with her grandparents to visit her dad in his new apartment. Grandpa took Misty to the pool one afternoon and held out his arms for her to jump. Misty loved to swim, but she was suddenly very frightened and wouldn't jump into her grandfather's arms. He insisted that he would catch her, but she stood trembling on the sidewalk. Grandpa repeatedly tried to persuade her to jump in, but she refused. He finally asked, "Misty, do you think I won't catch you? Do you think I'll just walk away?" Misty began sobbing and said, "Daddy did!" Research from the American Psychological Association shows that adults who grew up in broken homes are four times more likely to become divorced. Of this staggering problem, Dr. Silvio Silvestri of the Center for Adult Children of Divorce in South Lake Tahoe, California, has said, "There's a self-perpetuating cycle going on that's very alarming. We need to intervene."[225]

**Divorce** We've been desensitized by the statistic of a 50 percent divorce rate in America. It makes divorce seem normal if you think every other couple breaks up. Based on the 1990 Census Bureau records, that notion is erroneous. A new category tracks who has been married and who has been divorced. According to those figures, less than 20 percent have been divorced. What has inflated the figures to the 50 percent rate are those who have been divorced multiple times. Thus, the newlyweds of today can be encouraged by the fact that 80 percent of those who marry, do so for life.[226]

**Doctor's Orders** Untold billions are spent in the area of medicine each year, but ironically, "more than half of all patients fail to follow their physician's instructions." What occurs in the doctor's office also occurs in the Church. God's prescription for well-being is outlined in scripture, but many choose to ignore the Great Physician's orders.[227]

**Domestic Violence** The problem of domestic violence is a front page issue. One of the startling statistics now surfacing is this: "During the Vietnam era 58,000 American service persons died from combat related injuries. During those same years 54,000 women in the United States were murdered by their husbands, ex-husbands, or boyfriends." Court records reveal that men who murder their female partners receive a prison sentence of two to six years. Women who kill their partners get an average prison sentence of fifteen years.[228]

**Doubt** Some Christians fear they are the only believers who wrestle with doubts. Consequently they build façades of spiritual confidence, but feel like fakes. Fortunately, God understands such frustration and has provided stories of similar struggles to help us in the midst of our doubts. One of my favorites is found in Mark 9:24, but one that might hit closer to home comes from the founder of Methodism. Many people have heard of John Wesley's conversion at Aldersgate when he wrote of his experience as one in which his heart was "strangely warmed." He had previously taken a mission trip to America, only to discover he was not a minister but a lost soul. Most of the time the story ends at Aldersgate as if he lived "happily ever after." But less than a year later Wesley wrote in his journal, "I know that I am not a Christian. I know it because I do not feel that I love God and his Son Jesus Christ as my Savior." He would later lead England in a great spiritual awakening that sparked revival in America as well. In 1784 he established the formal beginnings of the Methodist denomination. Even great men of God have doubts. What we do with those doubts will dictate whether or not our faith is strengthened or weakened.[229]

**Dreams** Some people dream of worthy accomplishments, while others stay awake and do them.[230]

**Drink Offering** To celebrate the coming of Christian missionaries to a region of Zaire, a day-long event was filled with speeches, testimonies, and music. Judy, a missionary's daughter, recently recalled this event from years ago. That rally is best remembered for the way it ended. A very old man came before the crowd and insisted he be allowed to speak. He said his death was imminent and if he did not speak now the information he carried might never be known. He explained that when the missionaries first came a century ago, his people did not trust them. Missionaries were unusual and had a strange message. The tribal leaders decided to test the missionaries by slowly poisoning them to death. Over the months and years that followed, these tribesmen witnessed the fashion in which the missionary families handled death and grief. The old man said, "As we watched how they died, we decided we wanted to live as Christians." This story was unknown for a hundred years. Those who died painful, strange deaths never knew why they were dying or what impact their lives would have. Through it all, though, they stayed and preached their "strange" message. In Philippians 2:17, Paul mentioned the possibility of his life being a drink offering but rejoiced nonetheless. A drink offering appears to be a total waste of valuable resources, but if God is glorified, nothing is truly lost.[231]

**Drug Prevention** Parents cry, "How can we prevent our children from falling prey to drugs?" According to Steve Arterburn and Jim Burns, authors of *How to Drug-proof Your Kids*, significant studies indicate that kids who practice their faith in tangible ways (not merely church members) have less difficulty with drugs and alcohol. This same research reveals the propensity for substance abuse is significantly reduced when the parents, especially dads, have a visible and active spiritual life. When it comes to drug abuse prevention, "Just Say Yes" to the lordship of Jesus Christ.[232]

**Drunken Driving** When arrested for drunk driving in Malaysia, not only does the driver go to jail, but his or her spouse must serve jail time as well. Violation of the law is seen as a family problem.[233]

**Drunken Driving** One-quarter of your auto insurance premium goes toward drunken-driving claims. "Being filled with the Spirit" rather than "drunk with wine" (Eph. 5:18) would save about 25,000 lives each year in the U.S. and approximately $16 billion in insurance claims.[234]

**Dumpster Diving** Project Dignity produced a video called *The Fine Art of Dumpster Dining*. The Orange County, California, activist group made this unique video to provide health and safety advice for the homeless who salvage food from dumpsters. Among the tips is this advice, "Watch out for the broken glass and bleach many restaurants pour on discarded food to discourage scavengers." From 1965 to 1990, the Federal government spent over $3.4 trillion to help the poor. To spend that much money you would have to exhaust over $20,000 a minute for the next 274 years. Videos and money aren't the answer. The life-changing power of Jesus Christ is![235]

**Easter** During the days preceding Easter, Napoleon Bonaparte was about to overtake the Austrian village of Feldkirch. The villagers gathered to pray for deliverance on the Eve of Easter. On Easter morning the church bells rang to signal the day of worship. Napoleon heard the bells but didn't realize it was Easter. He thought those bells meant the Austrian armies had come to reinforce the village, so he sounded retreat. When the bells of Easter ring out, the enemies of God are forced to retreat.[236]

**Easter Celebration** The famed British minister, W. E. Sangster, began to lose his voice and mobility in the mid-1950s. His disease caused progressive muscular atrophy. He recognized the end was near, so he threw himself into writing and praying. In the midst of his suffering he pleaded, "Let me stay in the struggle, Lord. I don't mind if I can no longer be a general, but give me just a regiment to lead." Sangster's voice eventually failed completely, and his legs became useless. On Easter morning just a few weeks before his death, he took a pen and shakily wrote his daughter a letter. In it he said, "It is terrible to wake up on Easter morning and have no voice with which to shout, 'He is risen!'—but it would be still more terrible to have a voice and not want to shout." May every Easter bring many new voices that shout for the first time, "He is risen!"[237]

**Easter Eggs** Jeremy, a terminally ill student, was twelve years old and still in the second grade. He couldn't learn, made unusual noises, and often drooled. To most kids he was an object of humor;

to his teacher, Jeremy was an exasperatingly difficult student. Three months before he died, both students and teacher changed their opinion of him. Miss Miller gave an assignment before Easter that required all of the students to take an empty plastic egg and bring it back the next day with something in the egg that represented new life. The teacher planned to call Jeremy's parents that night and explain the assignment so that Jeremy would do what she asked, but several emergencies prevented her from calling. When she opened the nineteen eggs with the children, the first one had a flower in it, and the teacher affirmed the fact that a flower represents new life. The second egg contained a butterfly, which everyone agreed signified new life. A third egg with a moss-covered rock demonstrated new life as well. To the chagrin of Miss Miller, the fourth egg was empty. She quickly guessed it was Jeremy's egg and laid it down without comment. Jeremy piped up, "Miss Miller, aren't you going to talk about my egg?" Flustered, she said, "Jeremy, your egg is empty." He looked softly into her eyes and replied, "Yes, but Jesus' tomb was empty, too!" Miss Miller later spent the recess period crying with a softened heart. Three months later when Jeremy died, his theology was represented by nineteen plastic eggs on his casket—all of which were empty. The great hope of Easter is found in an empty tomb that promises new life. (The names have been changed for the sake of privacy.)[238]

**Easter Humor** In the tradition of the ancient Russian Orthodox church, the day after Easter was devoted to telling jokes. Priests would join with people in unveiling their best jokes for one another. It was an interesting tradition of imitating the cosmic joke that God pulled on Satan in the Resurrection. Satan thought he won on Friday but God had the last laugh on Easter Sunday. We would do well to laugh more often about the joyous victory we have through Christ.[239]

**Easter Lily** The Easter lily is the floral symbol of Easter, because its shape resembles a trumpet heralding the resurrection of Christ.[240]

**Easy Street** From the island of Oahu comes a little Hawaiian wisdom. If you take the Pali Highway north out of Honolulu, you come to Pali Pass. At Pali Pass you can turn right on Park Street. Go one block on Park Street, and you arrive at Easy Street. Turn left on Easy Street and drive one block. You then see a sign that reads, "Dead End." Those looking for the Easy Street of life are usually surprised by the road's predictable destination.[241]

**Education** Harvard has come a long way since its inception in 1636. The original stated purpose of the college was: "Let every student be plainly instructed and earnestly pressed to consider well that the main end of his life and studies is to know God, and Jesus Christ, which is eternal life (John 17:3). And therefore to lay Christ in the bottom is the only foundation of all sound knowledge and learning." The prestigious but now secular institution was initially founded to train ministers.[242]

**Effort** "There's no traffic jam on the second mile." —*Zig Ziglar*[243]

**Effort** To a friend who was a pathologist in Philadelphia, Howard Hendricks once asked, "Have you seen many brains?" "Hundreds of them," the pathologist responded. "Have you ever seen one worn out?" asked Hendricks. The pathologist friend answered, "I've never seen one even slightly used." As far as our brains are concerned, there's plenty of room for improvement.[244]

**Egotism** One nice thing you can say about egotists: they don't talk about other people.[245]

**Emotions** During World War II an American plane was flying a mission in Africa. Under the cloak of darkness they flew toward their destination of Benghazi in North Africa. A strong tail wind pushed the plane much faster than expected. When the instruments revealed they had reached their destination, the crew members apparently kept flying in disbelief of the gauges. They felt the instruments must be wrong, so they pressed on looking for a beacon light that was already miles behind. Eventually, the plane ran out of fuel, and the entire crew died when they crashed in the desert. Feelings can be a dangerous guide.[246]

**Emotions** Jessica Huffman's little two-year-old asked her for a Snoopy Band-Aid. Mrs. Huffman promised the needed first aid and asked, "What happened?" The child said, "I hurt my feelings." Physical hurts are usually obvious, but emotional hurts can be much more difficult to spot. When we become more sensitive to the feelings of others we will generally find there are many people around us who need a Snoopy Band-Aid for their hurt feelings.[247]

**Encouragement** Alexander Solzhenitsyn spent part of his life in a Soviet Siberian prison. At one point he was so physically weak and discouraged that he hoped for death. The hard labor, terrible conditions, and inhumane treatment had taken its toll. He knew the guards would beat him severely and probably kill him if he stopped working. So he planned to expedite his death by simply stopping his work and leaning on his shovel. But when he stopped, a fellow Christian reached over with his shovel and quickly drew a cross at the feet of Solzhenitsyn, then erased it before a guard could see it. He would later record that his entire being was energized by that little reminder of the hope and courage we find in Christ. He found the strength to continue because a fellow believer cared enough to remind him of our hope.[248]

**Encouragement** Mary Lincoln was the owner of a small box that contained the contents of her grandfather's pockets from the night he was assassinated. These effects were not publicly known until they came into possession of the Library of Congress. One of the items in the pocket of Abraham Lincoln on the occasion of his death was a letter to the editor praising Lincoln for his singleness of purpose. Everyone needs encouragement, even presidents as great as Lincoln.[249]

**Encouragement** Miss Thompson taught Teddy Stallard in the fourth grade. He was a slow, unkempt student, a loner shunned by his classmates. The previous year his mother died, and what little motivation for school he may have once had was now gone. Miss Thompson didn't particularly care for Teddy either, but at Christmas time he brought her a small present. Her desk was covered with well-wrapped presents from the other children, but Teddy's came in a brown sack. When she opened it there was a gaudy rhinestone bracelet with half the stones missing and a bottle of cheap perfume. The children began to snicker but Miss Thompson saw the importance of the moment. She quickly splashed on some perfume and put on the bracelet, pretending Teddy had given her something special. At the end of the day Teddy worked up enough courage to softly say, "Miss Thompson, you smell just like my mother . . . and her bracelet looks real pretty on you too. I'm glad you like my presents." After Teddy left, Miss Thompson got down on her knees and prayed for God's forgiveness. She prayed for God to use her as she sought to not only teach these children but to love them as well. She became a new teacher. She lovingly helped students like Teddy and by the end of the year he had caught up with most of the students. Miss Thompson didn't hear from Teddy for a long time. Then she received this note: "Dear Miss Thompson, I wanted you to be the first to know. I will be graduating second in my class. Love, Teddy Stallard." Four years later she got another note: "Dear Miss Thompson, They just told me I will be graduating first in my class. I wanted you to be the first to know. The university has not been easy, but I liked it. Love, Teddy Stallard." Four years later: "Dear Miss Thompson, As of today, I am Theodore Stallard, M.D. How about that? I wanted you to be the first to know. I am getting married next month. I want you to come and sit where my mother would sit if she were alive. You are the only family I have now; Dad died last year. Love, Teddy Stallard." Miss Thompson went to the wedding and sat where Teddy's mother would have sat, because she let God use her as an instrument of encouragement.[250]

**Encouragement** Someone noted, "Man doesn't live by bread alone. He also needs buttering up." [251]

**Encouragement** When asked why he did not give his son more early encouragement, Leonard Bernstein's father answered, "How was I to know he would grow up to be Leonard Bernstein?" [252]

**Envy** "Envy is the art of counting another's blessings instead of one's own!" —*Ruth M. Walsh*[253]

**Eternal Life** H. L. Hunt made millions of dollars as a Texas oilman. He was an aggressive businessman who had little regard for time. His chief confidant said he was just as apt to call in the middle of the night as he was to call in the middle of the day. One night Hunt called at 2:00 A.M. and said, "John, I just made the greatest trade of my life. I traded the here for the hereafter." That was the night H. L. Hunt had become a Christian.[254]

**Eternal Life** Steve McQueen was a top-billing actor who led a life as tough as the ones he portrayed on the screen. Success filled his life until alcohol and a failed marriage left him empty. In his despair he attended a crusade led by one of Billy Graham's associates. McQueen made a profession of faith and requested an opportunity to speak with Billy Graham. A connecting flight in Los Angeles allowed Dr. Graham to spend a couple of hours with Mr. McQueen in the actor's limousine. The great evangelist shared numerous scriptures in his quest to give spiritual hope and confidence. Steve McQueen struggled with the thought of God giving eternal life to a man who had such a checkered past. In Titus 1:2, Steve McQueen found his hope: "the hope of eternal life, which God, who cannot lie, promised long ages ago." He requested something to write down the verse, but Billy Graham gave McQueen his Bible instead. Later, Steve McQueen died in Mexico while seeking experimental treatment for his terminal cancer. He passed into eternal life with his Bible opened to Titus 1 and his finger resting on verse 2. Regardless of our past, we have the hope of God's eternal promise.[255]

**Eternal Life** Thelma Gruber's four-year-old grandson was memorizing John 3:16. He quoted what you would normally read from the fourth gospel until he made a slight manuscript change. He said, ". . . whoever believes in him should not perish, but shall live happily ever after." Not a bad paraphrase![256]

**Eternal Rewards** The widow's two small coins didn't appear to be worth much when she first offered them to God. A banker has shown otherwise. He estimated that had her monetary gift been placed in a bank drawing 4 percent interest compounded semi-annually, the account would now be worth 4.8 billion trillion dollars. (That's $4,800,000,000,000,000,000,000.) If a financial institution can multiply the value of two small coins like that, just think what God can do with our gifts.[257]

**Ethically Challenged** It is usually very difficult to admit dishonesty. One pundit has tried to salve the conscience by using the term "ethically challenged" instead of dishonest. It sounds better, but as the saying goes, "a mule in a tuxedo is still a mule."[258]

**Euthanasia** Derek Humphry wrote *Final Exit: The Practicalities of Self-Deliverance and Assisted Suicide for the Dying*. It quickly became number one in the hard-cover advice category on *The New York Times* best-seller list and sold out in virtually every bookstore across America. Humphry, president and principal founder of the Hemlock Society (an euthanasia organization founded in 1980), "thought the time was right for a responsible suicide manual." According to the Gallup poll you have to wonder: in 1975 only 41 percent of the respondents felt as though the terminally ill had the moral right to commit suicide. By 1990 that figure had increased to 66 percent. *Final Exit* gives detailed instructions on a variety of ways to commit suicide. It is filled with charts that specify drug overdoses and a variety of suicide techniques. Mr. Humphry says he prefers the technique of prescribed drugs used in combination with a plastic bag over the head.[259]

**Evangelical Warning** The 150th anniversary of the YMCA (Young Men's Christian Association) occurred in 1994. On June 4, 1844, twelve young men met in the bedroom of George Williams in London, England. They had come together to develop some strategies for evangelizing the masses of men who were coming to the city in search for work. Williams' plan was simple. He prayed with other Christians for the salvation of those with whom they worked. After three years of this practice, the drapery firm of Hitchcock and Rogers had shifted from being a place where it was "almost impossible for a young man to be a Christian" to becoming a working environment where it was "almost impossible to be anything else." The success of so many coming to Christ at his place of employment led Williams to expand the ministry to other shops. This expansion included lecture courses, libraries, reading rooms and sports facilities. In all of these activities, Williams and the other founders of the YMCA "regarded evangelism as foundational and indispensable." Fifty years later, in June of 1884, Queen Victoria bestowed the honor of knighthood upon Williams for his "distinguished service to the cause of humanity." Evangelism was the founding passion of the YMCA. Tremendous benefits have resulted from the 150 years of service the Y has provided. But today many do not even know what the C stands for, and fewer still have found Christ in their gyms. The edge of evangelism can be easily lost if it ever becomes a secondary goal. What will your church or denomination be like in 150 years? Will it be a place of the gospel, or just another humanitarian institution?[260]

**Evangelism** A client once wrote a company for information about their product. In the letter he specifically stated that he did not want a salesman to call on him. The information he requested was rather technical and could not be adequately communicated in a letter, so the company sent a sales representative anyway. When the rep showed up at the man's office, he received a cold reception. The potential client repeatedly reminded the salesman that his letter had stated, "No salesman!" The sales rep was a trainee with very little sales experience. He tried to calm the irate executive and assure him there would be nothing more than a simple exchange of information. The trainee finally said, "Mister, I'm about as close to a 'no-salesman' as they've got." Many of us feel "as close to a no-salesman as God's got," but he still has a place for each of us to share our faith. A lot of people aren't very good fishermen, but that doesn't stop them from going fishing. The same should hold true for our spiritual fishing trips as well.[261]

**Evangelism** C. T. Shedd, the renowned athlete and missionary, once said, "Some wish to live within the sound of a church or chapel bell; I want to run a rescue shop within a yard of hell."[262]

**Evangelism** D. L. Moody was known as "Crazy Moody" because of his zealous approach to evangelism. He resolved to speak with at least one person each day regarding his or her relationship to Jesus Christ. Most Christians recall at least something about this evangelist who dominated the last four decades of the nineteenth century. When a fellow minister told him, "The world has yet to see what God will do with a man fully consecrated to him," Moody resolved, "By the grace of God, I will be that man." He and Ira Sankey shook two continents for God, but what if Edward Kimball hadn't been obedient to God on April 21, 1855? On that day, Mr. Kimball led Moody to Christ. This very timid man was Moody's Sunday School teacher at a Congregational church where Moody's uncle forced him to attend. Mr. Kimball determined in his heart that he would go speak to his student at the shoe store in which he worked. With tears in his eyes, Kimball approached the seventeen-year-old shoe clerk. "I asked him to come to Christ, who loved him and who wanted his love and should have it," said Kimball. The surprised Moody opened his heart to Christ, and thousands of lives were transformed by his forty years of ministry. Only God knows what he has planned as a result of our obedience in sharing the gospel.[263]

**Evangelism** A bumper sticker I saw reminds us: "Friends don't let friends die without Jesus." [264]

**Evangelism** "God is not saving the world; it is done. Our business is to get men and women to realize it." —*Oswald Chambers*[265]

**Evangelism** In Chile, missionary Karen Wright experienced a bizarre tradition at the funeral of a Catholic neighbor. During the service an offering was collected. Then the priest said, "Thank you for your participation in the salvation of this man." After hearing these words and seeing only small change in the offering plate, Karen thought, "If these people really believed their offering would help save this man, wouldn't they sacrifice and give more?" She then personalized this thought by saying, "I, and many others, profess the truth about salvation through faith in Christ. Yet, if I really believe it, wouldn't I be giving more than small coins for spreading the good news of Jesus Christ?"[266]

**Evangelism** Membership in many Korean churches involves more than "walking the aisle." In fact, a lot of American Christians would be wanting for a church if the same standards were utilized here in the United States. The requirement for membership in many Korean churches is not only a profession of faith in Jesus Christ, but a convert at your side as well. Not only must you believe in Christ, but you must lead someone else to the Savior before you can become a church member. Based upon our Korean brothers' standards, would you qualify for church membership?[267]

**Evangelism** Norman Cates shared the humorous story of a guy who prayed this prayer every morning: "Lord, if you want me to witness to someone today, please give me a sign to show me who it is." One day he found himself on a bus when a big, burly man sat next to him. The bus was nearly empty but this guy sat next to our praying friend. The timid Christian anxiously waited for his stop so he could exit the bus. But before he could get very nervous about the man next to him, the big guy burst into tears and began to weep. He then cried out with a loud voice, "I need to be saved. I'm a lost sinner and I need the Lord. Won't somebody tell me how to be saved?" He turned to the Christian and pleaded, "Can you show me how to be saved?" The believer immediately bowed his head and prayed, "Lord, is this a sign?" Are you looking for a "sign" to start witnessing? It can be found in Matthew 28:19–20 and Acts 1:8.[268]

**Evangelism** "Remember, unsaved people are not the enemy. They are victims of the enemy." —*Joe Aldrich*[269]

**Evangelism** The Persian Gulf War was a demonstration of military success, yet the greatest victory was not the liberation of Kuwait. According to official statistics, there were 141 casualties resulting from the Middle East crisis. During that same period of conflict, Southern Baptist chaplains recorded 1,200 professions of faith among the troops. As Dr. Rick Warren observed, "It was the first war in history where more people were saved than killed."[270]

**Evangelism** While speaking in London, evangelist D. L. Moody was approached by a British companion who wanted to know the secret of Moody's success in leading people to Christ. Moody directed the man to his hotel window and asked, "What do you see?" The man looked down on the square and reported a view of crowded streets. Moody suggested he look again. This time the man mentioned seeing people—men, women, and children. Moody then directed him to look a third time, and the man became frustrated that he was not seeing what Moody wanted him to see. The great evangelist came to the window with watery eyes and said, "I see people going to hell without Jesus. Until you see people like that, you will not lead them to Christ." What do you see in five o'clock traffic, a busy restaurant, a crowded waiting room, your neighborhood, or your extended family?[271]

**Evangelism** Witnessing is sidelined by fear more than any other reason. At every evangelistic training session, fear is mentioned as the greatest barrier to witnessing. Stan Clark, a Mission Service Corps volunteer with the Souther Baptist Home Mission Board's personal evangelism department, said, "Christians should not assume that fear is God's way of telling them that witnessing is not their gift. Fear is natural, but God intends for Christians to overcome it and share their faith with others." Fear can actually be beneficial, in that it keeps us humble and dependent upon God. So how do you overcome incapacitating fear? Clark suggests five ways:

1. Have a planned approach to witnessing.
2. Remember that witnessing is the fulfillment of God's plan for Christians.
3. Pray for sensitivity, direction and strength.
4. Presume all people are lost and receptive.
5. Practice to become more comfortable with witnessing.

Above all, Clark said, "It takes the same faith to witness that it does to receive Jesus as Savior." If you have faith in God to save you, have faith enough in God to believe he can use you as an effective witness for him.[272]

**Evangelistic Benefits** Billy Graham wrote about a woman who, after experiencing a death in her family, sensed a strong urgency to share her faith. When a repairman completed servicing her furnace, she backed him against the wall and asked, "If that furnace had blown up in your face and you had died, would you know for certain where you would spend eternity?" The guy was so startled by the inquiry, he forgot to leave her a bill. So many people worry about personal disadvantages that witnessing may cause. Here's a lady who shared her faith and got her furnace fixed free.[273]

**Evangelistic Concern** Darrell Robinson has reminded us of the spiritual crisis facing America. "The United States is third among nations with the most unsaved people. Only China and India have more." There is little question that our nation desperately needs both spiritual awakening and genuine revival.[274]

**Evangelistic Concern** Pastor Stephen Bly, of Winchester, Idaho, was fortunate to have witnessed the beauty of discipleship in one of his church members. August Jensen was an eighty-four-year-old widower who sat toward the back in church. Many perceived him as one who no longer had much to offer. His pastor learned otherwise. On a visit to Gus' house Pastor Bly saw the old man's daily regimen. He spent two and a half hours in Bible study and prayer followed by a three-mile walk where he conversed with God. Lately, he had been fasting two meals a day and praying for the salvation of Anthony, a neighborhood teen who was good for little more than mischief. The pastor asked, "How long have you been fasting and praying for him like that?" Gus replied, "Forty days." "How much longer will you continue?" wondered his pastor. With a smile, Gus said, "As long as it takes." On day fifty-one, Anthony committed his life to Christ.[275]

**Evangelistic Death Threat** Mordecai Ham emerged as an evangelist from Kentucky at the turn of the century. He had a background in business and the study of law. From the very beginning his approach was zealous and blunt. Rather than sit and talk with Christians at revival sites, Ham insisted on being taken to the worst sinners in the community. On one occasion a non-believer hid in a corn field, but Ham tracked him down. The man asked what his intentions were, and the evangelist said he was going to pray for God to kill him. When the man protested, Ham told him he shouldn't be bothered, since he didn't believe in God, anyway. But if there was a God, then death would be appropriate for a man who had poisoned his family's spiritual prospects. The lost man begged him not to pray for his death, so Ham relented and prayed for his salvation. At the final meeting Ham baptized the man and his family. The key to effective evangelism is not methodology (e.g., confrontation vs. friendship) but passion. Mordecai Ham had what many of us lack today, passion for the lost.[276]

**Evangelistic Priorities**  A few years ago when Bill McCartney was coaching the top-ranked Colorado Buffaloes, he had a leader of a nationally-known ministry speak to his players. For thirty minutes, the dynamic preacher pulled out all the stops and exhorted the young men to reach beyond themselves and unite for victory on the football field. When he finished his presentation he sat down next to McCartney and asked, "Well, Coach, what do you think of that?" The wise coach looked him in the eye and said, "You know, all you seem to care about is whether or not they win a football game. And all I care about is whether or not they know Jesus Christ. We should trade places."[277]

**Evolutionary Change**  On July 21, 1925, the "Monkey Trial" ended in Dayton, Tennessee. John T. Scopes was convicted of violating state law by teaching Darwin's theory of evolution. The conviction was later overturned, but it reveals a stark difference between then and now. Today it is the creationist who must stand trial, while the evolutionist controls the gavel of educational laws. An optimist would note that if that much change could take place in seventy years, we can reverse the current trends and bring about positive, revolutionary changes for our children and grandchildren to enjoy.[278]

**Excellence**  In 1993, commemorations marked the twenty-fifth anniversary of Bobby Kennedy's assassination. Before Sirhan Bishara took Bobby's life in 1968, JFK's younger brother was amassing a large following with his theme, "America can do better." What Kennedy said of America, is what Jesus says to the Church and Christians today: "We can do better."[279]

**Excellence**  A slovenly-dressed soldier appeared before his commander, Alexander the Great. The mighty leader asked the soldier for his name. The unimpressive soldier responded, "Alexander, sir." Alexander the Great commanded, "Change your name or change your ways." With the title of Christian comes a level of excellence that must be observed.[280]

**Excellence**  During his service in the Navy, Jimmy Carter applied for the nuclear submarine program. The legendary Admiral Hyman Rickover interviewed him for the job. Toward the end of the interview the Admiral asked, "How did you stand in your class at the Naval Academy?" Carter proudly answered, "Sir, I stood fifty-ninth in a class of 820." He fully expected congratulations from his superior but got a much different response. Rickover asked, "Did you do your best?" The former president started to say, "Yes, sir," but when he took a moment to reflect he had to admit there were times when he had not given his best. He finally replied, "No, sir, I didn't always do my best." Admiral Rickover looked at Carter for a long time, then asked one final question, "Why not?" Are you giving God your best? If not, why?[281]

**Excellence**  Howard Hendricks is a big fan of Van Cliburn. On one occasion a friend arranged for Dr. Hendricks to meet the famed pianist after attending a concert. Dr. Hendricks expressed great admiration for Cliburn's remarkable musical abilities and asked how much time he spent practicing. Without hesitation Van Cliburn said, "I practice eight to nine hours a day." He noted that two of those hours were invested in nothing more than scales and fingering exercises, the basics. The price tag of excellence is high.[282]

**Excellence**  "It's not good enough that we do our best; sometimes we have to do what is required." — *Winston Churchill*[283]

**Excellence**  On June 17, 1885, the Statue of Liberty arrived in New York City aboard the French ship *Isere*. Miss Liberty's sculptor was the noted Frenchman, Frederic-Auguste Bartholdi.

Together with his crew, Bartholdi created a masterpiece of excellence. The intricacies of this statue are incredible. One intriguing aspect of this commitment to excellence can be found atop her head. The detail given to this section of the statue makes you think the sculptor planned for the whole world to frequently gaze down at Lady Liberty's head. The fact is, once she was raised to her full height of more than 151 feet, only the seagulls could appreciate the artist's propensity for excellence. Bartholdi didn't think anyone would notice his work up top, but he still wanted every inch to be finished with the best he had to offer. Good thing, because in 1903, Orville and Wilbur Wright created a new avenue for the world to examine Bartholdi's work. Excellence starts when we're committed to doing our best, whether or not anybody else will ever notice. Besides, somebody like Orville or Wilbur may come along and make sure the whole world takes notice of your work.[284]

**Excitement**  The Bethany Missionary Baptist Church in Dallas was taken to court by one of the church's deacons. This man had a herniated disc and blamed the church for his problem. He claimed his back injury occurred when he was assisting a fellow church member who became "overly excited during the sermon." Many churches would welcome a lawsuit like that.[285]

**Excuses**  Excuses abound for not attending church. The Tenth Presbyterian Church in Philadelphia ran an ad targeted for excuse-prone professionals living downtown. The lead line read, "Jesus Hated Church, Too!" The following lines said, "It's boring. The people are phony. The politics are less than righteous. Jesus hated the same things. But he never used it as an excuse not to worship. Maybe he knew something you don't. Find out this Sunday." The church wasn't perfect when the only perfect man walked this earth, but he never let that keep him away on the Sabbath.[286]

**Excuses**  Pastor Greg Gearing of Greater Valley Baptist Church in Phoenix put together an analogy of a sold-out football game and a less-than-sold-out church. He refers to it as "Ten Reasons For Never Attending Another Game":

1. I was taken to too many games by my parents when I was growing up.
2. It seems that the games are always scheduled when I want to do other things.
3. Every time I go to a football game, somebody asks for money.
4. Although I go to the game often, most of the people aren't even friendly enough to speak to me.
5. The seats are too hard and uncomfortable. Besides, I often have to sit right down in front, on the 50-yard line.
6. I suspect that there are a lot of hypocrites sitting nearby who come to see their friends and what others are wearing rather than to see the game.
7. The referee says things I don't agree with.
8. The band plays songs that I've never heard before.
9. Some games last too long, and I'm late getting home.
10. I have a book on football. I can stay at home and read it.[287]

**Exercise**   Please take time to exercise each week. Sixty-two percent of ministers who died in 1992 died as a result of heart attacks. Dr. Kenneth Cooper, the internationally-known founder of the aerobics movement, reminds ministers, "Of professional groups, pastors are the most deconditioned people I see." He further notes, "Dedication of thirty minutes three times a week to some type of sustained physical activity will improve the quantity as well as the quality of your life." We want you to be around a long time so please take this message to heart—literally.[288]

**Expectancy**   George and Jeanie Douglas were bankrupt just fifteen years ago. Today they enjoy the benefits of being co-founders of the $40 million company Computer Business Services. When George lost his job and was trying to figure out what his future would hold, he decided to change his attitude about life and become more of an optimist. As part of his new commitment to living with greater expectancy, Douglas took a spiral notebook and drew a line down the middle of one page. On one side he wrote "yes" and on the other he put "no." He then stuck that notebook in their car as a reminder to look for opportunities. Every time they drove into a parking lot they quit taking the open parking spaces far from the door and started driving up toward the front with expectations of finding a place. They tracked their results from every parking lot for seven years. If they found a spot close to the door they marked it on the "yes" side of the notebook. If they had to take a place that wasn't near the door then they marked "no." They compiled the results of their little seven-year experiment and found that 67 percent of the time there was a parking space near the door. Life has similarities to parking lots. Opportunities await those people who live with expectancy. Those who live without it may never realize the potential they possess.[289]

**Expectancy** If you bring a thimble to God, he'll fill it. If you bring a bucket to God, he'll fill that. If you bring a fifty-gallon barrel to God, he'll fill that, too. Which best describes your expectations of God? A thimble, a bucket, or a barrel?[290]

**Expectations** School children were used for an experiment in education. The children in three groups were equally average students. Controllers of the study made a significant change, though. They placed the three groups with three different teachers and told each teacher the status of the students. One teacher was told her group consisted of "exceptional" students. Another teacher was given average students and the third acquired slow children. All of the students were equal but classified differently. Throughout the school year each of the three teachers subconsciously treated their students just like they had been classified. At the end of the year the students were tested, and the results were startling. Although they began the school year as equals, at the end of the year each group scored exactly as they had been classified and treated. The exceptional students tested above average, the average scored in the middle and the slow students ended up with below-average grades. In essence, each student lived up to the expectations and treatment of the teachers. What we receive from others and from life will generally be no more than what we expect or give.[291]

**Experience** When a person with experience meets a person with money, the person with experience will end up with the money and the person with money will end up with experience. Experience isn't always fun, but it can be valuable.[292]

**Experiencing God** "Not by might nor by power, but by my Spirit, says the LORD of hosts" (Zech. 4:6). Henry Blackaby understood this verse when Expo '86 came to Vancouver. He and the 2,000 people in Vancouver's association of churches were convinced God wanted to use them to reach the twenty-two million people that would come to the fair. Two years before the fair they began making plans. At that time the total income for the entire association was $9,000. Yet, for the year of the World's Fair, they set a budget of $202,000. They had commitments which would provide about 35 percent of that budget. The remaining 65 percent depended completely on prayer. As an association, they fervently prayed for God to provide what they felt he desired. By the end of that year, $264,000 had come in from all over the world, and God used that group of believers to be the catalyst for almost twenty thousand people coming to know Jesus Christ. Blackaby said, "You cannot explain that except in terms of God's intervention. Only God could have done that. God did it with a people who had determined to be servants who were moldable and remained available for the Master's use."[293]

**Extravagance** In 1626, Peter Minuit, the director-general of Dutch West India Company's settlement in North America, made what he thought was a very good deal. He bought Manhattan Island from native Indian chiefs for $24. Unfortunately for him, company headquarters didn't think it was such a bargain and charged him a fine for his "extravagance." Mr. Minuit's extravagance would not purchase a square inch of Manhattan Island today. What we see as extravagant today may someday be seen as cheap.[294]

**Faith** Faith can never be exercised by proxy. You must actively develop it yourself. Spiritual growth begins when we move beyond the futile attempts to grow passively and start actively engaging our faith. Howard Hendricks has correctly discovered, "There is no such thing as a correspondence course for swimming." If you want to swim you must get in the pool. Proactive faith requires "getting wet." Maybe that is why "only 4 out of every 100 Southern Baptists have ever shared their faith in Jesus Christ."[295]

**Faith** "Faith is the refusal to panic." —*Martin Lloyd-Jones*[296]

**Faith** "God can't steer a parked car." —*Norman Wharr*[297]

**Faithfulness** Yellowstone National Park's most featured attraction is a geyser named Old Faithful, which earned its name by consistently erupting like clockwork. Millions of visitors come to view the geyser. Three hotels are located for clear viewing of Old Faithful; folks who can't get reservations in them fill the huge parking lot in anticipation of witnessing this natural phenomenon. But Old Faithful is losing its faithfulness. In the 1960s it erupted an average of every 64 minutes. Now it kicks up about every 80 minutes, and often waits 90 minutes. Its name hasn't changed but its behavior has. Christians and churches can do the same thing. The term "faithful" may apply more to what we used to be than to what we are now. As with manna, we cannot live on yesterday's supply. Faithfulness is a name we keep by demonstrating it every day.[298]

**Fake Mousetrap** Our artificial fixations may be best epitomized by the guy who tried to rid his house of mice. He bought a mouse trap but had no cheese. To remedy the problem, cut out a picture of cheese from a magazine. He loaded the trap with the artificial cheese and went to bed. When he checked the mousetrap that following morning he was quite surprised to find a picture of a mouse in the trap. A counterfeit lifestyle produces artificial results![299]

**False Gods** Jemima Wilkinson was born in Rhode Island during 1752. Her Quaker parents provided a religious education, but she later became a religion unto herself. She was a very capable speaker who convinced a following of 250 people that she had been raised from the dead at age twenty. They thought she was the Messiah. At one point in her ministry she took her flock to a lake and begged the question, "Do you think I can walk on this water like Jesus did?" They affirmed she could, so the "spiritual leader" said, "Then there is no point in me doing it." When she died in 1820, the sect followed her strict orders, "Don't bury me, because God is going to raise me from the dead." As Wilkinson's body decomposed, her following died off as well. False gods give false hopes, but Jesus Christ is the Truth that can set you free.[300]

**Fame** Erma Bombeck offered some good advice to those graduates of Meredith College in Raleigh, North Carolina. At their Commencement Ceremonies in May of 1995, Bombeck gave this maternal advice: "Don't confuse fame with success. Madonna is one; Helen Keller is the other."[301]

**Family** In 1992, the third edition of the *American Heritage Dictionary* was released with sixteen thousand new entries. Many things have changed since the last revision ten years earlier. Unfortunately, one definition has been given a new meaning that seems to reflect both the further attempts to dilute Judeo-Christian values and the results of a nation that has partially rejected this value system. Family is now defined as "a fundamental social group typically consisting of a man and woman and their offspring."[302]

**Family** In December 1994, *USA Weekend* ran a cover story about Anna Quindlen. She was working on the fast track with *The New York Times* when she made the decision to leave the office and stay home with her children. She now enjoys the life of a full-time mom and utilizes her professional skills by writing novels from her home. The feature article contained a question for readers to answer through a phone survey. To the question, "Would you take a job demotion and/or pay cut in exchange for more family or personal time?" Ninety-six percent said yes. Only 4 percent voted no. Once again, an indicator points toward the resurging priority of family.[303]

**Family** Professor Nick Stinnett, chairman of the Department of Human Development and the Family at the University of Nebraska, headed a research project to "discover what makes families strong." Their team observed and interviewed three thousand strong families in South America, Switzerland, Austria, Germany, South Africa, and the United States. From all of this research they concluded that strong families have six main qualities:

1. Family members are committed to the family
2. They spend time together
3. They have good family communication
4. They express appreciation to each other
5. They have a spiritual commitment
6. They are able to solve problems in a crisis.

Strong family ties don't just happen—they take work![304]

**Family** "The concepts of marriage and parenthood were not human inventions. Seek divine assistance." —*James Dobson*[305]

**Family** There is good news concerning the family. According to the Gallup Poll, America feels stronger about the family in 1991 than it did in 1981. Eighty-two percent of Americans said the family is "very important" in 1981. By 1991 that percentage had grown to 93 percent. At that rate, we could hypothetically have 100 percent by the turn of the century![306]

**Family** Vince Foster was the deputy presidential counsel to President Clinton. He spoke to the 1993 graduating class of Arkansas University School of Law six weeks before his controversial death. In his speech he spoke of his love for family and his wife of twenty-five years. He encouraged the graduates to "balance wisely your professional life and your family life. No one was ever heard to say on a death bed, 'I wish I had spent more time at the office.'"[307]

**Family Feud** Just about everyone has heard of the feud between the Hatfields and the McCoys. What they might not know is how it all started. In 1878 they had a dispute over the ownership of a hog. That led to a twelve-year war which resulted in the deaths of three Hatfields, seven McCoys, and two outsiders. Disagreement over that one hog stole twelve years and twelve lives. Most family feuds today are equally ridiculous.[308]

**Family Rental** In Japan, you can rent a family. Elderly Japanese who are isolated from their children by the frantic pace of modern life can rent a "family" for lunch and a few hours. Just call Nippon Kokasei Honbu (Japan Effectiveness Headquarters) and ask for a son, daughter, grandchild, whatever relative you want, and that type will show up at your door and greet you as if they haven't seen you in years. Of course the service isn't cheap: three hours with your family cost $1,130, plus transportation. Satsuki Ohiwa founded the business in 1990 when a businessman was too busy to visit his mother. Company staff visited her instead, and Ohiwa deemed it a success. Ohiwa's observation of the recipients is not surprising. She said, "What is common about our clients is that they are thirsty for human love." Aren't you glad God didn't call this service when we needed a Savior? Love can't be marketed, only unconditionally given.[309]

**Family Resemblance** Near the main entrance to the Alamo there is a portrait with the inscription: "James Butler Bonham— no portrait of him exists. This is a portrait of his nephew, Major James Bonham, deceased, who greatly resembled his uncle. It is placed here by the family that people may know the appearance of the man who died for freedom." A portrait of another who died for freedom is missing as well. Jesus Christ died to free us from the captive forces of sin, yet no picture of him remains. May we, his redeemed, bear the likeness of our Lord.[310]

**Fatalism** Actor James Dean died in a car crash on September 15, 1955. He was only twenty-four and had made but three movies. Still, he had become a lasting icon in American culture. For three years after his death, six thousand letters a week arrived at Warner Brothers Studios for him, more than any living star received. Each year thousands of fans descend on his hometown of Fairmont, Indiana to mark his death. Hopefully, these fans aren't adhering to one of Dean's favorite sayings: "Live fast, die young, and leave a good-lookin' corpse." God's purpose for us extends far beyond Dean's philosophy. Psalm 139 reveals the beauty of God's desire.[311]

**Father's Day** Brian Schmitz of the Orlando, Florida *Sentinel* sent a Father's Day card to his dad that said, "Being a father can be expensive, time-consuming, frustrating, confusing and emotionally draining. . . . Actually it's a lot like golf." How are you shooting on the "home" course?[312]

**Father's Day** Dorothy Law Nolte noted, "If a child lives with criticism, he learns to condemn. If a child lives with hostility, he learns violence. If a child lives with ridicule, he learns to be shy. If a child lives with shame, he learns to feel guilty. If a child lives with encouragement, he learns confidence. If a child lives with praise, he learns to appreciate. If a child lives with fairness, he learns justice. If a child lives with approval, he learns to like himself. If a child lives with acceptance and friendship, he learns to love the world." [313]

**Father's Day** In 1909, Mrs. James Bruce Dodd thought of her father as she listened to a Mother's Day sermon in Spokane, Washington. She felt the need for a similar day to honor fathers, so she initiated the process. The mayor set aside the third Sunday in June as "Father's Day." The governor of Washington then made a statewide proclamation to celebrate fatherhood. In 1972, President Nixon made it permanent by signing a congressional resolution which called for the official recognition of Father's Day.[314]

**Father's Perspective** Tim Kimmel is a well known Christian author. He does much of his work at a large roll-top desk in his office. On the top of this desk are a unique set of pictures. To the far left is a photo of the place where he was born—Jamison Memorial Hospital. At the far right is a picture of the place where he will most likely be buried—Graceland Cemetery. Between those two pictures is a photograph of his wife and children. It's a daily reminder of where life began, where it will end, and what really matters during the in-between time. Life is short, so seize the moments with your family.[315]

**Fatherhood** Forget the spotted owl; responsible fathers are a far more important endangered species:
- About 36 percent of American children live apart from their biological father.
- About 70 percent of juveniles and young adults in long-term correctional facilities did not live with both parents while growing up.
- Fatherlessness is judged a contributing factor in as many as 3 out of 4 teen suicides and 4 of 5 teen psychiatric admissions.
- More than 30 percent of births today are to unmarried women; most of these children will always live in mother-only homes.
- About half of all children in the United States will experience parental divorce. [316]

**Fatherhood** It was a typical scenario of young boys debating whose father was the best. This discussion highlighted who their fathers knew. The first boy started the debate by claiming his father knew the mayor. He was soon topped by the second boy who said, "That's nothing. My dad knows the governor." The stakes were getting pretty high, and the eavesdropping father wondered what his young son would say about him. The little boy shot back, "So what! My dad knows God!" Would your son say the same thing? May our children always be able to say, "My dad knows God!" [317]

**Fatherhood** "One size of fathering does not fit all." —*Paul Lewis* [318]

**Fatherhood** "The best thing fathers can spend on their children is time." [319]

**Fatherhood** The most important thing a father can do for his children is to love their mother. [320]

**Fatherhood** The research of Dr. Urie Bronfenbrenner showed the dichotomy of how much time fathers think they spend with their children and how much time they actually share. Fathers were asked to estimate how much time they spent playing and interacting with their small children. Estimates averaged from fifteen to twenty minutes per day. Microphones were then attached to the fathers and the results were astounding: "The average dad-child times was thirty-seven seconds a day." Maybe that is why one cartoonist drew the characterization of a young boy standing next to his father's recliner. The father was engrossed in the sports page, while the impatient boy pounded the leather of his baseball glove. Finally the energetic little guy said, "Play with me or trade me!" [321]

**Fatherly Example** First-graders were asked to draw a picture of God in their Sunday School class. Their finished products contained some interesting theology. One child depicted God in the form of a brightly colored rainbow. Another presented him as an old man coming out of the clouds. An intense little boy drew God with a remarkable resemblance to Superman. The best snapshot came from a little girl. She said, "I didn't know what God looked like, so I just drew a picture of my daddy." When we live godly lives, people will see God.[322]

**Fatherly Love** Phil Littleford took his son on an Alaskan fishing trip with two other men. In a quest to find some running salmon, they flew their seaplane to a secluded bay. The fishing was every thing they had dreamed. When they finished for the day, their plane was on dry ground. The fluctuating tide left their plane twenty-three feet from the water so they cooked some of their fish for dinner and slept in the plane. When they awoke, the tide had come in and their plane was drifting in the water. They cranked the engine and took off. Unknown to them, one of the pontoons had been punctured and was filled with water. The extra weight caused the seaplane to crash within moments. Everyone survived, but they had no safety equipment on board. They used their waders as floating devices but the frigid water was a deadly threat. The current was too strong for Dr. Littleford's twelve-year-old son to swim against. The other two men fought their way against the tide and barely made it to shore. The two survivors looked back from shore to see Dr. Littleford and his son Mark being swept out to sea, arm-in-arm. The Coast Guard reported that they probably lasted no more than an hour in the freezing waters. The hypothermia would chill the body functions and put them to sleep. Mark, with a smaller body mass would fall asleep first and die in his father's arms. Dr. Littleford could have made it to shore, but that would have meant abandoning his son. He chose to die with his boy.[323]

**Fathers** A little girl looked her dad in the face and said, "You're better than just a father. You're a DADDY!"[324]

**Fathers** In 1960, only 7 percent of all children in America lived in households without an adult male present. By 1992, that figure had tripled.[325]

**Fathers** Madison Avenue has killed the Yuppies and resurrected fathers. "We're redefining success," said Mal MacDougall, chairman of The MacDougall Company, a New York advertising agency. "The ultimate hero of the '90s will be the best dad. The Yuppie, the macho man are both dead." Instead, agencies are creating ads like his agency did for Quorum cologne. In a pin-striped suit a man was shown carrying a baby instead of a briefcase with the caption reading, "Success is knowing which appointments to keep."[326]

**Fear** Remember that everyone you meet is afraid of something, loves something, and has lost something.[327]

**Feast** Have you ever wondered what it takes to feed all of the athletes involved in the Olympic Games? ARA Services was the official food service manager of the 1992 Olympic games in Barcelona. Here's a sample of the supplies they needed to feed all of the those medal-hungry athletes. A half million pounds of meat and poultry; 50,000 gallons of milk; 275 tons of fresh fruit; 110,000 loaves of bread (enough to make more than one million sandwiches), and one million tomatoes. That grocery bill may seem incredible, yet it pales in comparison to the wedding feast planned for Christ and his bride (Rev. 19:7–9).[328]

**Fighting** "Never get into fights with ugly people because they have nothing to lose."[329]

**Financial Contentment** A survey by the Barna Research Group revealed the average American adult believes he or she needs an additional $8,000–$11,000 per year to live comfortably. Tracking studies show, however, that even when adults reach or exceed the income levels to which they aspired, they still claim they need another $8,000–$11,000 to live comfortably.[330]

**Financial Planning** Willie Nelson made millions of dollars but ended up owing the IRS $16.7 million, even after a serious negotiation which lowered his taxes and penalties from $32 million. Most of us think just $1 million would set us for life, but without careful planning we could just as easily go the way of Willie. "Financial planning, of course, had no place in Willie's worldview. His belief that you should spend your way through life and die a pauper kept him forever at odds with his moneymen," wrote author Robert Draper. One of Nelson's accountants, Havery Corn, voiced similar sentiments: "Willie's sense of responsibility about his wealth was not what I thought it should be." To another adviser he simply said, "It's more fun if we don't plan." The management of the resources God has entrusted to us require prudent plans. Without a plan we will never accomplish the tasks set before us. Incidentally, few people tithe unless they plan on it.[331]

**Financial Woes** Have you ever thought a little more money would solve some of your problems? Phyllis Cohen isn't so sure money will solve hers. This Durham, North Carolina, resident was the only million-dollar winner in McDonald's first round of Monopoly. She won the instant prize when she picked up a Big Mac and Coke on her way home from a round of chemotherapy. Ms. Cohen was receiving treatment for kidney and breast cancer. The sixty-nine-year-old woman said, "I'm worried I won't live to collect it. With all that's happened to me, I'll be glad if I reach seventy." We wish Ms. Cohen improved health, because her situation reminds all of us that money won't solve most of life's problems.[332]

**Flexibility** Although his daughter's name is more widely recognized than his, this famed ventriloquist would have died in obscurity had he not exercised flexibility in his youth. This young boy from Decatur, Illinois, was very interested in photography. He carefully saved his money to buy a photography book from a mail-order cata-log. The publisher mistakenly sent a book on ventriloquism instead. The boy had no idea what the book was about and was saddened that he had not received his long-awaited book on photography. He didn't know he could send the book back, so he felt as though he was stuck with the wrong book. He opened the strange book and began to read about a subject he had never heard of. His interest grew and he soon learned to masterfully throw his voice. He eventually got a dummy that he named Charlie McCarthy, and Edgar Bergen was on his way to international fame. Needless to say, his daughter, Candice Bergen, has enjoyed the fame of that name as well.[333]

**Foreign Missions** In proportion to its Christian population, India now sends out more missionaries than the United States. Twenty years ago there were only 420 missionaries from India. Today there are more than 11,000.[334]

**Forgiveness** A man was awakened in the middle of the night by a phone call. On the other end a frantic, sobbing girl managed to get out the words, "Daddy, I'm pregnant." He was groggy and stunned but communicated his forgiveness and prayed with her. The next day he and his wife wrote their daughter two letters of counsel and love. Three days later the man received another phone call. His daughter was shocked by the letters, because she was not the one who had called. Some other distraught girl had dialed a wrong number. Nonetheless, the letters were not wasted. Their expres-sions of unconditional love and forgiveness are now a treasured possession. Here are a few excerpts: "Though I weep inside, I can't condemn you, because I sin too. Your transgression is no worse than mine. It's just different. It all comes from the same sin pack-age you inherited through us. We're praying much. We love you more than I can say. And respect you, too, as always. Remember, God's love is in even this, maybe especially in this. This is a day of testing, but hold our ground we must. God will give us the victory. We're looking forward to your being at home. Love, Dad."[335]

**Forgiveness** Bob Hoover was a famous test pilot and a frequent performer at air shows. Once when he returned to his home in Los Angeles from an air show in San Diego, both engines of his World War II propeller plane suddenly stopped. With skill and a lot of luck, he safely landed the plane without injury to himself or the other two passengers. After the emergency landing he inspected the airplane's fuel. As he suspected, the plane had been filled with jet fuel rather than gasoline. He then asked to see the mechanic who serviced his plane. The mechanic, horrified at the prospect of seeing the man he had nearly killed, anticipated the full force of Hoover's anger. But Hoover put his arm around the mechanic and said, "To show you I'm sure you'll never do this again, I want you to service my F-51 tomorrow." Forgiveness isn't an occasional act; it's a permanent attitude.[336]

**Forgiveness** "Everyone says forgiveness is a lovely idea, until they have something to forgive." —*C. S. Lewis*[337]

**Forgiveness** From the land in which our Lord walked comes a story of mercy and forgiveness. In November of 1989, Sergeant Zeev Traum was patrolling the beachfront road south of Gaza City. He and another Israeli soldier were ambushed in their jeep by Palestinian gunmen. The forty-year-old's death brought a unique dilemma for his widow. She could simple bury her husband, or donate his heart to an ailing Palestinian. Bittersweet revenge could be found if she denied the request and let *one of them* die, since *they* killed her husband. Instead, she opted to forgive. So outside the city walls where Jesus Christ replaced our heart with his, fifty-four-year-old Hanna Khader, who had waited four months for a heart, received new life from his political enemy. In response, Zeev's widow said, "If it's possible to save a man's life, I think it's a *mitzvah*" (commandment of Jewish law, or meritorious act).[338]

**Forgiveness** If you live in a large city, you know the frustration of dodging non-yielding motorists while trying to exit from the freeway. On the frontage road there are two yield signs to remind drivers that the exiting freeway traffic has the right of way to any lane on the frontage road. Technically, you can exit from the freeway and take out any car that fails to yield. Unfortunately, though, such vindication brings damage to your car, too. That's the way forgiveness works. When someone fails to observe our rights we are tempted to inflict "justifiable" pain. Yet, like the freeway, such action brings personal loss as well. Forgiveness is a much better option![339]

**Forgiveness** Mitsuo Fuchida was a staunch military pilot who led the attack on Pearl Harbor. He was a proud Japanese warmonger who admired Adolf Hitler. He wore his hair like Hitler and sported the same little mustache. Fuchida took part in the Battle of Midway, the Marianas Turkey Shoot, Leyte Gulf and other major engagements of the Pacific war. He stood on the deck of the USS *Missouri* at the surrender ceremonies. Though defeated, he was pleased with his behavior as a pilot. After the war, though, he became disillusioned. He was surprised to learn that Japanese POWs were treated humanely—a sharp contrast to the Japanese treatment of Allied prisoners. He also learned of a woman who ministered to the Japanese prisoners. Her parents were missionaries to Japan but had been beheaded by his countrymen. She had forgiven the Japanese and met the needs of their captured soldiers. Such love led him to the Bible. He eventually became a Christian, and later an evangelist. Before his death in 1976, he led many to Christ through his preaching in Japan and the United States. Transformation started when one woman chose to forgive like Christ.[340]

**Fornication** The first school in the United States to distribute free condoms was Adams City High School, Commerce City, Colorado. After doing so, the birth rate of students from Adam City High soared to 31 percent above the national average of 58.1 births per 1,000 students. Likewise, an informal study conducted by M. B. Fletcher, a psychology professor at Carson Newman

College, showed that premarital sexual intercourse among Christian adolescents has risen dramatically since 1984. Among males, 70 percent acknowledged having premarital intercourse. The figure was 53 percent among the females.[341]

**Freedom** A spy was captured and sentenced to death by a general in the Persian army. Before execution, the general would go through a rather unusual ritual. He would give the criminal a choice between the firing squad or the big, black door. This spy was given the usual choice. He deliberated for a long time then finally decided on the firing squad. Moments later his life was extinguished. The general turned to his aide and said, "They always prefer the known way to the unknown. It is characteristic of people to be afraid of the undefined. Yet, we gave him a choice." The aide himself did not know what fate lay behind the big, black door so he asked his commander. "Freedom," replied the general, "and I've only known a few brave enough to take it." Freedom can be a frightening endeavor. Far too many choose familiar slavery rather than taking a risk for freedom.[342]

**Freedom** "Every generation of Americans needs to know that freedom consists not in doing what we like, but in having the right to do what we ought." —*Pope John Paul II*[343]

**Friends** A cartoon depicted a man being held up by a thief. The robber shoved a sack in the victim's chest and said, "Put all of your valuables in the bag." The next frame showed the man stuffing his friends in the sack. Friends are indeed a valuable asset.[344]

**Friendship** It has been said that friendship between two persons depends upon the patience of one. As you reflect upon your friendships, does it require greater patience on the part of others? True friendship shares this responsibility and forgets when patience was exercised on behalf of others but keeps a steady check on how often others need to display their patience.[345]

**Fudging** In England, nearly three hundred years ago, there was a merchant commander named Captain Fudge. This historical figure became famous for his lies and exaggerations about adventures on the high seas. His crew members were so accustomed to his tales that they would call each other "Fudge" when one was straying from the truth. By the mid-1800s, children in America were readily referring to cheating as "fudging." Today many people still use the term when dealing with deception. Exaggerations are just as deceptive as blatant lies. "Therefore, laying aside falsehood, speak truth." (Eph. 4:25)[346]

**Funeral Custom** Black Muslims have a unique funeral custom. Close friends and relatives circle around the casket and stand quietly as they look at the corpse. There is no singing, no flowers, and no tears. A peppermint candy is passed to everyone present. At the given signal each one puts the candy in his or her mouth. The symbolic candy helps them reflect on the sweetness of the life of the deceased. When the candy is gone each participant is reminded that life for this person is over. In their belief system life simply dissolves. There is no hope of eternal life. The candy idea might not be such a bad thought if there was something beyond the grave. With Christ the sweetness both continues and improves.[347]

**Futility** In Proverbs 6:6, Solomon advised learning from the ants. A modern twist to Solomon's adage occurred during 1990 at the National Zoo in Washington, D.C. Worker ants in a zoo display accidentally beheaded their queen but continued to serve her as if the head were still in place. Sometimes our approach to ministry is about as healthy as a beheaded queen but, because that is what we are accustomed to doing, we continue to feed it, prop it up, and act like it is alive and well. Like the ants, an occasional evaluation may prove we have been oblivious to the need for a decent burial.[348]

**Gambling** A person has a much better chance of getting murdered on the way to a convenience store to buy a lottery ticket than he/she has of winning the multi-million dollar prize. Note the following odds:

- Seeing a no-hitter: 1 in 1,347.
- Having a royal flush in a poker game: 1 in 649,739.
- Having quadruplets: 1 in 705,000.
- Being struck by lightning: 1 in 1,900,000.
- Winning the California Lottery: 1 in 23,000,000.[349]

**Gambling** In 1987, Richard Kommit lost $8,000 at an Atlantic City casino. The money had been advanced to him from his credit card through an ATM machine. Kommit couldn't repay his debt, so . . . he sued the bank. State law prohibits the lending of money for gambling, and Kommit's lawyer argued that the bank encouraged just that by placing machines near casinos. Mr. Kommit and his lawyer won! Gambling breeds irresponsible behavior. (It's usually the responsible folks who get stuck with the tab.)[350]

**Gambling** It's been said that common-sense is called horse-sense because you never see a horse betting on a man. Such logic has gone to the wind as Americans are wagering $400 billion dollars per year on horses, casinos, lotteries, and sundry other legalized forms of gambling. (This does not include the mountain of money spent on illegal bets.) To put that in perspective, in 1992 Americans gave $56.7 billion to churches and religious organizations. Too bad we can't convince more Americans to gamble on eternal rewards instead of earthly jackpots.[351]

**Gambling** When a vacationing family drove by a large dog racing track the little boy asked what it was. The father explained, "It's a place where people go to race dogs." After a long pause the six year old said, "I bet the dogs always win."[352]

**Generosity** Gallup recently determined that 84 percent of the "generous givers attend church regularly." Regular worship tends to breed more consistent generosity.[353]

**Get To vs. Got To** Pastor Charles Roesel reminds pastors and laity alike that the success of ministry depends upon one's perspective. Roesel says, "People have been deceived into thinking the Lord's work is Got-to." Is God's work something you *get* to do, or is it something you feel you've *got* to do? How you answer that question will help you determine the treasure of your heart. Pastors need to present ministry as a privilege, and laity need to be encouraged to see it as such.[354]

**Girl Scout Pledge** On October 23, 1993, the Girl Scouts voted 1,560 to 375 to allow girls to pledge their service to "God, Allah, the Creator, or anyone else they please." The Girl Scout promise now states: "On my honor I will try to serve God (or whomever) and my country, to help people at all times, and to live by the Girl Scout Law." B. LaRae Orullian, the national president, said, "It's a very strong statement that Girl Scouts continue to be on the cutting edge, and this is a continuing effort to show that we do have strength in diversity and that we are an inclusive organization." It appears that a select few Americans think being on the "cutting edge" means cutting out the Christian concept of God.[355]

**Giving** "Annually, Americans spend more on dog food than on church contributions." We might want to review some priorities! [356]

**Giving** "The finest gifts are given, not after waiting until need has to ask, but by the person whose eye sees, whose heart feels, and whose hand is stretched out even before any request is made." —*William Barclay*[357]

**Goals** From 1923 to 1955, Robert Woodruff was the president of Coca-Cola. After World War II he led the company to adopt his goal, succinctly stated as, "During my lifetime I want every person in the world to taste Coca-Cola." If one man can dream about the world tasting Coke, shouldn't Christians pursue a similar goal of providing the opportunity for everyone to taste Living Water? [358]

**Goals** Lily Tomlin humorously reminds us all of the necessity for goals. She said, "I always wanted to be somebody, but I should have been more specific." As Christians we share the common goal of being more like Christ, but if we aren't deliberate and specific about it, we might end up looking more like somebody else instead of Christ.[360]

**God** C. S. Lewis wrote about an erroneous but prevalent view of God: "We regard God as an airman regards his parachute; it's there for emergencies, but he hopes he'll never have to use it."[361]

**God** During Lincoln's tenure as president, he was visited by a guest who sought to flatter him by saying, "Back in my home state people say the welfare of the nation depends on God and Abraham Lincoln." Humbly, Lincoln responded, "You are half right." He later said, "Without divine assistance I cannot succeed. With it I cannot fail." The welfare of our country is in the hands of God; therefore, said Paul, "I urge that entreaties and prayers, petitions and thanksgivings, be made on behalf of all men." (1 Tim. 2:1)[362]

**God** "God really is God, he's not just applying for the job." —*Leighton Ford*[363]

**God** Early in the sixteenth century, Martin Luther debated with Desiderius Erasmus and told him, "Your thoughts of God are too human." Regardless of our theological background or educational status, we are all like Erasmus. Our thoughts of God are restricted by our finite faculties. That is why we must regularly seek the Holy Spirit's help in expanding our view of God (John 16:13).[364]

**God** There is a God. You're not him. —*Gary K. Odle*[365]

**God** Yandall Woodfin has noted, "The most basic religious question anyone can ask is, 'Does God know my name?' The answer is yes, for Christ teaches, 'Pray then like this: Our Father . . .'"[366]

**God's Blessings** Augustine (A.D. 354–430) said, "God wants to give us something, but cannot, because our hands are full—there's nowhere for him to put it." When we feel as though God's blessings are missing from our lives, we need to examine our hands and see if they are open to receive, or clutched around something that we refuse to let go.[367]

**God's Faithfulness** Hudson Taylor had complete confidence in God. He once wrote in his journal: "Our heavenly Father is a very experienced One. He knows very well that his children wake up with a good appetite every morning. He sustained three million Israelites in the wilderness for forty years. We do not expect he will send three million missionaries to China: but if he did, he would have ample means to sustain them all. Depend on it, God's work done in God's way will never lack God's supply." (See Lamentations 3:23.)[368]

**God's Presence** From his deathbed, John Wesley said, "The greatest of all, is, God with us." His brother, Charles, lived out that truth when he spent a night locked in a cell with a group of prisoners scheduled to die the next day. His testimony and presence were so effective that these men went to their execution "assuredly persuaded that Christ had died for them and waited to receive them into paradise." The present of Christmas is God's presence. "They shall call his name Immanuel, which translated means, 'God with us'" (Matt. 1:23).[369]

**God's Presence** When Donald and Simmie Godwin took their four-year-old grandson camping at Lake Superior, they got a basic theology lesson. When a bad thunderstorm came up, the little guy was fascinated by the flashes of "whitening." He watched the sky light up for several minutes then gave his commentary: "Look! Jesus is taking my picture." Our activities and attitudes never escape the attention of God. It's as if God were constantly taking our picture. May lightning remind us of this truth.[370]

**God's Provision** When you hear the names Rodgers and Hart what comes to mind? What about Rodgers and Hammerstein? Richard Rodgers' first partner was Lorenz Hart. These two men enjoyed tremendous popularity while writing songs for twenty-three musicals on Broadway and eighteen films in Hollywood. Lorenz Hart died prematurely in 1943, and Rodgers was left without a partner. The future seemed less promising than the past, but a partnership with Oscar Hammerstein eventually proved to be much more successful than that of Rodgers and Hart. Rodgers and Hammerstein became inseparable friends and created unforgettable classics, like *Oklahoma, The Sound of Music, Carousel, South Pacific, The King and I,* and *Cinderella.* When the past seems to offer more than the future, remember God can cause all things to work together for good.[371]

**God's Recipe** Lehman Strauss has known the heartache of suffering and loss. In the midst of his wife's stroke, he wrote an excellent book, *In God's Waiting Room: Learning Through Suffering.* As he attempted to better understand the events of pain which moved into their lives, he likened their experiences to childhood memories of his mother making a cake. Dr. Strauss recalled the various ingredients that went into the cake. Flour, baking powder, shortening, and raw eggs were all part of the cake, but by themselves they aren't very enjoyable snacks. When they are properly mixed together with all of the other ingredients and baked for the correct length of time, they collectively produce a delicious dessert. In our lives we experience ingredients that seem unpalatable, and our temptation is to tell God he's ruining everything. At those times we will find greater strength and peace when we acknowledge God's perfection and trust him for the finished product.[372]

**God's Will** A thirty-six-year-old unmarried woman came to her pastor with a very stressful dilemma. She explained, "Pastor, to put it simply, I want to be married. I'm approaching forty and I think it's time." The understanding pastor tried to exercise wisdom in consoling the anxious single. He reminded her that God had a perfect plan for her life and she could not improve on the will of God. She responded to his discourse on God's plan by saying, "Pastor, I'm not trying to improve on it, I just want to get in on it!" God's will doesn't need any improvements, it simply needs our "getting in on it." [373]

**God's Will** In 1945, a young associate pastor named Cliff married his fiancee, Billie. They had very little money but scraped up enough to take a honeymoon. When they arrived at the hotel, they were told it was now a rehabilitation center and not available to overnight guests. They hitchhiked to a grocery store several miles down the road. The owner was sympathetic to their situation and let them stay in a room over the store. The owner quickly caught on that they were Christians and referred them to a friend with a nicer place to spend the rest of their honeymoon. During the week their host invited them to attend a youth rally at a nearby Christian conference center. The regular song leader was ill that night, so Cliff was asked if he might take charge of the music service. He consented and led the music before a young evangelist named Billy stepped up to preach. Cliff Barrows met Billy Graham that night and formed a ministry team that has preached the gospel throughout the world for fifty years. When your plans don't seem to work out, maybe God has something better in mind. He sure did for Cliff and Billie Barrows! [374]

**God's Word** A letter to Billy Graham was quite telling of some societal thoughts about God's Word. The inquirer asked, "How many of the Ten Commandments does God expect us to keep today?" To the chagrin of this desirous compromiser, the wise evangelist said, "All ten!" Just because we have chosen to reduce our standards doesn't mean God has lowered his. [375]

**Godless Ambition** Years ago, a pregnant woman stood in the yard of her Baltimore, Maryland home and shook her fists at God.

In a torrential rainstorm she shouted vulgarities at God and taunted him to strike her dead if he did indeed exist. After lightning did not strike, she turned to her family who had witnessed the unusual ordeal and declared victory because she had proven God doesn't exist. She would later tell her son, Bill, that she didn't care if he became a drug addict, bank robber, or brought home a boyfriend instead of a girl friend, all she wanted was for him to never become a Christian. Bill Murray did become a Christian at the age of thirty-three, and his mother disowned him. He had done the one thing she had hoped he never would. His life had been transformed from addictions with pornography and alcohol. He came to know the peace that had alluded him all of his life. Bitterness began to loosen its stranglehold on his heart and he started giving for the first time in his life. But none of that mattered to his mom. The only ambition Madalyn Murray O'Hair had for her son was that he not become a Christian. The ambition of a godless philosophy definitely siphons any real meaning from life.[376]

**Godly Ambition** Bob Pierce founded World Vision over forty years ago. His heart of compassion was born out of the suffering he saw during the Korean War. As a young minister moved by the pain he witnessed in innocent children, Pierce wrote in the flyleaf of his Bible, "Let my heart be broken with the things that break the heart of God." When he returned home with a broken heart he knew what God wanted him to do. Godly ambition begins with a heart that is broken by the things that break the heart of God.[377]

**Good Friday** A visitor to the Passion Play in Spearfish, South Dakota, asked to see the cross which was used in the performance. He was shocked at the weight. He said, "I thought it would be hollow." The actor who portrayed Jesus replied, "I must feel the weight of the cross to effectively act like Christ." Today, crosses come in all shapes and sizes, and are usually designed for decoration or jewelry. Yet, to completely understand the magnitude of Jesus' cross, we must strive to feel the weight he bore on Calvary.[378]

**Good Old Days** Griff Niblack, in the *Indianapolis News*, has a clever way of reminding us that our idealistic perception of the past isn't always as realistic as we imagine: "If you're yearning for the good old days, just turn off the air conditioning." [379]

**Goodness** "Too much of a good thing is . . . wonderful!" —*Mae West* [380]

**Gospel** Asian missionary M. V. Varghese told of a commonplace tragedy in India. An Indian woman named Alila took her tiny infant to the River Ganges. With tears pouring from her eyes she stood there for a long time with the water lapping at the baby's feet. Then she threw her six-month-old baby into the river. Varghese found her weeping along the river's bank. Through her sobs she said, "The problems in my home are too many and my sins are heavy on my heart, so I offered the best I have to the goddess Ganges: my first-born son." The missionary gently told her of Jesus' love and forgiveness. She tearfully responded, "I have never heard that before. Why couldn't you have come thirty minutes earlier? My child would not have had to die." People are desperate for what only God can provide. [381]

**Gospel** During 1991, the Billy Graham Evangelistic Association was planning for their crusade in Buenos Aires. A local coordination meeting was held in a small Argentine town. The weather was terrible with heavy rains, strong winds, and hail. Nonetheless, pastors were gathered from all over the region. Halfway through the meeting a man slipped in, drenched and looking exhausted. The coordinators were concerned about why he was so late for this critical meeting. They later found out this man was tardy because he had actually walked 125 miles to attend the meeting. He did not have money for transportation, so he walked to make sure his town of fifteen thousand people was included in the evangelistic plan. The gospel was worth that kind of sacrifice for this dear saint. May the gospel move all of us to a similar commitment. [382]

**Gospel** "Why should so few hear the Gospel again and again when so many have never heard it once?" —*Oswald J. Smith* [383]

**Gossip** After three years of research, Indiana University sociologist Donna Eder has identified an important dynamic involved in gossip. Eder discovered that the initial negative statement was not the starting point for gossip. The critical turning point was found in the response to the initial negative statement. "She's a real snob" is not the start of gossip. It's when someone else agrees that the gossip fest begins. Eder found that the key is whether or not a negative statement is "seconded." If a second is provided, gossip ensues. If not, the conversation changes direction. "No one ever challenged an evaluation that had been seconded. Conversely, no matter how cutting the opening remark, an immediate quibble from a listener could send talk into a less critical direction." The moral: you can abort gossip-bound conversations by quickly affirming the person being targeted for negative comments. [384]

**Grace** George Wilson was sentenced to hang after he was convicted of killing a guard while robbing a federal payroll from a train. Public sentiment against capital punishment led to an eventual pardon by President Andrew Jackson. Unbelievably, Wilson refused to accept the pardon. Can one do that? The case became so legally confusing that the Supreme Court had to rule on it. Chief Justice John Marshall delivered the verdict: "A pardon is a parchment whose only value must be determined by the receiver of the pardon. It has no value apart from that which the receiver gives it. George Wilson has refused to accept the pardon. We cannot conceive why he would do so, but he has. Therefore, George Wilson must die." Consequently, Wilson was hanged. God's grace becomes a pardon from sin only to those who receive it. [385]

**Gratitude** A harried waitress approached the table where a young girl was sitting by herself. She quickly asked the girl what she wanted. "How much is an ice cream sundae?" the little girl inquired. The waitress snapped, "A dollar seventy-five." The girl looked at her fistful of change and then asked, "How much is a dish of just plain ice cream?" "One-fifty," retorted the waitress. "Then I'll take the plain ice cream, please," said the young customer. The waitress returned with the bowl of ice cream but delivered it in rude silence. After the little girl finished her ice cream and left, the waitress went to clean off the table. To her shame, she found two dimes and five pennies. Her tip was the exact amount the little girl needed to get a sundae rather than just plain ice cream. In each of our lives, others have made sacrifices for our well being. May we be grateful for even the smallest gesture of kindness we receive.[386]

**Gratitude** Matthew Henry (1662–1714) is remembered today for his commentary. During his lifetime he was known for his gratitude. Once, while walking down a street, he was robbed. The thieves took everything of value. Later that night, Matthew Henry wrote the following in his diary: "I am thankful that during these years I have never been robbed until now. Also, even though they took my money, they did not take my life. And although they took all I had, it was not much. Finally, I am grateful that it was I who was robbed, not I who robbed." True gratitude can be found in more places than we often look.[387]

**Gratitude** "The instant we are born, we already owe someone for nine months of room and board . . . and we never really pay that debt." This quote from John Maxwell reminds us that we all carry a debt of gratitude that cannot be repaid, but our gratitude can be passed on to others.[388]

**Greatness** Mother Teresa was a woman whose name has become synonymous with greatness. This correlation may have resulted from her philosophy of greatness. She simply believed, "We can do no great things; only small things with great love." Such words are reminiscent of our Lord's immortal words on greatness in Mark

10:43: "whoever wishes to become great among you shall be your servant." [389]

**Greed** A young man from a wealthy family was about to graduate from high school. The custom of this affluent neighborhood was the bestowal of a car once the student graduated from high school. The boy fully expected the norm would hold true for him as well. He had spent months talking about cars and looking at them with his father. Just a week before graduation this father and son found what appeared to be the perfect car. The young man was certain he would see the car in his driveway. Yet, when he opened his father's graduation present it was a Bible. He was so mad that he threw down the Bible and stormed out of the house. He never reconciled with his father and remained estranged until the father died. As the son went through his father's belongings, he came across the Bible his father had given him years ago. He brushed off the dust and opened it. To his surprise and horror he found a cashier's check between the pages of Scripture. It was dated the day of his graduation for the exact amount of the car he and his dad had chosen together. God's greatest gifts are still found in the pages of Scripture, but we sometimes allow greed to destroy relationships and divert our attention elsewhere. [390]

**Greed** Dr. Myron Madden tells the story of a man he knew who owned half of a piano. The father left this piano as an inheritance to his two sons. The piano was charged with history and tradition, as it had been carried from Virginia to Texas on a covered wagon by ancestors several generations before. The father intended for the sons to share it, but greed wouldn't permit such cooperation. So for fifteen years they kept it in a vacant rental house their father had owned. Finally, Dr. Madden's acquaintance experienced a financial setback and was forced to sell his half of the piano to his more fortunate brother. Had he been willing to share his half of the piano, they would not have needed to use the rental house for storage, and he could have prevented his financial problems by sharing fifteen years' worth of rent money. Greed eventually leads to our own destruction.[391]

**Grief** When C. S. Lewis lost his wife he recorded notes of his emotional pain. These notes eventually became a book that gives a very honest look at grief. In the middle of his hurt he wrote a very penetrating statement: "I need Christ, not something that resembles him." In the midst of grief, and every other aspect of life, we can't afford anything less than Christ.[392]

**Guilt** Some people are travel agents for guilt trips.[393]

**Guilty as Charged** In a San Diego courtroom two men were on trial for robbery. A witness to the crime was being examined by the prosecuting attorney when he asked the following sequence of questions. "Were you at the scene when the robbery took place?" "Yes," was the reply. "And did you observe the two robbers?" Again, the witness nodded, "Yes." The attorney then turned up the heat of his intensity and boomed out his last question. "Are these two men present in court today?" There was no need for the witness to answer, because the two defendants raised their hands. Although these two crooks might seem a little confused, they do represent a good spiritual truth. We start our journey toward God when we confess our sins and acknowledge our guilt.[394]

**Guilty Conscience** Arthur Conan Doyle found great humor in a practical joke he played on twelve famous friends. Doyle sent every one of these virtuous and highly respected men the same telegram: "Fly at once; all is discovered." Within twenty-four hours, the dozen men of reputation had taken a trip out of the country. (With a creative mind like that it is no wonder Sir Arthur Conan Doyle created Sherlock Holmes.) No matter how noble our reputation is, we all have areas of shame and deeds we hope no one discovers. The only lasting solution to a guilty conscience is the forgiveness of God himself. (See Romans 8:1.) [395]

**Happiness** "A happy person is not a person in a certain set of circumstances, but rather a person with a certain set of attitudes." —*Hugh Downs*[396]

**Happiness** "The Saints Among Us" was a poll completed by George Gallup. This survey reveals that fewer than 10 percent of Americans are deeply-committed Christians. Gallup says only 6 to 10 percent have what he termed a "high spiritual faith." The people of this minority group are categorized as particularly influential and happy. These folks are, as Gallup says, "a breed apart." "They are more tolerant of people of diverse backgrounds. They are more involved in charitable activities. They are more involved in practical Christianity. They are absolutely committed to prayer. They are far, far happier than the rest of the population." [397]

**Happiness** Two diametrically-opposed women have painted significant pictures about happiness. Mother Teresa devoted her entire life to serving God and others. As a result, this famous nun said she was incredibly happy. By contrast, Madonna has been on a hedonistic journey to satisfy little else than herself. On the topic of happiness, she said, "I don't even know anybody who is happy!" [398]

**Healing Attitude** The medical profession is filled with stress and adversity—especially with the current health care crisis. One doctor, though, found a way to handle some of the occupational hazards that accompany the medical community. When asked how he could carry a smile in the midst of so much suffering and disease, he replied, "I always look upon disease from the curative standpoint." Christians gain, and maintain, higher levels of effectiveness when they view themselves as carriers of the cure—Jesus Christ. It is easier to look around and curse the darkness, but it is far more helpful to light a candle and become "curative." [399]

**Health** Looking for a healthy edge? You may find it in the Church. According to *American Health*, "Godlessness may be harmful to your health." This claim was based on a recent study from Purdue University which involved 1,473 Americans similar in age, income, and education. Kenneth Ferraro, an associate professor of sociology, compared those who regularly participate in religious activities with those who don't. He found that those who don't regularly participate in religious activities were twice as likely to report health problems. Ferraro said, "We found that religion was almost as great an influence on health as age and social class." [400]

**Heaven** A little girl was walking with her father in the country. As she looked up into the star-studded sky, her eyes were filled with wonder. Turning to her father she asked, "Daddy, if the wrong side of heaven is so beautiful, what do you think the right side will be like?" [401]

**Heaven** Ralph Waldo Emerson was once approached by a concerned and inquiring person. He said, "Mr. Emerson, they tell me that the world is coming to an end." Emerson calmly replied, "Never mind, we can get along without it." The hope of heaven gives us confidence beyond this present world. [402]

**Heaven Can Wait** Calvin Miller teaches preaching at Southwestern Seminary. Before his professorship he pastored in Omaha, Nebraska. During that pastorate he talked with a new Christian about the glory of heaven. The man asked, "What are we going to do all day long for eternity?" Dr. Miller said, "We'll praise the Lord." The new disciple responded, "Forever—for ten million years—we're going to stand around and praise the Lord?" The pastor affirmed this truth, to which the young man replied, "Couldn't we just stop now and then and mess around a while?" The worship of heaven seems uninviting for many because we tend to compare it with the worship we experience at church each week. Multiply a typical worship service by eternity, and you've created a nightmare for the most righteous of us all. Our finite minds can't comprehend the grandeur of heaven, because we have trouble separating it from our experience on earth. Fortunately, though, we can never overestimate the wonder of heaven.[403]

**Heavenly Father** A little boy was standing on the sidewalk in the middle of a block. He was obviously waiting for something. An older man approached him and asked what he was waiting for. The little guy confidently told the older man that he was waiting for the bus. The man laughed and said the bus stop was in the next block. The boy acknowledged that fact but insisted the bus would stop for him right there. The older man became annoyed at what he thought was insolence. He raised his voice and told the boy he better start walking if he hoped to ride that bus. The boy politely turned down the suggestion and said he would wait for the bus where he stood. The man fumed at the little boy and started walking off. Before the man was too far away, he heard the screeching of brakes. He turned around and couldn't believe his eyes. The bus was actually stopping for the little boy. The bus door opened and the youngster started to board. Just before he did, he turned toward the man down the street and yelled, "My daddy is the bus driver." Our heavenly Father cares for his children in ways that seem impossible to those who don't understand his love.[404]

**Hell** In his insightful article, "Whatever Happened to Hell?" Larry Dixon raises his concern over Christians trying to soft-peddle the reality of hell. He says many think fear of hell is an outdated and terrible motive for moving one toward Christ. To counter this thought he notes, "Upon hearing the rattle of a diamondback, who would stand and debate the persuasive power of absolute terror? If running for one's life makes sense in the presence of a snake, how should we respond to the soul-threatening reality of hell?" His point is well taken, "If we neglect the bad news, some people won't listen to the good." [405]

**Hell** Some people don't believe in hell. They argue against such a place and claim they will simply "take their chances." Is that really a good gamble? Even if you're not religious, those kinds of odds are worth reevaluating. Consider the following analogy. Let's say a non-believer insists there is no hell but concedes there is a 10 percent chance he may be wrong. He still isn't worried about the odds but let's now ask him to board a jet that has a 1 in 10 chance of crashing. Will he buy a ticket to sit on that plane? Not likely because it isn't a "safe bet." Yet, he's hedging the same odds when he concedes there is a small chance a place called hell does indeed exist. Gambling with your soul is far more serious than taking a daring airline flight. If you won't fly a plane with a 10 percent chance of disaster, it's just not logical to "take your chances" that there is no hell.[406]

**Hell** "The safest road to hell is the gradual one—the gentle slope, soft underfoot, without sudden turnings, without milestones, without signposts." —*C. S. Lewis*[407]

**Heritage** In his will, Patrick Henry wrote, "I have now disposed of all my property to my family. There is one thing more I wish I could give them, and that is faith in Jesus Christ. If they had that and I had not given them one shilling, they would be rich; and if I had not given them that, and had given them all the world, they would be poor indeed." The bedrock of America is not her financial prosperity but her spirituality. Patrick Henry clearly understood this truth, and so should we.[408]

**Heroes** The pollsters at Gallup learned that among 13-to-17-year-olds, 51 percent do not have an adult role model. The other 49 percent were more likely to cite their parents rather than sports stars or entertainers as the adult role model(s) they hope to emulate. The void of heroes can and should be filled by parents.[409]

**Holiday Feasts** During the holidays, enjoy all those special dinners and subsequent leftovers. You won't be the only person who gains a little weight. Each year, Americans gain 1.1 billion pounds.[410]

**Holiness** Dr. M. R. DeHaan used a helpful illustration to communicate the value of holiness. A bar of steel worth $5 can yield any of the following: If made into horseshoes it will be worth $10. Manufacture needles, and the value becomes $350. Use it to create delicate springs for expensive watches and it will yield $250,000. We are like the $5 bar of steel. Our commitment to holiness will determine whether we become Christians of minimal, moderate, or significant spiritual influence.[411]

**Hollywood** The gap between the entertainment industry and the public seems to be widening. It may have started in 1939 when Clark Gable uttered his infamous expletive at the end of *Gone with the Wind.* Public outcry was expressed by people leaving theaters to show their disapproval. More recently, *Newsweek* reported a survey that compared the moral and religious attitudes of 104 top television writers and executives with the American public. The following data emerged: 49 percent of Hollywood believe adultery is wrong, as opposed to 85 percent of the public. Forty-five percent of Hollywood has no religious affiliation as opposed to 4 percent of the public. Twenty percent of Hollywood believes homosexual acts are wrong, as opposed to 76 percent of the public. Ninety-seven percent of Hollywood believe in a woman's right to an abortion, as opposed to 59 percent of the public. The entertainment industry is shaping and influencing the lives of many people. We must temper that influence with biblical morals and values.[412]

**Hollywood Morals** Goldie Hawn said her children decided it would be a mistake for her to marry longtime live-in partner, Kurt Russell. "They don't want us to get married because we're so happy. I've been married; they've been through that already." Hawn's way of life has become the readily-accepted norm of not just Hollywood, but America as well. But it seems many are not comfortable with such lax values. In the March 27, 1992 issue of *USA Weekend*, movie critic Michael Medved dominated the cover story. Medved succinctly said, "Hollywood no longer reflects—or even respects—the values of most American families." What followed was the largest caller response in the magazine's history. The phone lines were jammed with Americans agreeing with Mr. Medved. More than 54,000 callers noted their discontent with Hollywood. Twenty-one thousand felt Medved was wrong. Likewise, a *Houston Post* phone-in survey received over 12,000 calls (4,000 more calls than any previous survey) when readers were asked to agree or disagree with Vice President Quayle's criticism of Murphy Brown. Eighty-five percent of the callers agreed with Mr. Quayle and expressed concern over the TV character's moral message about unwed mothers. Thankfully, there are positive models in Tinsel Town. The marriage of John Tesh to Connie Sellecca made the cover of *People* magazine's April 20, 1992 edition. The feature article noted that both Tesh and Sellecca were "born-again Christians." It reported that the couple maintained premarital abstinence throughout their year-long courtship because of their religious convictions and Sellecca's desire "to be a good role model to my ten-year old son, Gib." Tesh was quoted as saying, "Even if Connie and I could not have sex for the rest of our lives, we would not leave this relationship." The entertainment industry may not be what we want, but positive change will only come through Christians voicing their concerns while seeking to touch the lives of movie makers with the redemptive message of Jesus Christ.[413]

**Holy Spirit** "Even though every believer has the Holy Spirit, it is possible to operate our lives apart from his control." —*Charles Swindoll*[414]

**Holy Spirit** For the shooting of *Ben Hur*, Charleton Heston was training to drive a chariot. Heston was having trouble with the apparatus, so he confided in his director, William Wyler. He said, "I can barely stay on this thing. I can't win the race." Wylar told Heston, "Your job is to stay on it. It's my job to make sure you win." The Holy Spirit orchestrates the victories for God's kingdom. Our job is to simply stay in the chariot of obedience.[415]

**Holy Spirit** Herschel Hobbs, the late Southern Baptist preacher, liked to quote the words of an old friend: "If the Holy Spirit were suddenly taken out of the world, 95 percent of the world would go on as usual." We cannot do "the Lord's work" without the Lord.[416]

**Holy Spirit** "Your life apart from the filling of the Holy Spirit may be spectacular, but it will never be miraculous." —*Ralph Smith*[417]

**Home** During World War II, housing was in short supply. A lady with good intentions expressed sympathy to a little girl whose family did not live in a house. She said, "It's too bad your family doesn't have a home." The five-year-old replied, "We have a home. We just don't have a house to put it in." In World War II there was a housing shortage; today we have a home shortage.[418]

**Home** Jonathan Edwards is known as one of the greatest theologians of American history. His voice played a significant role in America's first Great Awakening. He is remembered for his powerful sermons and his seventy "Resolutions." But one word from history that has long been neglected is his view of the home. He and his wife, the former Sarah Pierrepont, established something that is more noteworthy than the Northampton Church. Together, they formed a family. His value of this family, and all families, can be seen in a statement made during his "Farewell Sermon:" "Every Christian family ought to be as it were a little church, consecrated to Christ, and wholly influenced and governed by his rules." We have become very acquainted with the separation of Church and state. May we never allow such a separation to take place between the Church and the home because the home is "a little church."[419]

**Home** "The most influential of all educational factors is the conversation in a child's home." —*William Temple*[420]

**Home Life** Howard Hendricks has declared, "If your Christianity doesn't work at home, don't export it." More people are won or lost in the home than in the church. The home is either the greatest witness for Christ, or the worst.[421]

**Home Missions** Around the turn of this century, Annie Armstrong looked out of the bay window in her Philadelphia apartment and saw thousands of European immigrants streaming in from abroad. The experience of seeing all of these people led her to write in her diary. She noted there are two ways of winning the world: One is to go abroad and evangelize them. The second is to win them when they come to America. She sensed God's leadership to attempt the latter and became instrumental in establishing "Home Missions." Today, immigrants continue to seek the vast opportunities America has to offer. Our potential for global missions is far greater than it was during the time of Annie Armstrong. May we seize the moment and win those who are coming to America.[422]

**Homeless Help** On February 29, 1992, sixty-eight thousand people participated in *USA Weekend's* "Make A Difference Day." The idea was to take advantage of Leap Year's extra day and get volunteers to help others less fortunate than themselves. One eleven-year-old boy truly made a difference, even though he didn't win first place in the contest. Ryan Rigney of Manchester, Tennessee convinced his parents to let him use his Christmas money for the purchase of one hundred pairs of socks. On Leap Day, Ryan's parents drove him to the Nashville Union Mission an hour from their home. He there gave out the socks to homeless men who humbly and graciously accepted his gift of warmth to their feet. The eleven-year-old humanitarian said, "It sure makes you feel good when you know that, no matter how big or small you are, or what you do for someone less fortunate than yourself, you can make a difference." With his "runner-up" prize money of $250, Ryan planned to buy five hundred more pairs of socks for his homeless friends in Nashville. Let's hope Ryan's generosity is contagious![423]

**Homosexuality** On April 23, 1993, the homosexual community held a rally in Washington. They came to demand their "civil rights." What they actually did was demonstrate how immoral they are, and how inflated their statistics have been. Recent and extensive research has proven the Kinsey Report wrong. Homosexuals do not make up 10 percent of the population as Kinsey claimed. More accurately, only 1 percent are practicing homosexuals. The Institute of Sex Research has concluded through their studies, that of this small minority, only 10 percent of homosexuals are monogamous. Of the other 90 percent, the Institute says, it is not unusual for them to have hundreds of partners throughout their life. Many of these sexual encounters will take place with total strangers in public restrooms, locker rooms, and back rooms of gay bars. The Gay Agenda paints a picture of homosexuals being monogamous, loving people who are suffering terrible discrimination. In reality, monogamous homosexuals make up only one-tenth of 1 percent of the American population.[424]

**Homosexuality** The AIDS issue continues to dominate front-page attention. Nobody doubts the tragedy of this illness, but balanced perspective must be established. Figures provided by the Congressional Research Service in 1992 showed the U.S. spends nearly $2 billion a year of taxpayer's money on research and prevention of AIDS. That is equal to spending on *all* forms of cancer, and far more than the $686 million spent on heart disease, $280 million on diabetes, and $253 million for Alzheimer's disease. It should also be noted that in 1992 only two million people worldwide had AIDS (10–12 million people throughout the world have tested positive for HIV) and, according to the Census Bureau, same-sex households accounted for only 2 percent of all American households in 1991. The homosexual agenda is creating an enormous bill for the benefit of a tiny minority. Immorality does that![425]

**Honesty** William Willimon directs the Chapel at Duke University. Since students aren't required to attend the chapel services, he was humorously intrigued by one student's motivation for coming. Willimon approached this young man who had been ushering for several Sundays. He asked, "How do you like chapel?" The student politely said, "I like it." The chaplain then brashly inquired, "What do you think about the preaching?" "Well, I like that, too," said the collegiate. Willimon pressed on, and asked, "What do you like about it?" The young man stammered, "I just . . . I like it." Willimon held his feet to the fire until he confessed, "Look, Dr. Willimon, I'll be honest with you. I come to chapel to meet women." The good-hearted doctor appropriately responded, "Thank you. This has done me good. In case I should ever become presumptuous, I will remember this conversation."[426]

**Honeymoon Tip** Have you ever wondered why the guy is sup-posed to carry his bride over the threshold? Blame the Romans. They believed that good and evil spirits fought for control at a home's entrance. For good to prevail, Romans felt you must enter a room with your right foot first. Romans concluded that a new bride in a highly emotional state might be careless and forget about the "right foot" stuff. To prevent possible tragedy, they decided it best for the groom to carry his bride.[427]

**Hope** Bishop Arthur Moore told of a man who jumped to his death from the window of a high-rise building. A janitor in the building knew the man and commented on his suicide by saying, "When a man has lost God, there ain't nothing to do but jump." Fortunately, God will never be lost as long as we "seek him with all of our heart" (Jer. 29:13).[428]

**Hope** A great Scottish preacher said, "The most profane word we use is 'hopeless.' When you say a situation or a person is hopeless, you are slamming the door in the face of God." [428]

**Hope** At the famous Menninger Foundation, Dr. Bruce Larson asked some of the staff to identify the single most important ingredient in the treatment of the emotionally disturbed. The entire staff was unanimous in singling out hope as the most important factor in treatment. Regardless of one's mental status, hope is necessary for survival.[429]

8|64 **Hope** Best-selling author Barbara Johnson lives by the motto, "Life is about 10 percent how you make it, and 90 percent how you take it." With an Erma Bombeck style of writing, Johnson dips her pen in the ink of personal sorrow. Her husband was in a near-fatal accident and slowly recovered from severe and debilitating injuries. She lost one son in the Vietnam war, and another to a drunk driver. Her third son became a homosexual. With such a personal resumé you can more deeply appreciate her perspective on hope: "The cutest illustration of hope I've found is about a little boy who was standing at the foot of the escalator at a large department store, intently watching the handrail. He never took his eyes off the handrail as the escalator kept going around and around. A salesperson saw him and finally asked him if he was lost. The little fellow replied, 'Nope. I'm just waiting for my chewing gum to come back.'"[430]

**Hope** Years ago, a hydroelectric dam was to be built across a valley in Maine. The people in the town were to be relocated, and the town would be submerged. During the interim time between making the final decision and actually evacuating the people, the town, which had once been well-kept, fell into disrepair. The townspeople saw no reason for maintaining their town. One resident said, "Where there is no faith in the future, there is no work in the present." We must have some hope for the future. With Jesus Christ, we can![431]

**Hopelessness** Are you satisfied with your family life? On January 28, 1993, Steven Page told the world he was dissatisfied with his. Page and his wife had struggled to work out their marital differences over the holidays, but split up again. Although he was considered a "very nice guy" by his boss, Page became hopeless on that fateful Thursday. He killed his wife with a .12 gauge shotgun, then drove an hour to the Golden Gate Bridge. He walked onto the bridge holding his three-year-old daughter. When officers became suspicious of him, he threw his daughter into the San Francisco Bay, then jumped to his own death. What tragedy! Jesus Christ died so that we need not suffer such utter hopelessness.[432]

**Hospitality** In an article titled, "Where Are the Visitors?" Lyle Schaller says, "The most influential question that can be asked of a first-time visitor is, 'Would you like to come home with us for dinner?'" For those not interested in "knocking on doors," Schaller notes, "Just open your door."[433]

**Hostage Situation** A woman in Laingsburg, Michigan started 1993 uniquely. She heard "angry, accented voices" coming from her living room. Fearing her husband was being held hostage by terrorists, she hid in a bathroom closet and whispered to the police on her cellular phone. Sheriff's deputies and a state trooper surrounded the house as the woman stayed on the phone. They entered the house with guns drawn only to find a man sitting on the couch watching TV—alone! Police graciously did not release the woman's name. At least she was partially right. Television, and many other pastimes, do hold a lot of people hostage.[434]

**Housewife Comeback** Recent statistics reveal that the one-paycheck family with the father working and the mother staying at home is the fastest-growing type of household in America. This shift is occurring among women between the ages of twenty and twenty-four who grew up with both parents working. Trends like this reveal the renewed priority parents are placing on raising their children at home even if it means greater financial sacrifice.[435]

**Housework** A four-year study of couples found that men who do housework are healthier than those who don't. The theory is:

Willingness to do housework reflects a better ability to resolve marital conflicts and stress in general, thus providing better health. So at your house, who does the 2,000 pounds of laundry that the average American family of four washes each year? [436]

**Humility** A fan once pressed actor Don Johnson for an autograph while Johnson's eight-year-old son was there. After the autograph-seeker left, little Jesse looked at his famous dad and said, "Can you believe they want your autograph?" Some of the best teachers on humility live in our homes. [437]

**Humility** Alex Haley, the late author of *Roots,* had a unique picture in his office. Framed on his wall was a shot of a turtle sitting on top of a fence post. Haley prized the picture because it was a constant reminder of a lesson he had learned long ago: "If you see a turtle on a fence post, you know he had some help. Any time I start thinking, 'Wow, isn't this marvelous what I've done!' I look at that picture and remember how this turtle, me, got up on that post." If you're sitting on a fence post enjoying the view, remember, you had help! [438]

**Humility** Billy Graham was interviewed on *PrimeTime Live* in December of 1992. It replayed an impressive overview of his years in ministry and gave a very poignant conclusion. Dr. Graham was sitting somberly in a chair when he was asked, "What do you want people to say about you when you're gone?" He responded by saying, "I don't want people to say anything about me. I want them to talk about my Savior. The only thing I want to hear is Jesus saying, 'Well done, my good and faithful servant.' But I'm not sure I'm going to hear that." His genuine humility is one more reason why God has so powerfully used Billy Graham. [439]

**Humility** "Lord, when we are wrong, make us willing to change. When we are right, make us easy to live with." —*Peter Marshall* [440]

**Hunger Relief** In many places, a cold drink costs more than the average Southern Baptist church member gives toward worldwide hunger relief. According to figures provided by the Foreign and Home Mission Boards, each Baptist gives an average of 52 cents. Since bottled water often costs more than a Coke, someone might say we are no longer even providing "a cup of water in Jesus' name." [441]

**Hypocrisy** Although some people think the church owns exclusive rights to hypocrisy, a couple of stories from outside the church might shed a differing perspective. (1) St. Louis City Prosecutor George Peach once spearheaded a crusade against prostitution and pornography. He led a crackdown on the rental of adult movies at video stores and was a strong supporter of sting operations to prevent prostitution. In 1992, Peach was charged with soliciting an undercover police officer posing as a prostitute at the St. Louis Airport Marriot Hotel. (2) Mortimer Caplin was the head of the Internal Revenue Service from 1961 to 1964. After resisting the IRS for years, he finally agreed to pay $308,408 in back taxes for his federal income taxes from 1980 to 1982. [442]

**Hypocrisy** George Barna's research shows that 75 percent of Americans think it is important for people to read the Bible, but only 13 percent actually read the Bible daily. [443]

**If It Ain't Broken . . .** In Portugal there is a monastery perched high on a 3,000-foot cliff. Accessibility comes via a terrifying ride in a swaying basket that is pulled by several strong monks. One American tourist became quite nervous halfway up the cliff when he noticed the rope was old and frayed. In an attempt to find comfort for his fears, he asked the attending monk how often they replaced the rope. The monk's response provided little help: "Whenever it breaks!" "If it ain't broke, don't fix it" can be a useful philosophy for some things, but preventive maintenance is far better than trying to repair a disaster. [444]

**Ignorance** Josh Billings, a nineteenth-century humorist, said, "It is better not to know so much than to know so many things that just ain't so." Jaime O'Neil, a college professor, taught for more than twenty years. While teaching in the state of Washington he became very concerned that too many students knew too many things that "just ain't so." To help diagnose the problem he developed an eighty-six question quiz to test the general knowledge of his college students. Here are some of the responses to that quiz. "Charles Darwin invented gravity. Ralph Nader is a baseball player. Christ lived in the sixteenth century. Sid Caesar was an early Roman emperor. Mark Twain invented the cotton gin. Dwight Eisenhower served as president in the seventeenth century. Socrates was an Indian chief. Camp David is in Israel." More alarming than this knowledge of "things that just ain't so," is the "famine for hearing the words of the Lord" (Amos 8:11).[445]

**Illegitimacy** Illegitimacy is rapidly destroying the stability of our nation. Unless we change, early in the next century one out of every two American children will be born out of wedlock. Illegitimacy rates have already exceeded 50 percent in seven of our twenty largest cities: Baltimore, Chicago, Detroit, Memphis, Milwaukee, Philadelphia, and Washington.[446]

**Impossibilities** Until May 6, 1954, no human being had broken the four-minute mile. Many believed it impossible. Yet, when Roger Bannister broke the barrier of the four-minute mile, the "impossible" mindset was transformed. The following year, thirty-seven runners broke the four-minute mile. The next year, three hundred runners finished under four minutes. Today, in the New York Fifth Avenue Mile, it is not unusual for even the last place finisher to run the course in less than four minutes. Many of life's "impossibilities" are far more attainable than we think.[447]

**Inactive Members** The fastest growing segment of the Southern Baptist denomination is non-resident members. More than four million Baptists have left town and aren't returning to their Baptist roots, or any other roots. "They are no longer going to church anywhere, and they are harder to reach than non-Christians," says Tom Lee, coordinator of the Hello Baptists program for the Sunday School Board.[448]

**Inattentive Husbands** A recent study of fifteen thousand women by *Family Circle* magazine found that 69 percent would rather talk to their best friend than to their spouse when they feel unhappy. This is explained partially by a woman's unique ability to understand and empathize with other females. More importantly, it shows many women aren't getting empathy at home.[449]

**Indifference** On September 11, 1992, an unusual parking ticket was given on Piru Street in south-central Los Angeles. At 9:46 A.M. an officer wrote up the ticket for an illegally parked Cadillac. There was no question that the car was in violation. The driver did not object to the ticket. In fact, the driver didn't say a word. He couldn't. He was dead! The officer had taken time to observe the parking violation, write a ticket, then stick his hand through the open window (within inches of the body stiffly sitting upright behind the steering wheel) and place the $30 citation on the dashboard. He never noticed the man was dead. Paramedics said the man had been dead ten to twelve hours when the ticket was given. That officer shares a common trait with many Christians. We walk through life citing others with petty violations while remaining oblivious to the fact that they are spiritually dead. We're offended or repulsed by the behavior of some non-Christians and rebuke them for not acting more Christ-like. The fact is, they don't have the power to change. They are "illegally parked" and can't do a thing about it without Christ. Christians can help by personally introducing them to the love and power of Jesus.[450]

**Indifference** The Wisconsin Restaurant Association researched why people did not return to a specific restaurant. They discovered

1 percent did not return because they died, 3 percent moved, 5 percent formed other relationships, 9 percent preferred a competitor, 14 percent didn't like the product, and 68 percent did not return to that particular restaurant because they felt there was an attitude of neglect and indifference. People respond to churches in similar fashion. If they feel neglected or sense indifference, they will stop attending. Elie Wiesel, Holocaust survivor and winner of the 1986 Nobel Peace Prize, said, "The enemy is not love nor hate, but indifference." [451]

**Inerrancy** Add to your list of printing errors the "Wicked Bible." It left out "not" in the Seventh Commandment. That's the one on adultery. [452]

**Inerrancy** In the eighteenth century, the U.S. Congress issued a special edition of Thomas Jefferson's Bible. Jefferson had excised all references to the supernatural out of his Bible so that his Bible simply contained the moral teachings of Jesus. The closing words of this Bible were, "There laid they Jesus and rolled a great stone at the mouth of the sepulchre and departed." We end up with a dead philosopher rather than a risen Lord when we confine ourselves to only those sections of Scripture that accommodate our lifestyle or personal preferences. [453]

**Inexpensive Church** If you bring up the idea of starting a mission church, most people want to know how much it will cost. A deacon once told me we couldn't afford to think about starting a mission, because we were raising money for a new building. Robert Pride, Minister of Missions at Woodforest Baptist Church in Houston, Texas, is not fazed by lack of money. In 1995, he described how he started his newest congregation for just $3.17: "I bought a ream of paper for $3.17, printed up a few hundred flyers, passed them out all through the apartment complexes, and we had church the next Sunday." That first Sunday, ten people showed up; one made a profession of faith. If your congregation is waiting to start a mission because of financial restrictions, tell them about Robert and that $3.17 church.[454]

**Inflexibility** Charles Spurgeon became the pastor of the New Park Street Baptist Chapel in London when he was only nineteen years old. The building boasted a seating capacity of 1,500, but the attendance was less than 200. Within a few years, as many as 23,000 people had come to hear Spurgeon preach and his sermons were being published weekly in English-language newspapers around the world. Nine years after he came to New Park Street they built the large Metropolitan Tabernacle to accommodate the large crowds. They established a school to train pastors and began a book distribution business. Metropolitan became one of the most famous and significant religious institutions in nineteenth-century England. Spurgeon's ministry was particularly known for successfully attracting people from every walk of life, from the poor of London to members of Parliament. During his thirty-eight years as pastor, he built up the congregation to 6,000 and added 14,692 members to the church. When author and pastor Leith Anderson attended the Metropolitan Tabernacle in 1972, they had but eighty-seven worshipers present on that particular Sunday. The speaker lamented over the difficulty in reaching the people in the immediate community of the church. Much had changed in seventy-five years. London had changed, the neighborhood had changed, society had changed, all of the world had changed. But the church had failed to keep up with the changes. Consequently, the church lost in the battle of change.[455]

**Influence** In 1992, a store manager called his security officer with a problem. Such calls were not unusual in this Portland, Oregon store, but this time something very different was happening. The manager explained how someone had been in earlier and confessed to once switching price tags and wanted to make it right. One hour later another person came to the manager confessing, "I've stolen from your store. If you feel you must arrest me, then that's what you must do." Bewildered, the manager turned to the security officer and asked, "What's happening?" The officer simply responded, "Billy Graham is in town!" Let's live in such a way that our presence has a radical influence on those around us.[456]

**Influence** William Arthur Ward said, "Every person has the power to make others happy. One does it simply by entering a room; another by leaving the room." Which of these two actions makes those around you happy?[457]

**Information Overload** In 1989, Donnelly Marketing had detailed information on 85 million of the 92 million American households. Ten thousand magazines were published in the United States, 6,000 radio stations were operating along with 400 television stations, 100 different catalogs were printed for each household, and more than 1,000 pieces of unsolicited mail made it to the average home. In the midst of this inundation of information, futurist Roger Selbert has stated, "Although we have an incredible amount of information available already, the volume is just 3 percent of what we will have at our fingertips in the year 2010." The priorities of spiritual relevance must increase as we become more overwhelmed by this tidal wave of information.[458]

**Integrity** A man in Long Beach, California, went into a chicken franchise to buy lunch for himself and the lady with him. He took his order of chicken and drove to a nearby park for a picnic. When he opened the box, he was surprised to see money instead of chicken. The manager kept the earnings in a chicken box to prevent robbery but inadvertently handed the wrong box to this unsuspecting patron. The man quickly returned his picnic basket of cash to the store manager. The manager was elated. He said, "Stick around. I want to call the newspaper and have them take your picture. You're the most honest guy in town!" The man protested the idea of such publicity. When the manager pressed him for a reason, he ashamedly said, "I'm married, and the woman I'm with is not my wife." Integrity is much more than superficial honesty. It is a holistic commitment that directs every area of our lives.[459]

**Integrity** After the only year that Ted Williams' legendary batting average ever dropped below .300, he went to the management and demanded a pay cut: "I looked him straight in the eyes and said, 'I'm taking a $35,000 cut.'" Maybe that explains why he never again hit below .300.[460]

**Integrity** An unscrupulous salesman was delivering a bid that his company had made for an engineering firm. He was ushered into the office where he would present his bid to the firm. After a brief introduction, the firm's representative politely excused himself for a minute. The shady salesman quickly noticed the bid of his competitor lying on the desk. Unfortunately, there was a cold drink covering up the total amount. He gazed out into the inner office and noticed there was nobody to see him sneak a peek. He lifted the Coke and got the surprise of his life. Rather than a cold drink, it was a bottomless can filled with BBs. The quiet office was filled with the sound of BBs racing across the desk and spilling on to the floor. The firm's representative then returned to the office and showed the dishonest salesman the door. Integrity is demonstrated more when people are not looking than when they are.[461]

**Integrity** Dr. Bob Reccord tells of an experience he learned about while in the business world. A major institution that ranked among the Fortune 500 was working to make an unheard-of move. They were going to promote a thirty-eight-year-old vice president to president. The man was an impressive businessman who wooed and awed the board of directors. Upon completing the final interview process, the board broke for lunch, with plans to offer this man the prestigious position of president after they all returned from lunch. This young man went to lunch alone at a cafeteria, but was unintentionally followed by several of the board members, who stood in line behind him. When the young man came to the bread section, he placed two three-cent butters on his tray and covered them up with his napkin. As he checked out he never revealed the hidden six cents' worth of butter. When everyone returned to the boardroom for what was to be a joyous occasion, the mood had dramatically changed. The promising young man was not only denied the helm of the company but was fired from his position as vice president—all because of six cents' worth of butter.[462]

**Investment** "I would rather fail in a cause I knew someday will triumph than win in a cause I knew someday will fail." — *Woodrow Wilson*[463]

**Isaiah 40** In times of uncertainty it is good to know these simple facts from Isaiah 40:

- The oceans of the world contain more than 340 quintillion gallons of water, yet God holds them "in the hollow of his hand" (40:12).
- The earth weighs 6 sextillion metric tons, yet God says it is but "dust on the scales" (40:15).
- The known universe stretches more than 30 billion light years (200 sextillion miles), but God measures it by the width of his hand (40:12).
- Scientists claim there are at least 100 billion galaxies, and each galaxy is made up of about 100 billion stars. To such mind-boggling math Isaiah reminds us that God calls each star "by name" (40:26).

It's no small wonder that Isaiah ended such a chapter with those familiar words, "Those who wait for the Lord will gain new strength; they will mount up with wings like eagles, they will run and not get tired; they will walk and not become weary."[464]

**Islam** Of the world's 5.3 billion people, nearly one billion are now Muslims. Since the turn of the century, Islam has soared 468 percent worldwide, while Christianity has grown by 315 percent. Muslims comprise the majority in some forty countries and are increasing eight times faster than the populations of such developed countries as the United States.[465]

**Isolation** During the summer of 1995, Chicago experienced a severe and uncharacteristic heat wave which exacted a heavy toll. Hundreds of people died. Tragically, many died with no apparent trace of family or friends. After all of the contacts had been made, forty-one people were buried in a mass grave, because nobody came forward to claim their remains. No one grieved their passing. In your community, how many people could experience the same fate if similar circumstances arose? May we never allow anyone within our proximity to live or die in a vacuum of isolation.[466]

**Isolation** On March 17, 1992, an eighty-four-year-old woman was found dead on her balcony in Stockholm, Sweden. She was sitting on a chair, dressed in a coat and hat with her forehead leaning against the railing. Upon further research it was learned that she may have died as early as New Year's Eve while sitting on her balcony watching fireworks. Just inside the door of her apartment, policemen found untouched newspapers that dated back to the beginning of January. (In Sweden, papers are delivered to apartments through the mail slot in the door.) Margaretha Marsellas, a neighbor, realized something was wrong when she saw the woman on the balcony around the clock despite freezing temperatures. Marsellas said, "I accused myself for not having seen her earlier." In our quest to rest from our fast pace, too often we isolate ourselves from those around us. To everyone's detriment, this isolation can permit people to die, emotionally, spiritually, or even physically, without our even noticing.[467]

**It Is Well With My Soul** In 1873, Horatio Spafford was advised by his family doctor to take a European vacation in order to improve Mrs. Spafford's health. The Chicago lawyer responded to his doctor's wisdom by planning a trip overseas. Unexpected business matters forced Spafford to postpone his departure, but his wife and four daughters sailed as scheduled on the S.S. *Ville du Havre* in November of 1873. On November 22, an English ship, the *Lochearn,* collided with their ship, and it sank within just a few minutes. Mrs. Spafford was the only survivor of her family. On December 1, when the survivors had been brought to Cardiff in Wales, she sent a message to her husband: "Saved alone." On the high seas, near the place where his daughters lost their lives, Spafford wrote the words of this hymn while journeying to see his wife. The music was later composed by Philip Bliss and named *Ville du Havre* after the ill-fated ship.[468]

**Jamaican Proverb** An old Jamaican proverb does a good job of summarizing the biblical view of worry and prayer. It states, "If you're going to pray, don't worry; if you're going to worry, don't pray." [469]

**Jesus Christ** Jerome was a church father who translated the Greek manuscripts into Latin and put the Bible in the language of the people. He purposefully lived in Bethlehem where Jesus was born. One night, Jerome had a dream that Jesus visited him. In the dream, he collected all of his money and offered it to Jesus as a gift. The Lord said, "I don't want your money." So Jerome rounded up all of his possessions and tried to give them to Jesus. The Lord said, "I don't want your possessions." Jerome then recalled the moment in his dream when he turned to Christ and asked, "What can I give you? What do you want?" Jesus simply replied, "Give me your sin. That's what I came for; I came to take away your sin. Give me your sin." Jesus wants to give you the gift of eternal life in exchange for you giving him your sin. What an exchange of gifts! Are you willing to give Christ the gift he wants most?[470]

**Job Market** For the first time in American history, there are more workers with a white-collar job than a blue-collar job.[471]

**Job-Related Stress** From the book *Sports Shorts*, Jacques Plante, a former stand-out goalie for the Montreal Canadians, said of his career: "How would you like it in your job if every time you made a small mistake, a red light went on over your desk and fifteen thousand people stood up and yelled at you?" Try to relax; things could be worse at your office.[472]

**Jonah (Part 2)** In February 1891, the *Star of the East* was whale hunting off the Falkland Islands in the South Atlantic. While pursuing a large sperm whale, one of the two boats was capsized by the leviathan. The hunters went on to kill the whale but feared two of their men had drowned. James Bartley was one of the missing fishermen. The crew mourned their loss but also had a tremendous task of preparing this giant sea monster. They worked until midnight removing blubber from the eighty-foot long, eighty-ton fish. The next morning they hoisted the whale's stomach on deck. To their surprise, they saw faint movement. M. de Parville, science editor of the *Journal des Debats*, investigated the incident. He verified that James Bartley was indeed the reason for the movement. When the stomach was cut open, Bartley was found unconscious. He was bathed in seawater and placed in the captain's quarters for two weeks. He was confused and mentally disturbed. Yet, in four weeks he had fully recovered and was able to recount his experience. For the rest of his life he carried the scars of a bleached white face, neck and hands from the whale's gastric acid.[473]

**Joy** A ninety-year-old man approached his pastor after a meaningful time of worship. The man had been blind from birth and told the pastor he wanted to "see" him. He ran his fingers over the minister's face, then began to cry. He asked, "When I open my eyes for the first time, you know who I will be looking at, don't you?" The pastor said, "Yes, you will be looking at Jesus." The man then cried out with joy, "Pastor, it is worth being blind for ninety years to know that the first time I open my eyes, I will be looking at Jesus!"[474]

**Joy** Malcolm Muggeridge was a Marxist before he found Christ. His journalistic talent eventually led him to write some master-pieces for Christ, but he first wrote for Stalin. During the Cold War he went to Russia to do a story on the Communist party and the dying of religion in that atheistic empire. After completing his interviews with people in the Kremlin, he went to a Russian Orthodox service on Easter. The church was packed. At the end of the service a priest shouted, "Christ is risen!" The people yelled back, "He is risen indeed!" Muggeridge looked into their faces and instantly realized that they were right and Stalin was wrong. He said it was the reality of their joy that tipped the scales of his soul toward Christ. The reality of Christian joy is most compelling![475]

**Joy** Where does a person find joy? Possibly the best explanation comes from an acrostic using J.O.Y. The J represents Jesus, the Y stands for You, and the O signifies zero, or nothing. Joy is found when "nothing" comes between "Jesus" and "You." It's a great, bib-lical formula![476]

**Judging** D. L. Moody and Charles Spurgeon were great preachers of the nineteenth century. Moody admired Spurgeon from a distance and looked forward to the opportunity of meeting him in London. On that historic day, Spurgeon answered the door with a cigar in his mouth. Moody was aghast. "How could you, a man of God, smoke that?" Spurgeon took the cigar from his mouth, smiled, put his finger on Moody's inflated stomach, and said, "The same way you, a man of God, could be that fat." Since we are usually blind to our own vices, we are hardly qualified to judge others.[477]

**Judging** Tris Speaker was very critical of Babe Ruth's decision to quit pitching and become an outfielder. After Ruth made the tran-sition in 1921, Speaker said, "Ruth made a grave mistake when he gave up pitching. Working once a week, he might have lasted a long time and become a great star." Since our judgments are not infallible, we'd better leave that department to God.[478]

**Judgment** Dr. Arthur Glasser quotes an anonymous rabbi who has said, "A time is coming for all men when they will be either born again, or wish they had never been born at all." May we be faithful to our call, so that those with whom we have contact can know the joy of being born again.[479]

**Justice** With 70 percent of the world's lawyers practicing in America, you would think justice would prevail. That's not always the case. A burglar fell through a skylight while robbing a school. His attorneys charged the school with negligence and won $260,000 in damages. A man in Massachusetts stole a car from a parking lot, then died in a traffic accident. His estate sued the parking lot for letting him steal the car. In San Francisco a cab driver corralled a mugger by pinning him to a wall with his taxi. The thief ended up with a broken leg, so a jury ordered the cabbie to pay the crook $24,595 for using "excessive force." One lady claimed she lost her psychic powers after being injected with dye during a CAT scan. She was awarded nearly a million dollars in damages. Charles Colson says, "One wonders why she didn't foresee her problems and avoid the scan altogether." Thankfully we have a God who understands true justice: "Righteousness and justice are the foundation of thy throne" (Ps. 89:14).[480]

**Kissing Benefits** Some German psychologists, physicians, and insurance companies cooperated on a project to find secrets of longevity. According to West Germany's Dr. Arthur Szabo, the surprising results can be summarized, "Kiss your wife each morning when you leave for work!" Compared to their non-kissing counterparts, the kissing Germans had fewer automobile accidents on the way to work, missed less work due to sickness, earned 20 to 30 percent more money, and livd five years longer than stingy kissers. Dr. Szabo speculates, "A husband who kisses his wife every morning begins the day with a positive attitude." Generous display of matrimonial love is actually healthy! Does this have anything to do with Paul's admonition to "greet one another with a holy kiss"?[481]

**Kneeling** Joni Eareckson Tada is that beautiful woman who became a quadriplegic through a diving accident at age seventeen. She hasn't walked or known feeling in her legs for two decades. While attending a convention, the speaker closed his message with an appeal for everyone to kneel in prayer. Mrs. Tada was the only one unable to perform the task. Although God knew her heart was kneeling, she began to cry because she wanted to physically kneel before her Lord. Through tears of passion she prayed, "Lord Jesus, I can't wait for the day when I will rise up on resurrected legs. The first thing I will then do is to drop on grateful, glorified knees and worship you." Kneeling is but one expression of worship and can, like any other act of worship, be nothing more than a perfunctory and meaningless act. Yet, when we kneel out of true reverence for God we can experience a unique aspect of worship. Mrs. Tada desires to kneel, but can't; may those of us who can, earnestly desire to.[482]

**Koinonitis** Finding credit for who originally said it is tough, but the idea of "Koinonitis" is a clever thought. *Koinonia* is the Greek word for Christian fellowship. *Koinonitis* is the disease of becoming too inwardly focused as a church and getting out of balance in the area of fellowship. The church is called to nurture those within the Body of Christ *and* reach those outside the Body. A foreign missionary's daughter coined a phrase that may help us fight off the tendency toward koinonitis. Jeff and Nell Ginn have served as missionaries in Columbia. One morning Jeff entered his home study to find the world map had fallen off the wall. In the process of falling it became torn. Jeff was assisted in the repair of the map by his two-year-old daughter, Anna. Nell noticed the unusual quietness of her daughter so she called out from another room, "Honey, what are you doing?" Quickly and matter of factly, Anna replied, "We're fixin' the world, Mommy." If we will stay busy "fixin' the world" then our churches will enjoy rich and healthy *koinonia* while staying immunized from *koinonitis.*[483]

**Laughter** When Dan Jansen brought home a gold medal from the Winter Olympics in 1994, he did so with the help of a sports psychologist named James Loehr. In addition to the routine regimen of proper training, healthy eating, and adequate rest, Jansen was also instructed to lighten up and laugh more. Dr. Loehr noted studies that prove humor relaxes the body and relieves stress. He said a lot can be learned from children in that research shows children laugh an unbelievable four hundred times a day on average. This is compared to adults who average fifteen laughs a day. The writer of Proverbs 15:15 was right: "A cheerful heart has a continual feast." As for kids laughing more than adults, that could be one reason why Jesus said, "Let the children come to me." [484]

**Lawsuits** Bern Williams has summarized the modern trend of irresponsibility by speculating, "If Adam and Eve were alive today, they would probably sue the snake." More mirrors are needed in our increasingly irresponsible society.[485]

**Lawsuits** You don't need much of an IQ to see lawsuits have gotten out of hand. What could top the multi-million-dollar suit against McDonald's for coffee that's "too hot"? This could: as an inmate at the Indian Creek Correctional Center in Chesapeake, Virginia, Robert Brock sued *himself* for getting drunk and violating his civil rights. In 1995 he was serving twenty-three years for breaking and entering, plus grand larceny. In his handwritten suit he said: "I partook of alcoholic beverages in 1993. As a result I caused myself to violate my religious beliefs. This was done by my going out and getting arrested, which caused me to be in prison. For violating my religious beliefs, I want to pay myself $5 million, but I ask the state to pay it since I can't work and am a ward of the state." It didn't take Judge Rebecca Smith long to dismiss the suit. Her judgment read, "The plaintiff has presented an innovative approach to civil rights litigation. However, his claim, and especially the relief sought, are totally ludicrous." Sounds like we could use a lot more judges like Ms. Smith.[486]

**Leadership** The following five syndromes can stunt a leader's vision and growth:

1. *The Problem-Solving Syndrome:* More time is spent on problem solving than leading.
2. *The "Busy Enough Now" Syndrome:* An overloaded schedule restricts your ability to lead.
3. *The "No Vacancy" Syndrome:* Contentment with the current membership prevents wanting any more.
4. *The Nostalgia Syndrome:* More time goes into remembering the past than planning for the future.
5. *The Lazarus Syndrome:* Too much time and energy is spent on trying to recover inactive people.

A quick evaluation of your ministry might reveal a syndrome that is robbing you of energy and joy.[487]

**Leadership** Dr. Evan O'Neill Kane made history twice in the same day. The chief surgeon of Kane Summit Hospital in New York City was convinced that local anesthesia was a better option than the accepted practice of always using general anesthesia. Dr. Kane felt the patient sustained too many risks when completely put under. His plan was to find a volunteer who would allow him to perform an appendectomy (an operation he had performed nearly four thousand times) with local anesthesia. The search was difficult because prospects feared the local deadening might wear off, leaving them in great pain. Others did not believe it would work. At last, Dr. Kane found a willing volunteer. On February 15, 1921 the volunteer was prepared for surgery and given local anesthesia. The sixty-year-old surgeon performed the procedure without any complications. Dr. Kane proved his point, as the patient experienced only minor discomfort. Naturally, Dr. Kane became famous as a surgeon that day, but even more interesting is the fact that he became famous for being the patient as well. He proved his theory by operating on himself! Leadership shines brightest when the leader does what nobody else is willing to do.[488]

**Leadership** In a survey that compared the top ten priorities of leaders and followers, the top three for followers were appreciation, recognition of work, and genuine concern for employees. Leaders listed the above three priorities at the bottom of their list. Leaders would do well to reconsider what motivates those whom they attempt to lead.[489]

**Leadership** Robert Clinton has done extensive research in the area of biblical leadership. He has determined that there are approximately three hundred leaders chronicled in the Bible. In 1990 he studied one hundred of the most prominent of them. To his dismay, he discovered that less than one in four of these leaders finished well. Leadership in any arena is difficult, but it is especially rough among spiritual leaders because of the Satanic attacks which accompany the job. The odds of finishing well are clearly against those in ministry, so we must constantly seek spiritual empowerment and protection from God.[490]

**Leadership** "The best test of whether one is a qualified leader is to find out whether anyone is following him." —*Oswald Sanders*[491]

**Learning** "The only things worth learning are the things you learn after you know it all." —*Harry Truman*[492]

**Legacy** What organization, above all other interest groups, can generate the most calls to Congress in a single day? Focus on the Family. When they contact their grassroots, Congress is inundated with calls. Maybe the reason for such results should be credited to James Dobson . . . Senior! No doubt, James Dobson, Jr. has done a remarkable job, but would he be in such a position, had his father not been a man of prayer? Engraved on the tomb of James Dobson, Sr. are two special words: "He Prayed." Because he fervently prayed, this man of God has left a legacy of prayer that will continue to impact the American family for years to come. Are you leaving a similar legacy?[493]

**Letters to God** Not far from Jerusalem, Israeli postal workers sort through huge piles of undeliverable mail. Included among these dead letters are many addressed to God. Some have been forwarded by foreign postal workers who think someone in Israel might know what to do with them. Eventually, all of these petitions end up at a recycling plant in central Israel. Unless our communications to God are addressed "c/o Jesus" (see John 14:6), they're sure to suffer the same fate as those dead letters in Israel.[494]

**Lies** "Half-right is not right at all." —*J.B. Gambrell*[495]

**Lies** In the premier issue of *Full Armor*, Gunnery Sergeant Tom Shanks told about the Iraqis' response to the Marine invasion during the Persian Gulf War. "The Iraqis were told that to be a U.S. Marine we had to kill one of our relatives," said Shanks. No wonder we saw Iraqi soldiers surrendering in groveling fear! Likewise, Satan has spread lies about Christians and their faith that has given many people a distorted view of the gospel. As soldiers of the cross, we must make sure God's truth is effectively communicated.[496]

**Lies** "It is twice as hard to crush a half-truth as a whole lie." —*Austin O'Malley*[497]

**Life** "Don't be afraid your life will end; be afraid it will never begin." —*Grace Hansen*[498]

**Life** Emerson said, "People are always getting ready to live but never living." Do you remember when you were a kid and you would race your friends on the playground? You would say, "On your mark, get set, GO!" Then you became an adult, and all you've been saying since is, "On your mark, get set . . ." The hearse will soon be here, so "GO!"[499]

**Life's Work** April 9, 1995 marked the 130th anniversary of the Civil War's ending. On that historic day in 1865, Confederate

General Robert E. Lee surrendered to Union General Ulysses S. Grant at Appomattox, Virginia. Because of the four-year conflict 600,000 people were killed and 3.6 million slaves were set free. Abraham Lincoln's greatest contribution as our sixteenth President was his ability to end the war and keep our nation together. Appomattox marked the end of this national calamity. It also marked the end of Lincoln—he was murdered just five days later. Although Lincoln is one of the most well-known figures in history, he only occupied center stage for six years, from his famous debates with Stephen Douglas in late 1858 to his assassination in April 1865. We may not live long enough to see the fruit of our life's work, but we should nonetheless "not lose heart in doing good" (Gal. 6:9).[500]

**Life's Work** Horace Mann truly experienced life. Although he had very little formal education while growing up, he learned enough on his own to gain entrance into Brown University and was graduated with highest honors. Mann practiced law, taught in the university, served in the Massachusetts legislature, and became secretary of the Board of Education. His educational program in Massachusetts became a prototype for the rest of our country. At age fifty-two he became a U.S. Congressman and later assumed the presidency of Antioch College in Ohio. In a baccalaureate address just a few weeks before his death, he closed his speech with these words: "Be ashamed to die until you have won some victory for humanity." Life is not to be casually spent. It is a gift from God that is too valuable to waste. Mr. Mann was right, we should be ashamed to die until we have won some victory for humanity. As Christians we can most successfully accomplish this goal by winning some victory for Christ.[501]

**Lifestyle Evangelism** According to Rick Warren, there are two basic reasons people don't know Jesus Christ as their Lord and Savior: (1) they have never met a Christian; and (2) they *have* met a Christian. Christian influence is no small matter.[502]

**Light and Darkness** An article in *Newsweek* titled "The Fall of the Dinosaurs" explored the downfall of corporate giants such as General Motors, IBM, and Sears. Tucked away in the opening remarks were these words: "The institutions of family, church and government have long since lost their luster." Whether the diminished luster is perceived or real, an illustration from Russian scientists may contain the answer. On February 4, 1993, officials at the Flight Control Center near Moscow reported the successful deployment of a space reflector. This aluminum-covered disc was used by cosmonauts in the space station Mir to reflect light from the sun to the dark side of Earth. With a twenty-five-foot disc in space, they were able to produce a two-mile circle of light on earth. Such a move placed Russia in the forefront of this reflective technology. If the church has lost its luster, it may be due to our feeble attempts to produce light rather than reflect the Light. How much greater would be our impact if we started being better mirrors of the Son![503]

**Listening** A poor listener seldom hears a good sermon.[504]

**Listening** Research indicates there are three primary elements that cause us to listen. Our attention is enhanced when the topic at hand is something of value, something unusual, or something that seems threatening. If any or all of those elements are present, we will most likely pay attention. Ironically, the gospel carries all three elements. Salvation is of utmost value. The fact that a holy God would initiate a loving relationship with sinful people is unusual. The consequences of rejecting Christ's sacrifice on the cross is very threatening.[505]

**Listening** Which organ of the body requires the most energy? The first two obvious guesses might be the heart or brain. Actually, the inner ear demands the most bodily energy. Attentive listening can be a draining experience, so God made sure the ears got all of the necessary power to carry out this important task.[506]

**Listening Skills** President Roosevelt once grew tired of the smiling superficiality that accompanied many White House receptions. One particular evening, he decided to see whether or not anyone actually paid attention to what he said. As he shook hands with each guest filing through the line, he smiled real big and said, "I murdered my grandmother this morning." No one even noticed. They just gave the usual protocol, "How lovely!" or "Keep up the good work." One foreign diplomat was listening and added humor to the night as well. When FDR told of his scandalous deed, the diplomat tactfully commented, "I'm sure she had it coming to her." Jesus' half-brother, James, initially had trouble hearing his brother's message (John 7:5). Perhaps that's why James later wrote, "Everyone should be quick to listen" (James 1:19).[507]

**Listening to God** Before refrigerators were invented, icehouses were used to preserve foods. These icehouses had thick walls, no windows, and a tightly-fitted door. Large blocks of ice were obtained during the winter and covered with sawdust to prevent melting. This would allow the ice to last well into summer. One day a man lost his valuable watch while working in the icehouse. He and his fellow workers diligently searched for the valued time-piece without success. A small boy heard of the problem and slipped into the icehouse. He soon emerged from the cold with the man's watch. The men were amazed and asked the boy how he found it. He said, "I closed the door, laid down in the sawdust, and kept very still. Soon I heard the watch ticking." From the cool darkness of this dated icehouse comes the timeless reminder of Psalm 46:10: "Be still and know that I am God."[508]

**Living Water** During the days of sailing merchant ships, one such vessel becalmed off the coast of South America. Weeks went by without the slightest movement of wind. The ship was helpless and couldn't move. The sailors were dying of thirst, when another ship drifted close enough to read their frantic signs for help. "Let down your buckets," was the reply. They then found water suitable for drinking right beneath their keel. Although adrift at sea, they were surrounded by the fresh water current that came from the mighty Amazon River. All they had to do was reach for it. People don't need to thirst for true life because we are surrounded by Jesus' offer of Living Water.[509]

**Loneliness** An eleven-year-old orphan had known nothing but institutional life. She had been shuffled from one orphanage to the next. She defied authority and maintained very poor manners. Her friends were few because of her social ineptitude. On one occasion her roommates saw her write a note and hide it in a tree that overhung the orphanage wall. Such a practice was strictly forbidden, so the two girls ran to retrieve the letter once the poor misfit had gone. Their thoughts of blackmail were soon daunted when they read these simple words: "To whoever finds this—I love you!" Each day millions of lonely and hurting people are looking for a way to let the world know they need love. Don't miss an opportunity to share some of God's love with them.[510]

**Loneliness** Of Americans who ate dinner last night, 22 percent ate alone. Nearly one-quarter of our nation experiences regular levels of isolation and loneliness. Those who ate in the company of others would do well to remember their neighbors who walk through life alone. Mother Teresa said, "The most terrible poverty is loneliness and the feeling of being unwanted." [511]

**Loopholes** The late W .C. Fields (1880–1946) was a familiar and famous face among entertainers. Not as famous were his thoughts on God. As an illness began to overtake him in his final days, he opened a Bible. A friend was surprised by the sight and asked the dying actor what he was doing. Fields replied in his characteristic style, "Looking for loopholes, my man, looking for loopholes." God provided the largest loophole man could ever find when he sacrificed his son for our sins. That's the only loophole. There are no others. (See John 14:6.)[512]

**Lord's Prayer** A young boy from New Haven, Connecticut was struggling to memorize the Lord's Prayer. His mother was concerned by the child's erroneous recitation of the prayer and sought counsel from her pastor. The minister had the boy recite what he knew and here's what the little guy said, "Our Father who art in New Haven, how'd you know my name?" The minister chuckled at the twisted phrases and complimented the boy on his work. Turning to the distraught mother, the minister commended her son for his brilliant theology. He said, "Your son has embraced two important truths: God is near, and he knows our names." The boy misquoted the verse but communicated biblical truth. God knows where we are and he cares about our lives.[513]

**Lord's Supper** Each time we partake of the Lord's Supper we remind ourselves that the elements are symbolic of what Christ has done for us. New research accentuates this symbolism. Dr. Leroy Creasy of Cornell University has identified a chemical in grapes that the Journal of Applied Cardiology says reduces the risk of heart disease. "Resveratrol" lowers cholesterol in humans and is found in Concord grape juice. Now as we drink a substance that helps cleanse the physical heart of life-threatening impurities, we can be reminded in a new way that it is the blood of Christ that cleanses our spiritual hearts of sin's deadly effects.[514]

**Lotto Bucks** Stewardship appeals are continuously met with the phrase, "Times are tough." But is it valid? After Texas voters approved a state lottery, people from the Lone Star state came up with an additional $3,738,273,287 to play the game of chance between May 1992 and February 1994. In just twenty-one months the gambling industry found the equivalent of an extra $207 in *every* Texans' pocket. During that same period of time total giving to Texas Baptist churches equaled $1,681,904,800. That's less than half the amount spent on the lottery, or $93 per Texan. The truth remains: people have money for what they want. Unfortunately, God's work is not usually what they want.[515]

**Love** Nelson and Virginia Bell had a beautiful and lengthy marriage. All through their married life they did things together as often as possible. When they got older, Dr. Bell had to care for his wife. One day Ruth Graham entered her parents' home and found her father on his hands and knees putting on Mrs. Bell's stockings. Dr. Bell looked up at his daughter and said, "You know, the greatest privilege of my life is taking care of your mother." True love sees service as a privilege.[516]

**Love** "The one who loves least controls the relationship." —*Robert Anthony*[517]

**Lying** *The Day America Told the Truth* came out in 1991. In this work, research showed 91 percent of Americans lie routinely, while 36 percent confess to dark, important lies. Eighty-six percent lie regularly to parents, 75 percent lie to friends, 73 percent to siblings, 69 percent to spouses, 81 percent lie about feelings, 43 percent concerning income, and 40 percent about sex. Psychologist Michael Lewis of Rutgers University says there are three types of lies: (1) Lies to protect feelings, such as saying a gift is nice when you actually hate it; (2) Lies to avoid punishment; and (3) Lies of self-deception. Our behavior repulses others, but we lie to ourselves and blame the rejection on something or someone else. A woman gives herself a breast exam and notices an unusual lump but tells herself everything is fine. Lewis feels these lies of self-deception may be the most frequent lies. That could explain why so many people reject the gospel. They've lied to themselves about their need for forgiveness and God's requirement of commitment to Christ. In this age of obsessive lying, remember who is the "father of lies" (John 8:44), and who promised to give the "truth that shall make you free" (John 8:32). C. S. Lewis noted, "We often err either by ascribing too much or too little power to the father of lies."[518]

**Marathon Living** Noel Johnson was in sad shape at age seventy-two. He was smoking and drinking, was forty pounds overweight, had high blood pressure, gout, arthritis, bursitis, and a heart ailment. His life insurance was canceled because he was such a bad risk and his doctor warned him not to attempt anything strenuous. His son challenged him to start walking, so he defied his doctor's warning and began to take short walks. His walks developed into runs, and now the San Diego resident hopes to be the first one to run the New York City Marathon at age one hundred. He's already run it eight times with a personal best of 5 hours, 42 minutes. At ninety-two years old he feels like a kid. His only regret is that his doctor didn't live long enough to cheer him on. In the U.S. there are one million people over ninety years of age and only one-third of them are in nursing homes.[519]

**Marital Responsibility** In Russia, the best man in a wedding must sign the marriage register guaranteeing that the union will last at least six months or he'll pay a fine of 150 rubles.[520]

**Marriage** Every marriage is composed of two sinners—so remember the thoughts of Gigi Graham Tchividjian: "A good marriage is made up of two good forgivers."[521]

**Marriage** "I do not believe there is a marriage in existence today that would not benefit from both partners asking themselves: 'What is it like being married to me?'" —*Ed Young*[522]

**Marriage** Upon the occasion of celebrating his fiftieth wedding anniversary, Henry Ford told a reporter the secret of his successful marriage. "The formula is the same as in car manufacturing. I stick to one model." It may not be the best strategy for selling cars in today's changing economy, but it will always be great advice for marriage.[523]

**Marriage** When Mr. and Mrs. Kenneth Kantzer were about to celebrate their forty-eighth wedding anniversary, they shared their joyous news with a lady assisting them at the cash register. Amazed, the young cashier said, "I can't think of any man I'd like to live with for forty-eight years!" Mrs. Kantzer replied, "Well, don't marry until you do."[524]

**Marriage Plans** When women marry, they think their husbands will change. When men marry, they think their wives will never change. Both are wrong.[525]

**Marriage Survival Tip** A man came to his pastor for help because he was considering a divorce. The pastor counseled him to stay in the marriage and began to show the man scriptures which spoke to the issue of marital commitment. He first used Ephesians 5:25, "Husbands love your wives." The man responded by saying, "I don't love her." The pastor then turned to John 13:35, "By this all men will know that you are my disciples, if you love one another." The minister noted that they were both Christians and should be able to at least love each other as fellow believers. The husband replied, "We fight all the time. The longer I stay with her the less I like her." The determined man of God then scrambled to Matthew 22:39, "Love your neighbor as yourself." Pleadingly he asked, "Will you at least try loving her as your next door neighbor?" In response the man said, "Pastor, you just don't understand. We're not even friends anymore." The pastor's face lighted up with relief. "Well, then, I've got just the verse you need." Triumphantly he read Matthew 5:44, "Love your enemies, and pray for those who persecute you." Sometimes a marriage needs Matthew 5:44.[526]

**Marshmallow Test** In the 1960s, researchers at Stanford University ran the "marshmallow test." A researcher would tell a four-year-old the following: "I am leaving for a few minutes to run an errand, and you can have this marshmallow while I am gone, but if you wait until I return, you can have two marshmallows." After a dozen years they restudied the same children and found that those who had grabbed the single marshmallow tended to be more troubled as adolescents. The kids who wolfed down one marshmallow instead of waiting for two, scored an average of 210 points less on SAT tests. There is real and documented value to controlling and disciplining our desires.[527]

**Martyrs** They are known as the forty martyrs of Sebaste. In the famed Twelfth Legion of Rome's imperial army there were forty soldiers who professed their faith in Jesus Christ. One day their captain informed them that Emperor Licinius had sent out an edict commanding all soldiers to offer a sacrifice to pagan gods. These Christian warriors said, "You can have our armor and even our bodies, but our hearts' allegiance belongs to Jesus Christ." Because of their stance they were marched onto a frozen lake in the midwinter of A.D. 320 and stripped of their clothes. At any time they could renounce Christ and be spared from death. Instead, they huddled close together and sang their song of victory, "Forty martyrs for Christ." That freezing night saw thirty nine men fall to their icy graves. When there was but one man left he stumbled to the shore and renounced Christ. The officer in charge of guarding these men had secretly come to believe in Christ. He then replaced the man who had broken rank and walked out onto the ice. He threw off his clothes and confessed his faith in Christ. At sunrise the Roman soldiers found forty men who gave their all for the cause of Christ.[528]

**Materialism** "Focusing on material things is the greatest danger we face. What makes it seem so normal today is that virtually everyone in America is doing it." —*Larry Burkett*[529]

**Materialism** In a typical week, about eight hundred Americans are injured by their own jewelry. If you're not careful, luxury items can hurt you physically, as well as financially or otherwise.[530]

**Materialism** Larry Burkett has said, "We are so caught up in making more money and buying bigger things that we have lost most of our thrust to reach the unsaved world."[531]

**Materialism** Several years ago, construction workers happened upon a corpse outside the city of Pompeii. The evidence surrounding this woman's demise was interesting. Apparently, she had been fleeing from the eruption of Mt. Vesuvius in A.D. 79. Overtaken by the molten lava, she died in the hot ashes. The corpse revealed hands that were clutched around jewels. The jewels had survived, but the woman had not. The same is true today. Death will overtake us all and strip us of our earthly wealth.[532]

**Maturity** John Maxwell has identified four levels of maturity for Christians. They are given in progressive order with the least mature viewpoint listed first: (1) I'm going to do what I want, regardless of any thought for God; (2) If God gives me what I want, then I will give him what he wants; (3) I will give God what he wants, with faith that he will give me what I want; and (4) I will give God what he wants, regardless of any thought for myself. Many Christians spend the balance of their life at level two or three but the greatest joy is found at level four.[533]

**Maturity** Rick Warren notes the mark of spiritual maturity occurs when a believer "takes off the bib and puts on an apron." Immature children wear bibs and expect others to meet their needs. Those who don aprons have learned the joy of serving others. Which attire are you wearing?[534]

**Meditation** "This book of the law shall not depart from your mouth, but you shall meditate on it day and night, so that you may be careful to do according to all that is written in it" (Joshua 1:8). New Agers have stolen and perverted the concept of meditation so that many contemporary Christians seem uneasy with the term. Joshua noted the need for it centuries ago. Liu Chi Kung placed second to Van Cliburn in the 1958 Tchaikovsky Competition. A year later he was imprisoned during the Cultural Revolution in China. For seven years he was denied the use of a piano. Soon after his release from prison he was back on tour, and the critics were astonished that "his musicianship was better than ever." The obvious question was, "How?" One critic said, "You had no chance to practice for seven years." Liu replied, "I did practice, every day. I rehearsed every piece I had ever played, note by note, in my mind." Meditating on God's Word allows us to live above our circumstances.[535]

**Meekness** Ken Medema is a Christian musician whose ministry has impacted millions. He was born blind, but his parents never allowed his blindness to exclude him from activities. They taught him to ride a bike, water ski, and do many other things which are normally "off limits" for the visually impaired. One day while on his college campus, Ken accidentally bumped into another blind student. The guy yelled, "Hey, watch it. Don't you know I'm blind?" Medema didn't rail back or even mention his own disability. He simply said, "I'm sorry. I didn't see you." Meekness remains gracious even when one's rights have been violated.[536]

**Memory** The author of "Amazing Grace," John Newton, had great difficulty with his memory. In the later days of his life a friend asked if he still had a bad memory. Newton replied, "Yes, I do, but I remember two things: I am a great sinner and I have a great Savior; and I don't suppose an old slave trader needs to remember much more than that."[537]

**Mercy** When the Confederate Army was finally defeated, Abraham Lincoln was asked how he would treat the rebellious Southerners. The question hinted at the desire to see the South severely punished. Unexpectedly, though, the merciful President said, "I will treat them as if they had never been away."[538]

**Mercy Killing** Take note of the Dutch; America tends to be just a few years behind them, mirroring their trends. On October 20, 1994, Dutch television aired a one-hour documentary, *Death Upon Request.* It chronicled the story of a wheelchair-bound sixtythreeyear-old man named Cees van Wendel de Joode who suffered from ALS (also known as Lou Gehrig's Disease). He desired active euthanasia. So on his birthday, March 4, 1994, his physician administered a lethal injection. Such action is both legal and accepted in the Netherlands. Now it is becoming widely publicized as well.[539]

**Military Price Tag** When Desert Storm was the focus of our nation, we were reminded of our military's tremendous price tag. U.S. expenditures, combined with the rest of the world, equals $1 trillion a year on global weaponry and death machines. "Wisdom is better than weapons of war." (Eccles. 9:13).[540]

**Ministry** "We need the Lord high and lifted up, so we can get things in perspective. We are called to minister in a sense of awe, of reverence, of holy fear." *—John MacArthur*[541]

**Miracles** "Miracles sometimes happen, but many a life has been wasted waiting for one." Miracles are God's prerogative, not ours. If he chooses not to provide the tangible miracle you have requested, accept the far greater miracle of his presence in your life.[542]

**Miscalculation** Four days after the Watergate burglary of 1972, President Nixon recorded the following statement on a tape that was released to the public for the first time in May of 1993: "I don't think you're going to see a great, great uproar in this country about the Republican committee trying to bug the Democratic headquarters." God said "the wages of sin is death," but a lot of people are miscalculating and underestimating the magnitude of those wages.[543]

**Mistakes** Are you afraid to make a mistake? If you are, think about a lady who made a fortune off of other people's mistakes. Bette Nesmith had a good secretarial job at a bank in Dallas when she began thinking of ways she could more effectively correct typing errors. She knew that artists who worked with oil paintings just painted over their mistakes. She applied her art experience and concocted a white mixture to paint over her typing errors. Soon, all the secretaries in her building were using what she then called "MistakeOut." She felt it was a proven product, so she attempted to sell the idea to marketing agencies and various companies (including IBM), but they all turned her down. She then assumed the marketing role herself. Her kitchen became her factory. Bette Nesmith finally got the attention of Gillette; they bought her out for $47.5 million. Those little .6 ounce bottles of Liquid Paper turned out to be quite valuable. If a company was willing to pay nearly $50 million for a product that covers mistakes, rest assured, there are a lot of people besides you who make mistakes.[544]

**Misunderstandings** Have you ever heard of children playing Cowboys and Americans? Probably not, but it's closer to the truth than Cowboys and Indians. As you will recall from elementary school, this little misunderstanding started back in 1492. Columbus was sure he had landed in the West Indies so he referred to the native residents as Indians. Even though Columbus' misunderstanding has been known to be wrong for centuries, we still propagate his error five hundred years later. In fact, Americans have made this misunderstanding even more confusing by calling our earliest residents American Indians. This brief reminder from history warns us to be careful with our words. A little misunderstanding may be around for a long time.[545]

**Mom's Picnic** Jill and Pat Williams are parents of twelve children. Four are biologically theirs, four were adopted from Korea, and four were adopted from the Philippines. In 1990 they were also parenting two foster daughters. Mrs. Williams says most of the time people ask, "Are all of these kids yours, or is this some kind of picnic?" She quickly assures them, "They're all mine, and believe me, it's no picnic."[546]

**Money** After serving on the stewardship committee, a lay-leader became very aware of his church's financial condition. He saw the figures of the budget in a different light and understood the lack of giving among his fellow church members. The perceptive leader then hit on an idea that could revolutionize the financial status of American churches. He told his pastor, "The greatest thing the federal government could do for the church is to stop printing one-dollar bills." The man's idea would probably improve every church offering.[547]

**Money** In 1815, the Duke of Wellington defeated Napoleon in the battle of Waterloo. When Godfrey Davis wrote a biography about the famous general he had an advantage over previous biographers. Davis was exposed to the Iron Duke's personal financial records. Of this privileged information he made the following observation: "I found an old account ledger that showed how the Duke spent his money. It was a far better clue to what he thought was really important than the reading of his letters or speeches." If a biography were written about you, what would we learn from studying your checkbook?[548]

**Money** In 1986, Chris Evert was still a commanding figure among women's tennis. At age thirty-one she was internationally famous, had a three million dollar annual salary, and had homes in England, California, and Florida. At that stage of her life she told an interviewer from *Life* magazine, "I've had enormous success, but you have to find your own happiness and peace. You can't find it in other things and other people. I'm still searching." Likewise, before O. J. Simpson became known for anything but football and Hertz, he was rich and famous but "lonely and bored." In an interview with *People* magazine he spoke of his bouts with depression and said, "I often wondered why so many rich people commit suicide. Money sure isn't a cure-all." Not even a thesaurus lists money as a synonym for happiness and contentment.[549]

**Money** "Money ranks with love as man's greatest source of joy. And with death as his greatest source of anxiety." —*John Galbraith*[550]

**Money** What would you be willing to do for $10 million? From survey results found in *The Day America Told the Truth*, 1 of 4 respondents would abandon their entire family, 23 percent said they would become a prostitute for a week, 16 percent noted they would leave their spouse, and 3 percent confided they would put their children up for adoption. Sergio Hernandez, 28, was arrested and charged with stealing television sets and other electronics during the 1992 rioting in Los Angeles. This appears rather strange for a man who won $3 million in the 1989 California lottery. Kathleen Pizzi was a restaurant hostess when she won a $3.2 million jackpot in the 1985 Connecticut lottery. In 1992, Miss Pizzi wound up facing attorneys in a Palm Beach, Florida bankruptcy court. Many folks seem to think money is the cure-all to their problems. More correctly, Paul said, "the love of money is a root of all sorts of evil, and some by longing for it have wandered away from the faith, and pierced themselves with many a pang" (1 Tim. 6:10).[551]

**Money Crunch** Donald Trump had to cancel singing lessons for his wife, Marla, because her teacher, eighty-one-year-old David Sorin Collyer, refused to give them a discount. The Trumps said they did not have enough money to pay full price for the lessons. Collyer's other students include Paul Simon, Bette Midler, Michael Bolton, and Melissa Manchester.[552]

**Monopoly** In 1935, Charles Darrow brought his invention of *Monopoly* to Parker Brothers. The experts at Parker Brothers rejected the game for "containing fifty-two fundamental errors." Ironically, in 1936, Mr. Darrow was well-received by the embarrassed Parker Brothers. The persistent Charles Darrow had spent the year after his rejection demonstrating the potential success of the game by selling numerous editions of the board game himself. Parker

Brothers helped make the unemployed heating engineer from Germantown, Pennsylvania, a multi-millionaire. Since that time, over 100 million copies of *Monopoly* have been sold in 31 countries. Each year Parker Brothers prints more than $40 billion worth of *Monopoly* money—more than twice the amount printed annually by the U.S. Mint. *Monopoly's* success has produced 3.2 billion of those little green houses, enough to circle the globe. Persistence does have its benefits![553]

**Moral Majority** "Americans show much greater interest in religion than sports, but it receives far less attention from the news media." So began an article about discoveries by Robert Bellah, a sociologist at the University of California in Berkeley. He collected comparative statistics on the two most defining areas: financial participation and personal involvement. In 1992, Americans gave $56.7 billion to religious groups. That compares with $4 billion spent on major league baseball, football, and basketball. (That's fourteen times as much money given toward religion). In attendance, Gallup revealed that 5.6 billion seats were filled for church in 1993. During the same time period 103 million went to watch the three main professional sports leagues. Total attendance for *all* college and professional sporting events, including everything from tennis to dog racing, was 388 million. That is still thirteen times fewer people in the ballpark than in the church. In one month more people turned out for worship—about 433 million—than the 388 million spectators who attended all college and professional sporting events in one year. We live in a sports-crazed culture, but the statistics reveal most Americans are still very interested in God.[554]

**Morality** Few would argue with Gene Kasmar's belief that sex, child abuse, incest, and prostitution are unfit for children. The problem lies in his petition to the Brooklyn Center Independent School District in Minnesota. It seems Mr. Kasmar feels the dangerous medium by which these vices are foisted on children is none other than the Bible. "The lewd, indecent and violent contents of that book are hardly suitable for young students. The Bible quickly reveals its unsuitability in a school and learning environment," wrote Kasmar. Are you surprised he is an avowed atheist? A battle cry of late is, "You can't legislate morality." Actually, we can and we do. Phrased more accurately, the question is, "Whose morality will be legislated?"[555]

**Morals** Sometimes our personal views of morality smack of vile hypocrisy. Terry Richardson, while serving as the president of the Houston Gay and Lesbian Political Caucus, was interviewed about a trend toward violence against homosexuals. Such violence is unquestionably wrong, but Richardson's comment was hard to reconcile. The openly gay activist said, "We're seeing a generation without morals."[556]

**Mormonism** The Mormon Tabernacle at Salt Lake City, Utah reveals a significant truth about this deceptive religion. When the initial band of Mormons set out to construct a tabernacle, they were disheartened to find that their favorite materials from their homelands of Missouri and Illinois, marble and oak, where not readily available in the valley of the great Salt Lake. The only resource of abundance was pine. The industrious Mormons used the pine wood but added their own special touch. They utilized expert craftsmanship to paint the pine columns to look like marble and artistically converted the pine panels to appear as though oak. To the human eye their cover up is most impressive. Yet, when one closely examines this material impersonation the truth becomes known. This physical illusion in the Mormon Church is indicative of what they also portray in the spiritual realm. They claim to believe in Jesus Christ but, like the "marble and oak," it's just another facade.[557]

**Mother's Day** Mother's Day is the third most-celebrated holiday in the world. Only Christmas and Easter are more popular. This big day started in the heart of Anna M. Jarvis, one of twelve siblings and one of the only four who lived to adulthood. After her mother's death in 1905, Miss Jarvis dedicated the rest of her life to carrying out her mother's wishes for a special day to honor all mothers. Anna Jarvis made speeches, wrote thousands of letters, traveled countless miles, and spent a fortune on the Mother's Day idea. On May 10, 1908 she organized the first Mother's Day celebration at the Andrews Methodist Church in Grafton, West Virginia. The service ran from 8:00 A.M. until noon and included the fourfold purpose of Mother's Day:

1. to honor our mothers,
2. to bring families together,
3. to make us better children,
4. to brighten the lives of good mothers.

In 1914, President Woodrow Wilson proclaimed that the second Sunday in May (the Sunday closest to Miss Jarvis' mother's death) should be celebrated as Mother's Day. Carnations were also included in the festive day. Miss Jarvis donated white carnations and asked people to wear a red carnation if their mother was living and a white carnation if she was dead.[558]

**Mother's Worth** Sylvia Porter is a noted financial analyst. Mrs. Porter took her calculations to the computer and punched in an average hourly fee for a nursemaid, housekeeper, cook, dishwasher, laundress, food buyer, chauffeur, gardener, maintenance person, seamstress, dietitian, and practical nurse. She found that the labor performed by a mother each year at home would cost a family $23,580 in Greensboro, South Carolina, $26,962 in Los Angeles, and $28,735 in Chicago. Even at that, the list is not exhaustive. In addition to the roles cited above, most moms also function as coach, teacher, interior decorator, religious educator, mediator, counselor, and child psychologist. Punch up salaries for all of those professions, and mom's worth at least six figures![559]

**Motherhood** "A mother can get her children's complete attention just by sitting down and looking comfortable." —*Sam Ewing*[560]

**Motherhood** "There is nothing easy about good mothering. It can be backbreaking, heart wrenching, and anxiety producing. And that's just the morning." A *good* mom:

- Never bakes biscuits from a cardboard tube that goes "pow!"
- Appears instantly whenever any family member yells, "Mom!"
- Knows exactly which garment each child wants to wear every day and has it washed and hung in the closet.
- Is always home when you call.
- Uses coupons to save at least $15 every time she buys groceries.
- Never raises her voice.
- Never dreads teacher conferences.
- Attends every T-ball and soccer game in hose and heels after a productive day at the office or some other world-expanding venture.
- Never leaves kids with a runny nose in the church nursery.
- Never says no to the PTA.
- Keeps a regimented family schedule of daily tooth flossing and Bible memorization.[561]

**Motherhood** When Abraham Lincoln was asked, "What is the greatest book you've ever read?" he succinctly replied, "My mother!" Many people would say the same.[562]

**Motivation** Can you remember the last time you washed a rental car? Probably not. People don't wash rental cars. The motivation of ownership is missing. The same principle is true in churches. Until people feel a degree of ownership, they're going to treat the church like they treat a rented car.[563]

**Motivation** Leaders are always looking for ways to motivate people. Unfortunately, the two most frequently employed tactics are guilt and fear. According to a Gallup poll conducted for *Newsweek,* the best way to "motivate a person to work hard and succeed" is through "increased self-value." Eighty-nine percent of the adults surveyed said motivation was most effective when it enhanced their self-esteem.[564]

**Mummy's Burial** After sixty-six years, Henry Atkins finally got a decent burial. You may think he is an old war hero, but he's not. "Speedy" Atkins was an employee of Dixon Tobacco Company and had a good friend named A. Z. Hamock. Hamock was an undertaker with a secret, homemade embalming fluid. When Atkins died in 1928, he had no living family. Hamock embalmed Atkins and kept him around to monitor the permanence of his embalming fluid. Hamock and his secret embalming fluid died in 1948. Since that time the mummified Atkins had been kept in a closet. The tuxedo-clad corpse has been on national TV three times and was a regular tourist attraction, but all that changed. Hamock's widow, Velma, said, "It is time, after all these years, that he be buried. He is a dead person, and there is no need to keep on keeping on." So, after sixty-six years, Speedy Atkins was buried on August 5, 1994 in Paducah, Kentucky. Whether you disguise it, deny it, or embalm it, death is still a reality we must all face. With Christ this reality takes on new meaning: "If anyone keeps my word, he will never see death" (John 8:51).[565]

**My Fair Lady** In the play *Pygmalion* (brought to the screen as the movie *My Fair Lady),* Eliza Doolittle expresses the sentiment of many when she cries out, "Don't tell me you love me, show me! Show me!" Saint Francis of Assisi said it succinctly when he declared, "Preach the gospel at all times. If necessary, use words." Emmanuel Suhard wrote, "To be a witness means to live in such a way that one's life would not make sense if God did not exist." Although words are a necessary part of evangelism, we could all probably stand a little improvement in the area of communicating love through deeds.[566]

**New Age** Iowa State University math professor, Alexander Abian, has proposed we blow up the moon with nuclear warheads so that the Earth's tilt will be reduced and the global climate can be improved. Satan's initial temptation enticed man to "be like God" so he could make "improvements." New Age theology is causing people to fall for that same temptation and believe God needs their expertise.[567]

**New Name** Seventeen-year-old Peter Eastman Jr. got tired of his name so he changed it. On April 22, 1994, the California teenager officially became "Trout Fishing In America." The name came from the title of Richard Brautigan's 1967 counterculture book. Peter, who is now Trout, said, "I am just saying I am not this little kid anymore. I want to be my own person." Peter Eastman Sr. said, "I am proud of Trout. I will address him as Trout, because that honors his choice." I sure hope the references to a "new name" in Revelation refer to something else. Could you imagine being called Trout Fishing In America for all of eternity?[568]

**New Year's Resolution** "The trouble with turning over a new leaf is that once you've done it twice, you're right back where you started." There's a big difference between turning over a new leaf and turning over your life to Jesus Christ.[569]

**Nintendo** Significant research has been uncovered by John and Sylvia Ronsvalle of Empty Tomb, Inc., an Illinois-based research organization. The Ronsvalles discovered that total Protestant support of foreign missions in 1991 amounted to almost $1.7 billion per year—precisely the same amount Americans spent on Nintendo games. Is Nintendo of equal value to the gospel?[570]

**Numbering Our Days** In Psalm 90:12, Moses said, "Teach us to number our days . . ." Leslie Weatherhead, who pastored the City Temple in London for twenty five years, wrote a book entitled *Time for God*. In this book, Weatherhead helps us to number our days by mathematically calculating a "one-day lifetime" for a person living an average life span. (His calculations are actually for only the waking hours of 6:00 A.M. to 11:00 P.M.). If you're fifteen years old, it is 10:25 A.M.. If you are 20, it's 11:34 A.M. If you're 25, the time is 12:42 P.M. It's 1:51 P.M. for a 30-year-old. At 35 it's 3:00 P.M. If you are 40, it is 4:00 P.M. At 45 the clock reads 5:16 P.M. For a person of 50, it's 6:25 P.M. It's 7:34 P.M. for those at 55. A 60-year-old is looking at 8:42 P.M. Retiring at 65 means it's 9:51 P.M. And if you're 70, it is 11:00 P.M. Look at the clock and live each day to the fullest![571]

**Obedience** In March of 1986, a twenty-five-year-old man named Roger Moore was given a traffic ticket for not having his toddler secured in a car seat. The young man grumbled about the ticket and fastened his son into the appropriate restraint. The ticket was begrudgingly stuffed in the glove compartment. Nineteen minutes later, Mr. Moore and his young son were involved in an accident. The little toddler sustained a few minor injuries but was protected by the restraints of his car seat. Unfortunately, the father was killed. Although he heeded the warning to fasten his son's seat belt, Moore never buckled his own. James 1:23 paraphrased: "For if anyone is a hearer of the word and not a doer, he is like a man who . . . died in Bel Air, Maryland, in 1986."[572]

**Obedience** The only part of the Bible you truly believe is the part you obey.[573]

**Obedience** Which version of the Bible do you prefer? Some advocate the King James; others, the New International Version. One likes the New American Standard while another chooses the Living Bible. The question isn't really which version of the Bible you read, but which version you prefer. Dr. Howard Hendricks notes that many of us actually prefer the Reversed Standard Version. When we read God's Word and recognize a call for change, we often choose to do the reverse and go against God's clear call.[574]

**Obstacles** In 1992, Kristi Yamaguchi won the gold medal in figure skating. That was quite an accomplishment, when you consider what she had to overcome. Her legs were incorrectly developed at birth, so she was placed in corrective casts at two weeks of age. The casts were changed every two weeks until she was one. For the next four years she wore corrective shoes. Skating was later introduced as a method to strengthen her legs. Then at age twenty, she became the reigning queen of figure-skating.[575]

**Occult** Most people have heard of the Salem witch hunts in 1692. During that year, fourteen women and six men were executed by those who believed they had engaged in witchcraft. Today in Salem, Massachusetts (population forty thousand) there are three thousand people who practice witchcraft. In 1692 the documentation and evidence of those involved with witchcraft was questionable. Today it is not only accurately documented, but tolerated as well.[576]

**Offering Applause** Norman Whan has had the opportunity of ministering in both Korea and Nigeria. In these two countries he had the privilege of seeing a unique demonstration of Christian giving. Before the offering plates are passed the minister announces, "We will now take up God's tithes and our offerings." This statement is met with resounding applause from the congregation. Giving to God is a blessed opportunity for which we should always be gratefully applauding.[577]

**Open Minded** For more than a century the Swiss dominated the watch industry. In 1968, they commanded 65 percent of the world market and 80 percent of the profits. Within ten years those figures had plummeted. By 1978, Japan had assumed world dominance, and the Swiss held just 10 percent of the watch market. This led to a three-year process of laying off 50,000 of their 65,000 watch workers. So what happened? In 1967 the Japanese were open-minded and the Swiss weren't. In that year Swiss researchers invented the quartz watch. The Swiss watch manufacturers rejected it because it had no gears or springs. In short, it wasn't made like a watch is "supposed" to be made. The Swiss were so certain the quartz watch would never sell, they didn't even protect their invention. They displayed it at the Annual Watch Congress in 1967. The open-minded Japanese saw the potential of a watch that is one thousand times more accurate than conventional watches and went from zero percent of the world watch market to global dominance in less than a decade.[578]

**Opinions** In 1968, producer Don Hewitt asked Harry Reasoner to make a pilot for a new show called *60 Minutes.* Reasoner agreed to the project but predicted it wouldn't fly. "I said, 'Sure,' but I also said I didn't think it would fly." Twenty-three successful years later, Harry Reasoner retired to "editor emeritus" at age sixty-eight. The late reporter's experience with *60 Minutes* taught him something about opinions. When God asks us to do something it is wise to remember, "'My thoughts are not your thoughts, neither are your ways my ways,' declares the Lord" (Isaiah 55:8).[579]

**Opportunistic** Do you see ways to reduce the frustrations of problems in everyday life? Sometimes it is as simple as just changing the focal point from "broken" to "different." A Hong Kong shopping center did this when one of their escalators broke down. Rather than putting up a sign that read, "Out of Order," they cleverly displayed a sign highlighting the negative in a positive manner. It read, "This escalator is temporarily a stairway." When things go wrong we will move through the difficulty much easier if we try to be opportunistic and turn negative situations into positive ones. That's what Jesus did![580]

**Opportunities** "A wise man makes more opportunities than he finds." —*Francis Bacon*[581]

**Opportunity** Have you ever heard of Elisha Gray? Probably not because he was late for a golden opportunity. On March 7, 1876,

Mr. Gray submitted his brilliant idea to the U.S. Patent Office. The only problem was, Patent #174,465 was given to another man with the same invention just a few hours earlier. Elisha Gray was a few hours late, so we now remember Alexander Graham Bell as the inventor of the telephone.[582]

**Opportunity** "No one can go back and have a new beginning, but everyone can start now and have a new ending." —*Buckner Fanning*[583]

**Opportunity** Opportunity seldom knocks twice, so Levi Strauss opened the door after that first knock. Like many other men, Strauss went to California in hopes of making his fortune there. He did make a fortune, but not the way he had planned. He set out with a load of heavy canvas fabric, from which he planned to sell sections for tents and wagon covers. Upon arrival, the first miner who saw his product said, "You should have brought pants." The seasoned miner further explained how there weren't any pants strong enough to endure the arduous conditions of mining. Levi Strauss immediately made the miner a pair of work pants, and struck gold. Opportunities only become opportunities when we embrace them as such.[584]

**Opportunity** "The reason so many people never get anywhere in life is because when opportunity knocks, they are out in the backyard looking for four-leaf clovers." —*Walter Chrysler*[585]

**Optimism** The late Norman Vincent Peale once asked a doctor what he thought were the physiological advantages of optimism over depression. This physician said, "Depression in the mind increases the possibility of infection by at least tenfold." This truth was statistically confirmed by a study from Harvard. In 1946, researchers interviewed ninety-nine Harvard graduates. For the next thirty-five years these graduates were monitored. Those who were pessimistic in nature incurred substantially more illness than those with an optimistic outlook. "A cheerful heart is good medicine, but a crushed spirit dries up the bones" (Prov. 17:22).[586]

**Others** It is both humbling and sobering to reflect on the following statement by J. A. Holmes: "It is well to remember that the entire population of the universe, with one trifling exception, is composed of others."[587]

**Outreach** It's the persevering salesperson who closes the most deals. Thomas Publishing found that 80 percent of all new sales are closed on the fifth sales call. However, their study showed that only 10 percent of all salespeople make more than three calls. When seeking to reach people for Christ and win an audience with the unchurched, we would do well to remember this truth from the world of sales.[588]

**Outreach** Of all church-going Americans who consider themselves Christians, only 36 percent have invited someone who was not already a part of another congregation. Among Evangelicals the percentage is higher, 46 percent, but it still means 54 percent aren't inviting people without a church.[589]

**Outreach** Eighty percent of all the people who have come forward to receive Christ during a Billy Graham crusade were brought by a friend or relative. That is the figure Billy Graham's Association has determined through decades of research. Elmer Towns affirms this statistic with his own research. Dr. Towns has been taking a personal survey in his seminars for twelve years, all across America. The results of these surveys reveal the following about how people have come to Christ: 2 percent through non-personal advertising (TV, radio, literature, etc.), 6 percent because of the personal influence of a pastor, 6 percent came to Christ through the intentional evangelistic efforts of a church, and 86 percent found Jesus as a result of a friend or relative. Unfortunately, the Church appears to be missing this important truth, because a recent Gallup poll showed that 63 percent of unchurched Americans have not been invited to church by their friends. Slick marketing will never replace a personal relationship.[590]

**Outreach** The advertising industry uses the term "six sticks." This means people need to be presented with a new idea many times before they are ready to consider the concept. People generally need at least six exposures to a product before they will seriously consider making a purchase. If that's true with laundry detergent and peanuts, it stands to reason that churches need to take the same approach and make at least six significant contacts with non-churched friends or acquaintances.[591]

**Overload** On the desk of Dr. John Maxwell is a humorous reminder he uses to lighten up times of stress. It reads, "God put me on earth to accomplish a certain number of things. Right now I'm so far behind, I know I'll never die."[592]

**Pace of Life** It is hard enough to get people involved in regular worship attendance, but when you start looking to develop additional ministries, it seems as though nobody wants to get involved. Such a pattern usually results in some browbeating, a few good guilt trips concerning commitment, and a truck load of frustration for everyone. Dr. James Dobson seems to think commitment, or the lack of it, isn't the real issue. "Most of us in North America live every day on the ragged edge, holding down multiple jobs and running full tilt from morning to night. Surviving another day takes priority..." In a *Time*/CNN poll of 500 adults, 69 percent said they would "like to slow down and live a more relaxed life." Maybe we have experienced a regression in Abraham Maslow's Hierarchy of Needs. Maslow noted our needs follow a progression of (1) Physiological (the basic needs of food, sleep, sexual release, physical activity), (2) Safety (protection from bodily harm), (3) Love and Belonging (warmth and affection, acceptance, approval and connection with others), (4) Esteem (status and self-respect, feeling adequate and worthwhile), (5) Self-Development (personal growth, fulfilling one's potential), (6) Knowledge/ Understanding (to value knowledge for its own sake), and (7) Spiritual (a need to rise above the boundaries of oneself). Involvement and commitment increase when we help people to do more than simply "survive."[593]

**Paradigm Shift** When Mickey Mantle was sixty-one, he was approached by an autograph-seeking middle-aged man and his little boy. The man had tears in his eyes when he said, "Son, it took me thirty years to get here to shake this man's hand. This is the greatest baseball player who ever lived." The little boy looked at Mantle then turned back to his dad and said, "Daddy, that's an old man." The heroes of yesterday have aged, and their mortality reminds us that age and change occur more rapidly than we think or desire.[594]

**Parental Advice** Doug Larson said, "The smartest advice on raising children is to enjoy them while they're still on your side."[595]

**Parental Encouragement** Despite all of their gripes, most teenagers get along fine with their parents. In a recent poll, 71 percent rated their relationship with Mom and Dad as "good" or "excellent." Eighty-four percent said they confide in their parents. The teenage years can be difficult for the parents and the teen, so stats like this should bolster some confidence on both sides of the relationship.[596]

**Parenting** "By the time we realize our parents were right, we have children who think we're wrong." —*Guillermo Hernandez*[597]

**Parenting** If you want to take Dr. James Dobson out to eat, you better not be hoping for a Tuesday engagement. In October of 1971, Dr. Dobson made a commitment to fast one day a week on behalf of his children. Prayer replaces food every seventh day as he intercedes for his two children. "It is very difficult to forget your highest values when one day out of seven is spent concentrating on them," he says. Dr. Dobson is a Christian leader who truly does focus on the family.[598]

**Parenting** Live in such a way that your children can look to you as an example, not an object lesson.[599]

**Parenting** Parenting is compared to building a home in Cheri Fuller's book *Helping Your Child Succeed in Public School.* In the building process of a home there is a general contractor and various subcontractors. The general contractor maintains relationships with the subcontractors and makes certain they understand his expectations as he is ultimately responsible for the proper construction of the home. Parents are "general contractors" of their children's education. Parents "sub out" parts of the educating tasks, but they must oversee, provide support, and take the initiative to keep in touch with what is happening at school. This translates to the church as well. Spiritual development is the duty of parents, even if they take their children to church. Sunday School teachers, youth workers, and ministers are "sub contractors" who are working with the parents to build spiritually healthy children.[600]

**Parenting** Penelope Leach is a well-known British expert in the area of parenting. In 1994, she released a book titled *Children First: What Society Must Do—and Is Not Doing—for Children Today.* Ms. Leach uses her book to say, "Let's pay attention to children now, because if we could get it right for a generation, we could make a difference." Her logic is reasonable as she notes most parents who are not doing a good job now were once children who were not parented well. If we could break the cycle of poor parenting, the next generation could experience radical and positive reform.[601]

**Parenting** Socrates (469–399 B.C.) said, "Could I climb the highest place in Athens, I would lift my voice and proclaim: Fellow citizens, why do you turn and scrape every stone to gather wealth, and take so little care of your children, to whom one day you must relinquish it all?" [602]

**Parenting** "Sometimes we're so concerned about giving our children what we never had growing up, we neglect to give them what we did have growing up." —*James Dobson*[603]

**Parenting** Training a child to follow the straight and narrow way is easy for parents. All they have to do is lead the way.[604]

**Parenting** When Harmon Killebrew was elected to the Baseball Hall of Fame in 1984, he said, "My father taught me and my brother to play ball in the front yard. One day my mother came out and told him we were ruining the lawn. My father told her, 'We're raising kids, not grass.'" [605]

**Parenting at 35,000 Feet** Each time you fly you'll hear a little spiel that almost anyone can recite. "In the unlikely event that we should lose cabin pressure, an oxygen mask will drop in front of you. Place the mask securely over your nose and pull firmly to activate the flow of oxygen. If you are traveling with a child, place the mask over your face first, then proceed to place a mask over your child." It's a nice speech, but it goes against our nature. As parents we tend to think we must take care of our children first. Yet the airline says take care of yourself first. Their reasoning is simple; our children depend on us. If we don't receive the breath of life to sustain us, we won't be able to assist our children, and both lives will be lost. By taking care of ourselves first, we will be able to save both them and us. The spiritual connection is obvious. If we neglect the life-sustaining breath of God in our lives, then we will promote the spiritual destruction of both parent and child. So take a deep spiritual breath today—your children are counting on it.[606]

**Passion** Life's heaviest burden is having nothing to carry.[607]

**Pastoral Advice** Richard Jackson is pastor emeritus of the North Phoenix Baptist Church. During his tenure, the church baptized over 20,000 people. In an interview with the *Arizona Baptist Beacon*, Dr. Jackson attributed his success to loving the people and centering his ministry on winning the lost. He acknowledged some wise counsel he received from his father. The senior Jackson said, "If you love the people and preach, they'll forgive half your mistakes, and if you keep the baptistry water hot, they'll forgive the other half." [608]

**Pastoral Advice** What doctors have learned about their patients can certainly assist pastors with their congregations. Dr. John Wasson and his colleagues at Dartmouth Medical School in Hanover, New Hampshire tracked 497 men ages fifty-four and older with chronic problems such as high blood pressure, diabetes, and heart disease. Half the men regularly visited their doctors. The other half had visits scheduled farther apart but received three phone calls from their doctors between visits. Over a two-year period of time the men who received less visits but more phone calls spent 28 percent fewer days in the hospital, took 14 percent less medication, had 41 percent fewer days in intensive care, and 28 percent lower medical expenses. Likewise in ministry, more frequent contact over the phone can enhance the care of your congregation, keep you more in touch with your people, and lower the pastoral strain of feeling as though you never make enough visits. [609]

**Pastoral Study** Doctoral research on growing churches revealed numerous methods and principles for growth, but one constant surfaced in all growing churches: a senior pastor with an uninterruptable devotional life. [610]

**Pastoring** The Charles E. Fuller Institute of Evangelism and Church Growth recently released these survey results: 90 percent of pastors work more than 46 hours per week. One out of three pastors say, "Being in the ministry is clearly a hazard to my family."

One out of three pastors feel burned out within the first five years of ministry. Seventy percent of pastors do not have someone they would consider a close friend. Ninety percent of pastors feel they were not adequately trained to cope with the ministry demands placed upon them. Seventy-five percent of pastors have reported a significant crisis due to stress at least once in their ministry. Forty percent of pastors have reported a serious conflict with a parishioner at least once a month.[611]

**Patience** Do you ever get impatient? Uh, not you, of course, but someone you know? Well the next time you run into your impatient friend, tell him about Walter Shane of Alaska. The Shane family lives on St. Paul Island in the Bering Sea. When they get the urge for a pizza, Walter calls in their order and patiently waits . . . three days. The "fast" food is jetted to them via a Reeve Aleutian Airways flight from Anchorage. It costs them the price of the pizza plus $23 for shipping. And, unless the weather is bad or a flight is canceled, it usually takes only three days to arrive. Some things may seem awfully slow until you talk with Walter![612]

**Peace** Father's Day was an enjoyable day for the Simonton family in 1990. The day that followed was not. Lee Simonton left for work with his new Father's Day wing-tip shoes and a promise to be home for lunch. At 10:40 A.M. his promise to return was broken. An irate customer stormed into the Jacksonville, Florida, General Motors Acceptance Corporation office where Lee worked and opened fire with a semi-automatic rifle and a handgun. He shot two customers and twelve employees before turning the gun on himself. Lee became a fatality, because he shielded a female co-worker from the gunfire. His tragic death brought unbearable pain to his wife and two children. The loss of both love and security were terribly frightening for them. They were hurt, scared, and angry over the lot they had received. Yet, from the pages of God's Word they found divine peace and hope. Psalm 37 gave Debra the strength to forgive the man who took her husband and replaced her bitterness with peace. Six-year-old Melissa took comfort in verse 25 of her mother's Psalm: "I have never seen the righteous forsaken or their children begging bread." In Exodus 22:22–24 the little man of the house, eight-year-old Josh, claimed the promise of God to defend widows and orphans. Together they bravely walked the pathway of sorrow and along their journey they found "the peace which passes all understanding." It is only God who can provide such peace in the midst of painful sorrow.[613]

**Peace** "God cannot give us happiness and peace apart from himself, because it is not there. There is no such thing." —*C. S. Lewis*[614]

**Peace-Making** H. L. Mencken was a newspaperman and magazine editor in the first half of this century. His critiques of American life often drew letters expressing outrage and indignation. He answered every critical letter and handled each one the same way. Mencken simply wrote back, "You may be right." Peace settlements start with the acknowledgment that the other party "may be right."[615]

**Peer Pressure** Several years ago, Dr. Ruth Berenda and a group of fellow psychologists rediscovered the dramatic power of societal pressure. In an experiment they invited ten teenagers into a room where three charts were displayed. Each chart had three lines of different lengths. The group members were asked to raise their hands when the teacher pointed to the longest line on each chart. One teen in each group did not know that the other nine teens had been instructed to raise their hands when the teacher pointed to the second longest line. The lone teen frequently looked somewhat confused but cast a wrong vote with the other nine students. Dr. Berenda's data revealed that 75 percent of the teens allowed peer pressure to override their own better judgment. We all need the affirmation to choose what is right rather than what is popular.[616]

**People and Pets** Frederick the Great said, "The more I get to know people, the more I love my dog." Although it may be true, God has commanded us to love people, not dogs.[617]

**People Development** Andrew Carnegie felt you develop people the same way you mine for gold: "In gold mining you literally move tons of dirt to find a single ounce of gold. However, you don't look for the dirt—you look for the gold."[618]

**Perception** Picture yourself after a long, hot day in the yard. You have mowed the yard, edged the lawn, run your weed-eater, planted a few new flowers, and absorbed a lot more sun than you had planned. At the door you are greeted with a cordial proposition, "Would you like some chilled dihydrogen oxide or a glass of cold water?" Without hesitation you would probably ask for the water. The truth is, they're both the same thing: $H_2O$. What makes them different is one's perception. How do you perceive God? Many people perceive God as unfamiliar and undesirable, just like dihydrogen oxide. Our job is to make sure they understand he is really Living Water.[619]

**Perfection** In our hi-tech culture, sin's definition of "missing the mark" can be illustrated with help from the computer industry. T. J. Rodgers, founder and CEO of Cypress Semiconductor, told his employees, "A computer chip is the result of literally a thousand multidisciplinary tasks; doing 999 of them right guarantees failure, not success." Just one defect on a computer chip renders it useless. Likewise, those who seek salvation apart from Christ must perform with the efficiency of a computer chip and never fail to do all that God requires. It is an impossible task that humbly points us to Jesus.[620]

**Perseverance** Barry Sanders, an exciting running back for the Detroit Lions, is also a deeply-committed Christian who has learned to trust God's perfect timing. He didn't start for his high-school team until midway through his senior season. When he made it to Oklahoma State, he didn't start until his junior year of college football. His football career with the Lions is encouragement enough to persevere, but his spiritual zeal in an arena that can be hostile to one's faith is a real encouragement to persevere for the cause of Christ. (In 1991, Sanders commented about a Bible on the desk of his head coach, Wayne Fontes. He said, "Coach, the bookmark in your Bible hasn't moved.")[621]

**Perseverance** It was a miserable time of ministry. Something just didn't seem to be working. After several years of rather unsuccessful ministry, it might have seemed as though he wasn't really designed for preaching. Nonetheless, he stuck it out in the pastorate and sought another place of ministry in a different part of the country. This time he tried Fullerton, California. Good thing he did; otherwise, the world might have missed out on the ministry of Charles Swindoll.[622]

**Perseverance** Just say his name and most Christian readers will know who you're talking about. In fact, they've probably read at least one of his books. His book sales are exceeded only by the likes of Billy Graham and Charles Swindoll. Max Lucado has a last name many people struggle to correctly pronounce, but they sure know who he is and they love his books. His book *When God Whispers Your Name* was named the top-selling book of 1994. Word Publishing Company considers a book to be successful when a first-time author sells 50,000 copies and an established author sells 100,000. Each of Lucado's fourteen books have sold more than 300,000 copies. But it hasn't always been that way for the Church of Christ minister. In 1985 he put together his first book while serving as a missionary in Brazil. That book, *On the Anvil: Thoughts on Being Shaped Into God's Image*, was rejected by fifteen publishers. What a treasure the world would have missed had he given up on writing.[623]

**Persistence** "Consider the postage stamp: its usefulness consists in the ability to stick to one thing until it gets there." —*Josh Billings*[624]

**Persistence** General Douglas MacArthur's most famous words are probably those three he uttered in the Philippines during March of 1942, "I shall return." He lived up to his promise and did indeed return. More significantly, though, is when and where that persistence was first forged. He was a West Point graduate and no doubt learned about diligence while serving as a cadet. But MacArthur learned persistence before he ever entered West Point. You see, West Point turned him down not just once, but twice.[625]

**Persistence** Jim was weary of the bedtime struggle with his five-year-old son, Paulie. To eliminate the cat-and-mouse game of repeated trips back to Paulie's bedroom, one evening Jim lay down the law. He told Paulie there would be no more talk after they had said their prayers together, had the last glass of water, told each other "good-night," and turned off the light. Jim was certain his parental authority had corrected the problem when he left Paulie's bedside. In five minutes, though, Paulie was calling out for another glass of water. Jim went in, reviewed the rules, and told Paulie he'd better go to sleep. Within five minutes Paulie was requesting more water. Jim increased his intensity this time and told Paulie he would get a spanking if he asked for water once more. This time Jim was convinced the issue was resolved. His confidence was shattered about five minutes later when little Paulie said, "Daddy, when you come in here to spank me would you bring me a glass of water, please?" Paulie's persistence paid off. He got the water, and his dad didn't follow through on the predicted punishment.[626]

**Persistence** The late Jonas Salk failed two hundred times before he found the right vaccine for polio.[627]

**Personal Contacts** When Todd Hundley was struggling with his hitting as catcher for the Mets, New York broadcaster Ralph Kiner commented on Hundley's .209 batting average: "The only thing bothering him as a hitter is making contact." (Was he repeating Yogi Berra?) Some churches are a lot like Hundley. The only thing bothering them is they aren't making contact with people. Each Sunday your number of contacts should exceed your Sunday School enrollment.[628]

**Personal Reflection** Joseph Stowell is the president of Moody Bible Institute. The job is obviously very demanding. As a result, people frequently ask him what his biggest challenge is at Moody. Dr. Stowell could share about many great challenges, but his standard answer to that question is, "Me!" When we take the time to humbly and truthfully reflect on the circumstances of life, we must honestly admit our greatest challenge is generally "Me!" [629]

**Personal Touch** Jerry Rice is one of the greatest receivers in the National Football League. His abilities have been showcased by the winning tradition of the San Francisco Forty-Niners. During an interview with the Black Entertainment Television, Rice was asked why he attended such a small and obscure college like Mississippi Valley State University in Itta Bena, Mississippi. It was obvious his talent could have taken him to major universities. Rice said, "Out of all the big-time schools (such as UCLA) to recruit me, MVSU was the only school to come to my house and give me a personal visit." The big schools sent cards, letters, and advertisements, but just one school gave him personal attention. Even in a high-tech society, people still crave the attention of a personal visit.[630]

**Personal Touch** The Department of Social Services in Greenville County, South Carolina sent the following letter to a deceased individual. "Your food stamps will be stopped effective March, 1992, because we received notice that you passed away. May God bless you. You may reapply if there is a change in your circumstances." It can be a very impersonal world out there. People are looking for a church that will care, and take notice of their needs.[631]

**Personal Worth** The 1992 November ballot in the state of Washington carried a candidate named "Absolutely Nobody." David Powers had his name legally changed to capitalize on voter frustration and promised to abolish the office of Lieutenant Governor if elected. He lost with 6 percent of the vote, but what if he had won? "Absolutely Nobody Wins!" Fortunately, there's absolutely nobody God doesn't love.[632]

**Perspective** A mortician has the following sign on his desk to keep his perspective in the workplace: "Any day above ground is a good one!"[633]

**Perspective** A preacher from the Deep South once jolted a famous contemporary pastor. This bold minister told Bill Hybels, "Bill, you're going to be dead a whole lot longer than you're going to be alive." Since this fact is true, which side of the grave are you giving greater attention and energy?[634]

**Perspective** Dan Jansen was the favored gold-medalist in speed-skating for three consecutive Olympics. In 1988, he was favored to take the gold in the 500- and 1,000-meter sprints. Instead, his sister died of leukemia just hours before he had to compete, and he ended up falling to the ice in both of his events. Four years later he was still recognized as a contender for the gold, but the medal eluded him again. Nonetheless, his perspective changed. In Calgary (1988), winning was everything. In 1992 at Albertville he said, "Losing a sister was a lot bigger deal than winning a medal could ever be. Winning the gold can never again be the most important thing in my life." It wasn't until two years later at Lillehammer that he won a gold medal, but it meant more in 1994 because of his new perspective on life.[635]

**Perspective** "We can complain because rosebushes bear thorns, or we can rejoice because thorn bushes bear roses." —*A. L. Todd*[636]

**Perspective** When things aren't going well it can be difficult to see the whole picture clearly. Paul Tournier, the famous Swiss physician and theologian, provided an illustration that helps us understand circumstances from a more objective perspective. Think of yourself sitting at a train crossing while waiting for a train to pass. As the train approaches the crossing, the conductor blows the whistle continuously. The approaching train whistle has a unique sound. When the train passes directly in front of you the pitch of the whistle changes. Then a third distinct sound is heard from the whistle when the train moves past the crossing. The whistle itself never changed its pitch. The perspective changed the pitch. When circumstances seem less than ideal it can be difficult to maintain a clear perspective. In such times it is helpful to remember that things will appear differently when viewed from various perspectives. Approaching difficulties may now appear ominous, but may seem much different once they have passed.[637]

**Perspective on Love** God's gift of Christ seems all the more significant when you consider the vastness of our universe and our small role in it. If we were to experience a holocaust that destroyed our entire solar system, the massive inferno would be barely visible from the Andromeda galaxy. It would look like a match flaring faintly in the distance, then imploding into permanent darkness. Within this solar system which seems so large and incomprehensible to us, there lives only 5.4 billion people. To put that in further perspective, all of these people could stand shoulder to shoulder in an area about the size of Jacksonville, Florida (800 square miles). From the viewpoint of one galaxy among many, we are but a small spark on a flickering match. Yet, it was for this minuscule speck of humanity that Jesus Christ wrapped Himself in flesh so that we could unwrap the bounty of God's unlimited grace.[638]

**Physical Maintenance** Mickey Mantle never expected to live beyond the age of forty. His father and grandfather both died by forty. Unfortunately, Mantle abused his body with alcohol for forty-three years. Upon reflection, at age sixty-two Mantle said, "If I'd known I was going to live this long, I'd have taken better care of myself." Now is a great time to start taking better care of yourself.[639]

**Playboy Advice** *Playboy* magazine discovered something that contradicts their promiscuous philosophy. Through a carefully selected survey, the less-than-maritally-supportive periodical learned that the "overwhelming majority" of both men and women are against extramarital sex for people in general and for themselves in particular. Even *Playboy* admits faithfulness is still in vogue. (Don't forget to say you got this illustration secondhand!)[640]

**Pleasing God** "When you please God, it doesn't matter whom you displease. When you displease God, it doesn't matter whom you please." Whom are you seeking to please?[641]

**Pledge of Allegiance** We've each said it a thousand times but who started it? Our country's pledge was written especially for children in 1892 as part of a celebration for Columbus Day in public schools across our land. The original verse first appeared in an educational publication called *The Youth's Companion* on September 8, 1892. It then read, "I pledge allegiance to my Flag and the Republic for which it stands—one nation indivisible—with liberty and justice for all." The author, Francis Bellamy, was an assistant editor for the *Companion*. It was intended to be used just for the four hundredth anniversary of Columbus' discovery but its popularity led to an annual tradition. The pledge later became a daily ritual in schoolrooms throughout the land. In 1923, the first revision was made. "My Flag" was replaced by "the Flag of the United States of America." Then in 1954, President Eisenhower signed a bill that added the words, "under God."[642]

**Political Insight** Billy Graham received some strong criticism for praying at President Clinton's 1992 Inauguration. Regardless of party preference, we can all benefit from Dr. Graham's words of defense. He said, "I'm praying for the president, not for a party or platform. We're told to pray for the people in authority. Jacob prayed for Pharoah, and Daniel prayed for Nebuchadnezzar." Christians, and political leaders, would all benefit from less complaining, blaming, and name calling, and a lot more praying.[643]

**Pornography** A few statistics provide a snapshot of America's obsession with pornography:

- There are more outlets for hard-core pornography in America than there are McDonald's restaurants.
- According to the FBI, the porno industry grosses $8–10 billion per year and is dominated by organized crime.
- Pornography's number-one consumer group is adolescent boys between twelve and seventeen years old.
- In 1994 Iran's Parliament approved the death penalty for producers and dealers of pornographic videos on their third conviction. A third offense places the culprit in a category, "corrupt on Earth," and is punishable by death.[644]

**Pornography** All pornography is built upon the "Rape Myth." This myth deceptively communicates the message that all women are sexually starved and are actively seeking men to fulfill their need. To escalate their sexual stimulation they initially pretend they are not interested so that the man will actively pursue them. When the man then initiates she temporarily resists but is quickly overcome by her obsession for sex and ends up begging the man for more. Our communities are filled with pornography-reading men who have been led to believe this myth. These men are looking at our wives and daughters and thinking they have an open invitation for rape.[645]

**Pornography** In an interview with James Dobson just hours before his execution, serial killer Ted Bundy said, "Those of us who have been so much influenced by violence in the media, particularly pornographic violence, are not some kind of inherent monsters. We are your sons, and we are your husbands. We grew up in regular families. And pornography can reach out and snatch a kid out of any house today." [646]

**Positive Attitude** Todd Hunter conducted an in-depth survey on pastoral success. All of the pastors he researched were hard and diligent workers. Some of these pastors experienced success, while others did not. After compiling the results, Hunter noted a curious phenomenon concerning attitudes. Ninety-five percent of the successful pastors had continual positive attitudes, while 82 percent of the unsuccessful pastors had continual negative attitudes. If you feel unsuccessful today, check your attitude. [647]

**Possessions** Mother Teresa said, "If it takes you more than fifteen minutes to pack, you have too much stuff." To most Americans this would probably sound ridiculous, but it is a sobering reminder that we are usually guilty of accumulating far more than we need. [648]

**Potential** Educator Rene Voeltzel said, "We must not look too soon in the child for the person he will later become." In both the physical and spiritual realm, we must look beyond the present to see in others what God knows they can become through his Son, Jesus Christ. [649]

**Potential** "One of the greatest sins we commit against God is not reaching the potential he has placed in us." —*John Maxwell* [650]

**Potential** American artist James Whistler was never known for his modesty. On one occasion, he was advised that a shipment of blank canvases had been lost in the mail. When the authorities asked him if the canvases were of any great value, Whistler replied, "Not yet, not yet." Like a blank canvas, the value of our lives can be limitless if we allow God to create his masterpiece in us. [651]

**Potential** The Dead Sea is appropriately named. Nothing grows or lives in it. The consistency of the water is like none other in the world. Its only outlet is evaporation, so heavily-concentrated compounds remain after the water is lifted to the sky. The potential of such a lake seems limited. To the contrary, engineers estimate that if the potash around the Dead Sea could be mixed and distributed, there would be enough fertilizer created to supply the whole surface of the earth for at least five years. Some people or situations feel like dead ends. Allow God to help you see the potential that your eyes may be missing.[652]

**Potential** "We were created in God's image, and God is no weakling." —*Charles Atlas*[653]

**Poverty** On August 20, 1964, President Lyndon Johnson declared "war on poverty" by signing an anti-poverty measure costing nearly one billion dollars. Since that declaration, untold billions have been spent. Today 36.8 million Americans live below the poverty level. In 1964, the figure was 36 million. This war of money against poverty has dropped the percentage of Americans living under the poverty level just 4.5 percent. In 1964, 19 percent were in poverty and today the percentage is 14.5 percent. Our compassion for the poor should never decline, but we might want to reconsider our approaches to relieving the pain. Attempted physical transformation without spiritual transformation is futile.[654]

**Prayer** A few years ago a fascinating experiment was conducted on the power of prayer. Dr. Randolph Byrd, a cardiologist with the San Francisco General Medical Center's Coronary Care unit, did a scientific study on prayer involving heart patients. Nearly four hundred patients participated in a ten-month, double-blind experiment, scientifically controlled and documented. The patients were divided into two groups with no statistical difference between group A or B. The patients were not told which group they were in. Group B received no prayer support. Each patient in Group A had two people praying for them. Those who prayed for the patients were scattered throughout the country and did not know the patient's name—only the person's medical problem. When the results were tabulated, the findings revealed that patients in Group A did as well or better in virtually every comparison. The conclusion drawn by those who analyzed the study was, "Intercessory prayer appears to have a beneficial effect in patients in a Coronary Care Unit." [655]

**Prayer** A tavern was being built in a town that had previously been dry. In opposition to the tavern, a group of Christians began an all night prayer meeting and asked God to intervene. Lightning struck the tavern and burned it down. The owner then brought a lawsuit against the church and held them responsible. The Christians hired a lawyer and denied responsibility. In response to this unusual scenario, the judge said, "No matter how this case comes out, one thing is clear. The tavern owner believes in prayer, and the Christians do not." [656]

**Prayer** "Behind every work of God you will always find some kneeling form." —*D. L. Moody* [657]

**Prayer** Dr. David Yonggi Cho pastors the world's largest church in Korea. He averages about three hours in prayer every day. When he has to speak before a large group he prays five hours a day. When he was recently asked how the church in Korea differs from the church in America, he said, "While Americans are sleeping, many of us in Korea have been up for several hours praying." It's strange how often we neglect the one resource that promises to yield the greatest return. [658]

**Prayer** During the Apollo missions to the moon, the spaceships were off course more than 90 percent of the time. Yet, through continual communication with Mission Control they were able to make necessary corrections. In our journey through life, we too are off course most of the time. By staying in constant contact with God we can correct our course, stay headed in the right direction, and succeed in our mission.[659]

**Prayer** During the pioneer days, a family lost all of their possessions to a fire. In response, the church called for a special prayer meeting in their behalf. As the people came together for prayer, a young man rode up with a wagon full of supplies. He had canned goods, staples, building materials, tools, and sundry other items. The young man said, "My father couldn't make it today, but he sent his prayers." Prayer involves much more than words![660]

**Prayer** Every Friday night, a prayer group meets in Rivera, Uruguay. Such fervency would usually be applauded, but such is not the case. These Friday-night warriors are the leaders of spiritist groups who meet for the purpose of calling on the forces of evil to hinder and destroy the efforts of local Christian churches and pastors. Additionally, they attend worship services in hopes of disrupting them. To counter these attacks, Pastor Nelson Fernandez and his wife, Maria, have established daily prayer groups of Christians. May the tenacious zeal of these non-believers challenge us to more faithfully utilize the power, opportunity, privilege, and responsibility of prayer.[661]

**Prayer** John Bayer is now a Southern Baptist Foreign Missionary in Panama. His calling to foreign missions began on a mission trip to Australia. During that trip he encountered an elderly Catholic woman. When the subject of prayer was discussed the woman said, "I have to pray to Mother Mary every day, or my day just won't go right." Bayer shared the promise of Scripture that we can pray directly to Jesus. The woman replied, "But Mary is close to Jesus. She is his mother, and she will take my prayer to him." Bayer then felt prompted by the Holy Spirit to gently ask, "If you were sick and you had your choice of calling the doctor or the doctor's mother, who would you call?" She acknowledged she had never thought about it that way. They then prayed together and that dear woman heard a prayer directed to Jesus for the very first time. When she opened her eyes, tears trickled down her cheeks as she said, "Thank you for coming." "Since we have confidence to enter the Most Holy Place by the blood of Jesus . . . let us draw near to God with a sincere heart in full assurance of faith." (Heb. 10:19-22).[662]

**Prayer** Minette Drumwright works with the Southern Baptist Foreign Mission Board. She is truly a woman of prayer. She recently expressed her concern for the place of prayer in too many churches. She noted, "We spend more time praying to keep sick saints out of heaven than we do praying lost people into heaven." Drumwright went on to say, "At Pentecost they prayed ten days and preached ten minutes, and three thousand were saved. We reverse it. We pray ten minutes, preach ten days, and of course, we don't have that kind of results." Ruth Graham has said, "We are to take care of the possible and let God take care of the impossible." Keeping prayer in a position of priority is a spiritual necessity.[663]

**Prayer** "Prayer may not change things for you, but it sure changes you for things." When Paul prayed for his thorn to be removed, he asked God to "change things." Instead, God changed him so that he could handle his pain and suffering.[664]

**Prayer** R. C. Sproul has noted, "To pray without action is hypocrisy. To act without prayer is pagan." Effective prayer involves the balanced tension between total dependence on God and responsible action by the one who prays.[665]

**Prayer** T. W. Hunt is a prayer specialist for the Southern Baptist Sunday School Board. While evaluating a recently published Gallup poll on prayer, Hunt noted, "The biggest single non-biblical aspect of American praying today is lack of intercession or praying for others." He went on to say, "The majority of teachings in the Bible are for intercession. The Bible tells you to pray for other people, and this is where Americans fail most dismally." If we're not careful, even our prayers can become selfish.[666]

**Prayer** "The power of prayer is not in the one who prays but in the one who hears it." —*Max Lucado*[667]

**Prayer** "The three secrets to successful ministry are: prayer, prayer, and more prayer." —*Billy Graham*[668]

**Prayer** "We will never have time for prayer, we must make time." —*Richard Foster*[669]

**Prayer Experiment** The late Sam Shoemaker was an Episcopal minister in New York City during the first half of this century. When he encountered someone who did not believe in God he would suggest they enter a Thirty-Day Prayer Experiment. He would instruct them, "Don't pay any attention to whether you believe or not. Just pray every day for thirty days that God will meet you at the point of your greatest need, and see what happens to you." From Reverend Shoemaker's little experiment, literally hundreds of people were transformed from staunch skeptics to committed Christians. Give God a chance, and he will turn a sinner in to a saint![670]

**Pre-Marital Counseling** "No one is automatically equipped by a marriage ceremony to function at the maximum effectiveness in marriage," says Dr. Cecil Osborne, Marriage Counselor. Marriage counseling can be time-consuming as well as taxing, and very few young couples want it—but young couples are not known for thinking far ahead. Pre-marital counseling may very well prevent future problems which require marriage counseling.[671]

**Preaching** "One of the best proofs of the inspiration of the Bible is that it has withstood so much preaching." —*A. T. Robertson*[672]

**Preaching** "Preaching a sermon that is strong on information but weak on application, is like shouting to a drowning man, 'SWIM! SWIM!' The message is true, but it's not helpful." —*Jay Kesler*[673]

**Preaching** "The devil will let a preacher prepare a sermon if it will keep him from preparing himself." — *Vance Havner*[674]

**Preaching** "Use me, O God, not because it's the hour for the message, but because you've given me a message for the hour." —*Ed Towne*[675]

**Preaching** While speaking in a church on the West Coast, Howard Hendricks found this sign on the pulpit from which he was to speak: "What in the world are you trying to do to these people?" It's a good question to ask each time we preach.[676]

**Prenuptial Agreement** Need a definition for "Prenuptial Agreement?" Try this one: "A legal document that says, 'I love you almost as much as my money.'"[677]

**Pride** A rabbi was preparing for the Day of Atonement. He paraded around beating his breast and saying, "I am nothing, I am nothing." A cantor followed suit and did as his rabbi. The two marched through the synagogue demonstrating their "humility." The janitor witnessed this ritual and was reminded of his own sinfulness. He too began to beat his breast and cry out in attrition, "I am nothing." When the rabbi heard the janitor, he turned to the cantor and smugly said, "Now look who thinks he's nothing." As we approach the Cross of Christ, we do so with one of these two attitudes. We are either like the rabbi who only pretended to need God, or like the janitor who truly saw himself as nothing without Christ.[678]

**Pride** Captain James Cook was an English explorer and navigator (1728–1779). He is the man credited with discovering Hawaii.

When he first landed on those Pacific islands the natives thought he was a god and gave him divine treatment. He did nothing to discourage their perception; he embraced the role of god. All worked well for Cook until he left the isles. A storm forced him to sail back to the island for shelter. The natives believed no god would be hindered by a storm, so they felt betrayed and killed Captain Cook for pretending to be a god. When we assume the role of deity our destiny is death.[679]

**Pride** "Nothing so needs reforming as other people's habits." —*Mark Twain*[680]

**Pride** Raymond Cuthbert wasn't too bright when he exercised a bit of his pride, but then again, exercising your pride is never very bright. On January 6, 1995, Cuthbert entered a drug store in Vernon, British Columbia. He bragged to employees that he would be back in thirty minutes to rob them. The employees of Nolan's Pharmacy then called the Royal Canadian Mounted Police. Cuthbert returned thirty minutes later and was arrested with his accomplice. Sounds pretty dumb, doesn't it? But don't you imagine God thinks *all* pride is that dumb?[681]

**Pride** Romanian ruler Nikolai Ceausescu was one of the cruelest dictators of this century. After years of viciously persecuting Christians and killing all potential threats to his power, he instructed the National Opera to produce a song in his honor. Included in this song were to be the words, "Ceausescu is good, righteous, and holy." He wanted this sung at his seventy-second birthday on January 26, 1990. Instead, he and his wife were executed a month earlier on December 25, 1989. "God opposes the proud" (James 4:6).[682]

**Pride** "What will finally destroy us is not communism nor fascism, but man acting like God." —*Malcolm Muggeridge*[683]

**Priorities** Dr. Stephen Hawking is an astrophysicist at the University of Cambridge in England. He is generally believed to be the most brilliant scientist since Einstein. Dr. Hawking has what is commonly called Lou Gehrig's disease. This incredible mind is locked in a body that is rapidly deteriorating. He can only speak through the aid of a computer, and this process of communication is very laborious. He is too weak to feed himself, comb his hair, or fix his glasses. Yet, with his mind he memorizes long equations and contemplates amazing thoughts. Before this debilitating illness, Hawking floundered with his life. He claims he was bored with his profession, and life in general. He drank too much and did very little work. After the illness Hawking found a new interest and zest for life. He said, "When one's expectations [for life] are reduced to zero, one really appreciates everything that one does have." Sometimes it takes a catastrophic event to arouse the right priorities. For those of us who still have our health, we don't have to wait for an illness to rethink our values.[684]

**Priorities** When Greg Swindell pitched for the Cleveland Indians, he wore a modern day "phylactery." Greg was the proud father of Sydney, born January 21, 1991. That's an important date to Swindell. On the back of his baseball cap he had her name inscribed in tiny little white letters and her birth date was written out on the underside of his cap's bill. "When things are going badly or when I'm getting shelled, I can take it off and look at it and know what I have to look forward to when I get home." You may not wear a baseball cap to work, but such vital statistics can be etched onto a briefcase or hard hat along with such reminders as: "You shall love the Lord your God with all your heart and with all your soul and with all your might. . . . and they shall be as frontals on your forehead." (See Deuteronomy 6:4–9.)[685]

**Prison Reform** Research by the Children's Defense Fund produced an interesting comparative statistic. A year in a United States prison costs $28,000. A year at Harvard University costs the same.[686]

**Pro-Life** On February 3, 1994, Mother Teresa was the keynote speaker at a National Prayer Breakfast in Washington. President and Mrs. Clinton, Vice President and Mrs. Gore, and three thousand others were present to hear this eighty-three-year-old nun. She spoke forthrightly against abortion: "If we accept that a mother can kill even her own child, how can we tell other people not to kill each other? Any country that accepts abortion is not teaching its people to love but to use any violence to get what they want." Although the current administration has advocated abortion, they can't dismiss the logic they heard. Violence in America goes much deeper than drugs, gun control, and gangs. It is rooted in a philosophy that cheapens life from the moment of conception.[687]

**Problem Solving** "All of us might as well swap problems, because we all know exactly how to solve other people's problems." I don't know who said it, but it sure is true. Just tell someone you're sick and they'll start treating you like you're their patient. Tell someone you've just spent ten hours underneath the hood of your car, and they'll tell you how to fix it in less than five minutes. Talk about a child's disciplinary problem, and they'll give you the best-kept secret on raising kids—even if they don't have children. Yes, indeed, we could solve all of the world's troubles if we just rearranged the ownership of our problems.[688]

**Problems** A businessman hit a terrible turn in the economy. When a friend asked him how business was doing, he said, "My business is so bad I'm getting two and three calls a day from President Clinton and Boris Yeltsin." The friend asked, "Why are they calling you?" The hard-luck executive answered, "They like to talk with someone who has more problems than they do." When problems get you down, just set them down and let Jesus carry them for you (1 Pet. 5:7).[689]

**Problems** "I know God will not give me anything I can't handle. I just wish that he didn't trust me so much." —*Mother Teresa*[690]

**Problems** "In times like these, it helps to recall that there have always been times like these." —*Paul Harvey*[691]

**Professional Passengers** If you think traffic is bad in your city you should get a glimpse of the problems in Indonesia. Their transportation gridlock has gotten so bad that vehicles with fewer than three passengers have been banned from public roads. This new law has spawned an innovative niche in the job market. A whole new employment opportunity is being discovered by "professional passengers." These entrepreneurs can be hired by the hour to help you reach your quota of three passengers so you can navigate on public roads. Although this is a new phenomenon in Indonesia it's been going on in the church for centuries. The pews have plenty of people who are professional passengers. For a price they will ride with you in ministry, but there is always a price and their only interest is in what they will get in return.[692]

**Prophecy** In 1993, the TV show *Rowan and Martin's Laugh-In* had its twenty-fifth anniversary show. As part of the commemoration, segments from that first season in 1968 were shown. One clip included a segment called "News of the Future." This was a time in the show when two futuristic anchor men acted as though they were reporting current news from decades in the future. Each news item was designed to be as outlandish and crazy as possible. Two of those predictions didn't appear so crazy when the audience of 1993 looked back at what was said in 1968. They correctly forecasted that an actor named Ronald Reagan would be president of the United States from 1980–1988. They also reported in 1968 that the Berlin Wall would fall in 1989. False prophets are right some of the time, but God's prophets never miss.[693]

**Prophetic Words** Three hundred years before Christ, Plato, the Greek philosopher, predicted that "if ever the truly good man were to appear, a man who would tell the truth, he would have his eyes gouged out and in the end be crucified."[694]

**Purity** "Peace if possible, but purity at all costs." —*Martin Luther*[695]

**Purpose** Benjamin Franklin kept his life in constant evaluation by asking himself two questions every day of his adult life. In the morning he would ask, "What good shall I do today?" This was followed up by his evening question, "What good have I done today?" Mr. Franklin understood Socrates' warning, "The unexamined life is not worth living," yet he carried it a step further to add, neither is the unplanned life worth living.[696]

**Purpose** Pollsters say, "One out of five Americans feel life is meaningless." Jesus recognized such feelings among his countrymen when he noted they were like sheep without a shepherd. To all those people wandering in a wilderness without meaning, Jesus has promised purpose and hope.[697]

**Purpose** Steve Jobs is a whiz at making computers, but there was a time when he needed some help in marketing his incredible little "magic boxes." He was in need of an expert who could help him take his Apple Computers into the ring against IBM. John Sculley became the target of Steve Jobs' attention. Sculley, at age thirty-eight, had been Pepsi-Cola's youngest president. He masterminded the Pepsi Generation ad campaign that dethroned Coke from the number one position for the first time in history. Steve Jobs knew it would take a lot to get Sculley. He wined and dined him and made numerous offers with money he didn't even have, all to no avail. Sculley was content with his present and secure success. Finally, in desperation, Steve Jobs threw out a question of exasperation, "Do you want to spend the rest of your life selling sugared water, or do you want a chance to change the world?" It was that single, piercing question which leveraged the greatest weight in John Sculley's decision to leave his security at Pepsi and go to Apple for an opportunity to "change the world." Christians, more than computers, have the "real" opportunity to change the world.

Let's not miss our purpose by remaining content to simply sell "sugared water." [698]

**Quality Control** A zealous baker decided to advertise his goods. His campaign slogan was, "The finest pastries in Vienna." A competitor across the street countered with an ad claiming, "The finest pastries in Austria." A third baker watched the competition, then put up a sign which simply read, "The best pastries on this street." People aren't concerned if you are the biggest and best in their town or country. They want to know whether or not you will effectively meet their needs at home. [699]

**Racism** During the Civil Rights era, a first-grade white girl met a black girl on the first day of school. Segregation had prevented the white girl from associating with black people. Integration changed all of that and made both of the girls scared. When the white girl returned home after that historic day, she told her mother that she sat next to a black girl in school. The mother tensed, anticipating the worst. She asked her little girl what happened. The child said, "We were both so scared that we held hands all day." The problems of our day would move toward resolution if we could learn from these little girls and holds hands rather than making fists. [700]

**Racism** The tragedy of racism was not settled during the Civil Rights Movement. Unfortunately, it is still a major point of contention among divergent ethnic groups. How sad that six to ten pounds can so divide people. That's all it boils down to. Your skin accounts for between six to ten pounds of your total weight, yet because of those few pounds, many people destroy relationships. [701]

**Rat Race** "The trouble with the rat race is that even if you win, you're still a rat." —*Lily Tomlin* [702]

**Reading** Rick Warren has cleverly noted, "Americans spend more on beer than they do on books. No wonder their stomachs are bigger than their brains." The very successful and eternally opti-mistic Zig Ziglar also knows the value of reading. Mr. Ziglar has disciplined himself to read three hours a day for the past twenty-five years. It is no wonder he continues to be one of the most cap-tivating speakers in our land.[703]

**Reality Check** Peter Pan came back to the silver screen through the imaginative perspective of Steven Spielberg's *Hook.* When *Peter Pan* originally opened as a play in London, author Sir J. M. Barrie quickly found himself on the hot seat with parents. Initially, the script called for Peter to tell the Darling children they could fly if they believed strong enough. Some children believed the line and hurt themselves by leaping from high places in their attempts to fly. Barrie responded by placing a cautionary line in the scene. Peter's new discussion with the children included the now-famous element that they could fly *after* they had been sprinkled with pixie dust. Today's children are no less confused about reality than those kids who hurt themselves trying to fly. Our theology mustn't add to the confusion but prevent it.[704]

**Reconciliation** The Spanish have a story about a father and son who became estranged. The son left home, and the father later set out to find him. He searched for months with no success. Finally, in desperation, the father turned to the newspaper for help. His ad simply read, "Dear Paco, meet me in front of this newspaper office at noon on Saturday. All is forgiven. I love you. Your father." On Saturday, eight hundred young men named Paco showed up look-ing for forgiveness and love from their estranged fathers. The world is filled with people who desperately long for reconcilia-tion—with each other, and with God (2 Cor. 5:18–19).[705]

**Record Keeping** Sam Williams has said, "We count how many people come to church. God counts how many didn't show up." Our focus might be altered if our attendance records revealed "624,968 absent" rather than "157 present."[706]

**Recovering Hypocrite** Steve Green is a very successful Christian vocalist who has also succeeded in writing. In his book *Listening Heart*, he shares some insightful truths. Although he has a passion for holiness, he recognizes within his own life the tendency we all have of occasionally being dishonest spiritually. To remind himself of this tendency, he says, "I am still a recovering hypocrite." Although we quickly become defensive when someone says the church is full of hypocrites, we would do better to acknowledge that we are all "recovering hypocrites" who could very easily slip back into sin. For your friend who is concerned about the church being "full of hypocrites," just tell him it's true. Then invite him to church, because there's always room for one more.[707]

**Redemption** "For the Son of Man has come to seek and to save that which was lost" (Luke 19:10). The term "lost" subtly describes how much God loves us. As Rick Warren explains, "Our value is communicated by the word *lost*. When you can't find your car keys you've misplaced them. When you can't find the diamond on your ring you've lost it." When someone dear to you dies they aren't misplaced, you've lost them. Things of value are lost, not misplaced. Jesus came to save that which he lost, those whom he loves![708]

**Redemption** The Apostle Paul reminds us that we have been "bought with a price." Jesus' death paid the debt for our sins, but is Jesus getting what he paid for? Gauge your emotions in this scenario: You walk into a restaurant and pay full price for a hamburger, fries, and a drink. The counter attendant takes your money and slides you a tray of goods. As you unwrap your hamburger, you discover someone has already eaten half of it. A quick bite of your fries tells you they are cold, soggy, and limp. You sip on the straw to calm your nerves, but get a mouth full of melted ice. Immediately you race to the counter and claim you've been robbed. You complain that you "did not get your money's worth." You demand the goods for which you fully paid. If that ever happens to you, remember that's what happens to Jesus all the time.[709]

**Reincarnation** Garfield and his nerdy owner Jon were shown in one of their typical cartoon conversations. Jon poses the question as to whether or not he has lived any former lives. Garfield seriously doubts the prospect of Jon's reincarnation because, "You're not even living this life." Some folks are so preoccupied with "former" lives that they completely overlook this life.[710]

**Rejection** Michelangelo Buonarroti (1475–1564) was a masterful artist and sculptor. One of his most famous works stands in Florence, Italy. Nearly eighteen feet of finely-crafted stone bring to life the colossal figure of David. This incredible carving has been viewed by millions and is truly a masterpiece. Ironically, though, the huge marble stone from which Michelangelo chiseled away the young king was first rejected by other great artists like Duccio, Baccellino, and Rosellino. A stone of much greater significance was, and is, rejected by many. But it is this stone from which we all find ultimate beauty and worth. "The stone the builders rejected has become the cornerstone" (Mark 12:11).[711]

**Relationships** Darrell Robinson calls it "heresy" when lay people aren't included in ministry. To help church members see how important their role in the church is, ask them to raise their hands in response to this sequence of questions during a sermon. "How many of you came to Christ through the direct influence of a TV ministry? A radio program? A book? A pastor? A family member or friend?" Very few hands will go up until you ask about a family member or friend. This will help them to visibly see the importance of their role as a "minister." Their influence for Christ can be much greater than the pastor. According to Church Growth Institute: six out of every one hundred visitors to the church result from traditional organized visitations programs. Eighty-six out of one hundred visitors come at the invitation of a friend or relative. Of four thousand new converts who were surveyed, 75 percent indicated they were in church because they had been invited by a relative or friend.[712]

**Relationships** Former hostage Thomas Sutherland said he tried to kill himself three times during his six years of captivity in Lebanon. The suicide attempts came in late 1986 when Sutherland's captors moved him to a tiny underground cell, deprived him of light, and isolated him from his fellow hostages. He pulled a plastic bag over his head and tried to suffocate himself. "I found out on each try that it got very painful and as it got more painful, the vision of my wife and three daughters appeared before me ever more clearly. I decided each time, 'Gee, I can't go through with this,' and I would pull it off." We all need relationships that are strong enough to keep us from quitting when circumstances get tough, and we all need to care for others in such a way that when their life seems hopeless, they can think of us and be motivated to keep on going.[713]

**Relationships** If you were pressed to list the seven greatest problems a missionary faces you might very well list loneliness, financial pressures, marriage difficulties, raising children, managing general stress, and cultural adjustments. Cedric Johnson and David Penner surveyed fifty-five North American Protestant mission agencies with more than one hundred staff members overseas. The above list was the result of their research. This list is in rank order with loneliness in seventh place. You might be surprised to find that the number one problem missionaries face is "relationships with other missionaries." Satan knows the necessity and value of relationships, so he consequently focuses his greatest attention on destroying them. His success comes in distancing people from God, and from one another.[714]

**Relativism** Before Willie Nelson met up with the IRS, he owned his own golf course. Someone asked him about par. "Par is anything I want it to be," said Willie. "Do you see that hole over there? That's a par forty-seven, and yesterday I birdied it!" God has given us great freedom in life but not everything is relative. (See Romans 3:23.)[715]

**Relevance** A man was dying in the desert. As he stumbled over a sand dune he was greeted by a man selling ties. The dehydrated man begged for water, but the salesman said he only had ties. In frustration and anger the weakened man continued on his journey for survival. In an hour he reached an isolated restaurant in the middle of the desert. Was it a mirage? As he drew closer, he saw it was real. He was ecstatic. With renewed energy he ran for the door. He was stopped at the entrance by a security guard who denied him entry. The guard said, "I'm sorry, sir, but you need a necktie to eat here." Caution must be exercised in assessing relevance. We often discount the value and relevance of something without adequately studying our future needs.[716]

**Relevance** The Barna Research Group asked Americans, "Is the Christian church relevant for today?" In response, only 27 percent of the unchurched said yes. Possibly more significant was the reply of the churched. Less than half (46 percent) felt the Christian church is relevant for today. This means the majority of both the unchurched and the churched feel the Christian church has lost its relevance for today's society.[717]

**Religion** "Men will wrangle for religion, write for it, fight for it, die for it; anything but live for it." —*C. C. Colton*[718]

**Religion** "Religion is giving God what he wants." Peter Lord's definition of religion invokes a sobering question: "Am I giving God what he wants?" If not, my religion needs adjustments.[719]

**Repentance** A man continually rededicated his life and always prayed the same prayer, "Lord, take the cobwebs out of my life." His pastor had heard this prayer more times than he cared to remember. Finally, when the man uttered that prayer into his pastor's ear at the altar, the pastor responded with a prayer of his own, "Lord, kill the spider!" Repentance requires change in both our attitudes *and* our behavior.[720]

**Repentance** In our quest to reach people for Christ, we must caution ourselves to never compromise the gospel's standards in order to accommodate those people who are not interested in repentance. Billy Graham's sentiments on this concern are most appropriate: "We are dangerously near to saying to the prodigal son, 'It is not necessary to return to your father and home; we can make you comfortable in the pigpen.'"[721]

**Repentance** The promise of 2 Chronicles 7:14 was demonstrated at the Jersey Village Baptist Church in Houston, Texas on February 26, 1995. The congregation began their evening service at 6:30 P.M. expecting a routine worship service. During the invitation, a young girl walked the aisle, confessed her sin, sought the Lord's forgiveness, and sought encouragement from the church. After her response to God, other members started coming forward and confessing their sins. Around 9:00 P.M., some members relieved a couple working in the nursery so the workers could experience what God was doing. That couple went to the altar and asked for prayer. Their son had run away four months before because he wanted the freedom to live his life as he desired. While this church was praying, that young man was at Mardi Gras in Galveston. He felt God telling him to go home. He made the ninety-minute drive home, only to find a dark house. He wondered why his parents would still be at church, but he drove to the church anyway. A deacon recognized him at the door and pointed him to his parents, who were still kneeling at the altar. The son tapped them on the shoulder. In a tearful embrace he told of his desire to come home and recommit his life to Christ. What if that young girl had not been obedient to repent of her sins? That worship service may have just lasted the usual hour rather than going until 11:00 P.M., and one family might still be distant from each other and the Lord.[722]

**Resourcefulness** Martha Berry lived from 1866 to 1942. She founded the Berry School for needy children at Mount Berry,

Georgia. In 1932 she was named one of the twelve outstanding women in America. Upon one occasion she asked Henry Ford for one million dollars to assist her school. He coolly gave her a dime instead. She graciously accepted the dime and bought some peanuts for her schoolboys to plant. The next season they used the entire crop to plant a larger field. Eventually they sold enough peanuts to buy a piano for their music students. Martha Berry wrote a letter to Mr. Ford and told him what his dime had done. Ford was deeply impressed and invited her to Detroit where he gave a belated one million dollars. If we spent more time working with the dimes we have rather than complaining about the dollars we need, we might end up with a lot more in the long run.[723]

**Responsibility** Best-selling author and lecturer Denis Waitley has said, "There should be a Statue of Responsibility standing in Los Angeles or San Francisco Harbor, to match the Statue of Liberty in New York. Without individual self-control and responsibility, there can be no enduring liberty or freedom in our society." In Christ, we have not only received liberty from sin but the responsibility to share that gift of freedom with those who are still in bondage.[724]

**Responsibility** Leave the driving to us, or so the saying goes. On May 28, 1993, Greyhound bus driver J. Massenberg balked on his company's slogan and asked for a relief driver from the passengers on his bus. Thirty miles shy of his destination in Tallahassee, Massenberg said, "I quit. I can't handle this anymore. Does anyone have a Class B license to drive a bus?" Nobody was qualified, but an off-duty police officer got behind the wheel and drove about thirty minutes while Massenberg slept. He reclaimed the wheel just before arriving at the bus station and drove in for the last time. Needless to say, the rookie bus driver is no longer working for Greyhound. Responsibility involves completing a task, or making sure it is correctly completed by someone else.[725]

**Responsibility** One of the more interesting commencement speeches took place a few years ago at Talladega College in Alabama. Bill Cosby, the actor and strong advocate of education, was their graduation speaker in 1992. Although his speech was filled with the humor you might expect from such a man, some of his words were much more pointed. Dr. Cosby told the graduating class, "Get a job!" He went on to say, "Tomorrow is Monday and old people expect you to be out there looking for a job and they expect you to come back Monday evening with a job. Your family has done enough. Get a job." Bill Cosby's words are appropriate for many within the ranks of our churches as well. Others in the church family have done enough. It is now time for the "bench warmers, hitchhikers, and lifetime students" of our churches to carry their load and "get a job!" [726]

**Responsibility** We all know, "Humpty Dumpty sat on the wall. Humpty Dumpty had a great fall." But a modern twist to the traditional verse reflects some irresponsible thinking: "Humpty Dumpty was pushed." [727]

**Resurrection** During the early days of Sam Boyle's ministry in Japan, he hired a translator to assist him in preaching. The only translator Boyle could find was a Japanese man teaching English in a nearby junior high school. The teacher was not a Christian but agreed to translate Boyle's sermons. The relationship worked well through the first few sermons, but hit a snag when the missionary preached on the Resurrection. He proclaimed, "And on the third day Jesus arose from the dead." The translator looked at Boyle and said, "They're never going to believe this." May we never assume the position of this translator, deciding who will and who will not believe the gospel. God's invitation to hear the good news extends to everyone, regardless of how *we* think they will respond. [728]

**Retirement** Do you know anybody who is just living for the day they can retire and take it easy? Recent studies have been conducted by the insurance industry concerning retired military officers and businessmen who were looking forward to retiring and relaxing after thirty years of hard work. The results indicated that "just kicking back in retirement" leads to a funeral in four to seven years. Longevity requires a purposeful retirement with meaningful hobbies, ongoing relationships, and sustained involvement.[729]

**Revenge** Have you ever hungered for a little sweet revenge? In 1992, Lady Sarah Graham Moon, fifty-five, was dumped by her British aristocratic husband. She sought to get even with her unfaithful spouse and did so with a passion. First of all, she poured gallons of paint on his cherished BMW while it was parked in his girlfriend's driveway. A week later, she cut four inches off the left sleeve on thirty-two of her husband's custom-tailored, $1,600 Saville Row suits. The following week she gave away sixty bottles of her husband's finest wine. Her exploits got the attention of the press, and she became somewhat of a celebrity. One lady wrote her to share how she cleaned the toilet with her unfaithful husband's toothbrush, then watched with delight when her husband brushed his teeth. Of course none of these acts compares with the sweet revenge of Vera Czermak. Upon learning that her husband had betrayed her, Mrs. Czermak became suicidal and decided to jump to her death from their third floor apartment in Prague. Surprisingly, she survived the jump. because she landed on her husband and killed him, instead. True story![730]

**Righteousness** The Chinese language creates the word *righteousness* by placing the character for "lamb" above the character for the pronoun "I." Our righteousness is secured when we lift the Lamb of God high above ourselves and ask him to cleanse us with his blood (John 1:29).[731]

**Risks** On April 30, 1992 NBC aired the final episode of *The Cosby Show*. Since its premiere on September 20, 1984, the show was watched by more people than any other situation comedy in the history of television. It also propelled NBC to sixty-nine consecutive weeks at the top of the Nielsen ratings. Without question, this show was the mainstay of NBC for eight years. Looking back at the show's unprecedented success it would appear the initial decision to air Cosby's brainchild was easy. Such was not the case. The show was a risk, because ABC had already rejected it. As missiologist Ralph Winter said, "Risks are not to be evaluated by the probability of success, but by the value of the goal." [732]

**Role Model** In 1993, Willie Nelson was sixty and had some unusual advice for his twenty-three-year-old daughter. The singer said, "Paula, look at everything I do closely, and do exactly the opposite." Around the same age, Paul said, "Follow my example, as I follow the example of Christ" (1 Cor. 11:1). Maybe, in a roundabout way, that's what Willie was saying: follow the example of Christ. [733]

**Romanian Revolution** Pastor Laszlo Tokes became too successful in the eyes of his Romanian government. He preached the gospel boldly and within two years saw his small church grow to 5,000. The authorities confiscated his ration book so he couldn't buy fuel or food. Then in December 1989, they decided to exile him. When the police arrived they were stopped by an unmovable crowd of people. Members of other churches and denominations stood shoulder to shoulder in protest. All day, the police tried to disperse the crowd, but they wouldn't budge. Just after midnight a nineteen-year-old Baptist student named Daniel Garva, pulled out a packet of candles. He lit one and passed it to his neighbor. One by one the burning candles were passed through the crowd. The crowd stayed all through that night and the next. The police finally broke through and knocked in the church door. They bloodied Pastor Tokes' face, then paraded both him and his wife through the crowd. An outcry from the people led them to their city square of Timisoara, where they began a full-scale demonstration against the Communist government. Once again, Daniel Garva passed out his candles. Troops were brought in and ordered to shoot the crowd. Hundreds were shot, and Daniel's leg was blown off. Their brave example inspired the entire population of Romania, and within days the bloody dictator, Ceausescu, was dead. For the first time in half a century, Romania celebrated Christmas in freedom. In a world of hostile darkness, God has called us to light a candle of love. Although the presentation of his Light may not be favorably received, such faithfulness will yield results beyond our grandest dreams.[734]

**Rumors** Abraham Lincoln's coffin was opened in 1887 because a rumor had convinced many people that the pine box was empty. To the surprise of quite a few, Lincoln's body was found just as it had been buried twenty-two years earlier. Some good rumors never die, though. Fourteen years later the same rumor circulated again. The critics would not be silenced, so Lincoln's body was exhumed again. Facts can really mess up a good rumor![735]

**Rumors** Many Christians are still concerned that Madalyn Murray O'Hair is trying to stop religious programming. With a petition in hand, they are ready to take action against RM 2493. In this particular case, it is believed Mrs. O'Hair is "currently" seeking to take religious programming off the air. The fact of the matter is, RM 2493 was rejected in 1975 and has nothing to do with the atheistic O'Hair. In 1974, two broadcast producers in California filed a petition with the FCC asking the agency, among other things, to stop accepting applications by religious institutions for TV and FM channels that had been reserved for educational use. Their petition was routinely assigned a rule-making number, RM 2493. It died in 1975. Zora Kramer of the FCC office in Washington, D.C. said, "Over the years we have received twenty-five million pieces of mail on this issue. That is more mail than we have ever received on any issue." Rumors usually die long, slow deaths, with sporadic resurrections.[736]

**Russian Revival** The National Opinion Research Center at the University of Chicago recently released its finding from the first comprehensive study of spiritual beliefs in the former Soviet Union since the fall of communism. Among the most interesting findings is the large percentage of conversions from atheism. Twenty-two percent of the population at large said they were once atheists but now believe in God. Andrew Greeley, a sociologist at the University of Chicago, wrote a report on the findings and titled it "God Is Alive and Well and Living in Moscow" Greeley said, "It would seem, at least at first glance, to demonstrate that after the most serious attempt to obliterate religion in human history, they are experiencing the most dramatic religious revival in human history." [737]

**Sabbath** Voltaire predicted that within a hundred years of his life (the eighteenth century) Christianity would be nothing more than history. He admitted, though, for this to happen the world would first have to get rid of Sunday. He said, "There is no hope of destroying Christianity so long as the Christian Sabbath is acknowledged and kept as a sacred day." No doubt, Voltaire would be pleased with America's current thoughts about the Sabbath. [738]

**Sacrifice** Figure skater Nancy Kerrigan is most remembered for her run-in with Tonya Harding, but there is another part of her life that deserves far more attention. When Nancy was just a year old, her mother sustained nerve damage in her eyes from a virus and became legally blind. To watch her daughter perform, Brenda must press her nose against the TV screen and realize the blurred image is her daughter. Nonetheless, Brenda Kerrigan has always been her daughter's greatest fan. Each morning for the better part of the decade before she won a silver medal, the family started each day at 4:30 A.M. to practice at the ice rink. It cost the family more than $35,000 each year to train their daughter. That was more than Dan Kerrigan's annual salary. Of the sacrifices they made, Mrs. Kerrigan simply says, "It never made any sense. We just did it." Sacrifice doesn't always make sense, you can't always see the results, and it can often be quite expensive. But sacrifice doesn't secure all the answers; it simply responds in love.[739]

**Sacrificial Love** In March of 1991, Lisa Landry Childress (daughter of Tom Landry) found out she had a malignant tumor on her liver. This was just two months after she and her husband, Gary, had learned she was pregnant. The doctors counseled her to undergo an abortion so she could begin immediate chemotherapy. She rejected the thought of abortion, even though it meant she would most certainly die. She and her husband had for years tried to have a baby. On December 20, 1991, after the baby was born, Mrs. Childress said, "This baby was a blessing; a gift to me. It wasn't my right to deny this gift." She lived three years and nine months after receiving a liver transplant, but the legacy of her love and sacrificial gift of life will live forever.[740]

**Safe Sex** From 1970 to 1991, the federal government spent over two billion dollars to promote condom usage and safe sex. In 1992 alone, $450 million of our tax dollars were spent on this project, with only $8 million ear-marked for abstinence programs. Somehow the message hasn't caught on, because of sexually active teenagers, 57 percent never use contraceptives. They haven't bought in to the lie of safe sex — with good reason. At a recent conference, sexologists were asked to raise their hand if they would trust a condom to protect them during intercourse with a person known to be HIV-positive. Not one in eight hundred raised a hand. If eight hundred advocates of safe sex unanimously agree that it's not always safe, then why call it "safe," and why continue wasting so much money on a lie? Hollywood certainly hasn't helped, either. In the September 25, 1991 episode of *Doogie Howser*, the star said, "A man is a lot of things, but he's not a virgin."[741]

**Saint Patrick** In Chicago a whole river is turned green on St. Patrick's Day, but that hardly represents the significance of the man after whom the day is named. Patrick was a Scottish boy born in A.D. 389. He was the grandson of Christian landowners. Some Irish raiders invaded his homeland and took him as a prisoner. Patrick became an Irish slave for the next six years of his life. He later escaped and fled to a monastery on the southern coast of France. In 432 he was ordained as a missionary bishop and returned to Ireland. He preached throughout the land and was so successful that Ireland became known as the Isle of Saints. Patrick's unique contribution to the cause of Christ was his missionary strategy of sending missionaries from Ireland to other countries. St. Patrick turned converts into converters.[742]

**Saints and Sinners** Some folks would rather run with their sinful buddies than get mixed up with a bunch of saints. That's how Jesse James saw things before April 3, 1882. On that fateful day he wasn't gunned down by a law-abiding saint. James dropped dead from the slug of Robert Ford, a member of his own gang. There is value in associating with saints.[743]

**Salt** Marshall Shelley was reminded afresh of the meaning Jesus placed on being salt. In a conversation with an inner-city pastor, the topic turned to spiritual influence. The pastor told about his newfound understanding of salt. He described a scenario in which he might accidentally leave a steak on the kitchen counter just before leaving on vacation. Upon returning home, he would be welcomed with a horrendous odor. He would stumble to the kitchen, trying to imagine what could cause such a stench. When finding the meat he would not blame the meat for being a rotten slab of beef. He would kick himself for failing to preserve the meat in the refrigerator. Christians make plenty of negative comments and vent frustration over the putrefaction of our society. But our culture is simply doing what comes natural, rotting because it has no preservative. As hard as it is to admit, we should quit leveling the blame of decadence on pagans and start asking why the Church is not more effectively preventing decay from setting in.[744]

**Salvation** Ben Wofford caught a bass worth $21,786 on April 11, 1992 at the Texas Bass Championship Tournament on Lake Conroe. His 7.64 pound fish was the fourth largest fish overall but according to Rule Number 6, Ben's fish didn't qualify. The fish was fine but Ben wasn't. Rule 6 clearly stated that all contestants must wear the official tournament hat they were issued at check-in. Ben opted instead to wear his "lucky" cap and left the tournament headgear in his partner's truck. Because of Ben's small error he was denied any prize money. The Bible is clear, salvation requires identification with Jesus Christ as your Savior and Lord—you must wear his hat. Unfortunately, though, many people feel their "lucky" cap is a better option and they end up forfeiting the greatest prize of all, eternal life.[745]

**Salvation** Billy Graham has ministered to people throughout the world for five decades. He has preached to over 110 million people in eighty-four countries. In addition to these who have heard him in person, he has been heard by countless others through radio and television. Three million people have responded to his invitation to receive Christ or make a recommitment. There is no question that Billy Graham has made a significant impact for Christ. Yet, all of these efforts will not gain him entrance into the presence of Christ. Every person is saved by the grace of God, not good works (Eph. 2:8–9).[746]

**Salvation** During a Texas revival meeting led by Mordecai Ham, a man in the congregation was overcome by the love and mercy of God. He had killed four men and never dreamed God could care for him. This man was so touched by the gospel that he stood up during that revival in 1910 and shouted, "Saved! Saved! Saved!" Jack Scofield, the musician for the revival, was so moved by this joyful outburst that he used those words to write that popular hymn the next afternoon. The inspiration for this widely-sung hymn came from the enthused gratitude of a four-time murderer who found the grace of God.[747]

**Salvation** Maximilian Kolbe was a Catholic priest in Poland whom the Nazis arrested in February 1941 for publishing unapproved materials. By May, he was serving his sentence at Auschwitz. Life expectancy there for a priest was about a month. He soon faced imminent death after the guards beat him and left him for dead. Fellow prisoners nursed him to survival, and he was transferred to Barracks 14. In July, a prisoner escaped from Father Kolbe's barracks, and that meant death for some who remained. Commandant Fritsch made the prisoners of Barracks 14 stand at attention the entire day. Some passed out, but Father Kolbe endured the day. When the rest of the prisoners returned for evening roll call, the Commandant levied the sentence. Ten would die in the starvation bunker for the one who escaped. One of the ten cried out, "My poor wife! My poor children! What will they do?" Father Kolbe then broke rank and pleaded with the Commandant, "I would like to die in place of one of the men you condemned." Never had there been such a request. Nonetheless, he was permitted to die for the man he chose—prisoner 5659, the one who cried for his wife and family. Father Kolbe was then stripped of his clothes and marched with the other nine to their grave. The basement of Barracks 11 was dark and hot. No food or water was provided, because they were there to die. As days passed by, the usual screams were not heard. To the contrary, faint sounds of singing arose from the basement. By August 14, all but four prisoners were dead. The living skeleton of Father Kolbe was one still alive. He was propped against the wall with a ghost of a smile on his lips. His eyes were wide open as though fixed on a faraway vision. He, like the other three, was given a lethal injection, and death relieved his pain. Father Kolbe died with the victory he had prayed for earlier: "Christ's cross has triumphed over its enemies in every age. I believe, in the end, even in these darkest days in Poland, the cross will triumph over the swastika. I pray I can be faithful to that end." The triumph of the cross guarantees life for those destined to die.[748]

**Salvation** The Barna Research Group has noted, "Our surveys consistently show that more than two-thirds of all adults who have accepted Christ as their Savior made their decision to do so before the age of eighteen."[749]

**Sandwich Generation** Golda Meir said, "It's no crisis to be seventy, but it's no joke, either." To the generation that is sandwiched between the needs of their parents and the concerns of their children, life is no joke. "It is estimated that parents spend approximately seventeen years caring for their children and eighteen years caring for their own parents," says Ruth Bathauer in Parent Care. Strength for such a journey can only be found in Jesus Christ. (See Philippians 4:13.) Consequently, the church must give ample attention to this very pressing need that is sandwiching middle-aged Americans.[750]

**Satan** A missionary returned to his home in Africa, only to find a huge python inside. He ran back to his truck and got his .45-caliber pistol. He went to his home and carefully entered through the door. The man aimed with precision and fired a single shot into the snake's head. It was a mortal blow to the reptile, but it didn't die instantly. The missionary retreated from his house as the snake thrashed violently. The tremendous power of the snake's movement broke and damaged many items within the home. After the house finally became silent, he slowly entered the house to find the snake dead. The interior of the home was a disaster as the snake had unleashed all its fury in those moments of death. But now, there was peace. Satan received a fatal shot to his head when Christ conquered sin and death. Now as he writhes in the pain of his defeat, he is unleashing a few remaining destructive blows. He still seems dangerous, but his fate is sealed.[751]

**Satan** There is a humorous and poignant story from the early days of football in Dallas. The Dallas Texans were the first attempt at professional football in the Lone Star State. Their brief history lasted just one year, 1952, going 1–11. Their training camp was in Kerrville, Texas. Their equipment manager, Willie Garcia, had one wooden leg. The first time a football bounced off the playing field into the tall grass, no one wanted to go after it because of snakes. Garcia volunteered to retrieve the ball, quipping, "I've got a fifty-fifty chance the snake will go for the wrong leg." Many Christians underestimate the power of Satan and dash through the tall grass of life, thinking he will "go for the wrong leg." [752]

**Savior** In the Kremlin of Moscow is the preserved body of Vladimir Lenin. He has been dubiously named the father of Communism. Lenin died in 1924, but each day a long line of visitors still parade by to see his remains. His contribution to humanity was hardly benevolent, yet the inscription next to his body reads: "He was the greatest leader of all people of all time. He was the lord of the new humanity. He was the savior of the world." Fortunately, the nation that was crafted by Lenin is now recognizing the true Lord and Savior whose crypt is empty.[753]

**Schedules** Have you ever let your schedule lead you to make irrational decisions? It happened some years ago with the transportation system in Great Britain. Complaints were mounting over empty buses that were driving past bus stops full of people. After a thorough investigation the irrational logic was discovered. The bus drivers said they needed to pass up the crowded bus stops so they could stay on schedule. Schedules are a necessary part of life, but they must never override our primary objectives.[754]

**School Prayer** To those who fear that God no longer has access to schools, a recent T-shirt sums up the situation nicely; "As long as there are exams, there will be prayer in school." [755]

**Scrooge** Just for the record, from 1659–1681, the Puritans made it illegal to observe Christmas.[756]

**Second Coming** January 3, 1993 will certainly be remembered in both Houston and Buffalo. Houston Oilers' and Buffalo Bills' fans watched with NFL viewers from across the country, as the Bills engineered the greatest comeback in NFL history. The Oilers led the football game at half-time 28–3. Quarterback Warren Moon had just completed the best half of his career. The half-time show featured talk of whom Houston would play next week as their last stop before the Super Bowl. Boomer Esiason warned his presumptuous co-commentators that Frank Reich was just the man to perform a miraculous comeback. Even Warren Moon used half-time to warn his jubilant teammates that the game was far from over. But when Bubba McDowell opened the second-half with a 58-yard touch-down interception that boosted the Oilers to a 35–3 lead, a comeback seemed virtually impossible. Everything changed in just twenty-one minutes. The fans at Rich Stadium in Orchard Park, New York saw the most unbelievable event unfold before their eyes. The Bills overcame a 32-point deficit in the second half and won the ball game on an overtime field goal. Football fans everywhere will never forget that game. In a world full of sin, suffering, and injustice, it seems as if God has been convincingly outscored by Satan. Victory appears to be nothing more than a wistful dream. When such thoughts invade your mind, turn your attention to that football game. If such unlikely turnarounds can transpire in the world of sports, then you can rest assured that God is gearing up for the most incredible comeback of all times.[757]

**Second Coming** On November 2, 1992, the "Mission for the Coming Days" church disbanded after a very tough weekend. Lee Jang-rim, the Korean church's founder, was in jail and the embarrassed congregation returned to their respective homes and places of employment. The central message of this church had been Christ's imminent return on October 28, 1992. It was the largest of the South Korean churches that were predicting the impending end of the world. Hundreds, and possibly thousands of these believers sold property, left their families, quit schools and jobs, and deserted military duties. Of course, they should have checked the pastor's financial portfolio before banking on the October rapture date. Pastor Jang-rim had swindled four million dollars in donations and had $380,000 invested in bonds that wouldn't mature until the following May. I guess this explains why the good Reverend never preached from Jesus' words in Matthew 24:36.[758]

**Second Coming** Stephen Hawking, the British physicist whose book *A Brief History of Time* sold over three million copies, recently confessed that the end of the world will be later than he first thought. He now calculates the end won't happen for "at least ten billion years." More importantly than trying to guess what Jesus said "is not for you to know" (Acts 1:7), we should focus on the fact that our own end is imminent (2 Tim. 4:6).[759]

**Security of Believers** When the Golden Gate Bridge of San Francisco was being built, workers developed a great fear of falling. Bridge builders have a superstition that one man will die for every million dollars spent on the project. This bridge was budgeted for $35 million, so the fear was pervasive. The chief engineer, Joseph Strauss, also believed that three dozen men could fall to their deaths. The impact of falling from the bridge to the water below is equivalent to hitting a brick wall at eighty miles per hour. Strauss made an unprecedented move and ordered a large trapeze net to be placed under the workers. Bridge builders had never enjoyed such a luxury, so the added security made them feel as though they could, as one worker said, "dance on the steel." Christians can be immobilized from effectiveness by the fear of losing their salvation. God has promised the security net of his hand to prevent believers from fearing an eternal fall. Such luxurious security should cause Christians to "dance." (See John 10:28–30.)[760]

**Selective Listening** Selective listening is generally thought of with negative connotations. Marilyn vos Savant is listed in *The Guinness Book of World Records* Hall of Fame for "Highest IQ." In a recent article from her weekly column, she said, "Most of the stuff we hear is just audible junk mail." As Christians we need to be selective listeners and not allow our minds to be filled with "audible junk mail." [761]

**Self Image** It is unfortunate that most of us see ourselves as a composite of all our failures. When we look in the mirror we may only see a divorced person, or someone who lost his job, or an overweight loner. Even though many of us can't see beyond the failures, this is not the way God views us. As a loving Father, he looks past our failures. Can you imagine a loving father introducing his children by saying, "This is my daughter, Meagan, who stained the carpet with grape juice when she was two"? Or, "This is my son, Myles, who broke a valuable vase last week." If loving fathers don't have a need to memorize their children's failures, you can rest assured our loving Heavenly Father has no use for such memories either. When we accept God's forgiveness through Jesus Christ, he forgets our failures. [762]

**Self-Sufficiency** The Barna Research Group asked Americans about the importance of religion. The results say something significant about self-sufficiency. Here is how many people of various income brackets answered "yes" to the question, "Is religion very important in your life?":

- Less than $20,000 annual income: 71 percent
- $20,000 to $29,999: 69 percent
- $30,000 to $39,999: 62 percent
- $40,000 to $59,999: 61 percent
- $60,000 or more: 45 percent

It seems as though Americans think money diminishes one's need for God. [763]

**Selfishness** Robert Logan has pegged our society correctly by suggesting that most people are tuned in to channel WII FM—

"What's In It For Me?" Many of us need to hit the scan button and search for channel WCBG FM—"What Can Be Given From Me?" Switch to that station and you will gain a greater listening audience.[764]

**Senior Adults** The Olympic Games seem reserved for youth. And even then, "youth" is defined as "under 25." When youthful Melvin Stewart, 23, won the Gold Medal in the men's 200-meter butterfly he shared some keen insight on age. In 1988, Stewart finished a disappointing fifth at the games in Seoul. His family was there with a gentleman named George Baxter. Mr. B, as Stewart calls him, paid for his boarding school when he flunked out of school. "He gave me a chance to turn things around. I owe my education to him. He was, and is, my mentor." Stewart continued, "That day in Seoul, Mr. B took me aside and said, 'This is a blessing in disguise. Use this to fuel the fire toward the next Olympics.'" After emerging victorious in Barcelona, Melvin Stewart threw his victory flowers to Mr. B and "I told him, 'I love you.' I'm going to give him my gold medal, too. Mr. B is seventy-six years old and I don't do many things without talking with him first . . . He's incredible. And he's been married to the same woman for fifty-three years. It's too bad, but older people are a great resource that too many young people don't rely on today." Melvin Stewart appears to be a gold medalist outside of the pool as well. "You shall rise up before the gray-headed, and honor the aged" (Lev. 19:32).[765]

**Senior Advice** Mulligans are the mainstay for many amateur golfers. When a golfer makes a bad shot and wants to redo it without adding an additional shot to his score he simply calls it a mulligan and shoots again. Most of us would like a few mulligans in life. Tony Campolo noted this after reading a sociological study of fifty people over the age of ninety-five. Each of these seniors were asked one question: "If you could live your life over again, what would you do differently?" It was an open-ended question, so these

228 † SOMETHING TO THINK ABOUT

elderly people could provide any answer. Many different responses were tabulated, and from all of those there were three answers that consistently emerged. These three dominant thoughts were: "If I had to do it over again, I would . . . (1) reflect more, (2) risk more, (3) do more things that would live on after I am dead." Such counsel should be seriously heeded because it comes from people who have gone before us and have experientially observed the wisdom that we would all do well to observe. One sage said, "Our lives would run a lot smoother if second thoughts came first." These seniors have helped us to see some second thoughts first! [766]

**Senseless Kindness** We are repulsed by the all-too-familiar phrase, "random acts of senseless violence." It occurs daily in the newspapers and on TV. Chuck Wall, Professor of Human Relations at Bakersfield College in California, was repulsed enough to do something about it. He assigned his students to "do something out of the ordinary to help someone who isn't expecting it, then write about it." The essays included stories about a student who bought thirty blankets for the homeless, and a woman who reparked her car one-half mile from her destination so a frantic-looking motorist could park in her spot near the door. Bumper stickers were made and sold by the students to benefit the Kern County Braille Center. They read, "Today, I will commit one random act of senseless kindness . . . will you?" Professor Wall stumbled upon a new twist on an old message: "Let us consider how to stimulate one another to love and good deeds" (Heb. 10:24). [767]

**Serial Eater** Gangaram Mahes is no ordinary criminal. Although he's been arrested nearly three dozen times, you probably wouldn't be frightened by his presence. Unless of course you own a restaurant. He's known in New York as the "Serial Eater." This emigrant from Guyana likes elegant dining but doesn't have the budget to support his taste. So rather than deny his culinary desires, he simply treats himself to some of the finer restaurants. Mahes orders fine cuisine and top-shelf liquor. He then savors the meal until the check arrives. At that point he informs the waiter of his inability to pay the bill. The police then arrest him and Mahes ends up with at least a few days of regular meals in jail. His alibi is simple: "I like to live decent." Mr. Mahes' "decent" lifestyle has cost New York taxpayers more than $250,000. Although this type of activity seems rather unorthodox, it is most prevalent in every church. Plenty of people savor the menu of ministries and activities the church offers but leave the tab for someone else to pay.[768]

**Serial Polygamy** An African husband of several wives was approached by an American missionary and confronted about the scriptural mandate for monogamy. The African noted there was little difference between his marital status and that of Americans. He said, "In America you just marry one wife at a time. Here, we just keep our old wives while marrying new ones." Some have called our American trend, "Serial Polygamy." We're still polygamist; we just don't keep all of our wives at the same time. Mignon McLaughlin has some insight that may help all couples: "A successful marriage requires falling in love many times, always with the same person."[769]

**Servanthood** A rabbi dreamed he had been given the opportunity to see both heaven and hell. He was directed to a closed door and informed that hell existed beyond the doorway. As he entered he was surprised to see a banquet hall set for a feast. Everything was exquisitely prepared, but all of the diners moaned and wailed in agony. In the center of the table was a mouthwatering dish of food, and each person had a very long spoon set beside them. The spoon was long enough for one to dish out the food, but too long to reach one's mouth. Consequently, they were unable to eat and were shrieking with pains of hunger. The horror was more than the rabbi could bear, so he asked to leave. When he opened the door to heaven he was petrified to see the same scene. Everything was the same, except laughter replaced the pitiful cries. The difference in the two places was that those in heaven did not cry over their inability to feed themselves. They simply celebrated the privilege of feeding each other with the same long spoons. The law of the harvest promises joy to those who joyfully serve others.[770]

**Servanthood** Dr. Viktor Frankl was an Austrian physician who was imprisoned in one of Hitler's death camps. He and his fellow Jewish people suffered unbelievable atrocities. Everything about their living and working conditions were deplorable, including their medical care. Dr. Frankl offered what little medical help he could to the sick and dying. Over time, he discovered a unique phenomenon he recorded in his book *Man's Search for Meaning.* He said those people who kept their strength and sanity the longest were those who tried to help other prisoners and share what little they had. Their physical and mental condition seemed strengthened by their friendliness, compassion, and focus on something other than themselves. Dr. Frankl concluded that if someone responds to life by trying to make life better for others, that effort reinforces the individual's psychological and physical stamina. Ministry energizes, contrary to the great fear that resources will be depleted if we help others. No wonder Jesus, though initially very hungry, could say after his ministry to the woman at the well, "I have food to eat that you know nothing about" (John 4:32).[771]

**Servanthood** Mother Teresa was an icon of servanthood. On one occasion she was brought face to face with a man who had a rare and horrendous case of terminal cancer. One of the workers had vomited from the stench and could no longer continue. Mother Teresa then stepped in and kindly took over. The patient was mystified. "How can you stand the smell?" asked the patient. Mother Teresa replied, "It's nothing compared to the pain you must feel." Servanthood begins when we move beyond our own comfort to relief the discomfort of another.[772]

**Servanthood** "Servanthood is not difficult to define; it is only difficult to achieve." —*John Maxwell*[773]

**Servanthood** "The measure of a man is not how many servants he has, but how many men he serves." —*D. L. Moody*[774]

**Service** "Let no one come to you without feeling better and happier when they leave." —*Mother Teresa*[775]

**Service** "To harm one is way too many; to assist a thousand is way too few." —*Joe Hall*[776]

**Service** "Unless our belief in God causes us to help our fellow man, our faith stands condemned." —*Billy Graham*[777]

**Sex Education** According to Jim Dethmer, the problem with sex education being taught in schools is not that the children are told too much. "The problem is they are being told too little. Sex is reduced to just a physical act." Children are being taught the biological aspects of sex without the corresponding spiritual and emotional ramifications. No wonder sex is taken so lightly in our culture. To most students it's is nothing more than a physical transaction.[778]

**Sexual Promiscuity** Police reports show that the suicide rate of prostitutes is forty-five times greater than that of non-prostitutes. "Sexual freedom" doesn't exist outside of marriage![779]

**Shadow of Death** Dr. Donald Grey Barnhouse was one of America's great preachers. He lost his first wife to cancer when she was in her thirties. This left him with three children under the age of twelve. He chose to preach the funeral for his wife but wondered what he would say. His thoughts came together on the way to her funeral. A large truck passed them on the road and cast a shadow over their car. He turned to his oldest daughter and asked, "Tell me, sweetheart, would you rather be run over by that truck or its shadow?" The broken little girl looked curiously at her father and said, "By the shadow, I guess. It can't hurt you." The wise minister quietly told his three children, "Your mother has not been overrun by death, but by the shadow of death. That is nothing to fear." Although death usually feels like a truck running over your heart, in reality, the death of a believer can bring nothing more than a painful shadow. "Even though I walk through the valley of the shadow of death, I will fear no evil, for You are with me" (Psalm 23:4).[780]

**Sick Leave** We've all heard of calling in sick, but have you ever called in well? One manager boosts morale among his workers by allowing them to "call in well" one day a year. If an employee is just feeling too good to waste a day at work, he can call in well and head out to the golf course. It's nice to see a manager who recognizes there is much more to life than just work.[781]

**Sin** An athlete was pulled into an unusual experiment through a bet. A veteran on the subject bet this strong man that he could not endure one pint of water being dropped on his hand, one drop at a time, from a height of three feet. The big guy thought such a bet was a sure win so he accepted the challenge. A pint of water can produce 11,520 single drops. After 300 drops the athlete's hand was hurting, but he kept going because "no pain, no gain." By drop number 420 the battle was over. He quit. His hand was red and badly swollen. Sin is like that. One sin at a time may not seem like much, but the cumulative effect is painful and destructive.[782]

**Sin** Exxon was fined one billion dollars for their role in our nation's worst oil spill. When the *Exxon Valdez* dumped all of that oil in Prince William Sound, Alaska, the world watched in horror. What few of us realize, though, is how small that mess was when compared to the environmental disaster we recreate each year in the United States. American "do-it-yourselfers" (DIYs) annually dump 193 million gallons of motor oil in storm drains, trash receptacles, and back-lot alleys. That amount is nearly twenty times the amount spilled in Alaska on March 24, 1989. Don't we look at sin that way? When someone pulls a "Valdez" sin, we shriek in righteous disbelief but forget to see the sum total of all our "little" sins. Whether we commit an atrocity or only drive "a bit too fast," it always adds up to Romans 3:23.[783]

**Sin** Sin takes us farther than we want to go, costs more than we want to pay, and keeps us longer than we want to stay.[784]

**Sin** Jeffrey Dahmer's atrocities as one of this nation's worst serial killers will be woefully remembered for years to come. Although he was viciously murdered in prison, his death pales in comparison to the horror he inflicted on the seventeen people he admitted to killing over a thirteen-year period. Dr. David Abrahamsen, a psychiatrist who has advised courts on the psychology of killers like David (Son of Sam) Berkowitz, testified concerning Dahmer by saying, "He knew what he was doing, and he knew it was wrong." So if he knew he was wrong, why did he continue? "Once you've committed murder number one, murder number two is just a little bit easier and three and four and five and so on down the line," says Robert de Vito, chairman of psychiatry at Chicago's Loyola University and an expert on serial killers. Jeffrey Dahmer demonstrated the graphic reality of sin's snowballing effect. We may realize we are violating God's commands but each violation makes the next one that much easier for us to rationalize away.[785]

**Sin** When a man says he has a clear conscience, it often means he has a bad memory.[786]

**Sin** While working as a court-appointed attorney, Emory Potter was assigned a client who had been accused of criminal trespass. Mr. Potter probed his client with some general background questions. He asked if had any previous arrests or convictions. The man ashamedly said, "Yes, sir. "I've got quite a few." The thorough attorney then asked, "Any felonies?" The man indignantly replied, "No sir! I specialize in misdemeanors!" Some of us quickly

acknowledge the truth of Romans 3:23 but become quite indignant if anyone suggest we are "sinners." We agree we have sinned,
but our specialty is "misdemeanor" sin.[787]

**Sin's Passing Pleasure** In April 1988, a skydiver attempted to
film a number of fellow jumpers as they all leaped from the plane
and began their free-fall. The jump started well as the photographer secured some very exciting footage. The camera captured
each skydiver as he raced through the air, and then opened his
chute. The last segment of the film is one of total chaos as the cameraman makes a horrifying discovery. In his enthusiasm to film the
dive, the photographer forgot to put on his parachute. It wasn't
until he reached for the ripcord that he realized his error. His jump
was an eventful and exhilarating trip for a few fleeting moments.
The pursuits of sin can be temporarily thrilling, but the end result
is death. Hebrews 11:25 reminds us that sin produces a moment
of gratification and an eternity of remorse.[788]

**Sin's Price** The Israelites refused to follow God's plan for taking
the Promised Land. The consequence of such disobedience led to
forty years of purposeless wandering in the wilderness. The tragedy
of this sin may be seen when calculating the frequency of funerals
conducted by God's chosen but disobedient people. There was one
funeral every twenty minutes, twenty-four hours a day, for forty
years! Disobedience is costly![789]

**Sincerety** In ancient Rome, sculpting was a popular profession.
The culture flourished with statues, as nearly every public and
private building had numerous gods represented. The market was
flooded with sculptors, so quality was sometimes lacking. Less
qualified craftsmen would cover their errors with wax, and frequently the customer could not see the flaw. To compensate for
this practice, authentic sculptors would mark their statues with the
words *sine cera*—"without wax." Today we frequently use the same
term to close letters: "sincerely." As Christians we are called to live

authentic lives. Many churches have become showcases for saints rather than hospitals for sinners. It is time we started giving God and others a life that is *sine cera.*[790]

**Sinful Nature** In Victor Hugo's *Ninety-Three*, his novel about the French Revolutionary War, a ship is caught in a terrible storm. The crew's plight is further compounded by the realization that a cannon is loose below deck. Every wave turns the unchained cannon into an internal battering ram. Two brave sailors risk their lives to go below and secure the loose cannon. On their descent into the ship, they discuss the fact that the cannon within is more dangerous than the storm without. Although there is much to fear in life, our greatest danger is the sinful nature within us.[791]

**Single Parents** Currently, one out of every four children in the United States lives in a single parent home. This represents nearly a three-fold increase over the last twenty years. This phenomenon is not a respecter of race or socio-economic status. Among Anglo children, 1 out of every 5 live in a single parent home, among Hispanics the ratio is 1 in 3, and the African-American ratio is 1 in 2. The fastest growing segment of increase is among the Anglo population. Additionally, 60 percent of the children born today will live at least part of their first eighteen years in a single-parent environment. The Church must reach out with healing arms to embrace those who are hurting because of broken homes.[792]

**Single Parents** There are ten million single parents in America today. That means 29 percent of all American parents are single.[793]

**Smiling** Holiday Inn interviewed five thousand people to fill five hundred positions for the opening of a new Inn. When the hotel managers interviewed these candidates, they excluded anybody who smiled fewer than four times during their interview. This standard applied to every available job and to every prospective employee. How many of us would qualify for a job at Holiday Inn?[794]

**Smoking God's Word** Gaylord Kambarami, the General Secretary of the Bible Society in Zimbabwe, tried to give a New Testament to a very belligerent man. The man insisted he would roll the pages and use them to make cigarettes. Mr. Kambarami said, "I understand that, but at least promise to read the page of the New Testament before you smoke it." The man agreed, and the two went their separate ways. Fifteen years later, the two men met at a Methodist convention in Zimbabwe. The scripture-smoking pagan had found Christ and was now a full-time evangelist. He told the audience, "I smoked Matthew and I smoked Mark and I smoked Luke. But when I got to John 3:16, I couldn't smoke anymore. My life was changed from that moment." Aren't you glad God's book is more than just words on paper?[795]

**Smoking Sermons** Years ago when Exxon was Esso, they had an annual meeting in which all of their scientists would come together in New Jersey. Because there were so many attending, each scientist was given only five minutes to make a presentation. If anyone went over the allotted five minutes, smoke began emitting from the lectern and cartoons started showing on the screen behind the platform. Needless to say, most presenters finished on time. No doubt some deacons have already considered this idea.[796]

**Someone Else** The following is a eulogy for Someone Else: "Our church is deeply saddened by the passing of an irreplaceable member, Someone Else. For all of these years he did far more than any other church member. Whenever leadership was mentioned, Someone Else was looked to for inspiration and achievement. Whenever there was a job to do, a class to teach, or a meeting to attend, everybody always turned to Someone Else. It was common knowledge that Someone Else was among the largest contributors to the church. Whenever there was a financial need, everyone just assumed that Someone Else would make up the difference. Although we are grieved by the loss of Someone Else, his death comes as no big surprise. He was far too overworked and continually stretched too thinly. In fact, we may have contributed to his death by expecting too much out of Someone Else. He left a wonderful example to follow, but it appears there is nobody willing to fill the shoes of Someone Else. I shudder to think what will now happen to our church since we can no longer depend on Someone Else." [797]

**Spare Time** Do you ever get frustrated about not having enough time? The Chinese must have been very frustrated. At one point in their history they had fifteen-day weeks. True time management starts with "seeking God first" (Matt. 6:33).[798]

**Special Offering** Nobie McGill was an eighty-eight-year-old retiree from the Texas Woman's Missionary Union. During the Great Depression she set a personal goal of giving $1 to the Southern Baptists' Lottie Moon Christmas Offering. One hundred pennies doesn't sound like much, but it took all year for this mother of two to save a dollar. She remembers that offering as "the happiest money I ever gave to anything." In 1983 Mrs. McGill was inspired by a message from Minette Drumwright and asked God to permit her the opportunity of giving $1,000 above her tithes and offerings. That year she reached her goal and gave $1,000 to foreign missions. The next year she gave $2,000, then $3,000, then $4,000 and finally, (in her eighties) she was able to give $5,000 above her tithe to Lottie Moon. Upon reflection, Mrs. McGill simply said, "I can't do many things, but I can get money together, and the Lord has really blessed me. I could have lived better, but I got joy out of giving." In reality, we do live "better" when we find joy in giving, because "God loves a cheerful giver" (2 Cor. 9:7).[799]

**Spiritual Armor** At Scott Air Force base in Bellville, Illinois, there hangs this sign: "An Untrained Soldier Is Just a Target." Paul notes the same thought in Ephesians 6:10–18. Peter affirms this truth in 1 Peter 5:8. The adversary is looking for easy targets, and we become one every time we walk without our spiritual armor.[800]

**Spiritual Awakening** In 1985, a missions organization assigned a family to work in a predominantly Moslem city. After decades of work, this denomination had only produced five small churches in that unresponsive environment. Many thought their talents would be better used in another, more open, area. They were convinced of their call and committed themselves to the work. They didn't know how to reach the city, but they knew God did. So they joined fourteen other believers in praying for the city. During an all-night prayer meeting, they sensed God was telling them he "didn't have any clean vessels to use." They fell on the dirt floor and began confessing their sins. As they did, God revealed everything in their lives that was hindering his work. Revival broke out among this small group and quickly spread. They proclaimed the gospel with boldness. Over the next $3\frac{1}{2}$ years 132,000 people made professions of faith. When the family returned home for furlough in 1989, 156 churches had been started by new believers in that area which initially seemed so indifferent to the gospel. Spiritual awakening awaits those who seek God with *all* their hearts.[801]

**Spiritual Blindness** On November 9, 1991, thirty-four-year-old Lolita Arellano beheaded her three children and offered their heads to pacify the Mount Pinatubo volcano. The Philippine volcano began erupting the following summer and had numerous subsequent tremors. The spiritual blindness and superstitious fears of many people cause countless such tragedies.[802]

**Spiritual Decline** According to Gallup Poll research for 1993, the key indicators of religious beliefs and practices in America are at their lowest level since the collection of such data began five decades ago.[803]

**Spiritual Development** A plant nursery displayed this sign: "The best time to plant a tree was ten years ago. The next best time is today." Ten years of consistent devotion to spiritual disciplines would be ideal. If you haven't done that over the past decade, then next best is a commitment to start your spiritual development today.[804]

**Spiritual Food** "Do Not Feed the Bears." This sign is posted in Yellowstone National Park. Most tourists probably assume it's there to protect humans, thinking, "If you're close enough to feed a bear you could be in a position of real danger." Not true! The sign is posted to protect the bears. Each fall, when the feeding tourists have long since departed, the park service must carry off the remains of dead bears who became so dependent on tourists that they were no longer able to gather food for themselves. We can become like the Yellowstone bears if we depend on others to spiritually feed us. Each day we must take the initiative to gather spiritual nutrients for ourselves from God and his Word.[805]

**Spiritual Gifts** Do you know anyone who has struggled to find their spiritual gift on one of those "gifts tests"? They should be encouraged to know that God's personnel department has a wide variety of available jobs. Jesus told us to be the salt of the earth. If we take his analogy seriously, we should note there are fourteen thousand industrial uses for salt. That's a lot of possibilities![806]

**Spiritual Gifts** In 1 Corinthians 12:22, Paul noted that the gifts we often see as unimportant are truly most necessary. When President Reagan was shot in 1981, the nation's government continued to function as though the attempted assassination had never taken place. During that same year the garbage men of Philadelphia went on strike for three weeks and brought the city to its knees. Although most would say the Presidency is far more important than domestic sanitation, it was the trashmen who proved to be indispensable. Likewise, in the church there are those who appear to have "unnecessary" gifts, but the absence of their service might hurt more than you would expect.[807]

**Spiritual Gifts** Sometimes great workers are overlooked in certain areas of the church because they don't "look the part." Such "pigeonholing" can be a big mistake. History shows that some very famous inventors went out of their field to make a major contribution to society. John Dunlop invented the pneumatic tire, but he was a veterinarian. A cork salesman named King Gillette invented the safety razor for shaving. The founder of Kodak, George Eastman, was a bookkeeper. First Corinthians 12 uses the word "variety" three times in the context of spiritual gifts. We would do well to "experiment" more with this variety. God might use us to "invent" something that brings him great pleasure.[808]

**Spiritual Gifts** In 1934, Ward Kimball was a young artist working with an upstart named Walt Disney. They were working on a major project called *Snow White*. Kimball worked on a four and one-half minute sequence for 240 days. All day and many nights he labored to create this brief section where the dwarfs showed affection for Snow White by making her some soup. Once Kimball had completed his work, Disney called him into his office and said, "I don't know how to tell you this, because I love the sequence, but we're going to have to cut it out. It's getting in the way of the story." Ouch! As we exercise our gifts in God's kingdom, the goal is to use our gifts in such a way that they complement the picture God is making and never get in the way.[809]

**Spiritual Gratitude** James Calvert (1813–1892) was a zealous missionary to cannibals on the Fiji Islands. His faithful work bore fruit in the lives of those accustomed to taking the life of others. Years later, an English earl visited the Fiji Islands and was critical of a chief's conversion to Christianity: "You're a great leader, but it's a pity you've been taken in by those foreign missionaries. No one believes the Bible anymore. People are tired of the threadbare story of Christ dying on a cross for the sins of mankind. They know better now. I'm sorry you've been so foolish as to accept their story." The old chief responded with a gleam in his eyes, "See that great rock over there? On it we smashed the heads of our victims. Notice the furnace next to it. In that oven we formerly roasted the bodies of our enemies. If it hadn't been for those good missionaries and the love of Jesus that changed us from cannibals into Christians, you'd never leave this place! You'd better thank the Lord for the Gospel; otherwise, we'd already be feasting on you. If it weren't for the Bible and its salvation message, you'd now be our supper!" Those who take lightly the benefits of Christianity should reconsider the privileges they enjoy because of the transformation Christ has made in his believers.[810]

**Spiritual Growth** Executives from two hundred of the nation's largest companies were asked, "Of the successful people you have met over the years, which of the following is the main reason for their success: (a) contacts, (b) determination, (c) hard work, (d) knowledge, or (e) luck?" In response, 40 percent of these high-powered executives indicated success was due to hard work and 38 percent said determination. Seventy-eight percent of these who have succeeded in their professions said people achieve success through hard work and determination. We all have a tendency to look for the "magic bullet" that will give us immediate results. To such thinking we should expose our minds to the information above. Success usually requires a great deal of hard work and determination—not to mention, plenty of prayer.[811]

**Spiritual Growth** In the world of academics there is a specialty known as "cramming." It is the practice of procrastinating on studies until the last possible moment. When that day of reckoning arrives, the coffee pot is stoked and we strap ourselves to the desk for an all-night journey with our books. Cramming is a phenomenon unknown to the agricultural world. Farmers don't cram. They can't delay planting crops in the spring, then hit the ground really hard in the fall. If a harvest is expected in the fall, then scheduled procedures must take place throughout the year. Maybe that is why Jesus used so many agricultural illustrations. Spiritual growth doesn't come like grades that are salvaged by intensive periods of last-minute cramming. Christ-likeness comes from a lifetime spent with the Savior, not a night of cramming for sainthood.[812]

**Spiritual Growth** Lee Iacocca was, at one time, an American folk hero. He engineered Chrysler's return from oblivion in the early 1980s, but then Chrysler and Iacocca suffered some major set-backs. Eugene Jennings, a Michigan State University business professor, has extensively studied the man behind Chrysler's comeback. In the briefest summary of what he has researched, this statement may very well be the best analysis of what has happened: "He [Iacocca] is at his best when he's climbing the mountain. He gets careless when he's on top." Churches and Christians are at their best when they are "taking the mountain" for God. When we get too comfortable with our previous successes and stop climbing, we become careless. It happened to David with Bathsheba (2 Sam. 11:1), and it can happen to us as well.[813]

**Spiritual Hunger** According to the research of John Naisbitt and Patricia Aburdene, the fields of America are white for harvest. In *Megatrends 2000* these authors have cited several key indicators of spiritual hunger in America. Two such facts point to this truth:

- Between 1987 and 1989, four hundred new religious groups were formed.
- American corporations spend an estimated $4 billion per year on New Age consultants.

Unchurched America may not be knocking down the doors of our churches, but they sure are hungry for spiritual direction. Through prayerful creativity we can reach these soul-searching millions.[814]

**Spiritual Immunity** Halford Luccock noted the significant correlation between physical and spiritual immunity. In medicine, a person can develop an immunity against a disease by receiving a very mild dose of that disease. The same thing can be experienced with the soul. If a person receives nothing more than a small dose of God, he may develop an immunity against the life-changing relationship Jesus can provide. Leslie Weatherhead affirmed this when he said, "The trouble with some of us is that we have been inoculated with small doses of Christianity, which keep us from catching the real thing." One solution to this problem is greater vitality among believers. When someone sees the abundant life being experienced, they won't want to settle for anything less.[815]

**Spiritual Maturity** Pollster George Gallup is concerned about the maturity of American Christians. Although some 53 percent of the general public says religion is "very important," he found only 13 percent live the faith they profess. Gallup said, "There is not a spiritual vacuum in our country, but spiritual chaos." According to his research, "Americans need instruction badly in Bible study, prayer techniques, and how to share the gospel. People are trying to be Christian without the Bible." Gallup is a Christian who thinks Americans need more spiritual maturity because they have become consumer-oriented and are practicing what he calls "*a la carte* religion." He noted, "People want the fruits of faith but not the obligations." Spiritually speaking, we need to grow up![816]

**Spiritual Needs** In December 1990, George Gallup delivered a talk at Princeton Theological Seminary in which he shared six basic spiritual needs of Americans as revealed through surveys and research:

1. The need to believe that life is meaningful and has a purpose. (Two-thirds of those interviewed did not believe that churches were effectively meeting this need.)
2. The need for a sense of community and deeper relationships.
3. The need to be appreciated and respected.
4. The need to be listened to and heard.
5. The need to feel that one is growing in faith.
6. The need for practical help in developing a mature faith.[817]

**Spiritual Rejection** Archaeologists are excited about a recent discovery in Israel. After Israel fought Syria in 1967, a Benedictine monk and an archaeologist by the name of Bargil Pixner set out to find the lost city of Bethsaida. Amid the spent shells and abandoned rifles, Pixner found pieces of pottery that dated back to the time of Christ. The area was not actively pursued by archaeologists for another twenty years. Now they have uncovered the remains of three houses and numerous Jewish artifacts. Pixner noted, "We find a village that is practically the same as at the time of Jesus." Bethsaida was a central hub for Jesus' ministry but it was gradually abandoned by its residents in the latter half of the first century. An earthquake in A.D. 115 dealt this place its final blow. In Matthew 11:21, Jesus identified Bethsaida as a city of woe because they witnessed many of his miracles but did not repent. Whenever Christ is rejected death is sure to follow. What took place in Bethsaida will take place in any heart that rejects the Lord.[818]

**Spiritual Significance** After Hurricane Andrew ripped through Florida in 1992, Shawna Drew made an insightful observation. This Floridian beautician lived an hour north of the disaster. Life for her remained normal except for the unusually heavy traffic. Since her regular commute of fifteen minutes took ninety minutes, she had a lot of time to think. From her mobile think tank came these words: "At first, after the hurricane it was like, 'I'm alive, I'm alive. Heaven be praised.' Now it's like, I'm alive, and I have a home. But I'm stressed, and I'm sad and it seems real trivial to paint ladies' fingernails for a living." Such natural calamities should inspire soul-searching in us all. It should also remind us of another storm raging on the terrain of mankind. Satan's power far exceeds the swirling winds of any hurricane, and he exercises his destructive resources continually. Imagine the changes that would pummel our lives if a new hurricane landed every week. In essence, though, that is what is happening. Week in and week out, Satan is bearing down with all the forces of hell. The destruction is rampant. We too seldom take time to ask, "Am I just painting nails?"[819]

**Spiritual Vacuum** He has counseled millions on raising children, but perhaps Dr. Benjamin Spock's greatest advice came from his 1992 assessment of America's parental woe: "a lot of our problems are because of a dearth of spiritual values." [820]

**Spiritual Warfare** One hundred lightning bolts blast the earth every second. These eight million daily surges of power provide more energy than all of the electric generators combined in the United States. Even though three-quarters of the bolt's energy is used up in heat (the surrounding air heats up to 50,000 degrees Fahrenheit), enough energy remains to deliver a full 125 million volts of electricity. Ironically, lightning is much more than what our eyes see. With a lightning bolt traveling at 90,000 miles per second it's hard to realize what is actually happening. The bolt gets its start from channels of pulsing electric energy two inches across, going from the ground to the clouds. In Luke 10:18, Jesus says, "'I saw Satan fall like lightning from Heaven.'" Like the physical phenomenon of lightning, tremendous spiritual energy is released when the prayers of God's children start pulsating upward to Heaven. [821]

**Spiritual Warfare** "That this world is a playground instead of a battleground has now been accepted in practice by the vast majority of fundamentalist Christians." —*A. W. Tozer* [822]

**Spousal Concern** A woman wrote to Ann Landers concerning her husband's smoking habits. He was a human chimney for forty-three years, but didn't contract lung cancer—she did. His wife, a non-smoker, had one lung removed, yet he continued to smoke in her presence. Finally, he read an article which divulged some research on lung cancer in dogs. The veterinarian author noted that dogs living in a house with a smoker had a 30 percent higher incidence of lung cancer. After seeing this information, the man said, "My gosh! I've got to give these things up. If anything ever happened to Champ [their beagle], I'd never forgive myself." He threw out his cigarettes and hasn't touched them since. Isn't it strange how we sometimes show more concern for our pets than our spouse?[823]

**Spousal Responsibility** Howard Hendricks has a unique way of making you squirm on the horns of a dilemma. One of those unsettling dilemmas involves marriage partners who are frustrated with the way their spouse has turned out. One such guy approached Dr. Hendricks with a list of gripes about his wife. Hendricks consoled the guy with his Columbo-type tactics. He told the man he was really surprised that a man of his intelligence would marry a woman with so many blatant faults. The man quickly defended his prenuptial decision by declaring, "She wasn't that way when I married her!" Hendricks then retorted, "Then I guess it means you made her that way." The fault we often foist upon our spouse can frequently be the result of our own activities, or lack thereof. As one old cowboy put it, "A man who treats his wife like a thoroughbred will never end up with an old nag."[824]

**Statistics** Statistics can be made to say just about anything you want. For instance, research demonstrates that pickles cause cancer, Communism, airline tragedies, auto accidents, and death. About 99.9 percent of cancer victims have eaten pickles some time in their lives. One hundred percent of soldiers have eaten them, along with 96.8 percent of Communist sympathizers. In auto and air accidents, 99.7 percent of those involved downed a pickle at some point in their lives. Moreover, those born in 1839 who ate pickles have suffered a 100 percent mortality rate. Statistics and scripture share one particular similarity. You can twist them to your way of thinking. But as followers of David Koresh discovered, when you twist scripture, you risk becoming another statistic.[825]

**Stealing** Eric Morse lived in a rough section of Chicago. Many children die in such dangerous conditions, and he was no exception. On October 14, 1994, he was pushed to his death from the fourteenth floor of a South Side housing project. His crime? Refusing to steal. Two boys, ages ten and eleven, insisted that five-year-old Eric steal some candy for them. When he refused to steal the candy, these two boys then took Eric to their "clubhouse" and pushed him out of the window. How tragic that a child was killed because he refused to break the law and steal.[826]

**Stepfamilies** "Each day in the United States, 1,300–1,800 new stepfamilies are being formed."[827]

**Stewardship** Ron Blue, Certified Public Accountant and Christian Financial Advisor, has a unique way of updating the term "stewardship." Mr. Blue compares a steward to a banker. The money he uses to conduct business is not his own; he simply operates under the premise that he will manage the money of others. We would become quite angry if our banker began to use "our" money as though it were his own. Each time we write a check it would be wise to remember we are but bankers who manage the Lord's account.[828]

**Stewardship** George Burns has given an entertainer's perspective on stewardship: "It's easier to make a paying audience laugh. They get dressed and they put on a tie and they get in their cars and they pay so much that they like your act. An audience that doesn't pay is very critical." He's right! Critical church members seldom have many check stubs which bear the church's name.[829]

**Stewardship** "It's not how much of my money will I give to God, but how much of God's money will I keep for myself." —*Oswald Smith*[830]

**Stewardship** Ralph Waldo Beeson was a multimillionaire who never lost sight of his Christian stewardship. He lived a frugal lifestyle in a modest home with no air conditioning. He had no desire to spend the money on himself but wanted to give all he could "to the Lord's work." Mr. Beeson gave a large sum of money to help found a divinity school on the campus of Samford University in Birmingham, Alabama. His only stipulation for the gift was that he remain anonymous. Mr. Beeson said, "It's the Lord's money. He gave me the gift of making it. I am not smart enough to make that much money on my own. It's his money, and I am going to give it back to him." [831]

**Strength** Bob Wieland lost both his legs in Vietnam. For an athlete with dreams of a pro sports career, the tragedy was especially difficult to bear. Bob was spared the destruction of bitterness, though, by his reliance on God and his Word. "I do the best I can to apply the Word of God to my life, because I know it works." Bob took God at his word, "cast all his cares on Jesus" (1 Pet. 5:7), and claimed, "the weakness of God is stronger than man's strength" (1 Cor. 1:25). Maybe that explains why Bob, who walks on his hands, has completed a three-year walk across America, the Race Across America on a custom-made bicycle, the New York and Los Angeles marathons, the Hawaii Ironman Triathlon, and bench pressed a record 507 pounds. Bob Wieland has indeed found that God can perfect his strength through our weaknesses. [832]

**Stress** A typical concert piano has over 240 strings that, when tuned and tightened, create a pull of 40,000 pounds on the frame. Without the tension, there would be no beautiful music. Yet, too much exerted pressure can cause the piano to crack and will destroy its sound. The piano models a good strategy for stress. (Especially since Americans consume 20,000 pounds of aspirin a year). Balance in work, exercise, diet, recreation, worship, and relationships keeps us in harmony. Over-commitments can knock us out of tune and rob the music from our lives. [833]

**Stress** Each year the American Institute for Preventive Medicine issues a "Top Ten Most Healthy Resolutions." Number five for 1994 was stress management. Stress is responsible for two-thirds of all office visits to doctors and plays a role in our two major killers (heart disease and cancer). Sixty-two percent of Americans say they experience a great deal of stress at least once a week. Those most likely to experience stress almost every day are people in their forties. To manage stress, the institute recommends that people "practice a relaxation exercise, such as mental imagery, meditation, or yoga for at least twenty minutes every day." Ironically, twenty minutes alone with God each day would fit neatly into their prescription for stress reduction.[834]

**Stress** "For fast-acting relief, try slowing down." —*Lily Tomlin*[835]

**Stress** Several years ago a garbage truck exploded in Virginia. The trash crew had unknowingly picked up some calcium hypochlorite, and it blew up under the pressure of compaction. Two firemen ended up in the hospital and the poisonous gas forced many people to evacuate nearby office buildings. You might expect such an occurrence to take place outside an explosives plant, but these were swimming pool supplies. Calcium hypochlorite is a powder form of chlorine. It dissolves harmlessly in a swimming pool but explodes when placed under pressure. We share great similarities with this volatile chemical. When life's pressures are not given opportunity to harmlessly dissolve, we run the risk of exploding on our families, neighbors, or vocational colleagues.[836]

**Submission** "Lord, I am willing to receive what you give; to lack what you withhold; to relinquish what you take; to suffer what you inflict; to be what you require. And, Lord, if others are to be your messengers to me, I am willing to hear and heed what they have to say. Amen." —*Charles Swindoll*[837]

**Success** General H. Norman Schwarzkopf became a very popular man after the Gulf War. He published a book, *It Doesn't Take a Hero*, and was on the cover of *Newsweek*. He has toured the country giving lectures on leadership and has shared eleven principles that guided him to victory in the Persian Gulf. Principle number five is: "No repainting the flagpole." He says, "Make sure all the work your people are doing is essential to the organization." Church work can become just another coat of paint on the old pole if we're not careful. For this reason we should do as Rick Warren advocates: "A great commitment to the Great Commission and the Great Commandment will make a great Christian and a great church." [838]

**Success** "History's greatest accomplishments have been made by people who excelled only slightly over the masses of others in their field." —*John Maxwell*[839]

**Success** In 1972, Cathy Rigby was determined to win a gold medal at the Olympic Games in Munich. She had trained very hard for many years and did not want to disappoint herself or the United States gymnastics team. As she began the grueling regimen of performing under Olympic pressure, she prayed for the strength and control to get through her routines without making mistakes. She performed well but did not win. Cathy was crushed by the defeat. When she later joined her parents in the stands, she burst into tears and said, "I'm sorry, I did my best." Her mother gave these wise words of consolation, "You know that, and I know that, and I'm sure God knows that too. Doing your best is more important than being the best." Doing our best for the Master is all Jesus has asked. We won't always be the best, but we can always try to do our best.[840]

**Success** *Inc.* magazine crunched some serious numbers to provide a survey on "What Workers Want." In the category of success, respondents answered the question, "Which one of the following would most give you the feeling of success in your life?" "Happy family life" scored first place, with 62 percent. "Ability to do some good in the world" placed second, with 15 percent. The balance of the respondents picked less noble benchmarks of success like "earning lots of money, prestige, and fame." In summation, 77 percent of those surveyed defined success in terms of family and helping others.[841]

**Success** Success is sweet, but usually it has the scent of sweat about it.[842]

**Success** There is less to fear from outside competition than from inside inefficiency, discourtesy and bad service.[843]

**Success** "There's no place where success comes before work, except in the dictionary." —*Donald Kendall*[844]

**Success** "You can always tell when you are on the road to success; it's uphill all the way." —*Paul Harvey*[845]

**Suffering** Amy Carmichael was a missionary to South India. Had she never experienced suffering, her name would probably not be well known today. She spent fifty-six years on the mission field and never returned home to England on furlough. An accident damaged her leg and left her bedridden for the last twenty years of her life. It was during these years in bed that she wrote most of her forty books. God used her experience of suffering to bring encouragement to millions of people. It was this understanding of God's ability to fulfill the promise of Romans 8:28 that led Miss Carmichael to write, "A wise master never wastes his servant's time." No matter what set of circumstances we receive, God will not waste an experience if we remain obedient to him.[846]

**Suffering** In 1876, the British government passed the Merchant Shipping Act. This law required each ship to bear a mark on its bow to indicate when a vessel had received the maximum amount of cargo permitted for a safe voyage. If that mark fell below the waterline, the ship was required to unload enough cargo to bring the mark up to water level. This marking was called the "Plimsoll Mark," named after the British reformer who was instrumental in the passage of this law. God has placed a Plimsoll Mark on each of us. It signals the limit beyond which we cannot receive an additional load. God knows our limits and will not allow us to carry more than we can bear. We are sometimes tempted to question God's ability to read our "Plimsoll Mark," but he is faithful to keep us floating, even when we feel like our ship is going down.[847]

**Suicide** December can be a depressing month for many people who entertain thoughts of suicide. Each year, some 28,000 Americans take their lives, and a high percentage of those suicides occur around the Christmas holiday season. In San Francisco, the Golden Gate Bridge is not only the city's trademark, but it is also the final point of life for many people. Since the bridge opened in 1937, there have been nearly one thousand confirmed suicides. The bridge accounts for about 10 percent of all suicides in San Francisco. Significant is the side of the bridge from which so many people jump. Reports indicate that almost every person has jumped off looking at the city rather than the ocean. Their final gaze at the city seems to communicate that each one was taking one last look for hope. May we always be there to help broken people find hope when it seems like none exists, because, "Suicide is not a temporary solution to a permanent problem; it is a permanent solution to a temporary problem."[848]

**Superstition** Some people need to reconsider the value of good luck charms. Take the rabbit's foot, for instance; it sure didn't help the rabbit.[849]

**Support Groups** Is the gathering of Christians really needed every week? Some debate the value of such weekly support and worship. But have they read a recent study from Stanford University? Stanford recently conducted a study of terminally-ill cancer patients. They found that those who attended weekly support group meetings lived twice as long as those who did not. No wonder the Sabbath comes once a week.[850]

**Sweepstakes** Chances are pretty good that you haven't yet hit one of those big sweepstakes jackpots. Although the big sweepstakes publishers have stayed tight-lipped about your chances of winning, *Reader's Digest* did come clean on actual odds of winning the Grand Prize: 1 in 199.5 million. Of course, you might get lucky and cash in if the guy ahead of you fails to claim his winnings. You have a pretty good chance, presuming you're next in line behind Oscar Wilde. Wilde probably didn't submit his winning numbers by the deadline, even though he got an entry form like everyone else. *Reader's Digest* informed him that he had reached the third stage in the "Strike It Rich" contest. Not bad for the nineteenth-century writer, who died penniless in Paris during 1901.[851]

**Sweet Revenge** Ted Engstrom tells the story of a disgruntled husband named Joe. He was ready to end his three-year marriage, but since he was so angry with his wife, he wanted not only to leave her but to hurt her as well. Joe visited a psychologist and sought a professional opinion as to how he could most severely hurt his wife. The wise counselor sized up the situation and gave this advice: "Here's the perfect solution. Go home and start treating your wife like a goddess. Give her your undivided attention, take her out to eat, help around the house, compliment her every move, and just treat her like a queen. Do this for two months, then just pack your bags and walk out. When you leave her after treating her so well she will literally crumble." Joe thought it was a wonderful scheme. He put it into practice as soon as he got home. For two months he gave his wife the best he had to offer. After this eight-week setup, the marriage counselor called Joe and asked, "Well, did she crumble when you left?" Joe shot back, "Are you kidding? I wouldn't leave this woman for the world. I now have the best marriage a man could want. My wife *is* a goddess!" The marriage counselor hung up the phone with the satisfaction that he had accomplished what he set out to achieve, "sweet" revenge. When a spouse treats a mate like a prized treasure, the result is a beautiful and fulfilling marriage.[852]

**Syncretism** Syncretism is the act of combining different beliefs or practices. Americans seem to be immersed in this practice of picking and choosing their theology from an array of sources. This is illustrated by a service offered through Blockbuster Entertainment Corporation. A few of their more than five hundred stores are selling customized CDs. A customer can choose favorite songs from a computer library and then create a customized CD within seconds. Unfortunately, many people think this trend of picking only what you like should apply to God as well.[853]

**Talking to Yourself** Talking to yourself isn't always a sign of old age. In this day and time it may be the only way to be sure someone is listening.[854]

**Taxes** Call it adding insult to injury. A new IRS code implemented in 1994 causes 52 percent of married couples to pay $1,244 more in Federal Income Tax than an equal-earning non-married couple who live together. In other words, each year the majority of married couples in the United States will pay a $1,244 penalty for being married.[855]

**Teamwork** A business partner became very upset when he realized he was carrying more than half the work load. To vent some frustration he sought the counsel of a friend. Over lunch, the hard-working man shared his grievance. Quietly and patiently the friend heard out this distraught worker. He then reached for a glass of water and shared a significant truth. "Water is the foundation of life. All the planets we know about are barren, because they don't have water. For water to exist there must be teamwork, but that teamwork isn't mutually equal. Water is made up of two parts hydrogen and one part oxygen, $H_2O$. Hydrogen has to work twice as hard as oxygen. If a business (marriage, friendship, or church) is to thrive, we must be willing to sometimes work twice as hard as others."[856]

**Teamwork** Lou Holtz started his coaching career at the University of Minnesota. During his first year there, he distributed T-shirts with the word "TEAM" printed on them in big block letters. Underneath, in tiny print, was the word "me." Holtz understood the truth that success comes through placing the team's objectives above personal ambition. (See Philippians 2:3.)[857]

**Teamwork** On July 20, 1969, the world watched as astronaut Neil Armstrong became the first man to set foot on the moon. Who can forget the moment when he said, "That's one small step for man, one giant leap for mankind"? What we probably don't remember is how many people were involved in getting Mr. Armstrong to the moon. In all, there were 218,000 people working behind the scenes to make that historic moment possible.[858]

**Teenagers** "Few things are more satisfying than seeing your children have teenagers of their own." —*Doug Larson*[859]

**Teenagers** It never occurs to teenagers that someday they will know as little as their parents.[860]

**Teenagers** Mark Twain is often quoted for his "insight" on teenagers. The Mississippi folk hero said, "When I was a boy of fourteen, I thought my father was the most ignorant man in the world, but when I was twenty-four, I was amazed how much the old man had learned in ten years." If you have a teenager . . . hang in there. If you are a teenager . . . hang in there.[861]

**Television** In 1991, we passed the thirtieth anniversary of former FCC Chairman Newton Minow's famous speech which classified television as a "vast wasteland." He was definitely ahead of his time. Through the medium of T V, the average child in America today will view 25,000 murders by the age of eighteen. Minow, who is now a lawyer based in Chicago, feels things are only getting worse: "In 1961, I worried that my children would not benefit much from television," he told an audience at Columbia University. "In 1991, I worry that my grandchildren actually will be harmed by it." Television is a neutral tool. What we do with it determines its benefit or harm. Today's benefit may best be found in turning it off more often and using that time to write to a network and tell them what types of entertainment you would like to see and support. Who knows, the silent box may even inspire you to engage in a little daytime drama with your own family.[862]

**Temptation** In 1986, Gordon MacDonald was the president of InterVarsity Christian Fellowship. He was admired and respected by countless people throughout the Christian community. Within a year he was a broken man. He had committed adultery. By 1988, he was on the long road to healing and wrote a therapeutic book which dealt with his own brokenness, *Rebuilding Your Broken World*. In this book, MacDonald shared an experience which took place several years before his adulterous relationship. While on campus to speak at a college commencement, he struck up a conversation with a school board member. After some pleasantries the new acquaintance asked, "If Satan were to blow you out of the water, how do you think he would do it?" "I'm not sure I know," said MacDonald. "All sorts of ways, I suppose; but I know there's one way he wouldn't get me." "What's that?" "He'd never get me in the area of my personal relationships," answered MacDonald. "That's one place where I have no doubt I'm as strong as you can get." Satan is wise and powerful. That's why Paul wrote, "Therefore let him who thinks he stands take heed lest he fall" (1 Cor. 10:12).[863]

**Temptation** In 1995, the American Sociological Review reported on a recent study that revealed young married couples have a greater tendency to divorce if they live in an area with a high concentration of singles. The research was done by Scott South, a sociology professor at the State University of New York in Albany, and his colleague Kim Lloyd. They analyzed 2,592 married men and women in their twenties. These participants were interviewed annually for seven years, then that data was cross-referenced with the demographics of their area. Those surrounded by greater numbers of available partners had higher divorce rates. Temptation works like that. When the majority of those around us are doing things differently than we are, our temptation to join them increases. Sometimes we need to change the environment we are in, or make certain we have ample support to keep us from being adversely impacted by it.[864]

**Temptation** Satan, like a good fisherman, baits his hook according to the appetite of the fish.[865]

**Ten Commandments** On November 17, 1980, the Supreme Court struck down a Kentucky law that required the posting of the Ten Commandments in public school classrooms. The logic for such action can only be described as absurd. The high court noted the following reason for their "brilliant" decision. The Ten Commandments were "plainly religious and may induce children to read, meditate upon, perhaps to venerate and to obey the commandments." So, we remove the moral code of ethics which is the foundation of our society, and people wonder why students act the way they do. Does it take a rocket scientist to figure out why morality goes south when you scratch out "No Adultery" and hand out condoms instead?[866]

**Tenacity** Maxcy Filer of Compton, California is a firm believer in the adage, "If at first you don't succeed, try, try again." Mr. Filer began taking the California Bar Exam in the mid 1960s. He didn't pass it the first time or the second time. In fact, he didn't pass the exam until his forty-eighth try. Before earning a passing grade, he failed forty-seven times over a span of twenty-five years. Sometimes the tests of life seem "unpassable," but "Let us not lose heart in doing good, for in due time we shall reap if we do not grow weary" (Gal. 6:9).[867]

**Termination Policy** Some people are eager to see their pastor "find another church." In *Your Pastor and You*, author Richard DeHaan has some excellent tips for vacating the pulpit. First, say "Amen!" once in a while, and he'll preach himself to death. Second, encourage him and brag on his work, and he'll probably work himself to death. Third, offer to help out with the ministry of the church and request the name of a person with whom you could go share the Gospel—your pastor just might die of heart failure. Or, finally, get the church to unite in prayer for the preacher, and he'll soon become so effective that a larger church will take him off your hands. If we terminated more apathy and fewer pastors, we would see greater results.[868]

**Tetelestai** In 1992, Congressional records revealed that 296 of the 440 members and delegates overdrew their House accounts in varying amounts. During the 39-month period that was under investigation, 200 representatives had overdrawn their accounts by more than a month's salary (the bank's stated limit) at least once. Sixty-six of the worse offenders wrote about 20,000 bad checks with a face value of $10,846,856. This political folly came to be known as "Rubbergate" and had congressional representatives pleading for voter grace and sympathy. This whole scandal revolved around the issue of insufficient funds. When our Savior died on the cross, his last word was *tetelestai*. Its root meaning is that of completion. In the market place it was used as a receipt that one had "paid in full." Jesus communicated volumes with his last word. He not only "completed" all that the Father had assigned him, but he "paid in full" our debt of sin. Although Congress may write bad checks, God's payment for salvation will never be returned because of "insufficient funds."[869]

**Thankfulness** A visiting farmer stopped at a city restaurant to eat lunch. When he was served his food he bowed his head and gave thanks to the Lord. Some uncouth guys sitting at a nearby table noticed the farmer's prayer and shouted, "Hey, pops, back where you come from does everybody *pray* before they eat?" Their laughter was silenced when the unmoved farmer answered, "Everybody but the pigs." [870]

**Thankfulness** In her classic autobiography *The Hiding Place*, Corrie ten Boom tells of the time she and her sister were forced to take off all their clothes during Nazi inspections at a death camp. Miss ten Boom stood in line feeling forsaken and defiled. Suddenly she remembered that Jesus hung naked on the cross. Struck with wonder and worship during that seemingly forsaken moment, ten Boom leaned forward and whispered to her sister, "Betsie, they took his clothes, too." Betsie gasped and said, "Oh, Corrie, and I never thanked him." Thanksgiving does not require bounty—just recognition of what our Savior has already done.[871]

**Time** "It is only when we truly understand that we have a limited time on earth that we'll live each day to the fullest." —*Elisabeth Kubler-Ross*[872]

**Time** "Time is what we want most but use worst." —*William Penn*[873]

**Time Management** Mark McCormack wrote the book, *What They Don't Teach You at Harvard Business School*. His management techniques are widely accepted and highly acclaimed. He personally spends a full hour each day deciding how he'll invest the other twenty-three hours. Martha Stewart is another in the public eye who watches her time closely; in fact, she borders on obsession. She sleeps with a light on all night, so if she wakes up she can immediately start reading. It must work, because she finds time to have her own TV show, put out a magazine, write books, and be in American Express commercials.[874]

**Time Management** *Forbes* magazine researched the subject of success and failure and found that the number one factor for success or failure was time management. What is true in the business community can also be true among Christians and their spiritual maturity. Christian stewardship requires the effective management of one's time.[875]

**Time Management** In one year, the average American will read or complete 3,000 notices and forms, read 100 newspapers and 36 magazines, watch 2,463 hours of television, listen to 730 hours of radio, buy 20 CDs or cassettes, talk on the telephone almost 61 hours, and read 3 books.[876]

**Time Management** Vilfredo Pareto was an Italian economist (1848–1923) who devised the 80/20 Principle. He calculated that 80 percent of your progress comes from 20 percent of your efforts. Conversely, 80 percent of our tasks yield only 20 percent of the results. In a list of ten tasks, two will accomplish more than all of the other eight combined. The trick then is to focus on that which brings the greatest return. Bob Biehl has helped clarify this truth by noting that if the ark were sinking, Pareto would advise Noah to forget the gnats and look for the elephants. Good stewardship of our time requires discipline—focusing more on the "elephants" and less on the "gnats." [877]

***Titanic* Theology** The story of the *Titanic* may be a bit overworked, but here is one more clip worth noting. Survivor Eva Hart related the experience of what took place after the big ship sank. Twenty lifeboats were launched, but many people chose not to board one. Consequently, few of the rafts were filled. When the Titanic slipped from sight at 2:20 A.M., Lifeboat No. 14 rowed back to the scene. It paddled through the darkness, chasing cries and seeking to rescue those in the water. The other lifeboats remained distant because they feared if they rowed back to help, too many swimmers would converge on their boat and cause it to sink. Do you ever act like those in Lifeboat No. 14? Unfortunately, we sometimes act more like those in the other nineteen boats.[878]

**Tithing** Are most of your church members living beneath the poverty line? You may be surprised. In 1992, the Department of Health and Human Services released the following breakdown. For a single person the poverty line is $6,810; for a couple it's $9,190; a family of three is in poverty if they make less than $11,570; four in a family moves the line up to $13,950; and $23,470 is the break point for a family of eight. If you multiply by ten the total of what each church family "tithed" this past year, you might find that a clear majority are claiming by their "tithe" that they live below the poverty line. In general, the average church of 100 families could increase their weekly budget by $1000 if each family only made $20,000 and faithfully tithed. Such obedience would generate an extra $20 billion among all American churches. To put that in perspective, $20 billion would produce a stack of new $1,000 bills, two and one-half miles tall. With such commitment, more Americans might look to God's Church for solutions rather than turning to the government.[879]

**Tithing** James Lewis Kraft was the founder of the company which bears his name. His success in business is exemplary but his faith is even more impressive. His wealth served as a platform for giving money to the causes of God. Upon one occasion he spoke of his giving by saying, "I don't believe in tithing . . . but it's a good place to start."[880]

**Tithing** Once, Martin Luther railed against his congregation for being stingy givers. From the pulpit he said, "You ungrateful beasts! You are not worthy of the treasures of the Gospel. If you don't improve, I will stop preaching rather than cast pearls before swine."[881]

**Tithing** One advisor has counseled, "Let us at least give according to our income, lest God make our incomes match our gifts."[882]

**Tithing** Only about four percent of professing Christians tithe.[883]

**Tolerance** Ask any great cook about aluminum foil, and you're bound to get an opinion on which side is "best." Some swear the shiny side must always be on the outside of a baked potato, while others condemn such nonsense and emphatically claim the opposite. Meanwhile, the manufacturer stays amused and gives a good lesson in dogmatism and tolerance. When foil is made, it is rolled. One side of the foil gets shiny because it comes in contact with the heavy roller. The other side stays dull because it never makes contact with the roller. Both sides produce the same results! [884]

**Tolerance** Edgar Dunlap was an attorney who, years ago, served on the Board of Education in Gainesville, Georgia. While touring an elementary school one day, he saw a boy carving his initials on a desk. Dunlap shouted for the boy to stop. "What's the matter with you kids today? When I was in school, none of the boys dared to deface public property like this!" A few days later the chastised boy stumbled upon an old desk in the school basement. Carved on the top of the desk was the date 1905 and six names. The six-name list began with none other than Ed Dunlap. The old attorney took the desk top with him and mounted it on his office wall. He said, "I keep that there to remind me to be more tolerant about the things kids do." [885]

**Tolerance** "I like long walks, especially when they are taken by people who annoy me." —*Fred Allen*[886]

**Tolerance** "See everything, overlook a lot, correct a little." —*Pope John XXIII*[887]

**Tolerance** The next time you see a guy with a ponytail, you might feel more tolerant if you remember George Washington wore one, too.[888]

**Tough Day** We've all had tough days at the office. The next time things don't go so well, think of Mike Grady. He played third base for the New York Giants in 1895. In one play he (1) muffed a routine grounder, (2) overthrew first-base, (3) dropped the ball when the first baseman finally recovered the overthrown ball and threw it to him to catch the advancing runner, and (4) promptly threw the ball over the catcher's head as the runner raced for home. What should have been a routine ground ball for an easy out ended up being an error-laden home run for the opposing team. Things could be worse![889]

**Tragedy** The horrifying pictures from Oklahoma City's A. P. Murrah Federal Building will never be forgotten. On April 19, 1995, a truck filled with explosives ripped the building in half and created a massive concrete grave. The death toll eventually reached 169. America's heart was broken, and our country has desperately sought ways to overcome this national calamity. The motto of Oklahoma is *Labor Omnia Vincit* (Labor conquers all things). Hard work and labor are good and necessary parts of overcoming such adversity, but toil and labor will never replace the loss that occurred. Many people try to overcome the most difficult obstacles of life by just working harder. Reality reminds us that this method does not work. We overcome tragedy by allowing the Wonderful Counselor to initiate the healing process and walk with us through the valley of the shadow of death. Labor does not conquer all things, but the labor of Christ does![890]

**Training** On September 17, 1991, the three major airports in the New York City area were shut down for several hours by a telecommunications failure. AT&T was responsible for the mishap, but the real story is in how it happened. The call switching center responsible for the failure is usually monitored by trained technicians. When the warning lights flashed on that fateful Tuesday, those technicians were in class learning how to read warning lights so such a problem wouldn't happen. Although ministry requires a degree of knowledge, sometimes we get hung up in the classroom and actually miss the people we are "learning how to help." [891]

**Tranquility** In 1969, the "Eagle" landed on the moon and set up Tranquility Base. It was an ironic name for such a daring and dangerous mission. Neil Armstrong landed the spacecraft on the moon with just eleven seconds of fuel left, and he did it with less computer power than is contained in a new car today. NASA seemed to be communicating a biblical principle: you can have peace in the midst of turmoil. The same can be said on earth as well. Oceanographers say the sea remains tranquil below twenty-five feet. No matter how bad the storm rages on top of the ocean, the waters are peaceful down deep. The Christian finds peace in the same place—down deep. Shallow faith leaves you anxious and fearful when the storms arise, but a deep and stable faith provides tranquility in the midst of severe and threatening storms.[892]

**Transformation** Paul's admonition to be transformed (Rom. 12:2) can be better understood through the use of a thermometer and a thermostat. We are being conformed to the world when we live as a thermometer and simply reveal the climate around us. Transformation means living like a thermostat, so that God works through you to set the climate of the environment you live in.[893]

**Treasurer's Report** The treasurer of a rural church resigned and was replaced by a man who managed the local grain elevator. The grain operator agreed to the new position on one condition: the church could not require a financial statement or ask him any questions about the finances for one year. The church members were confused by the request but obliged him because he was a successful and trustworthy man. At the end of the year, this secretive treasurer gave his glowing financial report. The $25,000 debt had been paid off, there were no outstanding bills, and there was a cash balance of $12,000. The congregation was elated and wanted to know how he managed to accomplish such a great feat. He replied, "Most of you bring your grain to my elevator. When I paid you, I simply withheld ten percent on your behalf and gave it to the church in your name. You never missed it, and now you have seen what God can do when we each give back to God the tithe he has commanded of us all." Tithing provides a beautiful transformation in the life of a Christian who is obedient to God's command, and collectively, tithing transforms the entire scope and magnitude of a church's ministry.[894]

**Trivializing Death** Batesville, Arkansas, resident Johnny Harrington lost his mother in 1991. Before the funeral he threw a party for his dead mother. He propped her up in the casket and put a beer in one hand and a cigarette in her other hand. When questioned about what he had done, he simply said, "I did exactly what she told me to—and I would do it again." Although many would not espouse to Mr. Harrington's actions, many are adopting his trivialized view of death. Hebrews 9:27 reminds us that a beer can and a cigarette aren't what await us after death.[895]

**Trust** On the day before Easter, April 18, 1992, Madalyn Murray O'Hair kicked off the 22nd Annual National American Atheists Convention in Austin, Texas. She rallied atheists and said what you might expect: "As long as there is religious slavery, mental slavery, we're not going to get anywhere as a nation. So, we're calling for the total, complete and absolute elimination of religion in American culture. We would not be in difficulty [as a nation] if we weren't being ruled by those classes of persons who believe in fantasy." Why have the convention on Easter weekend? She responded, "We want to take back Easter and make it a celebration of the start of spring." A placard carried by an atheist marching to the state capitol stated the message succinctly: "In God We Trust. Not!" He was following the fad of negating a statement by tagging "not" on the end. This atheist was on to what we do, as well. We pledge our allegiance to God but reserve the right to tag on, "Not!" "God, I trust you with my money. Not!" "Lord, I give you complete control of my business. Not!" "Father, please be the God of our home. Not!" Thanks to an atheist, we may better understand trust, and our lack of it.[896]

**Truth** "Get your facts first, and then you can distort them as much as you please." —*Mark Twain*[897]

**Truth** In his best selling book *Apocalypse Next*, William Goetz illustrates how some people respond to truth. He tells of a man who smoked cigarettes. Through the reading of numerous articles he became alarmed over the strong relationship between smoking and lung cancer. He finally confided in a friend: "I've been reading so many articles about smoking and lung cancer that I've decided to quit reading." [898]

**Truth** "Some people are afraid of truth, but be it understood . . . the truth's not going to hurt you—unless, of course, it should." —*Sharon Briggs-Fanny*[899]

**Truth** The American people are spending fifty million dollars a year on a lie. A recent study on subliminal tapes was conducted by Dr. Robert Bjork, a UCLA Psychologist, and the National Research Council. The fashionable trend of listening to a tape of relaxing music with powerful hidden messages has been proven to be a hoax. In theory, these messages are repeated thousands of times and stored in the subconscious and then converted by the conscious mind into behavioral changes. With such a claim people have been buying these tapes to help them lose weight, stop smoking, quit drinking, think creatively, make friends, reduce pain, improve vision, cure acne, conquer fears, and become better athletes. To all of these promises Dr. Bjork says, "We find such claims unwarranted from both a theoretical and empirical standpoint. . . . Imagining yourself swinging a golf club like Jack Nicklaus is less helpful than hitting a bucket of balls." The American people are searching for a quick fix to their problems, and they're spending millions of dollars to prove it. The church has the hope for which they are looking, and we must bring the gospel truth out of the "subliminal" realm and into that of the conscious.[900]

**Truth Deficit** In America, 67 percent of the adults agree that there is no such thing as absolute truth. Much worse is the fact that 52 percent of born again Christians think truth is relative. The truth is, God's Word is not relative (Isaiah 40:8).[901]

**TV Sex** Research has revealed that 93 percent of the 10,000 sexual situations which occur on television each year involve non-married people. Even worse is the fact that nearly 50 percent of American teenagers believe TV accurately portrays the consequences of sex outside of marriage. Statistics show the average adult would gain thirty hours a week by turning off the TV. In reality, much more than time would be gained.[902]

**'Twas the Night Before . . .** On Christmas Eve of 1822, Clement Moore composed his famous poem. His heart was heavy for his six-year-old daughter, Charity. She had tuberculosis and her only request for Christmas was a new story. Moore wanted to create something that would bring joy to his ailing daughter's life. During his trip to town he heard the local woodcutter tell some children a story about a man in Denmark named St. Nicholas who gave children gifts on their birthday. This inspired Moore to create "A Visit from St. Nicholas." Despite the urgings of his family, he refused to write it down and would only recite his poem from memory. A cousin secretly sent this masterpiece to the New York Sentinel in 1823, and it became a huge success. It was published anonymously for the next twenty-five years, so Moore was never paid for his poem. As a renowned scholar who taught Greek, Latin, and ancient Hebrew at Columbia University, he wanted to be known for his academic excellence, not a story composed for his daughter. The title was changed to match the first phrase of the poem and has captured the attention of each generation for over 170 years. Maybe someday another anonymous poet will step forward and take credit for the following adaptation of Moore's original piece:

'Twas the night before Jesus came, and all through the house
Not a creature was praying, not one in the house.
Their Bibles were lain on the shelf without care
In hopes that Jesus wouldn't come there.
The children were dressing to crawl into bed
Not once ever kneeling or bowing a head.
And mom in her rocker with a baby on her lap
Was watching the Late Show while I took a nap.
When out of the East there arose such a clatter,
I sprang to my feet to see what was the matter.
Away to the window I flew like a flash
Tore open the shutters and threw up the sash.
When what to my wondering eyes should appear
But angels proclaiming that Jesus was here.
With a light like the sun sending forth a bright ray
I knew in a moment this must be The Day!
The light of his face made me cover my head
It was Jesus returning just like he had said.
And though I possessed worldly wisdom and wealth
I cried when I saw him in spite of myself.
In the Book of Life which he held in his hand
Was written the name of every saved man.
He spoke not a word as he searched for my name
When he said "It's not here" my head hung in shame.
The people whose names had been written with love
He gathered to take to his Father above.
With those who were ready he rose without a sound
While all the rest were left standing around.
I fell to my knees, but it was too late
I had waited too long and thus sealed my fate.
I stood and I cried as they rose out of sight
Oh, if only I had been ready tonight.
In the words of this poem the meaning is clear
The coming of Jesus is drawing near.
There's only one life and when comes the last call
We'll find that the Bible was true after all.[903]

**Uncertainty of Life** When the Estonia ferry sank in the Baltic Sea during 1994, it brought a chilling reminder of humanity's uncertain tenure on earth. The more than nine hundred people who lost their lives were caught by complete surprise when death came knocking. It is reminiscent of another boat that sank surprisingly in frigid waters. The *Titanic* sank in April of 1912. Countless stories abound from that maritime tragedy. When Robert Ballard discovered her wreckage in 1985, intrigue with the *Titanic* was rekindled. As to the point of uncertainty with life, Captain Edward J. Smith is a chilling example. He was honored with the distinct privilege of guiding the *Titanic* on her maiden voyage. It was scheduled to be his final act of duty before retiring after forty-three years at sea. No doubt many plans for retirement had already been made. But even though the *Titanic* was deemed "unsinkable" and Captain Smith's retirement was "certain," uncertainty of life prevailed, and, as the James Cameron film stirringly portrays, Captain Smith went down with his ship. Life is both temporary and fleeting. Consequently, adequate preparation for one's eternal destiny should be of greatest concern.[904]

**Unconditional Love** Greg Louganis recorded an unprecedented double/double in Olympic diving when he won gold medals in the men's 3-meter springboard and platform competition in both the 1984 and 1988 Olympics. Few will ever forget how he fought back in 1988. In the springboard event he missed one dive and hit the board with his head. Physicians stitched his cut, and he went on to win. In the platform diving he won the gold on his final performance with an incredible reverse three-and-a-half somersault tuck. It was a breathtaking finish that brought Americans to their feet. It was the same dive that clinched the gold for Louganis in the '84 games. When reporters hounded him in Los Angeles he gave them a very unusual response. They asked, "What were you thinking about as you prepared for your final dive?" Maybe they were referring to the pressure, or to the fact that that dive is extremely dangerous and killed a Soviet diver just a year before in 1983.

Louganis' simple answer was, "I was thinking that no matter what happens, my mother will still love me." When Greg was just eleven, he became very frustrated at his diving performance in an early and important meet. Frances Louganis took her son aside and said, "I do not come to see you win. I come to see you dive. Just do your best. I will love you no matter what." That unconditional love carried her son to forty-three national diving titles, six Pan-American gold medals, five world championships, one Olympic silver medal, and four Olympic golds. Unconditional love can cause anyone to excel.[905]

**Unity** At a county fair, the townspeople held a horse-pulling contest. The first-place horse ended up moving a sled weighing 4,500 pounds. The second-place finisher pulled 4,000 pounds. The owners of the two horses decided to see what these horses could pull together. They hitched them up and found that the team could move 12,000 pounds. By working separately, the two horses were good for only 8,500 pounds. When coupled together, their synergism produced an added 3,500 pounds. It's a hard lesson for us, but unity consistently produces greater results than individual endeavors. "Teamwork divides the effort and multiplies the effect." [906]

**Unity** In the late 1800s, there were just two deacons in a small Baptist church in Mayfield County, Kentucky. The two deacons hated each other and always opposed one another. On a particular Sunday, one deacon put up a small wooden peg in the back wall so the minister could hang his hat. When the other deacon discovered the peg, he was outraged that he had not been consulted. The church took sides and eventually split. The departing group formed a new church, called The Anti-peg Baptist Church.[907]

**Universalism** A survey taken at a recent Urbana missions convention revealed that only 37 percent of those attending believed that "a person who doesn't hear the gospel is eternally lost." The propagation of the gospel is seriously threatened when two-thirds of the most mission-minded young people in America don't affirm the lostness of mankind.[908]

**Universalism** As president of the Unitarian Universalist Association in 1992, William Schulz spoke at a dedication service for the Bay Area Unitarian Fellowship in Houston. Schulz said, "[Unitarian Universalism] is first and foremost a religious institution. We need to be proud of that and own it." The service concluded with a word from Leonora Montgomery, Senior Minister of the Bay Area Unitarian Fellowship. She noted, "The denomination's 1,015 congregations run the gamut from conservative to openly atheistic."[909]

**Unwed Mothers** The rate of U.S. births to unwed mothers has risen more than 50 percent since 1980. Demographer Stephanie Ventura said, "The rising out-of-wedlock birth rates point to a tremendous decline in the stigma society once attached to such births."[910]

**Urgency** In 1857, Hudson Taylor went to China as a missionary. One of his converts was a man named Nyi. Nyi, thrilled about his newfound faith, shared it with all his friends. He asked Taylor, "How long have you had this good news in England?" Taylor revealed the gospel had been in England for centuries. Nyi then asked the obvious: "Why didn't you come sooner? My father died seeking the truth." Delivering the gospel is urgent! It is time to obey and no longer delay.[911]

**Vacation Bible School** In 1991, Southern Baptists experienced the following results from Vacation Bible School:

- 61,420 Professions of Faith.
- The discovery of 512,429 prospects.
- More than $1 million given for mission causes through the Cooperative Program.

The average Bible School had 101 students and faculty.[912]

**Values** In a large city some very creative crooks broke in to a department store. They entered the store unnoticed and stayed long enough to accomplish their mission. You may wonder what they stole, but that's just the catch. They didn't take anything. Instead, these thieves switched the price tags. The tag on a $395.00 camera was removed and placed on a box of stationery. The $5.95 sticker on a paperback book was attached to an outboard motor. Everything was shuffled. When the store opened the next morning, you would have expected total chaos. Surprisingly, though, the store operated normally at first. Some customers literally got some steals while others felt the merchandise was overpriced. Incredibly, four hours slipped by before the hoax was discovered. In the department store of American Culture, Satan has deceptively switched the price tags. Far more than four hours have passed since he did it. Things are valued more than people, pleasure is priced higher than faithfulness, profits mean more than integrity, and God has been priced for clearance. The tags have been switched, and we need to sound the alarm.[913]

**Verbosity** The shortest inaugural address was given by the endeared George Washington. It contained only 135 words. William H. Harrison delivered the longest: 9,000 words that took two hours. A freezing northeast wind made everything about the speech seem *long.* Such verbosity caught up with President Harrison. The next day he came down with a cold and died a month later from pneumonia. "When words are many, sin is not absent, but he who holds his tongue is wise" (Prov. 10:19). Verbosity can be deadly.[914]

**Victorious Spirit** During the Gulf War, Americans got reacquainted with our military. Televised briefings and constant media coverage helped us see the intricacies of our national defense. One learning point came from the *Joint Chiefs of Staff Official Dictionary of Military Terms.* In this unabridged edition of technical military terminology, two rather common words don't exist. One is "surrender," and the other is "retreat." On the eve of D-Day, General Dwight Eisenhower closed his address to the troops by saying, "We will accept nothing less than full victory! Good luck! And let us all beseech the blessing of Almighty God upon this great and noble undertaking." We can learn from our military leaders. Remove the terminology of defeat, so the temptation to surrender or retreat will never impede our pursuit to accept nothing less than full victory![915]

**Violence** Did the Mighty Morphin' Power Rangers have anything to do with it? No one is certain, but Scandinavian network TV-3 dropped the widely popular U.S. children's show in Norway, Denmark, and Sweden after the tragic death of a five-year-old girl. Little Silje Marie Redergard froze to death on a playground in Norway after three boys (one five-year-old and two six-year-olds) kicked and stoned the girl while playing together. The boys were too young to be charged with any crime under Norwegian law, but their crime convicts us all. When children kill each other, something is desperately wrong with the society in which they live.[916]

**Vision** Philip Knight had a crazy idea in the early 1960s. He decided to sell imported running shoes from the back of his station wagon in Portland, Oregon. As an auditor he was financially astute and figured he could make money by purchasing shoes from Japan and selling them in the U.S. His shoes were improved in the later part of 1963 when he was joined in this venture by his college coach. Coach William Bowerman modified the imported shoes to make them better. Nike is now worth billions of dollars, but their start-up investment was just $1,000. When it comes to vision, "Just Do It!"[917]

**Visions** In 1991, Pizza Hut unknowingly offered some divine guidance through their Atlanta billboards. Joyce Simpson, an Atlanta fashion designer, claimed to receive an answer to her prayers in the middle of a forkful of Pizza Hut's spaghetti. She had prayed for a divine sign to help her decide on whether to stay in the church choir or quit and sing professionally. While driving past the billboard she claims to have seen Michelangelo's version of Christ's face in strands of spaghetti hanging from a fork. To her, it meant she should stay in the choir. Fortunately for Joyce, she saw Jesus. Other people claimed to see deceased rock star Jim Morrison, a puppet, or Willie Nelson. Wouldn't it be easier to find the face of Jesus in the pages of his eternal Word?[918]

**Voting** On Election Day, proportionately more people in mental institutions vote than do people that are not institutionalized. They also make fewer errors on their ballots.[919]

**War** The price of war is costly. After two decades of fighting, Cambodia is one the world's poorest countries. More than two million lives have been lost, and 500,000 people are homeless. The aftermath of all this fighting has also left a major threat to those trying to scratch out a living. Each month, remaining land mines cause up to three hundred amputees. In 1990, Henh Han, seventeen years of age, lost both his legs to a leftover land mine when he took his oxen out to graze. War between nations, groups, or individual family members not only destroys the present but also jeopardizes the future.[920]

**Wealth** Measure wealth not by the things you have, but by the things you have for which you would not take money.[921]

**Weddings** Harvard University performed a study on divorce and discovered the following: the national divorce rate is 1 in 3. The average for people who were married in a church ceremony is 1 in 50. For those couples who were married in a Christian wedding ceremony, attend church weekly, read the Bible and pray together, the divorce rate average is 1 in 1,105. Christianity can truly divorce-proof your marriage![922]

**Weekends** The Roper Organization recently released the findings of a national survey. Part of this survey dealt with the main purpose of the weekend. Thirty-five percent perceive the weekend as a time to recharge yourself for the coming work week. Fifty-one percent live for the weekend and view work as a necessity to make it possible to enjoy life on the weekend. Seventy-five percent said Sunday is the day to relax. Such mindsets must be considered when strategizing for growth and ministry.[923]

**Weight Loss** Americans spend thirty to fifty billion dollars per year on weight-loss products.[924]

**West Point Advice** In the football locker room of West Point there is a sign which simply reads: "Do not let what you cannot do, interfere with what you can do."[925]

**Winning** On February 4, 1993 Larry Bird said good-bye to his fans at the Boston Garden. A special 2½ hour affair marked the retiring of Bird's jersey and the ceremonial placing of number 33 in the Garden's famed Rafter Heaven. His words were chosen with the class he typically displayed on the court. Maybe the most significant words he said were, "I never put on a uniform to play a game. I put on a uniform to win." The former Hoosier, who worked on a garbage truck before finding his niche in basketball, is right. God hasn't called Christians to simply play in his Kingdom. He's called us to triumph over the strongholds of Satan.[926]

**Wisdom** "Every man is a fool for at least five minutes every day; wisdom consists of not exceeding the limit." —*Elbert Hubbard*[927]

**Witnessing** His syndicated cartoons are read daily in scores of newspapers. *B.C.* and *The Wizard of Id* are the brainchildren of Johnny Hart. It is not uncommon to see blatant reference to his faith in Christ through the characters he creates. Concerning his openness to witnessing through his cartoons, Johnny Hart says, "Some people try to make me into a hero for speaking up through a newspaper syndicate, but I don't see it that way. Too many Christians have bought into the lie that we shouldn't mention our beliefs."[928]

**Witnessing** Muhammad Ali no longer "floats like a butterfly" but he still "stings like a bee." The legendary boxer has turned his energies toward witnessing, but it's not for Christ. One reporter said, "This is a man who is as sure about his purpose in life as he was about his talents in the ring." Ali said, "I wasn't just put here to box. Boxing made me famous and gave people a reason to listen to me. But I was put here to teach the Islamic faith." Recently, two reporters jumped at Ali's invitation to come up to his private suite after a banquet. They went expecting to get an exclusive interview. Instead, they got an hour of preaching. The former three-time heavyweight champion had a twenty-one-page document containing what he believed to be discrepancies in the Bible. He then said, "People have argued for centuries about which religion is right and which religion is wrong. This [waving the Quran in front of him] is the truth." May we who believe in "the Way, the Truth, and the Life" recapture such enthusiasm, zeal, and purpose.[929]

**Women's Rights** Harry Truman said, "There's no reason why a woman shouldn't be in the White House as President, if she wants to be. But she'll be sorry when she gets there." Mr. Truman's humorous comment holds a kernel of truth for both women and men. Many in the workplace are painfully discovering that career-driven sacrifices don't always deliver on their apparent promise of contentment.[930]

**Word Association** Bil Keane continues to deliver poignant truths from his comic strip, *Family Circus*. Little Billy got caught saying something he shouldn't have. His sister quickly called his hand and told Mommy, "Billy said a television word." Why do we discipline our children to not use profanity but permit the viewing of shows which flippantly use unwholesome language?[931]

**Words** After Salman Rushdie wrote the novel *Satanic Verses,* Ayatollah Khomeini issued a religious edict that called for the death of this "renegade Moslem." Since then, the British novelist has lived in hiding. Now that Khomeini is dead, some have speculated Rushdie is no longer in danger. Iranian officials cautioned otherwise. "The Ayatollah is dead. Only he could have revoked the *fatwa* [religious edict]." So the sentence stands, even if Khomeini's successors disagree with it. Words are like that. You can apologize or try to correct your words, but in reality, you can't change what has already been said. Words are irrevocable. Likewise, if one religious leader can issue an edict that nobody can change, isn't it conceivable that God can be trusted when he declared his Word shall never change? (See Isaiah 40:8.)[932]

**Work** Some comments on the activity that takes so much of our time:

- Albert Polger said, "Work is what you do so that some time you won't have to do it anymore."
- Jerome K. Jerome noted, "I like work. It fascinates me. I can sit and look at it for hours."
- One friend asked another: "I remember your brother was trying to get a job with the government a few months ago. What's he doing now?" The friend said, "He's not doing anything now. He got the job."
- One woman jarred her workaholic husband by saying, "Honey, if you kill yourself with overwork, I just might have to enjoy all your hard-earned money with my second husband."
- Cliff Bakin has written a book titled, *We Are All Self-Employed.* He opposes bonuses and says workers should take personal responsibility for their job productivity and career mobility.
- A cartoon depicted a workaholic standing at a busy intersection with a sign that read, "Will work for the fun of it." [933]

**Work Ethic** Michael Jordan is truly one of the best basketball players of all time. Raw talent is a major contributing factor to the superstar's success, but what should not be overlooked is his work ethic on the practice court. In his autobiography, *Rare Air: Michael on Michael*, Jordan shared an insight he gleaned from the Olympics. "I saw some Dream Teamers dog it in practice before the Olympics. I looked at them, and I knew that's what separates me from them." Although he is a gifted athlete, he has worked very hard to excel in his field. Every Christian should do likewise while remembering, great performances require great practice! [934]

**Work Ethic** On May 1, 1991, Nolan Ryan threw his seventh no-hitter. His unprecedented achievement came at the age of forty-four. He struck out sixteen and walked but two in his nine-inning masterpiece. After the incredible feat reporters flocked to the locker room to hear his "secret." "The secret is that there is no secret," was Ryan's reply. He simply shared his belief in a strong work ethic that was handed down to him by his father. As the media questions continued, he politely excused himself and went to a stationary bike where he began preparing for his next start. "The routine never changes, that's all a part of this," said Ryan. When sports reporter and long-time friend Barry Warner called Ryan at 2:30 A.M., just four hours after Ryan finished his no-hitter, Ryan gave him a fifteen-minute interview. Ryan simply said, "Barry, it was just another day of work. It's 2:30, but I'll be back at the stadium by 9:30 in the morning to start my weight work." (He lifts 70,000 pounds of Nautilus and free weights in a given week and 100,000 pounds a week in the off-season.) The Ranger's pitching coach, Tom House, said, "He does three hours of preparation for every one that anyone else does." Ryan told Warner, "Just because you have a good night doesn't mean you change your routine." The secret of continued success is usually hard work! [935]

**Workaholism** Wayne Oates, a long-time professor at Southern Seminary, introduced the world to "workaholism." It was a word he coined in a 1968 article for *Pastoral Psychology.* A more recent discussion of the subject helps to further define the different types of workaholics. *Identity Workaholic:* work defines your life, so your best energy is spent there. *The Perfectionist:* long hours are required to make every task flawless. *Approval Seeker:* work piles up because you fear saying "no" to others' request for your time and energy. *Situational Workaholic:* long hours are perceived as only a temporary situation that will soon pass—there is always another situation looming, though. *The Escapist:* work provides an escape from painful relationships or other problems. *The Materialist:* an insatiable desire for possessions drives you to increase your workload. Workaholism has many faces, and we may be guilty of hiding behind one or more of them.[936]

**Worldliness** C. S. Lewis spoke to the issue of worldliness when he wrote, "If you read history you will find that the Christians who did most for the present world were just those who thought most of the next." He continues, "It is since Christians have largely ceased to think of the other world that they have become so ineffective in this one. Aim at Heaven and you will get earth thrown in: aim at earth and you will get neither." Where is your focus? Where is your aim?[937]

**Worry** An exasperated husband asked his wife, "Why are you always worrying when it doesn't do any good?" She quickly piped back, "Oh yes it does! Ninety percent of the things I worry about never happen." One minister saw worry in a different light. When asked whether or not he ever worried, the wise pastor said, "Of course not. Worry is sin. If I'm going to sin, I pick something a lot more fun than worry."[938]

**Worry** Through research it has been estimated that we perform a great deal of "unnecessary" worry. Things for which we worry can be broken down as follows:

- Things which never happen: 40 percent.
- Things past which can't be changed or corrected: 30 percent.
- Needless worry about our health: 12 percent.
- Petty miscellaneous worries: 10 percent.
- Real and legitimate worries: 8 percent.

Maybe that's why Jesus said, "Don't be anxious for tomorrow; for tomorrow will care for itself. Each day has enough trouble of its own. (See Matthew 6:34.)[939]

**Worship** Gordon Dahl once observed, "Our problem is that we worship our work, work at our play, and play at our worship."[940]

**Worship** "I think the highest form of worship takes place when you lead someone to faith in Christ." —*Jerry Vines*[941]

**Worship** "If worship does not change us, it has not been worship." —*Richard Foster*[942]

**Worship** Reverend Thaine Ford has succeeded in providing what many church members cherish most: a guarantee to be dismissed by noon. In fact, you can be home by noon. This pastor of the First American Baptist Church of Pensacola, Florida, has created the "Compact Mini 22-Minute Worship Service." In just 1,320 seconds, Ford delivers an eight-minute sermon, leads in the singing of one hymn, reads scripture and has a prayer. His logic is, "It's for people whose parents made them go to church all their lives and they thought they had all the church they could stand. Or, it's a good entry-level church for people to see if they can take religion in smaller doses." It may be a creative way to reach the unchurched, but I fear it is the dream of too many who are already in the church.[943]

**Worship** There is a great lesson to be learned from the dictionary. When things start going bad, we often fear they will only get worse. It seems the "worse" will take us to the "worst." To prevent the "worse" from turning in to the "worst," look at the unique setup God has provided in the English language. Any standard dictionary will separate the words "worse" (and its derivatives) and "worst" with one special word: "worship." When circumstances seem to be slipping in the wrong direction, remember that worship is the buffer between "worse" and "worst." [944]

**Worship** "We used to think that the chief end of man was to glorify God. Now we're tempted to say the chief end of God is to gratify man." —*Oswald Sanders*[945]

**Worship** When Albert Thorwaldsen had completed his famous statue of Christ, he invited a friend to see it. The Danish sculptor had created a portrayal of Christ with his arms outstretched and his head bowed. The friend looked at the figure but said, "I can't see his face." Thorwaldsen replied, "If you want to see the face of Christ, you must get on your knees." Only when we worship Christ as servants on bended knee can we see him clearly.[946]

**Zeal** In his book *The Crisis in the University*, Walter Moberly notes the failure of evangelicals to penetrate university campuses with the gospel. To the Christian community he writes, "If one-tenth of what you believe is true, you ought to be ten times as excited as you are." It's a rare soul who is interested in embracing a faith that doesn't move the person trying to share it.[947]

# MOTIVATIONAL HUMOR

**Adult Education** At age five, little Aaron attended his first football game with his father. Beforehand, his dad gave him careful instructions about behavior at the game. He said, "You will have to stay seated, be quiet, and act like an adult." Not long after kickoff Aaron noticed lots of people jumping up and down, screaming, and shaking their fists in the air. He turned to his dad and asked, "Are these adults?"[948]

**Aging Priorities** Two old golfing buddies were playing a water hole when one hit his shot into the drink. As the old-timers puttered around the pond to find the sunken ball, one of them ran across a talking frog. The female amphibian said, "If you kiss me I will turn into a beautiful princess." His partner heard the frog's proposition and was completely surprised when his buddy reached down, picked up the frog . . . then put her in his pocket. He asked, "Why didn't you kiss her?" The senior golfer replied, "At my age, I'd rather have a talking frog." [949]

**Aging Secret** Jack Gulledge is the retired editor of *Mature Living*. One of his favorite jokes goes like this. A mischievous man walked up to an elderly woman and asked, "Lady, how old are you?" She indignantly replied, "Sir, my age is my business!" The man then countered, "Lady, it looks like you've been in business a long time." [950]

**Answered Prayer** A very timid woman wanted to participate in the visitation program of her church, but was petrified by the thought of actually visiting somebody. The pastor, sensing her anxiety, recommended that she pray before each visit. He noted God's promise to give peace which surpasses all understanding. A week later the woman was walking on Cloud Nine. She jubilantly told her pastor, "You were right—prayer works! Before each one of my visits I prayed that the people wouldn't be home, and they weren't!" [951]

**Appropriate Eulogy** A very wealthy man lost his brother. The town considered it no great loss, because both men were ruthless, perverse scoundrels. The rub came when the community pastor was asked to do the funeral. The surviving brother said he would give the necessary funds to build a new sanctuary if the pastor would perform the ceremony and refer to his brother as a saint in the eulogy. It was a tough call for this uncompromising minister, but he did want that new church building, so he agreed to the challenge. The service flowed rather smoothly and the minister maintained his integrity by pointing out the sinful lifestyle of the deceased. His wife was impressed that he had not compromised, but wondered how he could call the man a saint after all he was saying about him. The honest pastor took care of that worry when he closed by saying, "There is no question this man was a friend of Satan, but compared to his brother . . . he was a saint!" [952]

**Attorney's Fees** The attorney pleaded with the judge for a greater settlement. His logic was profound: "$100,000 isn't much of a settlement, Your Honor. After all, my client deserves something, too." [953]

**Automated Driver** A car salesman was sure he could make a big sale to this unassuming man if he could just get him inside one of their new computerized cars. This model came complete with a computer generated voice that told you everything. The salesman noted the little voice would tell him how much gas was left, when he needed to turn on his lights, how far he had traveled, and how fast he was going. In an attempt to close the sale he said, "Sir, there's nothing this car won't tell you." To his surprise he lost the sale. The man quietly walked away and said, "Why would I need one of those? I've got a wife!" [954]

**Baby Attraction** West Virginia folklore has a tale about a couple who called for a doctor late one night as the wife was ready to deliver a baby. The country physician turned the rustic farmhouse into a makeshift delivery room. The husband was handed a lantern and instructed to hold it up so the doctor could see. After a healthy boy was born, the man lowered the lantern. The doctor shouted for this new father to get the lantern up as he delivered another baby, this time a girl. The father was thrown into shock when the doctor once again insisted that the light be held up. He said, "We can't stop now, it looks like there's another one." The shaky father then asked the doctor, "Do you think it's the light that's attracting them?" [955]

**Back Seat Drivers** A man with four teenage daughters and a rather bossy wife admitted, "I no longer drive, I just sit behind the steering wheel." [956]

**Bad Investment** During an IRS audit, the defendant was asked to explain a $5,000 write-off that was flagged, "Bad investment." It seemed obvious to the audit recipient. He explained, "That was when I paid my taxes last year." [957]

**Baldness** Bald guys need to remember what Howard Hendricks says: "All good men come out on top." [958]

**Baptism** The six-year-old grandson of Ruth Kirby told his mother that he had been baptized. Mom knew he hadn't been formally baptized, so she probed further into the issue. She asked him to explain what he meant by "baptized." Little Blake then enlightened his mom, "Last night in the bathtub I put my face under the water and thought about Jesus." [959]

**Baptist Vices** Two Baptist groups met in Europe, one from America and the other from Germany. At the dinner table several of the American Baptists began to smoke. The German Baptists were aghast. In fact, the Germans were so shocked, they almost dropped their beer. [960]

**Barbering Blues** Joy Terzich's grandson was preparing to get his first real haircut by his grandfather's barber. Big tears accompanied the event, so they assumed he was fearful of pain. They tried to assure him that the haircut would not hurt. Finally, the little guy whimpered, "I don't want to go to Grandpa's barber, because he cuts a big hole in the top of Grandpa's head, and I don't want a hole in mine."[961]

**Bargain Hunting** While shopping for a new automobile, the hard-working gentleman grew weary of an overly zealous and optimistic car salesman who kept pitching the idea that this new car was "only $29,995!" The frustrated potential car buyer replied, "Sir, that's a lot of only." [962]

**Baseball Blues** The baseball season was proving to be lousy. One curious spectator approached the coach and asked, "What's the score?" "Seventy-five to zero," was his reply. The fan then remarked, "Not much point in going on, is there?" The Coach hollered, "We won't know that until we get a turn to bat." [963]

**Bath Powder** A little three-year-old boy named Bobby did not enjoy baths. His mother coaxed, "Don't you want to be nice and clean?" Bobby replied, "Yes, but can't you just dust me off?" [964]

**Beauty and the Beast** A belligerent husband wised off to his wife by asking, "How can you be so pretty, yet so dumb?" She appropriately replied, "I'm pretty so that you will love me. I'm dumb so that I will love you." [965]

**Biblical Dyslexia** Be careful if your King James Bible was printed in 1716. That particular year the printer made a flagrant mistake. In John 5:14, the final copy read "sin on more" rather than "sin no more." That must have been a good year for Bible sales, because it seems like a lot of people are still heeding the advice of that old edition.[966]

**Bilingual Handicap** Chi Chi Rodriguez, a professional golfer, cited an example of how his Puerto Rican accent can cause some things to get lost in the translation: "I asked my caddie for a sand wedge, and ten minutes later he came back with a ham on rye." [967]

**Blame Game** While walking with his son on the beach, a father asked his three-year-old, "Tim, where do you think all this sand came from?" The little guy was accustomed to being guilty as charged so he quickly replied, "I don't know, Dad, but don't blame me." [968]

**Boredom Factor** What started off as an introductory compliment quickly developed into a dangerous play on words. While introducing the guest minister, the host proclaimed, "Our speaker has never bored anyone with a long sermon. He always does it quickly." [969]

**Bowling Words** In the humorous little book *Children's Letters to God*, one little girl was quite concerned about her dad's salvation. Anita wrote, "Dear God, Is it true my father won't get to heaven if he uses his bowling words in the house?" [970]

**Box Office Surprise** A rural Texan decided to splurge one weekend and take his family to the big city for a movie. After buying the tickets, he stopped by the concession stand for some popcorn. When he was told how much the popcorn cost, the man couldn't help but comment on the price. He said, "The last time I came to the movie, popcorn was only fifteen cents!" The concession attendant responded, "Well sir, you're really going to enjoy yourself tonight, because the movies now have sound." [971]

**Bragging Rights** A Texas rancher met up with a Wisconsin dairy farmer. The two men began talking about their land and the milkman told the cattleman that he operated his business on 125 acres. The Texan scoffed at such a small parcel of land. He said, "Yankee, that ain't nothin'. On my ranch I can get in my truck at sunrise and I won't reach the fence line of my property until sunset." The dairy farmer snorted, "Yeah, I used to have a truck like that." [972]

**Brain Dead** In the book *The 776 Stupidest Things Ever Said,* professional basketball player Chuck Nevitt is quoted saying, "My sister's expecting a baby, and I don't know if I'm going to be an uncle or an aunt." [973]

**Brains vs. Brawn** During a picnic in the park, a man noticed a strange sight across the road. Two men were working feverishly in the summer heat. One man would dig a rather large hole. Then his co-worker would immediately fill it in. After watching this happen all through his lunch, the taxpayer was too perplexed to just walk away. He approached the two men and asked, "What are you doing?" The hole digger caught his breath and responded, "We're a three-man crew in charge of planting trees in the park, and the guy who puts the trees in the holes is out sick today." [974]

**Breaking Bad News** After a very difficult day at the office, a psychologist walked through his front door and said, "Honey, I've had a terrible day. All I did was listen to one problem after another. So, please, don't tell me about any more problems. Talk to me, but just give me the good news." The wife quickly restrategized and said, "O.K. The good news is . . . two of our three children didn't break an arm today." [975]

**Card Trick** Kids make great parrots—especially when you don't want them to repeat what you say. One father learned the hard way when he invited his boss over for dinner. He was hoping to score a few extra points with his superior but ended up losing it all when his young son asked the boss, "Where are your cards? Dad says you're not playing with a full deck." [976]

**Christmas Presents** A middle-aged woman posted her Christmas wish list on the refrigerator for her husband to read. Rather than list certain items of desire, she simply requested "something that will make me look sexy and beautiful." When Christmas rolled around she expected to open a package with some fancy lingerie inside. To her surprise, he gave her an exercise bike instead.[977]

**Clowning Around** A professional clown was trying to do his job when a drunk heckler began to disrupt his performance. The drunk went from bad to worse and was truly ruining the evening. The clown finally went over to the inebriated man and slipped his arm around the guy's shoulder. The clown looked him in the eye and said, "Mister, I get paid to dress up and make a fool of myself. What's your excuse?" The drunk never said another word.[978]

**Coaching Fatigue** When John Ralston left his position as coach of the Denver Broncos, he said, "I left because of illness and fatigue. The fans were sick and tired of me."[979]

**Codependency** One woman was so entwined in other people's lives that when she had a near-death experience, someone else's life passed before her eyes.[980]

**College Concerns** A college freshman was giving her friend a tour of the college she attended. They saw very little of the classrooms or the library, as most of their time was spent observing the hot spots for finding men. She pointed out the various recreational sights in the area and the numerous places for eating out. When they returned to the dorm, the freshman reminded her visiting friend that they needed to be quiet because her roommates were studying. Before they entered the room she whispered to her friend, "All they do is study. Honestly, I don't even know why they came to college."[981]

**Commercial Cleaning** A visiting friend was impressed by the cleanliness of the house. She didn't picture her friend as a homemaker, so she asked how she kept the house looking so nice. The residing husband noted the house was commercially cleaned. The friend knew of their limited retirement budget and asked, "How can you afford commercial cleaning on your pension?" The husband replied with a smile, "My wife cleans the house during TV commercials." [982]

**Communication** One guy worried about his wife to a friend. He sighed, "My wife is talking to herself a lot these days." The friend was hardly concerned. He said, "My wife has been talking to herself for years, but she doesn't know it. She thinks I'm listening." [983]

**Communication** The beauty of effective communication can be seen in Leroy Lockhorn's response to his wife, Loretta. "Sure we can talk; just don't block the TV." [984]

**Complaining** An angry pastor's wife looked over the remains of a dinner that had long since turned cold. She intensely inquired of her husband, "Where have you been for the last two hours?" His hollow eyes gazed toward his wife; then he slowly responded, "I met Mrs. Burton on the street and asked her how she was feeling." [985]

**Confidence** When Ty Cobb was seventy, an interviewing reporter asked him, "What do you think you'd hit if you were playing in this era?" (Ty Cobb was a legend who had a career batting average of .367.) He told the reporter, "About .290, maybe .300." The sports caster thought he understood Cobb's answer: "That's because of the travel, the night games, the artificial turf and all the new pitches like the slider, right?" Cobb quickly corrected the misunderstanding: "No, it's because I'm seventy." [986]

**Conflict Resolution** Upon one occasion, Winston Churchill so angered Lady Astor that she said, "If I were your wife, I would give you arsenic to drink." Churchill angered her even more with his reply, "And if I were your husband, I would gladly drink it." [987]

**Consequences** A little five-year-old was watching his older brother get disciplined by their father. After a thorough lecture the dad reminded his elder son that he would now have to live with the consequences of his actions. A few minutes later little Larry spoke with his dad and made a special request, "Dad, if David has to go live with the consequences, can I have his room?" [988]

**Contemporary Preaching** A pastoral candidate had done a masterful job of preaching his initial sermon. He had exegeted the text, outlined his vision, and instilled the congregation with great hope for a promising future. He concluded his sermon by declaring, "With God's help, I intend to lead this church forward into the nineteenth century!" The chairman of the search committee quickly caught the candidate's apparent blunder and loudly whispered, "You mean the twentieth century!" The minister replied, "We're going to take this one century at a time!" [989]

**Contentment** Question: Who has greater contentment, a man with seven children or a man with seven million dollars? Answer: The man with seven children, because he doesn't want any more. [990]

**Cooperation** A pastor met with his deacons to discuss an important recommendation to the church. After a lively debate the deacons brought the issue to a vote. To the pastor's surprise the raised hands indicated all but one deacon favored the recommendation. The pastor was so pleased with the balloting that he asked the one dissenting deacon if he would reconsider his vote so they could come to the business meeting with a unanimous agreement. The cantankerous deacon gruffly replied, "Pastor, as long as I'm around, ain't nothin gonna be unanimous." What a legacy! [991]

**Couch Potato** The wife looked at her husband sleeping on the couch, then turned to her friend and said, "Leroy was half-way through life before he realized it was one of those 'do-it-yourself' deals." [992]

**Couch Potatoes** Children of couch potatoes can be affectionately called "tater-tots." [993]

**Credit Cards** She may have missed the point of New Year's Resolutions. With an eagerness to make some changes in the area of financial habits, the lady called her credit card company and said, "I'd like to pay off my Master Card. Do you take Visa?" [994]

**Cuckoo Cover-up** A teenager overextended his midnight curfew and came home two hours late. As he quietly crept up the stairs, one of the steps creaked. His dad called out from the darkness, "Is that you, Jim?" The boy confessed it was. The father asked, "What time is it?" Before Jim could respond, the cuckoo clock went off. Knowing that little mechanical bird would reveal his tardiness, Jim followed the two cuckoos of the clock with ten more of his own. His dad went back to sleep, and the cover-up was complete. [995]

**Daddy** Some kids talked their mother into getting a hamster. Everybody agreed to the acquisition as long as the children took care of their new pet named Danny. Within two months the little rat would have died had the mom not assumed full responsibility for his care. She then decided it was time to give Danny to a new owner and called the children in to break the news. One child commented, "I'll miss him; he's been around here a long time." The mother agreed, "Yes, but he's too much work for me, so he needs to go." Another child suggested he might be able to stay if he ate less and wasn't so messy. But Mom was firm and said, "Let's go! It's time to take Danny to his new home." Then in unison the kids wailed, "Danny? We thought you said Daddy!" [996]

**Daily Devotions** A daily time of worship with God is very important. So much so that when we miss it others can tell. Such was the case when four-year-old Andrew made an honest mistake and spilled something in his house. His mother responded in a screaming tirade. The little psychologist made an astute observation: "Mommy, you forgot to ask Jesus to help you be nice today, didn't you?" 997

**Dangerous Crowd** Three-year-old Shawn accompanied his dad to church on Easter. The father wanted his son to understand the meaning of Easter, so he tried to explain the significance of the cross which hung at the front of the church. He said, "Jesus died because people nailed him to the cross." The little boy's eyes widened as he scanned the church. He asked his dad, "You mean *these* people?" 998

**Dangerous Preacher** A guest minister was preaching his heart out at a revival meeting. Unfortunately, he was uncomfortable with the microphone setup. A cordless lapel mike was not available, so he had to wear one of those "leash-like" mikes. He continuously tugged, pulled, and adjusted the microphone cord throughout his entire message. After this tug of war had gone on for quite some time, he lunged forward to the front of the platform, loudly raised his voice and began waving his fist in the air to emphasize his point. His sudden outburst frightened a little girl near the front of the sanctuary. She leaned close to her mom for protection and asked, "Mommy, will he hurt us if he gets loose?" 999

**Death Bed Reflections** Nostalgia overtook a dying man as he contemplated his life. He turned to his wife and said, "Honey, you've always been there for me. You were there when I lost my job. When I was involved in that terrible accident, you were right by my side. That time I fell off the roof, you were there to call the ambulance. During those years of dark depression, you stood by me. And now as I lay here at death's door, you're right beside me, just like always." After a few moments of reflection the old man looked at his wife and said, "Gladys, I just realized something. You're bad luck!" 1000

**Depravity** Three-year-old Alyson was preparing to go with her mother for a hamburger. She told her mother she wanted a cookie before leaving, but the maternal answer was, "No, but if you are good, you may have some when we come home." When they got in the car, Alyson became fussy and started throwing a fit. When she calmed down and realized what had happened, she asked her mother, "Mama, have I blown my cookies?" [1001]

**Desserts** It's only natural that stressed-out people eat more desserts, because "stressed" spelled backwards is "desserts." If that's true, there's a lot of stress between Thanksgiving and New Year. [1002]

**Disappointing Cure** The psychiatrist told his patient that they seldom used the term "cure," but after five years of therapy he was pleased to pronounce her completely cured. He was surprised to see that the patient did not look pleased. The doctor asked, "What's wrong? I thought you would be thrilled." The woman said, "Try to look at it from my point of view. Five years ago I was Joan of Arc. Now I'm nobody." [1003]

**Discernment** A college coach was trying to convert one of his former players into a high school talent scout. The coach began talking about the kind of player they wanted. He was describing the kind of guy who gets hit and doesn't get up, when the enthusiastic scout jumped in, "We don't want him!" The coach agreed, and told of the guys who get up after getting hit once but who stay down after the next hit. The prospective scout knew that wasn't the guy they wanted either. Then the coach told about a player who just kept getting up after every time he got knocked down. The former athlete knew this was the player they wanted so he shouted, "That's the guy I'll look for!" The coach said, "No, don't you get it? We want the guy who's knocking everybody down!" [1004]

**Discernment** The husband commented to his wife, "You've got to admit it, men have better judgment than women." The wife readily agreed. "Oh, that's definitely true. Just look at us; you married me, and I married you." [1005]

**Disgruntled Church Member** A pastor was venting frustration to his wife about a disgruntled church member. The pastor summed up the perpetual griper by saying, "It doesn't take much to make him happy, and even less to make him unhappy." [1006]

**Dishonest Gain** A wealthy but eccentric man called his pastor, his doctor, and a political friend to his deathbed. He told them he disagreed with the conventional belief that you can't take your money with you when you die. He said, "I'm taking mine!" He pulled out three envelopes and handed one to each of the gathered trio. He explained how the envelopes contained $30,000 in cash, and he wanted each man to throw an envelope in when they lowered his casket. At the funeral all three men did as their dead friend had requested. Upon returning from the cemetery, the pastor's conscience got the best of him, and he confessed to the doctor and politician, saying, "I needed the money for our church so I took out $10,000 and threw $20,000 into the grave." The doctor then came clean and admitted to taking $20,000 for costs he had incurred at his clinic. The politician was appalled at their dishonesty. He pridefully said, "I'm ashamed of you gentlemen. I threw in a check for the full amount." [1007]

**Disposition** One woman commented on her husband's unsavory disposition: "He can be nice when he wants to . . . he just never wants to!" [1008]

**Doctor's Orders** A woman accompanied her husband to the doctor's office for a checkup. Afterwards, the doctor took the wife aside and said, "Unless you do the following things, your husband will surely die. Every morning make sure he gets a good healthy breakfast. Have him come home for lunch each day so you can feed him a well-balanced meal. Make sure you feed him a good, hot dinner every night. Don't overburden him with any household chores. Also, keep the house spotless and clean so he doesn't get exposed to any unnecessary germs." On the way home, the husband asked his wife what the doctor said. She replied, "You're going to die." [1009]

**Doctor's Orders** With medication costs soaring so rapidly, one futurist suggested that doctors will soon be giving prescriptions with the following notation: "Take one pill as often as you can afford it." [1010]

**Doctors** The signs of the times in both medicine and recession were summarized by the insightful characters of the comic strip, *B.C.* "Show me a doctor who makes house calls . . . and I'll show you a Ph.D. who's selling vacuum cleaners!" [1011]

**Dog-gone Sermon** A rural church was in need of a preacher, so they contacted the seminary. In the confusion of making assignments, the seminary sent a student who had never been outside of the city. When he arrived at the church, the city boy was taken aback by the greatest travesty he had ever seen. On the second row of the church sat a deacon with his hound dog at his side. In the heat of righteous indignation, the preacher went down scolded the dog, and kicked him out of the church. The entire church held their breath, but nothing happened. After the sermon everyone quickly scooted out the side door and waited for the deacon to come out. When the deacon greeted the pastor everyone was taken aback. He extended his hand and said, "I want to thank you for kicking my dog out of church." The pastor was equally shocked, saying, "You want to thank me?" "Yep," said the old deacon, "I wouldn'ta had my dog hear that sermon for nothin'." [1012]

**Dress** During the hustle of getting ready for church, my three-year-old daughter wanted me to play a game with her. I told her I couldn't because I had to get "dressed" for church. Somehow the communication broke down. She stared at me with a puzzled face and then said, "You mean you're going to wear a dress like me and Mommy?" [1013]

**Driving Lesson** Dad grabbed his little boy and took him for a drive in the new family car. He pointed out all of the cars that cost more than their new car. When they got back to the house, the mother wanted to know what they saw on their drive. The little guy piped up, "We saw one Porsche, three Mercedes, two BMWs, four idiots and two jerks." [1014]

**Driving Tips** Sandra King of Charlotte, Michigan, quizzed her perceptive two-year-old as they waited at a traffic light. Mom's pop quiz had three questions. "What does red mean?" The little girl correctly answered, "Stop!" Mom inquired, "And what does green mean?" Back came the reply, "Go!" The third question was the hardest but received the most honest response. "What does yellow mean?" The bright toddler answered, "Go faster!" [1015]

**Dumb Move** Christian comedian John Paite noted, "Satan has to be the dumbest creature. Just think about it. He's sitting in heaven thinking, 'God's the creator, he's omnipotent, he's invincible, nothing can hurt him. . . . I think I can take him!' " [1016]

**Early Bird Shopping** During Christmas season a judge found himself in a generous mood. With a seasonal smile he asked the defendant what charges had been brought against him. The man replied, "Doing my Christmas shopping early, Your Honor." The judge said, "That's not a crime. How early were you shopping?" The defendant reluctantly admitted, "Before the store opened." [1017]

**Easter Crowd** As the pastor introduced his children's sermon on Easter, he asked the little ones, "Do you see anything different about our church today?" Little Heather quickly figured out the difference and blurted out, "It's full!" [1018]

**Ecumenical Golf** A Catholic priest and a Baptist minister were playing golf. Each time the priest prepared to putt he would cross himself and tap the ball in on the first try. The Baptist minister watched this for the first nine holes and the priest never missed a putt. During a clubhouse break the Baptist asked, "If I said a little prayer like you do before I putt, do you think it would help?" The priest said, "No." "Why not?" questioned the Baptist. Answered the priest, "Because you don't know how to putt." [1019]

**Education** One elementary school teacher found it hard to maintain a straight face when a little boy told her: "Miss Hayes, I don't want to scare you, but my dad said if my grades don't improve, somebody is going to get a spanking." [1020]

**Elevator Magic** Jerry Clower tells of a sheltered man who came to the city for the first time. In the lobby of a beautiful hotel he stared at these incredible machines which kept opening and closing. He was amazed at what took place right before his eyes. Two men entered the machine dressed in suits. When the doors opened, three men came out in shorts. One man got in with three suitcases and then was completely gone when the doors opened again. The excitement of this machine got the best of him when an old and wrinkled lady climbed into the machine and shut the doors. In just a few moments a gorgeous young lady exited from the machine. He couldn't contain himself any longer. He yelled across the lobby to his son, "Boy, go get your momma!" [1021]

**Environmental Cuisine** A hiker was charged with eating an endangered species while tracking the woods of California. After hearing the man had eaten a condor, the judge quickly passed a harsh sentence of ten years behind bars. The man pleaded with the judge to hear his side of the story because he felt circumstances justified his actions. The judge was interested to hear how anyone could rationalize killing a protected bird, so he allowed the man to speak. The hiker explained how he had been lost in the wilderness for three days and nights without any food or water. He then spotted the bird sitting on a rock. With what little strength he had left, he threw a rock and killed the bird. After eating the condor he walked another three days and nights without food or water before being rescued. He said, "Your Honor, had I not eaten that bird, I wouldn't be here today." The judge was moved by the story and suspended the hiker's sentence. As they left the courtroom the judge asked the man what a condor tasted like. The man thought for a moment, and then said, "It's kind of a cross between a bald eagle and a spotted owl." [1022]

**Environmental Dilemmas** We should all exercise caution and concern over the treatment of our environment. Sometimes, though, it seems like there is no right answer. At the grocery store a sacker hit on this dilemma when he asked the customer, "Do you want to destroy a tree by using a paper bag or endanger the environment with plastic?" [1023]

**Epistles** A New England high school teacher taught a course entitled *The Bible as Literature.* Only seniors in the top 10 percent of the class could take this course. A pre-test was given to evaluate the students' biblical knowledge. One student defined the Epistles as "wives of the Apostles." A pastor was so humored by this answer that he shared it during his next sermon. One of the church members approached him afterwards and asked, "If the Epistles weren't the wives of the Apostles, whose wives were they?" [1256]

**Equality** A little boy returned home from his first day of the new school year. His mother asked him, "How's your new teacher?" "She's mean but fair," the boy said. "What do you mean?" questioned the confused mom. "She's mean to everyone," responded the boy. [1024]

**Eternal Optimist** In Larry Olsen's *Outdoor Survival Skills*, he tells of a guy who has been lost in the desert for days. His water and food have long since run out. His lips are parched, and his tongue is swollen. His legs are bruised and bleeding from dragging himself across the desert floor. His body is scorched from the sun and covered with insect bites and cactus pricks. As he props himself up on his bleeding elbow to look over a knoll, he sees nothing but wasteland through his sand-peppered eyes, and comments, "You know, a few more days like this and I might get discouraged." [1025]

**Eternal Smoke** A concerned church member asked his pastor, Rick Warren, if he would go to hell for smoking. Dr. Warren answered, "No, but you'll smell like you've been there." [1026]

**Ethics** A young boy asked his dad, "What does 'ethics' mean?" The father was a rather prosperous businessman and valued his son's question, so he gave it considerable thought. After contemplation he said, "Well, you know your uncle Billy and I are in business together. Suppose a customer comes in and buys something worth $10 but mistakenly gives me a $20 bill and leaves without his change. It's ethics if I split the extra $10 with Uncle Billy." [1027]

**Fact vs. Faith** A minister tried to illustrate the difference between fact and faith. He hit upon a brilliant analogy that involved the congregation to which he was speaking. He said, "It is indeed a fact that you are sitting in the pews. It is also a fact that I am standing behind this pulpit. But it is only by faith that I believe any of you are listening to me." [1028]

**Fairway Fathering** After spotting a guy playing golf with four caddies, another golfer curiously asked, "Why so many caddies?" The fellow golfer replied, "It's my wife's idea. She thinks I should spend more time with the kids." [1029]

**False Impressions** A major was assigned to a new office on a military base. While he worked to set up his office, a private knocked on the door. The major quickly picked up the phone and motioned for the private to enter. On the phone the major said, "Yes, General Schwarzkopf, I think that is an excellent idea. . . . No sir, that's fine, you feel free to call me any time. I'm glad I can help. . . . Yes sir, I will, and you give my best to your family as well. Thank you sir, and a good day to you too, General Schwarzkopf." As the major hung up the phone he turned to the private and asked, "What can I do for you, private?" Sheepishly, the private mumbled, "Um, sir, I'm just here to hook up your phone." [1030]

**Family Vacation** It was a typical vacation. The kids were complaining, fighting, and whining. Dad was holding his own until his burning fuse finally hit dry powder. He was tired of having his seat kicked by these cranky kids who were ruining his time away from work. The car pulled to a screeching stop, and the father pulled out his two delinquent sons for their woodshed experience. As he shoved them back in the car he warned them that they better not make a sound for the next thirty minutes. From their back seat cellblock the boys got the message and remained quiet. After thirty minutes had passed, one boy asked if was all right to talk now. The father sternly replied, "Yes. What do you want to say?" The little boy started, "Well, when you spanked us back there, my shoe fell off, and we left it in the road." [1031]

**Fancy Preaching** An inexperienced seminary graduate went to a church in hopes of becoming their next pastor. Figuring he'd impress them with his brilliance, he preached on the attributes of God, using as many theological terms as he could find in his books. He mispronounced a few of them, but figured none of the people would know the difference. This became most evident when a little old lady met him at the back door. She scolded, "Young man, I don't care what you say, I still believe in God!" [1032]

**Fast Food** The teacher knew there was a shortfall of intelligence after she asked the class to name the four major food groups. Suzie shot up her hand and quickly reeled them off: "Wendy's, McDonald's, Burger King, and Pizza Hut." [1033]

**Fat Count** A woman was trying on different dresses at the mall. She hit upon an outfit she liked but was concerned it might make her look too big. Her faithful husband was shopping with her, so she tried it on and asked for his opinion. "Does this dress make me look fat?" The husband gave a response he has been trying to buy back ever since. "No, honey, that dress doesn't make you look fat. It's your hips that make you look fat." [1034]

**Father Knows Best** A father, tired and exhausted from a long day at the office, had little desire to engage in any type of brain function. He lounged in his recliner chair while his son struggled with homework. The mother, busy in the kitchen, saw the lack of adult supervision taking place. She tried to nudge her husband into action by saying, "You'd better help him while you still can. Next year he'll be in the sixth grade." [1035]

**Fatherhood** While camping in a national park, Bill struck up a conversation with Ray, who was shaving in the campground restroom. Bill asked Ray what he did for a living. Ray replied, "I'm a juvenile rehabilitation counselor." After a little pause, Bill said, "Yep, I'm a parent too." [1036]

**Fatherly Example** A father was riding his son for not measuring up to his expectations. After a few choice words the elder said, "Frankly, I'm just ashamed of you. You still don't have a job. When George Washington was your age he was working hard as a surveyor in the wilderness." The boy quickly fired an arrow back: "That's true, and when he was your age he was President of the United States." [1037]

**Financial Freedom** A woman with a terrible credit history sought a loan from a financial officer. The woman's credit check revealed she was a bad risk, so the loan officer asked probing questions about outstanding debts. The woman became agitated with the questions and retorted, "I just filed for bankruptcy and now I don't owe anybody!" [1038]

**First Grade Blues** After three days of school the first grader approached his mom and said, "Mom, if it's all the same, I'd just as soon you wouldn't sign me up next year." [1039]

**First Love** A husband accompanied his wife to her thirty-fifth high school reunion. While the woman was reminiscing with some of her old friends, a man approached the husband and confessed, "Years ago I was madly in love with your wife." The dry-witted husband retorted, "So was I." [1040]

**First Sermon Jitters** A young man felt God was calling him to preach, so his pastor suggested the youngster be given the opportunity to deliver a sermon. The young man was petrified by the thought of preaching but knew this was what he needed to do if he was going to be a preacher. He spent weeks preparing his message so that he could follow his pastor's example and preach without notes. When his big day arrived, he was terribly nervous but confident he had adequately prepared. Unfortunately, his nerves got the best of him when he approached the pulpit. Panic set in, and he forgot everything he had hoped to say. After several moments of awkward silence, his quivering voice came over the sound system with these words: "This morning only God and I knew what I was going to say. Now only God knows." [1041]

**Floral "Mis"arrangement** A businessman wanted to send a floral arrangement to a friend who was opening a new branch office. His friend called later in the day to thank him for the considerate gesture but was a little confused about the accompanying card which read, "Rest in Peace." The businessman apologized for the mix-up and quickly called to chastise the florist. The florist tried to console the executive. He said, "That's nothing. Somewhere in the cemetery there's a bouquet with a note reading, 'Good luck in your new location.'" [1042]

**Following Directions** Jury duty can be a mundane task and frequently calls for answering some ridiculous questions. One such question came to a gentleman who chose to give something more than a simple yes or no answer as he went through the jury selection process. The judge asked, "If you were picked for this jury, do you think you could follow instructions?" The man humorously replied, "Why, yes, I think I could, Your Honor. I've been married for forty years." [1043]

**Football** Football combines the worst elements of society: violence and committee meetings. [1044]

**Football** Our offensive line was so good that even our backs couldn't get through it. [1044]

**Football Canine** A fan of the Houston Oilers took his dog, Bonkers, to Juan's house for an afternoon of watching their favorite team. Juan was surprised to see the dog, but didn't mind. When Houston kicked a field goal, Bonkers went crazy. He barked, ran around the room, and did several rolls and flips. Juan was amazed. He asked, "If Bonkers does that for a field goal, what does he do when they score a touchdown?" The fan replied, "I don't know, I've only had him two years." [1045]

**Fountain of Youth** A young grandson was full of questions when he came to visit his grandmother. One probing question came at the dinner table after a day filled with activities. Grandma never slowed down the whole day so the little guy asked, "Are you really my grandma?" The matriarch affirmed this truth and then asked, "Why do you ask?" The amazed youngster said, "Because you look too new to be a grandma." [1046]

**Foxhole Religion** A pilot and his navigator had been shot down and were adrift at sea in their tiny lifeboat. After several days without food, water, and any hope of rescue, the pilot began to pray. He said, "God, you know I haven't lived a very good life. I've been a miserable husband and a terrible father, I've cheated, lied and stolen, and haven't had any use for the church. But God, if you'll save us from dying out here, I promise I'll never—" The navigator interrupted, "*Don't say another word!* I think I see land!" [1047]

**Free Admission** Ruby Moore was preparing her visiting grand-daughter for worship when she gave little Marsha some money for the offering. The bright four-year old contemplated the situation for a minute and then said, "I'll just go to my church instead. They don't charge you to get in." [1048]

**Fundraising** A pastor was absorbed in trying to generate more money for a new building. His most passionate appeal was scheduled for a Sunday morning with a call to commitment following his sermon. He had planned out every detail, or so he thought. Upon entering the sanctuary he panicked. He had not instructed the pianist with a specific song for the time of commitment. His mind went blank as he desperately tried to think of some appropriate music. In frustration he simply told her to pick out a song that would accentuate his stewardship drive. When the moment of commitment arrived the pastor called for the congregation to give tangible expression of their support. He said, "If you are willing to shoulder greater financial responsibility by pledging at least $100 over and above your monthly tithe, stand to your feet." He then looked to the pianist for her to begin playing an appropriate song. To his delight she started playing "The Star-Spangled Banner." [1049]

**Funeral Costs** When asked to contribute a franc to cover a stranger's burial expenses, famous writer Pierre Dumont asked who had died. Upon learning he was a tax collector, Dumont said, "Here's another franc, bury two of them." [1050]

**Gambling** When a vacationing family drove past a large dog-racing track the little boy asked what it was. The father explained, "It's a place where people go to race dogs." After a long pause the six-year-old said, "I bet the dogs always win." [1051]

**Garage Sale** When the Harrisons moved into their new home ahead of schedule, they had to undergo some minor inconveniences. The problem of moving in before the carpet was laid meant they had to move their furniture out on the driveway for a day while the carpet was installed. Late in the afternoon, Mrs. Harrison noticed a lady looking over the furniture as though it were a garage sale. She rushed out to tell the woman nothing was for sale, but before she could get the words out, this lady said, "I see all the good stuff's already been sold." [1052]

**God Talk** How do you perceive God? Years ago a little girl rode a train with her family. At night they slept in the sleeping car with the little girl on the top bunk by herself. Mom assured her they would be right below her, and God would look after her. As the darkness became quiet the little girl got scared. She called out, "Mommy, are you there?" Her mother replied, "Yes, dear." A few minutes passed and she asked her father the same question. Dad let it be known he was right below her. Several minutes later the questions were repeated and she also asked about her brother and sister. After everybody answered, "Yes," she was quiet—for a while. Later she began asking the same questions again, and another passenger lost his patience. In a deep voice he said, "We're all here! Your father, your mother, your brother, and your sister. Now GO TO SLEEP!" Complete silence followed his pronouncement. Then the little girl whispered, "Mommy, was that God?" [1053]

**Golf** While sitting in the club house, an old friend asked Dave why he no longer played golf with George. Dave said, "Would you play golf with a guy who's always improving his ball position, occasionally slips a tee under his ball in the fairway, and regularly lies about his score?" The answer from his old friend was obvious: "Certainly not!" Dave said, "Well, George won't play with a guy like that either." [1054]

**Golfing Buddies** An eighty-year-old avid golfer was becoming increasingly frustrated at his inability to see where his ball went once he hit it. Poor eyesight was about to sideline him from the game. Upon sharing this dilemma with his doctor, the physician hooked him up with a ninety-year-old man who had excellent eyesight but periodic bouts of memory loss. The doctor thought the teamwork would be good for both men. When they made it to the golf course they were each excited about the game. The eighty-year-old teed up the ball and drove it down the fairway. He quickly asked the ninety-year-old, "Did you see where it landed?" The ninety-year-old said, "Yep." "Well, where did it go?" demanded the eighty-year-old. The ninety-year-old remorsefully said, "I can't remember!" [1055]

**Golfing Hiccups** A high-strung golfer was thrown off his game because his caddie had developed a loud case of the hiccups. The problem continued for several holes as the tension mounted. On the eighteenth hole the golfer sliced his drive into a thicket of trees. He slammed his driver on the ground and yelled at his caddie, "See what you and your hiccups did?" The caddie defended himself by saying, "But sir, I didn't hiccup that time." The golfer screamed back, "That's just the point! I was compensating for it!" [1056]

**Golfing Widow** A recent ad from Midland, Texas read, "Lost: Golfing husband and dog. Last seen at Ratliff Ranch Golf Links. Reward for dog." [1057]

**Good Intentions** A businessman was scheduled for a very important meeting that required him to take a late-night train to his destination. Knowing he would most certainly be asleep when the train came to his stop, he spoke with one of the attendants and requested his help. He said, "I have the most important meeting of my life in the morning, and I cannot afford to miss it. When the train pulls into Chattanooga at 2:00 A.M. wake me up and help me off the train. I will be grumpy and beg for sleep, but do whatever it takes to get me off this train." The next morning when the man awoke he was still on the train and had missed his stop. Livid, he raged all over the porter who was supposed to have assisted him off the train. When the irate passenger stormed away, a passenger who had witnessed this tirade commented, "In all my life I have never seen anybody get so upset." The porter replied, "That's nothin,' you should have seen the guy I threw off the train at 2:00 A.M. in Chattanooga." [1058]

**Good Loser** "Show me a man who is a good loser, and I'll show you a man who is playing golf with his boss." [1059]

**Good News/Bad News** While praying over his sermon notes just moments before the morning worship service, the pastor was interrupted by an usher who was knocking on his door. The enthusiastic usher told his minister, "Pastor, you won't believe the sanctuary! It's packed! There are people in the aisles and every-where. In fact, it's so full the Fire Marshall couldn't even get through the front door." [1060]

**Good Samaritan** Peter stopped a man at the Gate of Heaven and asked him to give an account of himself. "Tell me one good thing you did in your life," demanded Peter. The man paused for a moment and then responded, "I saw a gang harassing an elderly woman, so I kicked the leader in the shins." Peter asked, "When did this happen?" The man replied, "About forty seconds ago." [1061]

**Gossip Column** Three ministers gathered to form a support group. After several weeks of building trust in one another, they began to share some of their darkest secrets. One minister con-fessed to his problem with gambling and how he would sometimes lose his concentration in a sermon when he looked down at the offering plates. The second pastor admitted to his vice of alcohol and noted his fears of being found out by his congregation. The third minister quickly piped up, "I'm a gossip, and I can't wait to get out of here." [1062]

**Grace** What a nightmare! A nominal church member had lived with the philosophy that his good works would be more than enough to get him into Heaven. One night, he dreamed of the Judgment. He was standing behind Mother Teresa. As the saintly nun was called to stand before the Lord, this presumptuous sinner overheard God say, "Teresa, I was really expecting a lot more out of you." [1063]

**Grandparents** A fast-paced executive was hoping to get some work done on a cross-country flight. He had his laptop computer running when the lady next to him struck up a conversation. Although he had a great deal of work to attend, he welcomed the brief interchange with this pleasant older woman. After several minutes of enjoyable conversation, the executive politely excused himself and said he must get back to his work. The woman was apparently oblivious to the man's need to work and continued to talk. She went from one subject to the next. The businessman tried to remain polite, so he halfway listened while continuing with his work. After nearly an hour of constant talk, the woman started digging through her purse. When she found what she was looking for, she turned to the now stressed-out executive and asked, "Did I tell you about my grandchildren?" He quickly replied, "No ma'am. And I really appreciate it!" [1064]

**Grapevine Gossip** A visiting evangelist greeted people after the opening service of a revival. The people seemed very gracious and appreciative of the sermon they had just heard. But then one lady abruptly stated, "Too long!" as she filed past the minister. She then cycled back through the line and shouted, "Too loud!" The two negative comments unnerved him a bit, but he tried to maintain his composure. When she came through a third time her comments were no more flattering. She declared, "And it was also boring!" At this point the chairman of the deacons intervened and assured the evangelist that this woman's remarks should not be taken seriously. He whispered, "Don't pay any attention to her. She's a little senile and doesn't know what she's saying. She just repeats what other people say." [1065]

**Green Bananas** An old-timer was having fun at a senior citizen's seminar when the young moderator asked him what kind of plans he had for the future. The old man said, "Honey, at my age I don't even buy green bananas." [1066]

**Headache Remedy** Six-year-old Molly complained to her mommy that her stomach hurt. Realizing it was lunch time, Mom told Molly, "Your stomach is empty; you'll feel better after you put something in it." Later that evening the pastor came over for a visit. During the conversation he mentioned he had a headache. Molly piped up with the solution: "That's because it's empty. You'll feel better once you put something in it." [1067]

**Health Insurance** Great news from the government health care package. They have finally resolved our national medical problem and without bureaucratic red tape. To enroll in our new national health care system you sign one brief form. It reads, "I hereby declare that I am not sick, never was sick, and will never get sick." [1068]

**Healthy Self-Esteem** Six-year-old Ian enthusiastically agreed to pray when dinner included his favorite dessert, shepherd's pie. He went through the usual expressions of thanks for the food and highlights of the day. Ian then added, "And thank you, God, for the nice little boy you gave this family." His mother questioned, "Nice little boy, where?" He grinned, pointed to himself, and said, "Right here. I was thanking God for me!" [1069]

**Hearing Check** After encountering considerable trouble communicating with his wife, the husband concluded the poor old gal was losing her hearing. On a mission to prove his point, he conducted a personal hearing check. While she sat on the other side of the room with her back to him, he quietly asked, "Can you hear me?" There was no response. He then moved a little closer and repeated his question. Again, no response. The self-proclaimed audiologist got even closer and asked the same question. With no reply he took his test to the back of her chair and asked, "Can you hear me now?" To his total surprise, she responded with a twinge of irritation, "For the fourth time, yes!" [1070]

**Hearing Test** Eight-year-old Brian went with his grandfather to have the car inspected. Granddad had trouble hearing the attendant, so he asked the inspector to repeat his questions several times. As they drove home, Granddaddy said, "Well, Brian, we passed the inspection." Brian responded, "Yes, we passed everything but the hearing test." [1071]

**Heaven** A Sunday School teacher asked the children in her class, "How many of you would like to go to Heaven?" All the children raised a hand except little Derrick. The teacher diplomatically inquired why he didn't want to go to Heaven. Derrick replied, "I'm sorry, Mrs. Spellman, but my mommy told me to come right home after Sunday School." [1072]

**Heavenly Suggestion Box** A new arrival in Heaven was surprised to see a suggestion box along Main Street. He turned to a more seasoned resident and asked, "If everybody is supposed to be happy in heaven, why is there a suggestion box?" The experienced tenant replied, "Because some people aren't really happy unless they can complain." [1073]

**Heavenly Wedding** Just days before their wedding, a couple was tragically killed in a car crash. Upon entering Heaven they asked if it might be possible for them to be married, since death had denied them the opportunity. Peter had no previous experience in this matter so he promised to check it out. After five years of investigation, Peter returned and told the couple they could indeed be married. The prospective bride had used these five years to better acquaint herself with the husband-to-be. She also noted the scope of eternity. So before committing herself to the marriage, she asked Peter another question. "If it doesn't work out, can we get a divorce in heaven?" Peter became enraged. For a full five minutes he told them of all the obstacles and struggles he had overcome to secure their wedding. Then he blasted them with the real kicker. "It took me five years to find a preacher up here! How long do you think it will take me to find a lawyer?" [1074]

**Helping Zeke** Daniel Webster was a great orator with a quick mind. In his early years, Webster's father left specific instructions for Daniel and his brother Ezekiel. When the elder Webster returned from a trip, the job was still unfinished. He questioned his boys about their slothfulness. "What have you been doing, Ezekiel?" "Nothing, sir," was his son's reply. The father turned to his other boy and asked, "Well, Daniel, what have you been doing?" Webster answered, "Helping Zeke, sir." [1075]

**Heroes** A junior-high teacher asked his students to make a list of who they thought were the eleven greatest living Americans. Toward the end of class one student was still struggling to finish his list. The teacher asked him how close he was to finishing. The student said, "I've got the other ten figured out, but I'm having a tough time deciding on the fullback." [1076]

**History Lesson** An excited child rushed home to tell his mother he was going to be famous. "Mom, Mom!" he shouted. "My teacher thinks I'm going to be famous." The mother inquired further and got an interesting explanation. "She said all I have to do is mess up one more time and I'm history." [1077]

**History Lesson** A kindergarten teacher was telling her students all about the Pilgrims as she prepared them for the Thanksgiving season. After one little girl had gone home and shared the details she remembered from her teacher's lesson, her mother asked if she could tell her what the Pilgrims ate during that first Thanksgiving. The little girl was stumped so she said, "I can't remember, Mommy, but you can ask my teacher. She was there!" [1078]

**Holiday Spirit** After a long day of putting on a wonderful Christmas meal, Mom was standing over the kitchen sink wearily washing the mountain of dirty dishes. In the middle of this monumental task, her teenage daughter strolled into the kitchen and saw what her mother was doing. The thoughtful girl said, "Mom, today's a holiday, you shouldn't be doing that." The mother was taken aback by the seeming kindness of her daughter. She began to put down the dishrag and take off her Platex gloves. A sense of pride overtook her as she thought her little girl was now starting to show signs of maturity by helping out with the dishes. Her bubble was burst, though, when the teenager said, "Just do them tomorrow." [1079]

**Holiday Travel** A little boy was traveling with his mother over the holidays. As they approached the airline ticket counter the little guy informed the agent that he was two years old. Suspiciously, the agent looked down at the boy and asked, "Do you know what happens to little boys who lie?" The young traveler smiled, "Yep, they get to fly for half price!" [1080]

**Hollow Threat** Two boys got into one of those "My dad's better than your dad" arguments. One boy bragged, "My dad can beat up your dad." The other kid hollowed out the threat by saying, "Big deal. So can my mom!" [1081]

**Home Improvements** Portable telephones have created a new problem for people: losing the phone. One family got so fed up with the problem of losing their portable phone that they came up with a novel idea. The wife demonstrated their solution to a friend with this explanation: "We kept losing our cordless phone, so Howard took this cord and tied it to the wall." [1082]

**Home Library** This classified ad caught the attention of quite a few folks. "For sale by owner: Complete set of *Encyclopedia Britannica*. Excellent condition. Never used; wife knows everything." [1083]

**Homesickness** The parents of an eight-year-old were having a tough time with their son going off to summer camp. They had never been away from each other for a whole week. After they hadn't heard from him in several days, they called the camp to see if he was all right. The parents were disappointed to learn that he had not missed them. Prying for some more reassuring information, his mom and dad asked, "Have any of the other children gotten homesick?" The boy said, "Only the ones who have dogs." [1084]

**Honest Confession** The boss, who had caught Calvin gazing out the window, barked, "Why aren't you working?" Without thinking, Calvin blurted, "Because I didn't see you coming." [1085]

**Honest Confession** After following the regimen of his personal trainer, an honest athlete said, "I'm finally seeing some results from my new fitness program . . . aches, pains, stiffness, and fatigue." [1086]

**Honesty** Macie Colley was enjoying a visit by her five-year-old grandson. He sat by her side as she removed her makeup and applied face cream. He asked about the stuff she was smearing on her face. She explained that it was supposed to keep the wrinkles away. He looked a little closer and said, "It doesn't work, does it?" [1087]

**Honey-Do** A minister begrudgingly agreed to clean the carpets for his wife. She had been after him to do it for months, so he went to the store to rent a machine. On his way to the store he thought of all the things he would miss on his day off because he had to do this dreaded job. By the time he reached the store he was completely depressed. He dragged himself to the customer service counter and asked if they rented carpet cleaning machines. The clerk apologetically said, "We do, but they're all checked out right now." The pastor threw his arms in the air and yelled, "Praise the Lord!" [1088]

**Honking Samaritan** A woman's car died at a stop sign and wouldn't start. The driver behind her honked his horn incessantly. She helped him regain some patience by walking back to his car and saying, "I can't seem to get my car started. Would you please see if you can start it while I sit here and lean on your horn?" [1089]

**Hourly Wages** A feisty seventy-year-old woman named Frances had to call a repairman to service her furnace. He quickly located the problem and fixed it. He handed Frances an itemized bill, which included seventy dollars for labor. She exclaimed, "Seventy dollars for labor? It only took you five minutes!" The repairman explained his company had a one hour minimum charge. To that line of reasoning Frances said, "Then I want my remaining fifty-five minutes of labor!" With that she handed him a rake and he bagged leaves for the rest of the hour. [1090]

**House** Mom and Dad overheard their children playing one day. Both kids hovered over a page filled with numbers. Big brother turned to his sister and said, "Honey, I don't know how we're going to pay all of the bills this month." The wife turned to her husband and quipped, "It sounds like the kids are playing house again." [1091]

**Husband Swapping** Writer Adela Rogers St. John observes, "I learned that there is little difference in husbands. You might as well keep the first." [1092]

**Hypocrite** A hypocrite can be defined as someone who complains that there is too much sex and violence on his VCR. [1093]

**Ice Cream To Go** While buying an ice cream cone at a Thrifty Drug store in Beverly Hills, a woman was amazed when Paul Newman walked in and stood right behind her. Although quite rattled, she was determined to maintain her composure. She paid for her ice cream cone, then confidently walked out. Outside, she realized she didn't have her cone. Not wanting to look foolish, she waited a few minutes before reentering the store. When she didn't find her ice cream cone at the counter, she paused to contemplate where it could be. A soft tap on the shoulder interrupted her thoughts. She turned to find Paul Newman. He politely told her if she was looking for her ice cream cone, she had put it in her purse. [1094]

**Impoverished Pastor** As the offering plate was passed, a little boy held tightly to the money in his hand. After the service he headed straight for the pastor and handed him the quarter. The minister asked, "Why didn't you put this in the offering plate?" The little boy said, "I wanted to make sure you got it, because I know you really need it. My daddy said you're the poorest preacher he's ever heard." [1095]

**Income Tax** Albert Einstein once admitted, "Of all the things in this universe, the most difficult to understand is the income tax." [1096]

**Inerrancy** While reading her Bible on a public bus, a bashful Christian was confronted by a belligerent man. He boldly asked if she believed everything in the Bible. She affirmed she did. He then said, "If you believe everything, then explain to me how Jonah lived for three days in the belly of a whale!" The unassuming woman answered, "I don't know, but I believe he did." The man became more agitated. "Lady, you should be able to explain what you believe!" She quietly repeated her inability to know exactly how Jonah survived but noted she would ask him once she got to heaven. Sarcastically, the rude guy queried, "And what if Jonah didn't make it to heaven?" She replied, "Then you ask him." [1097]

**Inflation** A father aired some of his frustrations over the inflation of our economy. He said, "It doesn't bother me that my son makes more money per week than I did on my first job. What gripes me is he's just six years old, and we're talking about his allowance." [1098]

**Inflation** In response to his father's lecture on finances, the little boy said, "Of course I know the value of a dollar, Dad. That's why I asked for ten dollars." [1099]

**Inspired Resignation** At the close of their morning worship service, the pastor stood to read his resignation. It had all the usual rhetoric and platitudes you might expect. He then concluded his prepared statement by saying, "The same Jesus who led me to you, is now leading me to another church." The minister of music then stepped to the podium and led the congregation in singing, "What a Friend We Have in Jesus." [1100]

**Instant Recovery** A farmer was driving his pickup with his dog in the seat next to him and a horse trailer in tow behind him. On a dangerous curve, the farmer was forced off the road by a large truck. A highway patrolman happened upon the accident and quickly assessed the damages. When he saw that the dog and horse were suffering, the patrolman pulled out his revolver and put them out of their misery. He then walked over to the farmer and asked, "How are you doing?" The farmer looked at the smoking pistol and then quickly replied, "I've never felt better!" [1101]

**Invisible God** A Sunday School teacher tried to communicate that Jesus is always with us, even though we can't see him. One four-year-old claimed to understand the concept. He said, "I know who he is. He's the one who opens the doors at the grocery store." [1102]

**June Bride** A wedding guest bubbled over with accolades to the bride as she passed through the receiving line. She said, "Oh, you look so lovely, my dear. I'm so pleased that Jeff chose you to be his wife." Then she whispered into the young bride's ear, "Whatever happened to that dizzy blonde he used to date?" The new wife whispered back, "I dyed my hair." [1103]

**Junk Mail** In response to her husband's comment, a wife piped, "Junk mail? Are you kidding? This is from Ed McMahon!" [1104]

**Just Watch the Hair** Ordination services can be confusing for children. One child observed the process of men filing by to lay hands on a candidate. After watching this for several minutes, the little boy blurted out to his mother, "Mommy, why do they keep messing up that man's hair?" [1105]

**Language Barrier** Pancho was a well-known outlaw to Texans. One lesser-known story involves his near demise in a Mexican bar. A tough Texas Ranger had trailed him through the desert and caught up with Pancho in a small village. With both guns drawn, the ranger approached the criminal and ordered him to turn over the one million dollars he had recently robbed from a train. From the other side of the bar a small man said, "Señor, Pancho does not speak English. I am his translator." The ranger told the man, "Tell Pancho I came to get the one million dollars he robbed from that train. If he doesn't hand over the money, I'll fill him full of holes." The man translated. Frightened, Pancho told the interpreter the money was two miles outside of town buried thirty paces east of an old abandoned well. The translator turned to the armed ranger and said, "Pancho says, 'I'm not telling—go ahead and shoot.'" [1106]

**Last Shall Be First** Things didn't go so well during those early days of the Dallas Cowboys. The newly-formed expansion team endured some rather severe thrashings on the field. The numerous losses were often blamed on Tom Landry. His critics accused him of not having enough enthusiasm and not getting his players pumped up for the game. On one particular day the sportswriters were amazed to see the Cowboys come roaring out of the locker room and race across the field. The aggressive sports hounds caught Landry on his way to the field and asked what he said to get the players so charged up. Landry replied, "It was easy. I said, 'The last eleven guys to the bench have to start.'" [1107]

**Last Words** The smooth, debonair trickster had come to his end. His hands were tied, and he was led in front of the firing squad. The overweight officer who was supervising the execution asked the young man, "Do you have any last requests?" The ever-calm convict said, "I do. Would you stand in front of me?" [1108]

**Laziness** The retired husband was in his usual position—lying on the couch. When he awakened from his nap, he looked at his watch. The second hand was no longer moving, and the time was obviously wrong. He called out to his wife, who was working in the kitchen. He said, "This watch doesn't work anymore." She immediately shot back, "At least it's in good company!" [1109]

**Leadership** The trouble with being a leader today is that you can't be sure whether people are following you or chasing you. [1110]

**Learning Curve** Leonard Workman of Wichita, Kansas, asked his grandson each day after school what he had learned. After a few days of this regimen, the little student said, "Grandpa, I wish you would stop asking me that question. When I learn something, I'll tell you." [1111]

**Life Insurance** A very nervous airline passenger began pacing the terminal when the bad weather delayed his flight. During his walk, he ran across one of those life insurance machines. It offered $100,000 in the event of an untimely death aboard his flight. The policy was just three dollars. He looked out the window at the threatening clouds and thought of his family at home. For that price it was foolish not to buy, so he took out the coverage. He then looked for a place to eat. Airports now carry a good variety of eateries so he settled on his favorite, Chinese. It was a relaxing meal until he opened his fortune cookie. It read: "Your recent investment will pay big dividends." [1112]

**Listening Techniques** Two psychiatrists met at their twentieth college reunion. One looked as though he had just graduated. The other appeared weary, worn, and much older than his colleague. The aged one asked, "What's your secret? Listening to other people's problems every day for all of these years has made an old man out of me." The spry-looking doctor replied, "Who listens?" [1113]

**Long Hair** One father was in great anguish as he told his friend, "I finally talked my son into cutting his hair, but I'm sorry I did. Now I can see his earrings." [1114]

**Love Is Blind** As the daughter brought in her date to meet her parents, the mother was terrified by the young man's tattoos, long hair, beard, earring, heavy boots, and overall rough appearance. In concern, she pulled her daughter aside and asked, "Honey, is he nice?" The girl was taken aback by such a question from her mother. She said, "Of course he's nice. If he wasn't nice, why would he be doing five thousand hours of community service?" [1115]

**Loyalty** A young executive was on the fast track to success. The corporate boss liked his drive and tenacity. To show his approval of the up-and-coming young man, the president ceremoniously gave him a lapel pin with the company's logo. Several weeks later they passed in the hallway and the pin was not on the young man's suit. The senior executive was troubled and asked, "Did you lose your pin?" The young, aspiring executive looked at his lapel and said, "Whoops! I must have left it on my pajamas." [1116]

**Magnetic Mom** After an elementary teacher had given her class a science lesson on magnets, she gave them a quiz to see how much they had learned. One of the questions read: "My name starts with

'M,' has six letters, and I pick up things. What am I?" Half the class answered with the six-letter word, "Mother." [1117]

**Make-Believe** Little four-year-old Preston was being asked by his grandmother to pick up the toys that were cluttering his room. Preston then suggested they play "make-believe." He said, "Granny, why don't you play make-believe and pretend like someone is helping you pick up the toys?" [1118]

**Makeup Mileage** While watching their mother apply her makeup, the older and astute big brother gave his little sibling a comparative education: "It's sorta like turning back the mileage on a car." [1119]

**Manners** At a birthday party it was time to serve the cake. A little boy named Brian knew he wanted the biggest piece of cake so he blurted out, "I want the biggest piece!" His mother quickly said, "Brian, it's not polite to ask for the biggest piece." The little guy looked around in confusion and then asked, "Well, then, how do I get it?" [1120]

**Marital Mistake** Classified ad: "For sale, cheap, one wedding dress, size ten. Worn only once by mistake." [1121]

**Marital Virtues** Humorist W. E. Thorn has noted, "Marriage is an institution that teaches man regularity, frugality, temperance, forbearance, and many other splendid virtues he wouldn't need if he had stayed single." [1122]

**Marriage** "Man is not complete until he's married; then he's finished." — *W. E. Thorn* [1123]

**Marriage** Credit Alan King for saying, "Marriage is nature's way of keeping people from fighting strangers." [1124]

**Marriage Ability** Three-year-old Jeremy announced he was going to marry Amy, his ten-year-old sister. When his mother explained that brothers and sisters can't marry, he said, "Then I'll marry Jackie." Jackie was a neighborhood girl whom Mom thought might not be Jeremy's best choice, so she added, "But Jeremy, Jackie is kind of bossy." He got excited and said, "You mean the way you boss Daddy?" [1125]

**Marriage Compatibility** The couple was at their wit's end. They could not get along and were trying to communicate how frustrating their marriage had become. The woman finally blurted out to the counselor, "We have absolutely nothing in common. In fact, we don't even hate the same people!" [1126]

**Marriage Counseling** After months of working with a fighting couple, the marriage counselor saw a ray of hope when the wife addressed her husband as "Hon." "There's still hope for this marriage if you can call him 'Hon,'" the skilled counselor pointed out. "Huh! I've been calling him that for years," said the wife. "Attila the Hun." [1127]

**Marriage Counseling** Dr. Pullman's Marriage Counseling office is a frequently-visited cartoon frame for the struggling Lockhorns. Leroy's attitude gives you a pretty good idea why they see Dr. Pullman so often. Says the compassionate and sensitive husband, "I'm just here to find out what Loretta's problem is." [1128]

**Marriage Counseling** A distraught man brought his wife to see the pastor. The woman was listless and unresponsive. After about thirty minutes of futile attempts to counsel them, the pastor walked over to the woman, pulled her from the chair, wrapped his arms around her and gave her a passionate kiss. The pastor turned to the husband and said, "There, that's all she needs, about three times a week." The man replied, "But Pastor, I can only bring her in on Thursdays." [1129]

**Marriage Options** A frustrated young man was desperately pursuing the woman of his dreams. Unfortunately for him, he was not the man of her dreams. He pleaded with her to marry him but had no success. He asked, "Why won't you marry me? Is there someone else?" She promptly replied, "There's got to be!" [1130]

**McHeaven** When my daughter, Meagan, was four years old she asked a lot of questions about death. During a trip to Dallas, we promised her a roadside stop at McDonald's. Although we frequented the "Golden Arches" too regularly, each visit was a thrill to her. As we began our much-anticipated lunch, Meagan asked one of her profound questions. "When you die, does Jesus take you to McDonald's?" I'm sure Ray Kroc chuckled from his grave. [1131]

**Medical Bills** The doctor noticed his patient was concerned about the impending surgery. In an attempt to calm his patient, the doctor told this man he was not alone in his struggles. "I know the stress you must feel right now. Life is pinching in on me too. I'm trying to figure out how I will pay for my daughter's wedding and my son's college at the same time." The patient became rather still and quiet. He then broke the silence by asking the doctor, "Am I paying for the wedding or the college?" [1132]

**Medical Bills** A doctor demonstrated some creative bedside manners when he told his patient, "What you have is so rare, we have no idea how much to charge you." [1133]

**Memory Lapse** An employee returned to the same downstairs office three times in a matter of minutes. After the fourth trip to retrieve something else she had forgotten, the absentminded woman muttered, "Pretty soon I'll be able to hide my own Easter eggs." [1134]

**Men** Robert Orben noted, "In 1492, Columbus set out for the Orient and ended up in the Caribbean, and thus set a pattern that has continued for over five hundred years. Men still won't ask for directions." [1135]

**Men and Women** During a long-range planning meeting one woman came up with a great idea. One of the male committee members joked, "It's a miracle that a woman would have such a great idea." Another woman shot back, "The miracle is that a man would recognize such a great idea." [1136]

**Mid-life Crisis** A father asked his daughter, "What do you want to be when you grow up?" The pre-teen replied, "I don't know, Dad. . . . what do you want to be when you grow up?" [1137]

**Middle Names** Dennis Fakes noted, "Any child can tell you that the sole purpose of a middle name is so he can tell when he's really in trouble." [1138]

**Ministerial Cuisine** An old farmer invited the minister over for lunch after their Sunday morning service. Since the farmer lived in a rather hard to find place, he left his seven-year-old son to ride with the minister, while the farmer and his wife went home to set the table and prepare the lunch. After the minister had shaken everyone's hand and closed up the church, he and the little boy got into the car and started for the house. The minister, new to the area, was glad for the opportunity to get acquainted with the boy and his family. The minister asked what they were having for lunch. The boy said, "Buzzard." The minister asked the boy, "Are you sure? Buzzard?" The boy nodded and said, "Dad told Mom we were having the ol' buzzard for lunch today." [1139]

**Ministerial Dilemma** A little girl answered the phone when a marketing sales representative placed an unsolicited call to her house. The agent asked if the man of the house were home. The girl said, "My daddy is a minister and he's just been offered a church in another town that wants to pay him a lot more money than he makes here. So he's in his study praying about it." The salesperson en asked if her mother was available. The girl replied, "No, she's packing." [1140]

**Ministerially Speaking** A minister was making some repairs on his home when he noticed the neighbor's little boy was paying very close attention to the job. The pastor asked, "Are you getting some pointers on carpentry, Harold?" The little observer replied, "No sir. I'm just waiting to see what a preacher says when he smashes his thumb with a hammer." [1141]

**Miracles** An unchurched teenager attended worship services with his church-going friend. When he returned home, his dad asked him what he had learned. The student said, "Well, the pastor told about the Egyptians chasing the Jews to the Red Sea. Real fast, the Jews built a bridge and got over the water just before the Egyptians showed up. When Pharaoh's army tried to cross the bridge, the Jews blew it up and all the Egyptian soldiers drowned." The dad questioned his son, "You mean the pastor actually told you that?" The young man answered, "Not exactly, but the way he told it, you'd never believe it." [1142]

**Mom and Rover** A doting mother tried unsuccessfully to kiss her teenage son good-bye as he set off for school. She waved to him from the door as he walked across the yard. Just before reaching the gate, he bent over to give their dog a hug. As she stepped back into the house, she told her husband, "I guess tomorrow I'll try barking." [1143]

**Mom's Favorite Book** A demanding woman on the church roll insisted that the pastor come by to visit her. When he arrived, she sat on the couch and told of all her woes. After listening to her long monologue of complaints, the pastor suggested he read some scripture for consolation. The woman quickly agreed and piously called out for her daughter, "Honey, bring mother the book she loves so much." The little girl immediately returned with her mom's favorite book, the latest edition of *TV Guide.* [1144]

**Mom's Stress** Two husbands sat on the park bench watching their children play while their wives strolled along in the grass. One man commented on his wife's temper. He said, "She gets mad at little things . . . like, children." [1145]

**Mommy Noises** Chery Webster overheard her eighteen-month-old daughter rehearsing some noises she had learned. The little girl said, "Sheep . . . baaa. Cow . . . mooo. Doggie . . . woof woof. Mama . . . no, no, no!" [1146]

**Money** Jack Benny, that comedian who always acted the part of a miser, told of the time he was held up. The robber stuck a gun to his back and said, "Your money or your life." After a long pause the robber repeated his threat, to which Benny replied, "I'm thinking, I'm thinking!" [1147]

**Monogamy** A little boy was trying to impress his mother with a new word he picked up in Sunday School. He explained in serious tones to his mom, "A Christian man can only have one wife. That's called monotony." [1148]

**Motherhood** While standing at attention during a parade, a private started waving to someone in the audience. The drill sergeant sternly warned the private, "Jones, don't ever do that again!" A few minutes later, though, the private waved again. When the parade was over, the livid sergeant started screaming at Jones. He pointed out the dangers of disobeying a superior and gave a few severe threats. Jones still seemed unremorseful. The instructor then yelled, "Boy, aren't you afraid of me and what I could do to you?" Jones replied, "Oh, yes, sir! But you don't know my mother!" [1149]

**Motherhood** The mother of three notorious kids was asked, "If you had it to do all over again, would you have children?" "Sure," she said, "but not the same ones." [1150]

**Motherhood** A zealous little boy was pledging his devotion to his mother when he began to brag of what he would do for her when he grew up. "Mom, when I grow up I'm going to buy you an electric can opener, an electric toaster, an electric stove, and an electric chair." [1151]

**Motherhood** "The joy of motherhood is what a woman experiences when all the children have gone to bed." [1152]

**Motherhood** A little girl wanted her daddy to tell her a story. He wove together a fine tale that involved slaves. After he finished his story, she asked, "What's a slave, Daddy?" He explained it the best that he could. When he was through, the little girl looked up at her daddy and asked, "Is that what Mommy is?" [1153]

**Mothers** Ivern Ball of Mansfield, Arkansas tells the story of her grandson Kelly's experience in kindergarten. Kelly's teacher happened to walk by just as he was struggling with a pair of bulky rain boots. The teacher overheard Kelly muttering in disgust, "Mothers! They're never around when you need them." [1154]

**Namesake** "I'm sure glad Mommy named me Ashley." "Why?" asked her brother. "Because that's what everyone calls me!" [1155]

**Narcissism** A narcissist football player was standing on the sidelines when someone from the stands yelled out, "Hey, John." The player scanned the stadium but could not see the fan. Several minutes later the same thing happened again: "Hey, John!" Still no luck in locating the vocal fan. After this went on several more times the player turned to the calling fan and shouted back, "My name's not John!" [1156]

**Nativity Seat** A three-year-old was helping his mother unpack their nativity set. He announced each piece as he unwrapped it from the tissue paper. "Here's the donkey!" "Here's a king!" When he got to the infant molded in a manger he proclaimed, "Here's baby Jesus in his car seat!" [1157]

**Negative Imaging** A guy blew a tire while driving through the country. To his chagrin, there was no jack in his trunk. Looking down the dark road he saw a distant farmhouse with a light on. It was his only recourse, so he started walking. During his journey he started thinking, "What if nobody's home?" A little later he thought, "What if they're home, but they don't have a jack?" His adrenaline started pumping even more when he asked himself, "What if they have a jack but won't let me use it?" This private conversation escalated to the point that when he finally arrived at the house, he simply yelled at the farmer, "You can just keep your stupid jack!" [1158]

**Nest Egg** When a retired woman entered the door with arm-loads of packages, her husband became overly concerned about their financial well-being. He expressed his concern by saying, "With all of these packages I can't help but wonder what's happening to our nest egg." The woman snapped back, "I'll tell you what's happening to our nest egg. This old hen got tired of sitting on it!" [1159]

**New Year's Resolutions** As the couple sat with a marriage counselor for their first session, the good doctor asked them to identify what seemed to be the root of their problems. The wife responded, "It all started when we thought it would be cute to think up each other's New Year's resolutions." [1160]

**Nice Comeback** A priest badgered a rabbi friend of his, saying, "Come on, when are you going to let yourself go and enjoy a piece of ham?" The rabbi fired back, "At your wedding!" [1161]

**No-Win Situation** Old habits die hard. One guy invariably left off the cap to the toothpaste, and for years his wife hounded him about it. Finally, on their twenty-fifth anniversary, he privately committed to break the annoying habit. Faithfully and regularly, he screwed on the toothpaste cap every time he used it. After a week of unbroken success the poor guy was blindsided by his suspicious wife. She cornered him at the breakfast table and said, "Why did you stop brushing your teeth?" [1162]

**Noah Syndrome** The doctor told a bloated man that he had what was commonly called the "Noah Syndrome." The horrified patient relaxed when the doctor told him there was a cure: "When you sit down to eat, stop taking two of everything." [1163]

**Obligatory Prayer** When Russell Dilday was the President of Southwestern Seminary, he received letters from some young Girls in Action. Although grateful for the correspondence of these girls, Dr. Dilday humorously realized some letters were written out of obligation. This was best represented by a little Texan who wrote: "I am writing you because it is a step in my G.A. book. I'm supposed to pray for you, I will." [1164]

**Old Age** Inside every older person there's a younger person wondering, "What happened?" [1165]

**Old Age** One day after school, a boy from Moberly, Missouri struck up a conversation with his neighbor, the late P. R. Lucas. The boy asked Mr. Lucas how old he was. "Pap" Lucas volleyed the question back with, "How old do you think I am?" The young boy answered, "About thirty-seven." Mr. Lucas shocked him with the truth, "I'm eighty-six years old." In amazement the little guy said, "Golly Mister, you're old enough to be dead!" [1166]

**Old Age** Talk about old! One pastor was said to be so old that he knew the Dead Sea when it was just sick.[1167]

**Omnipresence** A burglar had done an excellent job of casing the house. When the family left on vacation, he knew his heist would be easy. He entered the house just like planned but was startled by an unsuspected voice. It said, "Jesus sees you." He initially panicked but realized nobody could be home. This voice repeated the phrase, and he shined his flashlight in the general direction. To his delight, it was nothing more than a talking parrot. He relaxed and turned on the main light switch. To his horror, he saw a huge Doberman pinscher crouched in the corner. Then came the voice of the parrot again: "Sic 'em, Jesus." [1168]

**Opposition** A man celebrating his hundredth birthday was approached by a news reporter who remarked, "I suppose you've seen a lot of changes in your day." "Yes," said the centenarian, "and I've been against every one of them." [1169]

**Optimism** You can call yourself an optimist if you think the "E" on your gas gauge stands for "Enough." [1170]

**Optimist** During a very trying deacons' meeting, the pastor, who was an eternal optimist, tried to break the tension by proclaiming, "We shouldn't look at our situation like this. These aren't problems, they're opportunities." The disgruntled chairman quickly stifled the pastor's enthusiasm by retorting, "If that's the case, then pastor—we've got a church full of opportunities." [1171]

**Optimist Hunters** The sum of five thousand dollars was offered as a bounty for each wolf captured alive. Sam and Jed saw dollar signs, so they became overnight bounty hunters. They scoured the mountains day and night in search of their fortune. After several days of unsuccessful hunting, they fell asleep from exhaustion. In the middle of the night, Sam suddenly awoke to see that they were surrounded by fifty wolves with flaming eyes and bared teeth. He nudged his partner and whispered, "Jed, wake up! We're rich!" [1172]

**Out-of-Body Experience** The large and flabby philosopher told his doctor he had had an out-of-body experience. The wise doctor fixed his gaze on the man's sagging stomach and replied, "I don't blame you!" [1173]

**Out of Shape** Some of us may feel like Jeremy Hyams, the English forty-eight-year-old marathon runner. When commenting on his physique Hyams said, "I have the body of a man half my age. Unfortunately, he's in terrible shape." [1174]

**Out of Sight, Out of Mind** Two friends were sitting together on a crowded city bus. One noticed that the other had his eyes closed. He was concerned that the large crowd and warm weather were making his friend ill. He quietly turned to his friend and asked, "Are you getting sick?" The other man never opened his eyes but solemnly responded, "I'm all right. I just hate to see so many ladies standing!" [1175]

**Over My Dead Body** A little boy was fascinated with motorcycles and always noticed them when they passed his way. Every time he saw one, he would get excited and say, "I'm going to get one of those someday." His dad's standard response was always, "Not as long as I'm alive." This dialogue transpired nearly every time the boy saw a motorcycle in his dad's presence. One day the little guy was with a friend when a motorcycle came screaming toward them. The young enthusiast pointed to the approaching bike and shouted, "Look at that motorcycle. I'm going to get one of those as soon as my dad dies." [1176]

**Overpriced Church** Pastor Bob Dodridge thought taking his two visiting nephews to church would be a great and noble deed. Neither of the boys, aged six and nine, had any church experience, so Bob looked forward to exposing them to spiritual matters. The stark reality of growing up outside of the church showed itself when the boys came down for the children's sermon. In the middle of Pastor Bob's homily to kids, his six-year-old nephew Eric raised his hand and blurted out, "How much longer do we have to stay up here?" Pastor Bob pressed on. Eric was still not impressed with what he had seen. This became most evident when the offering plates were passed. Little Eric watched with keen interest as the plate made its way toward him. When it reached his hands he asked in an audible voice, "You mean we gotta pay for this?" [1177]

**Painful Diet** An unmotivated husband joined his wife for a diet after their holiday eating binge. His wife was very zealous about losing weight, but her husband was not. She challenged him with motivational speeches that would have made Vince Lombardi proud. One night, she caught him eyeing a piece of pecan pie that was left over from their pre-diet days. She shouted with the force of a drill sergeant, "Remember, if you cheat on your diet you're only hurting yourself!" When she left the kitchen he stuck the pie in his mouth and said, "Ouch." [1178]

**Paperwork** An elderly woman was given a stack of papers to fill out when she entered the admitting office of a hospital. She patiently waited her turn for a hospital official to see her. When asked, she handed the official her insurance card and all of the admitting paper work. When she was asked to give the reason for coming to the hospital she said, "Just to visit a friend, but this has taken so long, I'm not sure I have time now." [1179]

**Pardon Me** While Ginny Dow's father was in the hospital he shared a room with a man who used vulgar language. Mr. Dow had a stream of visitors from church who noticed the man's expletives. After hearing a string of profanity during one visit, several men read Scripture and prayed . When the visitors left, the roommate uncorked some more words to accentuate his apology. "If I'd known one of those guys was a minister, I'd have watched my $%@#! language." You could hear him gulp when Dow replied, "They're the deacons in the church. I'm the minister." [1180]

**Parent Night** A Florida church holding monthly events for the entire family had trouble with parents dropping their kids off and not staying for the various events. They remedied the problem with this announcement: "*The Magic of Lassie*, a film for the whole family, will be shown Sunday at 5:00 P.M. Free puppies will be given to all children not accompanied by their parents." [1181]

**Parental Report Card** A teenage son came home with another bad report card. Although he didn't ace psychology, he'd learned enough to rattle his dad. "What do you think caused the bad grades this time, Dad? Heredity or environment?" [1182]

**Parking Spots** As an elderly woman prepared to park her large expensive car, a young college student cut her off and stole her parking spot. The young driver jumped from his car and sarcastically said, "Oh to be young and fast." But when the student returned to his car, he was appalled. The old woman was using her big car as a battering ram to demolish his little car. The lady powered down her window and smiled, "Oh to be old and rich." [1183]

**Pastors** Howard Hendricks summed up the difference between a pastor and a layman. "Pastors are paid to be good. Laymen are good for nothing." [1184]

**Peer Pressure** Sharon Clausen, of West Chicago, was having trouble with her five-year-old son, Taylor. He insisted on wearing the same types of clothes his friends wore. After many unsuccessful attempts to steel him against peer pressure, Sharon blurted, "Taylor, Jesus is our leader. We follow him, not our friends." After consideration, Taylor responded, "Okay, Mom, what's Jesus wearing?" [1185]

**Personnel Problems** This sign was posted in a personnel office: "We had to cancel our ad seeking responsible, mature adults. The court ruled that it discriminated against irresponsible, immature adults." [1186]

**Pessimism** An old grouch was approached by an equally-aged but far more enthusiastic friend. The lively senior asked his less cheerful friend why he always had to see the proverbial glass as half-empty. The pessimist quickly corrected his upbeat friend. "I don't always see the glass as half-empty. Most of the time, it's completely empty." [1187]

**Pessimist** Two duck hunters were known for their contrasting outlooks on life. One was an eternal optimist, while the other lived out the role of the ever-negative pessimist. The optimist set out to get a positive response from his hunting partner by taking the off-season to train his dog to retrieve fallen ducks by walking on water. His dog didn't just swim out to get the ducks, he literally walked on the water. When opening day arrived, the optimist couldn't wait to show off his dog. He got his chance as he shot down the first duck that flew over. Confident that his dog would generate a positive remark from his pessimistic friend, he sent his dog after the duck. Just like he had been trained, the dog walked out on the water and brought back the duck. The hunter beamed with pride at his negative pal only to hear him say, "Got a dog who can't swim, huh?" [1188]

**Pet Peeves** A first-grade teacher named Mrs. Foster had trouble with one of her students. She called the boy aside and chided him for his behavior, saying, "You've really hit on some of my pet peeves." The boy looked confused. Mrs. Foster asked him whether he knew anything about a pet peeve. He said, "No," so she explained, "A pet peeve is the thing that irritates a person the most. Do you know what my pet peeve is?" The little guy guessed, "Is it Mr. Foster?" [1189]

**Pilot's License** A newspaper photographer in Los Angeles was called in by his editor and told a fire was raging out of control in Palos Verdes, a hilly area south of L.A. The editor told him to board a waiting plane at a nearby airport and get some pictures for the evening edition. The reporter raced off to his assignment and found the plane just as his boss had described. He jumped into the plane and yelled, "Let's go." When they approached the raging fire, the reporter pulled out his camera and told the guy behind the controls to swoop down near the flames so he could get some good pictures. The man looked surprised and asked, "Why?" Rather perturbed at this inquiry the reporter snapped back, "Because I'm a newspaper photographer and photographers take pictures." After a few moments of deft silence his cockpit companion stuttered, "You-u-u mean you're not the flight instructor?" [1190]

**Pointless Preaching** A minister was conscious of the lengthy sermon he delivered last Sunday. In an attempt to console his congregation and assure them that this week would be different, he said, "To compensate for last week's sermon of twenty points, this week's sermon will be pointless." [1191]

**Political Jargon** In a political debate, a candidate rallied the crowd by setting up his opponent. The smooth politician said, "There are hundreds of ways to make money, but only one way is honest." His opponent retorted sarcastically, "And what way is that?" "Aha!" gloated the victorious candidate, "I knew you wouldn't know." [1192]

**Political Paradise** As fate would have it, George Bush, Bill Clinton, and Ross Perot died simultaneously. As they stood before Peter at the eternal gate, the former fisherman asked them their names. Bush gave his name and mentioned he had been President of the United States. Peter said, "You sit on my right side." Clinton identified himself and explained he was the current U.S. President. Peter instructed him to sit on his left side. The Apostle then turned to Perot and said, "Who are you?" The billionaire retorted, "I'm Ross Perot, and you're sitting in my seat!" [1193]

**Politically Correct** In case you are attempting to be "politically correct," here are a few corrections you might want to consider.

Say "vertically challenged" instead of "short." "Economically marginalized" replaces "poor." Just as the stupid are now "cerebrally challenged," the old are "chronologically gifted." Use "client of the correctional system" rather than "inmate." "Follicularly challenged" is preferred over "bald." There are no longer any lazy people, just those who are "motivationally dispossessed." Say "non-waged," never "unemployed." Someone you incorrectly called "fat" is now a "person of substance." Although it may look like a bankrupt savings and loan, it is actually a "fiscally challenged institution." And of course, your deacons are "aesthetically challenged"—not ugly. [1194]

**Politician** In a prestigious argument, a surgeon, an architect, and a politician debated over whose profession was the oldest. The surgeon boasted, "Eve was made from Adam's rib. That was surgery!" "Maybe so," said the architect, "but before that, order was created from chaos, and that was the work of an architect." The politician quickly saw his cue and said, "But who do you think created the chaos?" [1195]

**Possibility Thinking** During a late evening jog, a man took a shortcut to his house through a large cemetery. In the darkness of the night he did not see a freshly dug grave, and fell into it. For the better part of the next hour he struggled to climb out. He tried every conceivable maneuver but just couldn't escape. Finally, he resigned himself to curling up in the corner and waiting for morning. Within the next thirty minutes another late-night jogger suffered the same fate and fell into the same grave. He tried to quickly climb out but fell down on his first attempt. The first jogger then put his hand on the shoulder of the other man and said, "You can't get out." But he did! [1196]

**Postage Increase** When the postal service raised its first class postage from 29 cents to 32 cents, one guy figured out why they had an increase: "The extra three cents is for storage." [1197]

**Power Play** A father and son were discussing the difficulties of life in typical fashion: the son was complaining and the father was explaining how easy the boy had it compared to his early years. Dad pulled out the old, "When I was your age I had to walk five miles to school in the snow." From across the room, Granddad topped them both by saying, "That's nothing! When I was your age, they didn't even have school. We had to walk five miles in the snow, then turn around and come back home." [1198]

**Prayer** Betty Traver always tries to instill in her children the need for prayer. Years ago, a perfect opportunity for prayer arose in their 1956 station wagon. They were setting off on an errand when the old clunker refused to start. Seizing the moment, Betty turned to her four-year-old son and asked him to pray. Closing his eyes tightly, he prayed, "Dear Lord, please help this piece of junk start." [1199]

**Prayer** Dad thundered his intent to punish his misbehaving son with a good old-fashioned trip to the woodshed. The father grabbed his son by the arm, saying, "Boy, you'd better say your prayers." In response the boy said, "I need something faster than prayer. . . . Does God have a fax number?" [1200]

**Prayer** The small boy continued his bedtime prayers with, ". . . now I'd like to tell you about some things I'm *not* thankful for." [1201]

**Prayer Volunteer** When it was evident that the ship would not survive this storm, the captain called out to his crew, "Does anyone here know how to pray?" One man volunteered with, "Yes, sir, I know how to pray." "Good," the captain replied. "You pray while the rest of us put on our life jackets. We're one short." [1202]

**Pride** The legendary coach of the Green Bay Packers, Vince Lombardi, became accustomed to fans seeking his autograph. One day while eating at a public restaurant, he spotted a kid approaching his table. Lombardi grabbed a menu and quickly scribbled his name. When the kid got to Lombardi's table, the coach handed him the autographed menu. The youngster said, "I don't need a menu. I just need to borrow your ketchup." [1203]

**Prison Reform** A prison official met a busload of new prisoners in the main courtyard of the detention facility. He addressed them as follows: "Gentlemen, the world will be a better place because you are here today." [1204]

**Profanity** During his first day in school, a little boy was caught saying an inappropriate word. The teacher quickly scolded him and asked where he had heard such a word. The little boy said, "My daddy says it all the time." "Well, that doesn't matter. You shouldn't being using that word. Besides, you don't even know what it means," said the reprimanding teacher. "I do so," said the little boy. "It means the car won't start." [1205]

**Professional Student** A first-grader sullenly approached his teacher on the first day of school, obviously distraught. The teacher asked him about his problem. The little guy said, "I don't like school, and I just found out I have to stay until I'm eighteen." The teacher consoled him by sharing a little frustration of her own: "That's not that bad. I have to stay until I'm sixty-five!" [1206]

**Psychiatric Help** Two psychiatric patients had become friends through their mutual contact with the same doctor. Once they saw each other at the doctor's office. One asked the other, "Are you coming or going?" The other one grumped, "If I knew that, I wouldn't be here." [1207]

**Psychiatric Help** "Are your visits to the psychiatrist helping?" asked a friend. "Absolutely," was the reply. "Before I sought his help I was afraid to answer the phone. Now I answer it whether it's ringing or not." [1208]

**Punch Lines** A young minister was losing his congregation to sleep during a dry sermon. To revive the sleeping flock he said, "I lived with a woman for seventeen years who was not my wife." The crowd quickly woke up. He then said, "It was my mother." A visiting minister was amused by the tactic and planned to try it on his own congregation when he returned home from vacation. On his first Sunday back in the pulpit he opened with the same line he heard the other minister use. He said, "For seventeen years I lived with a woman who was not my wife." He then hesitated with the punch-line as his mind went blank. Finally, after an awkward silence, he confessed, "For the life of me, though, I can't remember who she was." [1209]

**Puppy Love** After Sunday School, two small boys were standing in the church lobby. As they were talking, a pretty girl from their class walked by them. One of the little guys said to the other, "When I stop hating girls, she's the first one I'm going to quit hating." [1210]

**Purpose Statement** While walking through the office of his boss, an employee turned and said, "I've been here fifteen years, Mr. Ferguson, and don't get me wrong, they've been wonderful years, but just exactly what is it we do around here?" [1211]

**Quick Education** Four-year-old Jack was screaming at the top of his lungs. When his mother came running into the bedroom, she found Jack's two-year-old sister pulling Jack's hair. The mother tried to calm Jack and help him understand the situation. She said, "Honey, your little sister doesn't know that hurts." Within a few minutes she heard Jack's little sister scream. Jack ran out of the bedroom with a big smile and told his mom, "She knows now." [1212]

**Quick Exit** A recent "scholar" has postulated the reasoning for Jesus ascending so quickly after giving the Great Commission. The scholar speculates Jesus made a quick exit because he didn't want to stick around for the debate. [1213]

**Quiet Please** A young man was enjoying the loud sound of his new car speakers when he pulled up to a stoplight. In the convertible next to him, a guy waved at him frantically, motioning for him to turn down the stereo. The neighboring driver shouted over the loud music, "Turn it down! Can't you see I'm on the phone?" [1214]

**Rationalization** Julie Bianchin's three-year-old daughter, Sarah, was caught jumping on the bed by her grandmother. When Grandmom asked if she was allowed to do this, Sarah replied, "Oh sure, as long as Mom isn't in the room." [1215]

**Recreational Adjustment** Retired sportswriter Jim Reed wrote a book entitled, *The Funny Side of Golf.* In these pages Reed tells of Billy Graham's comments on golf: "I never pray on a golf course. The Lord answers my prayers everywhere except on the course." Reed shares another experience where a guy had a terrible day on the course and finally lost it on the eighteenth hole. He broke his putter, threw the rest of his clubs in the lake, and started screaming, "I've got to give it up!" The caddie asked, "Give up golf?" "No," the duffer shouted back, "the ministry!" The seventy-nine-year-old Reed says he's personally given up golf. "I've taken up painting, because it requires a lot fewer strokes." [1216]

**Recycling** In defense of his lack-luster report card, a young boy pointed out to his dad, "I'm not as bad off as Karl. He's being re-cycled through second grade." [1217]

**Relaxation** A little girl asked her relaxing brother an interesting question. She wondered, "When you just lie around doing nothing, how do you know when you're done?" [1218]

**Religious Overtones** After growing exhausted with the pastor's lengthy sermon, a little girl turned to her mom and asked, "How much longer till we goeth home?" [1219]

**Religious Rest** Research has proven that if all the people who sleep in church were laid end to end . . . they would be a lot more comfortable.[1220]

**Remote Comeback** Our technological revolution has forever changed the way fathers talk to their sons. Dads used to say, "When I was your age I had to walk five miles to school in the snow." Now to the remote control generation, a father pulls out all the stops when he says, "When I was your age I had to walk clear across the room to change the channel." [1221]

**Responsibility** A little girl had been trying for months to learn the art of tying her shoes. She finally grasped the knack and was able to do it by herself. Her parents expected the child to be delighted, but were surprised by her disappointment. Her father asked why she was crying. She sobbed, "I just learned how to tie my shoes." He said, "That's wonderful, Honey, but why are you crying?" She replied, "Because now I'll have to do it all by myself for the rest of my life." [1222]

**Retirement** "Most wives define retirement as twice as much husband and half as much money." [1223]

**Revival Fatigue** During a Sunday evening revival service, the visiting evangelist was extending the invitation. The sermon had been longer than usual, and now the altar call was lengthening as well. In his appeal, this evangelist asked, "What do you want from God?" A tired little boy blurted, "I want God to let me go home." [1224]

**Rock-a-bye Baby** During the first year of life a child frequently wakes up crying in the middle of the night. It's usually a wake up call for more food or a new diaper. One parent described these middle of the night air-raids as the most difficult part of early parenthood. He said, "The hardest part of the whole thing is seeing which spouse can pretend to be asleep the longest." [1225]

**Rolex Ripoff** A materialistic yuppie was driving his new BMW on a winding mountain road in California. He hit a slick corner and lost control of the car. Just before the automobile tumbled over the roadside cliff, he jumped out. In the process of jumping, his arm was cut off. A trucker quickly ran to the young man and found him weeping over his lost car. The trucker tried to console him. "Don't worry about your car. The way your arm's bleeding you're lucky to be alive." The yuppie looked down at his severed arm and screamed, "No, not my Rolex, too!" [1226]

**Running on Empty** A stranded teenage motorist sat by the side of the rode with the car hood up. She knew nothing about cars, as she had just begun to drive. Her limited knowledge became more apparent when a helpful traveler stopped by to assist her. His background in auto mechanics allowed him to quickly troubleshoot the situation. He said, "Honey, the problem is, you're out of gas." The naive teenager was deeply concerned that she not ruin her chances for future driving by damaging her father's car, so she asked, "Will it hurt to drive it home like that?" [1227]

**Satisfaction Guaranteed** Clara Null asked her granddaughter how she liked her first trip to the circus. The little girl said, "Oh, Granny! If you ever went once you'd never be satisfied with church again!" [1228]

**Scrooge** Two ladies were shopping at the mall when they happened upon a large nativity scene in one of the department store windows. In disgust, one turned to the other and said, "Just look at that. Now the church is trying to horn in on Christmas!" [1229]

**Season Tickets** One year when the Houston Astros were not enjoying their best baseball season, a crime revealed the level of fan frustration. A woman left her season tickets on the dashboard of her locked car. While she was in the store shopping, someone broke into her car and left another set of season tickets on the dash. [1230]

**Second Best** Retired NFL referee Jim Tunney told of his experience with John Madden in the 1977 Super Bowl. Madden, then coaching the Oakland Raiders, said, "Jim, glad to have you here. I want you to know we think you're the second-best official in the league." Tunney thanked him and then walked away. Shortly before kickoff, his curiosity got the best of him, so he returned to Madden and asked who was number one. Madden answered, "It's a tie between the other eighty-nine." [1231]

**Second Opinion** A man anxiously waited for his doctor to give him the results of a critical medical test. The doctor called to tell his patient he had some good news and some bad news. The patient opted for the bad news first. The doctor said, "The bad news is your blood pressure is higher than we thought." The patient asked, "What's the good news?" The doctor said, "I just got back from the golf course and even though I played thirty-six holes, I still shot ten strokes under your blood pressure." [1232]

**Self-Help** Over a light lunch, one lady told her friend, "I finally got in touch with my inner self. She's just as confused as I am." [1233]

**Self-Righteous Driving** Comedian George Carlin has come up with an updated illustration for self-righteousness. He inquires, "Do you ever notice that when you're driving, anyone going slower than you is an idiot and everyone driving faster than you is a maniac?" [1234]

**Sermon Notes** A pastor became very disturbed by the lack of attention his congregation was giving to his sermons. To remedy the problem he issued a mandate from the pulpit that everyone was to take notes when he preached. The following week a visitor took notice of this phenomenon. Sitting in front of him was a man writing feverishly while the pastor spoke, but the visitor detected nothing in the sermon that was worthy of noting. The newcomer was finally overcome by curiosity and leaned forward to see the extensive notes of this faithful member. To his surprise he saw a page full of notes which simply read, "Don't fall asleep, don't fall asleep . . ." [1235]

**Sermonic Anesthesia** The first recorded operation took place when God created Eve from Adam's rib. A Sunday School teacher quizzed her students about this surgery by asking them how they thought God put Adam to sleep before He operated. One boy was confident he had the answer: "By preaching a long sermon." [1236]

**Sermons** During a dry sermon a man heaved a sigh and died in the sanctuary. An usher quickly called an ambulance. When the paramedics arrived, they quietly did their job while the minister droned on. When the emergency team left, the usher overheard the medic talking on the ambulance radio: "We picked up six people before we got the right one." [1237]

**Shopping** It was a man's nightmare. As he sat contemplating the impending expenses of Christmas, his wife burst through the door with an armload of packages. She gleefully remarked, "You told me to stay away from all of those sales—so I bought everything at full price." [1238]

**Side Effects** The suave medical doctor tried to calm his irate patient over the phone. "Of course you're furious about the price of your medicine, Mrs. Martin; that's one of the side effects." [1239]

**Silent Night** A little boy and girl were singing their favorite Christmas carol, "Silent Night." The boy concluded the rendition with the words, "Sleep in heavenly beans." His sister quickly corrected him: "It's not beans, it's peas." [1240]

**Single Life** An old spinster watched a woman cry over the ashes of her fourth husband. She turned to a friend and whispered, "She has husbands to burn, while I can't even find one." [1241]

**Single-Hearted Devotion** As the soldiers prepared for a front-line attack from the enemy, a young private handed his buddy a letter. "If I don't make it back and you do, would you take this letter and see that Sally gets it? Tell her my last thoughts were of her, and her name was the last word on my lips. And here's a letter for Helen, too. Tell her the same thing." [1242]

**Sleepless Nights** The counseling session had been filled with loud verbal attacks and several near-outbreaks of hand-to-hand combat. As the couple jockeyed for position in getting out the door, their marriage counselor gave them one last platitude and some hard-core help: "Remember, never go to bed mad. Here's some No-Doz." [1243]

**Son-in-law Mystery** "One of the greatest mysteries in life is how the idiot that your daughter married can be the father of the world's smartest grandchildren." [1244]

**Source of Love** In exasperation, a middle-aged woman unloaded years of frustration when she told her husband of a recent insight she gained. "The reason our marriage has stayed together all of these years is because we're both in love with the same person—YOU!" [1245]

**Spellcheck** When Elizabeth found out she was going to the library she was ecstatic. "Oh boy," said the four-year-old, "I'm going to the liberry." Her grandmother noticed an opportunity to correct her pronunciation and said, "I'm going to the *library,* Elizabeth." The little girl responded with further excitement, "Oh, are you going too, Nana?" [1246]

**Stress Relief** While checking his bags at the airport, a man became indignant with the employee who handled luggage. For several minutes he belittled the young man and criticized his every move. Surprisingly, the curbside porter didn't seem troubled by this man's verbal abuse. After the angry man entered the airport, a woman approached the luggage handler and asked, "How do you put up with such injustice?" The young man said, "It's easy. That guy's going to New York, but I'm sending his bags to Brazil." [1247]

**Sunday Morning Rush** It was a typical Sunday morning. The husband was ready to go and his wife was still making cosmetic adjustments. The man paced the floor while repeatedly glancing at his watch and giving his wife up-to-the-minute time reports. He finally went to the garage and started the car. After a couple of minutes he came in and said, "Honey, you look nice, but you'd look a lot nicer in the car." [1248]

**Sweepstakes** Each Christmas season everybody gets a letter from Ed McMahon trying to convince them they will be a millionaire by the end of January. Last year a West Texas farmer thought it was his turn to get rich. Ed showed up on the front porch of his rural farmhouse. The farmer could hardly contain himself. When he finally composed himself enough to open the door, to his dismay, all Ed wanted was directions to his neighbor's house. [1249]

**Taxes** Overheard at an audit from the Internal Revenue Service: "Our records show that you still have some money left after paying your taxes. How do you explain that?" Incidentally, $100 billion of income tax goes uncollected each year. Aren't you glad you paid yours? [1250]

**Teenage Crowd Control** Teenagers can be difficult to discipline. One mother complained that although her three teenage sons did not get along very well, they would never confess or tell on each other when punishment was in order. A friend asked the woman, "How do you find out which one to punish?" The clever mother said, "Simple. I send all three to bed without supper. Then the next morning, I ground the one with a black eye." [1251]

**Teenage Shopping** A teenage girl was pleased with her trip to the mall but was concerned about one of her potential buys. Carrying a garment up to the boutique clerk, she asked, "If my parents like this shirt, can I return it?" [1252]

**Teenagers** The comic strip *Kudzu* opened with a pastoral counseling session involving the minister and Kudzu's mother. The woman said, "Preacher, I'm at my wit's end with my boy, Kudzu! I fear my parenting skills just aren't what they should be! In fact, sometimes I feel like a complete failure at parenting." The pastor then calmly assured her with these words, "Mrs. Dubose, I'm sure your parenting is fine. But even the best of parenting is no match for ordinary teenagering!" [1253]

**Telephone Etiquette** While reclining in his chair and reading the newspaper, a father was glad to have his young son answer the phone. He became a little less relaxed when he overheard his son's receptionist skills. The little guy told the caller, "I don't know if he's home or not—hold on while I ask him." [1254]

**Ten "Yellow" Commandments** Finding the Ten Commandments can be a challenge for many adults (Exod. 20). Imagine the looks a Sunday School teacher got when she inquired of their whereabouts in a class for five-year-olds. After a few moments of blank stares she asked again, "Can anybody tell me where to find the Ten Commandments?" Finally, a little kid offered, "Have you looked them up in the Yellow Pages?" [1255]

**The Phone's for You** Norman Whan is the mastermind behind the Christian telemarketing strategy called "The Phone's for You." He has been involved in churches calling literally millions of people. Several humorous responses have resulted from the question, "Could we ask you a few quick questions that will help us in putting our program together?" One lady said, "We're Episcopalians, and we don't help anybody!" "We're Jewish! We don't have anything to do with religion," responded a man. Another lady said, "We're Catholic, so obviously we don't go to church." [1257]

**Thunder** A burst of thunder caused the three-year-old to race into her parents' bedroom. "Mommy, I'm scared," she said. Her sleepy mother responded by saying, "Go back to your bed. God will be there with you." The little girl stopped at the doorway, turned and said, "Mommy, why don't I sleep here with Daddy, and you go in there with God?" [1258]

**Tough Course** Jim was not a good golfer, but he wanted to fit in with the guys who did golf well, so he began to invent stories about his prowess on the course. After listening to Jim's tales, some of the guys invited him to join them for a round of golf. No amount of practice would prepare him for the big day so, as usual, he used his mouth more than his clubs. On the first tee he addressed the ball three times and missed each time. After missing the ball for the fourth time, Jim turned to his foursome and remarked, "This is really a tough course!" [1259]

**Tricky Teeth** When little eight-year-old Ashley took a trip to see her grandmother in Albuquerque, New Mexico, she got a crash course in dentures. Early one morning she rushed into her grandmother's bedroom to wake her up. Grandma Edna Heard quickly reached for her denture container and tried to slip them in before Ashley noticed. Grandma was too slow for her perceptive little granddaughter. With large eyes of astonishment, Ashley asked, "Grandma, how old do you have to be before your teeth will come in and out like that?" [1260]

**Truck Driver** A truck driver was eating at a diner when three sneering motorcycle hoodlums came in. The first took the truck driver's hamburger, the second drank his coffee, and the third one wolfed down his pie. Quietly, the truck driver got up from the table and left the diner. One of the bikers said, "He's not much of a man, is he?" The cashier replied, "He's not much of a driver, either. He just ran his truck over three motorcycles." [1261]

**TV vs. Books** A couch-potato husband was amazed at his wife's preoccupation with a book while he was watching TV. After nearly an hour of watching her read without showing any interest in his show, he blurted out, "How can you just sit there and read when we have over forty channels of TV?" [1262]

**Umbiblical Cord** The children of *Family Circus* were in a lively discussion about babies. Two truths were unleashed by the little "experts." "Storks don't bring babies. They come UPS." And, "Babies are connected to their mothers by a biblical cord." Good insight! [1263]

**Unresolved Conflict** A couple had been arguing about everything for years. Both spouses were tired of living in their state of perpetual conflict. Finally, the wife tipped off her husband about her prayer life. She said, "I've been praying for God to help us stop all of this arguing by taking one of us to Heaven. When he answers my prayer, I'm moving in with my sister." [1264]

**Vacation Bible School** When Vacation Bible School rolled around, a woman who was new to the community came to enroll her son. The boy was extremely active, very curious, and had the energy to outlast most adults. When the mother came to that section of the enrollment card called "Remarks," she wrote in large, block letters, "BRACE YOURSELF!" [1265]

**Vacation Fatigue** Vacations are great fun but can also have their fair share of stress and fatigue. One family rediscovered this truth on a two-week vacation to the Grand Canyon. The father was a camera buff. The Grand Canyon is photographer's paradise because of the limitless potential for beautiful shots. This man pulled in to every lookout point for a few pictures. The whole family got out of the car for the first ten lookouts, but the mother became tired of the in-and-out routine. At the next stop the dad jumped out and the two boys started to follow. The mother wasn't about to move and didn't want to see any more air-conditioning go out the door. She snapped, "Boys, stay in the car. You can see the pictures when we get home." [1266]

**Value** A little boy was accustomed to being praised by his doting grandmother. On one particular visit she kept telling him that he was "priceless." When he finished a drawing of which he was very proud, he excitedly ran to his grandmother's side and yelled, "Look, Grandma, I'm worthless!" [1267]

**Waiter's Tip** One guy was reminded of his over-indulgence when he opened his menu and asked the waiter, "What do you recommend?" The waiter looked him over, then answered, "A diet!" [1268]

**Wedding Blues** When six-year-old Andy's grandmother informed him that someday he would get married, Andy declared his independence from women and denied he would ever marry. His grandmother persisted, saying, "Most people get married when they get older." Andy succumbed grudgingly with, "Okay, maybe I'll get married, but don't expect me to kiss her!" [1269]

**Wedding Colors** While attending her first wedding, a little girl whispered to her mother, "Why is the bride dressed in white?" The mother responded, "Because white is the color of happiness, and this is the happiest day of her life." The girl thought about this for a moment, then asked, "So why is the groom wearing black?" [1270]

**Weighing In** A young mother was trying desperately to lose weight. Each morning she woke up before the children and got on the scales. She kept a record of her weight and tracked her progress. One day the family went to visit Grandma so the dieting mom weighed herself on different scales. Since scales typically vary, when she saw the scales' verdict she indignantly said, "I don't weigh that much!" Little Christine watched the whole weigh-in and replied, "Mommy, you sure look like you do." [1271]

**Weight Watcher** An engaged daughter requested the privilege of wearing her mother's wedding gown for her wedding. The mother obviously consented. When the new bride tried on the dress, it fit her petite figure beautifully. She walked into the room looking like a dream. Tears began streaming down the mother's face. The daughter put her arm around her mother and said, "Don't cry, Mom. You're not losing a daughter, you're gaining a son." With a sob, the mother replied, "Forget that. I was remembering how I used to fit into that dress!" [1272]

**West Texas Preaching** A visiting preacher was concerned when he began the first night of a revival meeting and noticed all of the men wearing guns. Although rattled, he did the best he could with his sermon. When finished, his anxieties heightened as several of the men approached with their guns drawn. In panic, he turned to the chairman of the deacons, sitting next to him. The deacon calmed his fears: "Don't you worry. They ain't coming after you. They're looking for the cuss who invited you to preach." [1273]

**Wife's Crack** A successful CEO had the opportunity of going to his wife's hometown and meeting her high school boyfriend. The CEO couldn't wait to see what kind of guy his wife dated in school. As it turned out, her old flame had become the night manager of a gas station. After they met, the CEO could hardly wait to get back in the car and hear his wife's reaction. "Well, what did you think?" he asked. She said, "Nothing much." After a long silence he couldn't contain himself. "Honey, aren't you glad you're married to the CEO of a successful company instead of a manager at a gas station?" She responded as only a wife can. "Get this straight. If I'd married Billy Bob, he'd be the CEO of a successful company, and *you* would be managing a gas station." [1274]

**Will Changes** Grandpa was well into his eighties before he decided to try a hearing aid. He was amazed at the fancy gadget's capabilities, and stopped by to thank the audiologist who had assisted him. Grandpa told of his new ability to easily hear conversations, even in the next room. The hearing specialist was delighted. "Your relatives must be happy to know you can now hear so well." The wise elder replied with a smile, "Oh, I ain't told 'em. I just been sittin' around the house listenin' to 'em. Y'know what, I've changed my will twice already." [1275]

**Wish You Were Here** Heeding his psychiatrist's advice to take a vacation, an executive went to Hawaii. Halfway through his vacation the executive wrote his doctor a postcard. It read, "Having a wonderful time. Wish you were here to tell me why." [1276]

**Work Ethic** The CEO of a large corporation was asked, "How many people work in your company?" The dry-witted leader replied, "Not many." [1277]

**Worry** The doctor finished the exam and talked with his patient, who suffered from an ulcer. The patient was quite concerned, saying, "Doctor, I'm worried about the fact that worrying about my ulcer might make it worse!" [1278]

**Zoo Work** During some desperate times, a zoo advertised for needed help. A well-built man was rather disappointed to find the only job left was that of impersonating a gorilla. The gorilla had died, and the zoo was expecting some VIP visitors so they needed an impostor. Money was tight, so he took the job. All went well for the first few hours—until the heat started taking its toll. As he tried to swing from one tree to another, he lost his grip and went flying into the lion's den. He immediately started shouting, "Help! Help!" The lion leaned over and said, "Stop that screaming, or we'll both lose our jobs." [1279]

# INDEXES

# SOURCE INDEX

1. *The Secret Power of Evangelism*, Leighton Ford, 1962, p. 3
2. *Focus on the Family*, Dec. 1992, p. 12
3. *The Rebirth of America*, Arthur S. DeMoss Foundation, 1986, p. 113
4. Author's files
5. "The Sexual Side of Love," Lee Strobel, Seeds Tape Ministry, Jan. 30, 1994
6. *Sanctity of Life*, Charles Swindoll, 1990, p. 12-23
7. *U.S. News & World Report*, June 20, 1994, p. 24
8. *Disappointment with God*, Philip Yancey, 1988, p. 160
9. *Reader's Digest*, Aug. 1990
10. *Houston Chronicle*, July 30, 1992, p. 17C
11. *Baptist Beacon*, April 26, 1992, p. 8
12. *Houston Post*, Oct. 30, 1992, p. A-2
13. Author's files
14. *MissionsUSA*, Feb. 1991, p. 2
15. *Illustrations for Biblical Preaching*, Michael Green, editor, 1989, p. 394
16. *Lead the Field*, Earl Nightingale, 1990, p. 11
17. *When God Doesn't Make Sense*, James Dobson, 1993, p. 147; *Leadership Journal*, Summer 1991, p. 71
18. *Christian Reader*, July/Aug. 1993, p. 80
19. *Houston Chronicle*, Feb. 20, 1993, p. 3E
20. *The Rewards of Positive Living*, Norman Vincent Peale, 1981, p. 26-27
21. *Ministry Currents*, Jan.-March, 1992, p. 5
22. *Houston Post*, March 13, 1992, p. A-15
23. *Country*, Premiere Edition, p. 16, 48, 61, 62, 65
24. *Houston Chronicle*, Aug. 26, 1992, p. D-2
25. "Saddleback's Core Values: We Are a Value-Driven Church," Rick Warren, *Leadership Lifter* no. 49
26. *Disguised*, Pat Moore, 1985, p. 165-167
27. *Strengthening Your Grip*, Charles Swindoll, 1982, p. 128-129; *Houston Post*, April 24, 1994, p. D-7
28. *Houston Chronicle*, Nov. 29, 1991, p. 22A
29. *Houston Chronicle*, March 25, 1992, p. 2D
30. *The Top 10 of Everything*, Russell Ash, 1994, p. 79
31. *U.S. News & World Report*, June 20, 1994, p. 21
32. *Leadership*, Feb. 16, 1993, p. 21-22
33. Author's files
34. *Fatherless America*, David Blankenhorn, 1995, p. 227
35. *Moody*, March 1993, p. 74
36. *Southwestern News*, Nov./Dec. 1992, p. 16
37. Author's files
38. *Forrest Gump*, Robert Zemeckis, dir.; motion picture
39. *Houston Post*, Jan. 2, 1995, p. C-4
40. "How to Win Over Worry," John Maxwell, Dec. 1991

357

41. *Three Steps Forward, Two Steps Back*, Charles Swindoll, 1980, p. 32
42. *Houston Chronicle*, May 26, 1992, p. 4A
43. *Bits & Pieces*, Dec. 10, 1992, p. 15
44. *Guiness Book of World Records*, Norris McWhirter, 1984, p. 556
45. "Mirror, Mirror, in the Garden," Charles Swindoll, Orlando Conference, 1992
46. *Church Around the World*, Dec. 1993, p. 1
47. "So What?" Bill Hybels, Easter 1992, Seeds Tape Ministry
48. *Lead On!*, John Haggai, 1986, p. 77
49. *Baptist Standard*, Rick Warren, Nov. 13, 1991, p. 17
50. *The Seven Habits Report*, Stephen Covey, Fall 1991, p. 14
51. *The Seven Habits of Highly Effective People*, Stephen R. Covey, 1989, p. 32-33
52. *Executive Speechwriter Newsletter*, Vol. 8 No. 1
53. *Guiness Book of World Records*, 1984, p. 583
54. *Baptist Standard*, Jan. 6, 1993, p. 5
55. *Leadership*, Aug. 1993, p. 4
56. Author's files
57. *Baptist Program*, Nov. 1992, p. 5
58. *Missions USA*, Sept./Oct. 1991, p. 18
59. *Sports Spectrum*, Dec. 1993, p. 27; *Guideposts*, May 1992, p. 14-17
60. *Leadership*, March 16, 1993, p. 18-19
61. "How to Double Your Attendance," Elmer Towns, Church Growth Institute, 1995
62. *Decision*, June 1995, p. 13-14
63. *AFA Journal*, March 1995, p. 32
64. *Houston Chronicle*, May 5, 1992, p. 10A
65. *The Almanac of the Christian World*, 1993-1994 Edition, p. 240
66. *Commission*, Dec. 1993, p. 55
67. "Seven Habits of Effective Church Leaders," Robert Clinton, July 1991, Charles E. Fuller, Tape UO22
68. *Pastor's Story File*, Oct. 1993, p. 7
69. *Humorous Notes, Quotes, and Anecdotes*, Leslie & Bernice Flynn, 1973, p. 72
70. *Research in Christian Evidences*, Josh McDowell, 1979, p. 25
71. *What Americans Believe*, George Barna, 1991, p. 284; *Parade*, Dec. 29, 1991, p. 20; *Our Daily Bread*, Oct. 2, 1991
72. *Houston Post*, April 24 and 25, 1992, Front page
73. *Leadership*, Nov. 1993, p. 4
74. *U.S. News & World Report*, Jan. 3, 1994, p. 40
75. *Parade*, Dec. 13, 1992, p. 18
76. Author's files
77. "Critical Habits of Christ Followers: A Mind-Expanding Faith," John Ortberg, Seeds Tape Ministry, Sept. 22, 1993
78. *When God Doesn't Make Sense*, James Dobson, 1993, p. 182
79. *Special Sermons for Special Days*, Paul Powell, 1993, p. 104
80. "Discipline—You Can't Succeed Without It!" Hank Tate
81. *Newsweek*, Oct. 14, 1991, p. 6
82. *Hopeline*, Nov. 1992, p. 4
83. *Laugh Again*, Charles Swindoll, 1992, p. 120-121
84. *Houston Post*, July 29, 1994, p. A-19 and July 19, 1994, p. A-10
85. *Sagemont Challenger*, July 27, 1992, p. 2
86. *Fresh Beginnings*, Ecuador, Mission Vision Network, 1994
87. *Inc.*, Dec. 1992, p. 16
88. Author's files
89. *USA Weekend*, July 12, 1991, p. 18

90. *Living Biographies of Great Composers*, Henry and Dana Lee Thomas, 1940, p. 13-33

91. *Proclaim*, Spring 1994, p. 8

92. "Our Business Is Pleasing Customers," *The Economic Press*, 1992, p. 5

93. *Christian History*, Issue 23 (Vol. 8, No. 3)

94. *Leadership Journal*, date unknown

95. "How to Recruit Today's Volunteers," Marlene Wilson, 1991

96. *To Dream Again*, Robert D. Dale, 1981, p. 20

97. *Houston Post*, April 14, 1995, p. A-10; *U.S. News & World Report*, May 8, 1995, p. 14; *Guideposts*, July 1995, p. 15

98. *Newsweek*, June 8, 1992, p. 51

99. *Crossroads*, Vol. 1, No. 4, p. 23

100. *Newsweek*, April 29, 1991, p. 10

101. *Our Daily Bread*, Dec. 27, 1992

102. *All Things Are Possible Through Prayer*, Charles Allen, 1958, p. 28-29

103. "How God Uses Suffering In Our Lives," Rick Warren, *The Encouraging Word*

104. *TableTalk*, Sept. 1992, p. 10

105. *Today in the Word*, Sept.1991, p. 32

106. "The Church's Mission," Bill Donahue, Seeds Tape Ministry, Feb. 3, 1992

107. Author's files

108. *Houston Chronicle*, March 1, 1991; *Houston Post*, April 18, 1995, p. A-6

109. *Newsweek*, Nov. 30, 1992, p. 25

110. "Authentic Ministry," Bill Hybels, Willow Creek Pastor's Conference, May 17, 1990

111. *Humorous Notes, Quotes, and Anecdotes*, Leslie & Bernice Flynn, 1973, p. 27

112. *Progress*, Dec. 1992/Jan. 1993, p. 27

113. *Where Is the Child?*, Luis Palau, 1988, p. 1-2

114. *Maybe (Maybe Not)*, Robert Fulghum, 1993, p. 63-65

115. *Handbook to The Baptist Hymnal*, Wesley Forbis, editor, 1992, p. 175

116. *Decision*, Dec. 1992, p. 33

117. "The Innovating Man," Tony Evans, The Innovative Church Growth Conference, 1994; *Houston Post*, May 1, 1994, p. A-32

118. *Saturday Evening Post*, Nov./Dec. 1992, p. 34

119. Author's files

120. Author's files

121. *Houston Post*, Nov. 20, 1991, p. 2

122. *Executive Speechwriter Newsletter*, Vol. 8, No. 1

123. *Houston Chronicle*, April 4, 1987

124. *Jesus the Teacher*, J. M. Price, 1946, p. 47

125. *Church Administration*, Oct. 1995, p. 36

126. *Living Obediently*, Brian Harbour, 1992, p. 118

127. Author's files

128. *Church Growth Newsletter*, Vol. 2, No. 1, p. 3

129. *Facing Death and the Life After*, Billy Graham, 1987, p. 230

130. *Leadership Journal*, Summer '92, p. 41

131. *The New Realities*, Peter F. Drucker, 1989, p. 198-199

132. Author's files

133. *Houston Chronicle*, May 4, 1992, p. 3A

134. Ibid, Feb. 18, 1993, p. 8A

135. Ibid, Aug. 2, 1992, p. 3A

136. *Progress*, June/July 1992, p. 17

137. Author's files

138. *Houston Post*, Jan. 23, 1994, p. E-8

139. *Houston Chronicle*, June 22, 1995, p. 5D

140. Ibid, Feb. 1, 1993, p. C7

141. *SBC Life*, June/July 1995, p. 20

142. *Special Sermons for Special Days*, Paul Powell, 1993, p. 106

143. Author's files
144. Author's files
145. *USA Weekend*, Dec. 24, 1993, p. 4
146. *Home Life*, July 1991, p. 6
147. *Reader's Digest*, Dec. 1988, p. 93
148. Author's files
149. *Teaching to Change Lives*, Howard Hendricks, 1987, p. 107; *Reader's Digest*, July 1989, p. 8
150. *Ministry Currents*, Fall 1991
151. Author's files
152. "Compassion in a Discompassionate World," Joseph Stowell, Seeds Tape Ministry, Dec. 8, 1993
153. Author's files
154. *USA Today*, Sept. 16, 1994
155. *Christian Reader*, Jan./Feb. 1990, p. 22
156. *The Seven Habits of Highly Effective People*, Stephen R. Covey, 1989, p. 31
157. *Our Daily Bread*, March 29, 1992
158. *Houston Post*, April 25, 1991, p. 2
159. *Homemade*, March 1992, p. 1
160. *Newsweek*, April 13, 1992, p. 8; *Houston Post*, May 9, 1992, p. A-6; *Houston Chronicle*, May 16, 1992, p. 17A
161. *Houston Chronicle*, Jan. 30, 1993, p. 3E
162. Author's files
163. *Houston Post*, Oct. 1993
164. *Pryor Report*, Vol. 8, No. 1A, p. 2
165. *Houston Chronicle*, Feb. 24, 1993, p. 10D
166. *Focus on the Family Bulletin*, Aug. 1993
167. *Houston Post*, June 30, 1991, p. A-17
168. *Jubilee*, July 1992, p. 3; *Pastor to Pastor*, H. B. London, April 1993, p. 2
169. *Houston Post*, Dec. 14, 1992, p. A-11
170. Author's files
171. *Houston Post*
172. Founders Day Address, Russell Dilday, Southwestern Seminary, March 12, 1993
173. *Home Life*, Nov. 1993, p. 24
174. *American Health*, July/Aug. 1992, p. 48
175. *Houston Chronicle*, Aug. 2, 1992, p. 14B
176. Author's files
177. *Laugh Again*, Charles Swindoll, 1992, p. 50-51
178. *Decision*, Sept. 1991, p. 34
179. *Houston Chronicle*, April 1991
180. *Working Well*, Sept. 1995, p. 4
181. "Believing the Unbelievable: The Case for Creation," Lee Strobel, Seeds Tape Ministry M9045
182. Author's files
183. *Rotarian*, Aug. 1994, p. 56
184. *How to Win Friends and Influence People*, Dale Carnegie, 1981, p. 9-10
185. *Newsweek*, June 29, 1992, p. 56
186. *Working Well*, July 1995, p. 4
187. Contributed by Colonel Joe Long
188. *Houston Chronicle*, May 13, 1993, p. 22A
189. *Moody*, April 1993, p. 13
190. Contributed by Lauretta Reynolds
191. Contributed by Martha McHenry
192. Author's files
193. *Family Research Council*, Feb. 7, 1994, p. 4
194. *Houston Post*, Dec. 13, 1993, p. C1
195. Ibid, May 21, 1992, p. A-12
196. *Understanding Suffering*, B. W. Woods, 1974, p. 170
197. *Parade*, July 19, 1992, p. 16
198. *Houston Post*, Jan. 29, 1994, p. A-17
199. *Living Obediently*, Brian Harbour, 1992, p. 13, 15
200. Author's files
201. *Leadership*, Winter 1987, p. 41
202. *Parade*, Aug. 13, 1989, p. 8
203. *Houston Post*, Jan. 26, 1992, p. A-2
204. Author's files
205. "Passages that Pump Me Up," Bob Hendricks, Seeds Tape Ministry, May 29, 1994

206. *Psychology Today*, Oct. 88; "The Power to Overcome Adversity," Bill Hybels, Seeds Tape Ministry, Nov. 5, 1995

207. *Homemade*, May 1991

208. *Houston Chronicle*, 1991

209. *Ministry Currents*, April/May/June 1994, p. 13

210. *U.S. News & World Report*, July 31, 1995, p. 14

211. "The Greatest Sermon in History," Bill Hybels, Seeds Tape Ministry, Jan. 16, 1994

212. *Watching the World Go By*, W. E. Thorn, 1987, p. 125

213. *Understanding Church Growth*, Dr. Donald McGavran, 1970, p. 150-152

214. *Focus on the Family Newsletter*, Sept. 1991

215. Author's files

216. *Houston Post*, Dec. 21, 1991, p. A-20

217. *Injoy*, John Maxwell, Sept. 1992

218. *Houston Chronicle*, Oct. 1, 1992, p. 3G

219. Author's files

220. *Houston Zoo*, Aug. 1993

221. Author's files

222. *Houston Chronicle*, Jan. 17, 1992, p. 10B

223. *Angels: God's Secret Agents*, Billy Graham, 1975, p. 3

224. *Sermon Notes and Illustrations*, Oct. 1995, p. 30

225. *Words in Season*, P. Stokes, p. 63

226. *Homemade*, March 1993, p. 1

227. *We Are Not Alone: Learning to Live with Chronic Illness*, Sefra Pitzele, 1986, p. 113

228. *Therefore . . .* , Christian Life Commission, June 1995

229. *All Things Are Possible through Prayer*, Charles Allen, 1958, p. 48

230. Author's files

231. Leith Anderson, "Can Jesus Trust Us?" Preaching Today, Tape 126

232. *Focus on the Family Bulletin*, Aug. 1993

233. *Houston Post*, Nov. 20, 1991, p. D-9

234. *State Farm Insurance Good Neighbor News*, Fall 1992, p. 3; *Houston Metropolitan*, Dec. 1992, p. 12

235. *Newsweek*, March 16, 1992, p. 4; *TableTalk*, Sept. 1992, p. 9

236. Author's files

237. *Leadership*, Winter 1987, p. 40

238. *Focus on the Family*, April 1988, p. 2-3

239. *Christian Reader*, March/April 1990, p. 12

240. *Saturday Evening Post*, March/April 1995, p. 44

241. *Bits & Pieces*, Nov. 14, 1991, p. 1

242. *Christian History*, No. 21, p. 2

243. Author's files

244. *Teaching to Change Lives*, Howard Hendricks, 1987, p. 61

245. Author's files

246. "Signposts Aloft," Moody Institute of Science

247. *Christian Parenting Today*, Nov./Dec. 1992, p. 107

248. *NEWSLETTER Newsletter*, May 1993

249. *Leadership*, June 8, 1994, p. 1-2

250. *Who Switched the Price Tags?*, Tony Campolo, 1986, p. 69-72

251. *Preacher Talk*, Brian Harbour, Vol. 1, No. 3

252. *Reader's Digest*, Aug. 1990

253. Author's files

254. "Bivocational Ministers," Paul Powell

255. Ike Reighard, 1993 SBC Pastor's Conference

256. *The Best of Grandparents' Brag Board*, Judy Pregel & Robin Riley, 1993, p. 52

257. *NEWSLETTER Newsletter*, June 1994, p. 1

258. *Reader's Digest*, Jan. 1993, p. 169; Oct. 1992, p. 110

259. *Newsweek*, Aug. 19, 1991, p. 57; Aug. 26, 1991, p. 40-41; *Houston Chronicle*, Aug. 9, 1991, p. 20A; *Houston Post*, Aug. 9, 1991, p. A-6
260. *Decision*, June 1994, p. 28-29
261. *Bits & Pieces*, July 21, 1994, p. 4
262. Author's files
263. *Decision*, Feb. 1987, p. 23-24
264. Author's files
265. Author's files
266. *Baptist Program*, 1991
267. "The Acts of a Growing Church," Rick Warren, *Leadership Lifters* 50
268. *Deacon*, Jan.-March 1995, p. 34
269. Author's files
270. "Taking Orange County by Storm: Lessons We Can Learn from the Gulf War," Rick Warren, *Leadership Lifters,* Tape 42
271. Rodney Gage, 1993 SBC Pastor's Conference
272. *Baptist Standard*, Aug. 4, 1993
273. *Facing Death and the Life After*, Billy Graham, 1987, p. 215
274. *MissionsUSA*, Nov./Dec. 1993, p. 54
275. *Moody*, June 1992, p. 16
276. *Leadership Journal*, Fall 1988, p. 32
277. *Sports Spectrum*, Nov./Dec. 1991, p. 10
278. *Houston Post*, July 21, 1994, p. A-20
279. *Newsweek*, May 31, 1993, p. 26
280. "Studying Adult Life and Work Lessons," Herschel Hobbs, March 6, 1994, p. 92
281. *Executive Speechwriter Newsletter*, Vol.8, No. 4
282. Howard Hendricks, 1991 Leighton Ford Evangelism Leadership Seminar
283. Author's files
284. *Houston Post*, June 17, 1993, p. A-25; *Insight for Living*, Charles Swindoll, June 1987; *The Timetables of History*, Bernard Grun, 1982, p. 457
285. *Preacher Talk*, Brian Harbor, Vol. 2, Tape 4, 1994

286. *Houston Chronicle*, Sept. 16, 1995, p. 3E
287. *Baptist Beacon*, Oct. 29, 1992, p. 4
288. Kenneth Cooper
289. *Computer Business Services*, Inc., Vol. 16, Tape 2, 1995
290. *Too Busy Not to Pray*, Bill Hybels, 1988, p. 89
291. "Seeking, Finding, and Developing Leaders," Robert Logan, *The Pastor's Update*, March 1992
292. "Doing Big Things for God," John Maxwell, *Injoy,* Feb. 1993
293. *Experiencing God*, Henry Blackaby & Claude King, 1990, p. 7
294. *The Timetables of History*, Bernard Grun, 1975, p. 283; *Houston Post*, Nov. 11, 1992, p. 2
295. "Discipleship," Howard Hendricks, Dallas Theological Seminary, Tape T42D6Y; "Seven Characteristics of Effective Churches," Ken Hemphill, 1994 Texas Baptist Evangelism Conference
296. Author's files
297. Author's files
298. *Houston Chronicle*, Aug. 24, 1995, p. 12H
299. *Proclaim*, Jack Gulledge
300. Lee Strobel, Seeds Tape Ministry
301. *Houston Chronicle*, May 91, p. 2
302. *Christian Reader*, Nov./Dec. 1992, p. 75
303. *USA Weekend*, Jan. 13, 1995, p. 22
304. *Insight for Living Newsletter*, Charles Swindoll, Sept. 1991
305. Author's files
306. *Focus on the Family*, Jan. 1992, p. 1
307. Ibid, April 1994, p. 4
308. *Houston Post*, April 8, 1994, p. A-18
309. Ibid, May 20, 1992, p. D-10
310. *Break Point*, May 1992, p. 2
311. *Houston Chronicle*, May 14, 1992, p. 1E
312. *Houston Post*, June 12, 1994, p. B-2

313. "Children Live What They Learn," Dorothy Law Nolte

314. *Brian's Lines*, May/June 1994

315. *Pastor to Pastor*, H. B. London, Vol. 13

316. *Houston Post*, April 3, 1995, p. D-3

317. *Pulpit Helps*, Feb. 1994, p. 14

318. Author's files

319. *LifeWalk*, Nov./Dec. 1992

320. Author's files

321. *Focus on the Family*, June 1994, p. 1; *Decision*, June 1994, back page

322. *Today in the Word*, July 1992, p. 15

323. *The Man in the Mirror*, Patrick Morely, 1989, p. 89-90

324. *1993 Dayspring Calendar*, Father's Day

325. *Houston Chronicle*, Jan. 3, 1992, p. 3A

326. *Newsweek*, Nov. 12, 1990, p. 54

327. Author's files

328. *Houston Chronicle*, July 29, 1992, p. 9F

329. *Speaker's Idea File*, p. 5

330. *Pastor's Update*, July 1991, p. 2

331. *Texas Monthly*, May 1991, p. 174; *USA Weekend*, July 19, 1991, p. 5

332. *Houston Chronicle*, June 9, 1995, p. 3A

333. *All Things Are Possible through Prayer*, Charles Allen, 1958, p. 79-80

334. *Church Around the World*, Sept. 1994, p. 2

335. *Moody*, Sept. 1991, p. 6

336. *How to Win Friends and Influence People*, D. Carnegie, 1981, p. 14-15

337. Author's files

338. *Houston Chronicle*, Nov. 17, 1992, p. 24A

339. *Defensive Driving*

340. *Houston Chronicle*, Sept. 30, 1990, book review of *God's Samurai*, Gordon Prange

341. *Life Advocate*, Sept./Oct. 1992, p. 1; *The Baptist Standard*, Jan. 22, 1992, p. 8

342. "Reasons to Fear Easter," Don McCullough, *Preaching Today*, Tape 116

343. Author's files

344. "How to Double Your Attendance," Elmer Towns, Church Growth Institute, 1995

345. *Bits & Pieces*, March 30, 1995, p. 1

346. "The Greatest Sermon in History," Lee Strobel, Seeds Tape Ministry, Nov. 7, 1993

347. *Where Is God When It Hurts?*, Philip Yancey, 1977, p. 174

348. *Houston Chronicle*, July 31, 1991, p. 16A

349. *Lottery Action Guide*, 1991, p. 7, 15

350. *Newsweek*, Sept. 23, 1991, p. 6

351. *U.S. News & World Report*, June 12, 1995, p. 42

352. *Reader's Digest*, Nov. 1992, p. 128

353. *Leadership*, Jan. 1993, p. 3

354. *MissionsUSA*, Winter 1994, p. 1

355. *Houston Post*, Oct. 24, 1993, p. A-17

356. Ibid, June 26, 1994, p. E-14

357. Author's files

358. *Injoy Life*, John Maxwell, Oct. 1991

360. "Win or Lose? The Choice Is Yours," John Maxwell, Injoy, March 1993

361. *The Problem of Pain*, C. S. Lewis, 1962, p. 96

362. *Today in the Word*, May 1991, p. 30; *Executive Speechwriter Newsletter*, Religion & Philosophy, Vol. 1

363. Author's files

364. *Martin Luther on the Bondage of the Will*, J. I. Packer & O. R. Johnston, 1957, p. 87

365. Author's files

366. *With All Your Mind*, Yandall Woodfin, 1980, p. 237

367. *The Problem of Pain*, C. S. Lewis, 1962, p. 96

368. *Our Daily Bread*, May 16, 1992

369. Ibid, Dec. 6, 1992

370. *Mature Living*, June 1992, p. 49

371. *Rodgers and Hammerstein's The Sound of Music*, Souvenir Program, 1991, p. 26

372. *In God's Waiting Room: Learning through Suffering*, Lehman Strauss, 1984, p. 75-76

373. *Watching the World Go By*, W. E. Thorn, 1987, p. 51

374. *When God Doesn't Make Sense*, James Dobson, 1993, p. 135-6

375. *Houston Post*, Jan. 8, 1994, p. E-2

376. "God Talk: What Jesus Would Say to Robert Sherman," Lee Strobel, Seeds Tape Ministry, 8/2/92

377. *Marriage Partnership*, Fall 1992, p. 59

378. *Christian Reader*, March 1992, p. 37

379. *Reader's Digest*, Aug. 1991, p. 13

380. Author's files

381. *Moody*, Oct. 1991, p. 87

382. *Billy Graham Evangelistic Association Newsletter*, Jan. 1992, p. 1

383. Author's files

384. *Health*, April 1992, p. 9

385. *Leadership*, Summer 1991, p. 49

386. *NEWSLETTER Newsletter*, Nov. 1992, p. 1

387. *Have a Good Day*, Nov. 1993, p. 4

388. "What Leaders Expect from Followers," John Maxwell, April 1993

389. *All I Really Need to Know I Learned in Kindergarten*, Robert Fulghum, 1989, p. 192

390. *Houston Post,* Sept. 2, 1992, p. D3

391. *Home Life*, March 1992, p. 12

392. *A Grief Observed*, C. S. Lewis, 1961, p. 51

393. Author's files

394. *Reader's Digest*, Sept. 1991, p. 32

395. *This Way to Happiness*, Clyde Narramore, p. 13

396. Author's files

397. *Houston Post*, July 6, 1991, p. E-3

398. "Yea God . . . for Being A Servant," Lee Strobel, Seeds Tape Ministry, April 9, 1995

399. *Preaching from Ecclesiastes*, G. Avery Lee, 1958, p. 17

400. *American Health*, March 1993, p. 27

401. *Facing Death and the Life After*, Billy Graham, 1987, p. 237

402. *Christ and Human Suffering*, E. Stanley Jones, 1933, p. 198

403. *Leadership Journal*, Fall 1988

404. "God's Outrageous Claims," Lee Strobel, Seeds Tape Ministry, July 8, 1990

405. *Moody*, June 1993, p. 25

406. *Houston Post*, June 18, 1994, p. E-2

407. Author's files

408. *Facing Death and the Life After*, Billy Graham, 1987, p. 31

409. *Better Families*, June 1994, p. 1

410. *Leadership Journal*, Summer 1992, p. 41

411. *Broken Things*, M. R. DeHaan, 1948, p. 29

412. *Newsweek*, July 20, 1992, p. 55

413. *People*, April 20, 1992, p. 108-114; *Houston Post*, May 22, 1992, p. A-11; *Houston Chronicle*, May 16, 1992, p. 2A; *USA Weekend,* April 24, 1992, p. 24

414. Author's files

415. *Leadership Journal*, Max Lucado, Summer 1992, p. 22

416. *Studying Adult Life and Work Lessons*, Oct.-Dec. 1991, p. 70

417. Author's files

418. *Christian Reader*, Nov./Dec. 1994, p. 47

419. *TableTalk*, June 1991, p. 12

420. Author's files

421. *Focus on the Family*, Dec. 1993, p. 1

422. *A Missions People: The Southern Baptist Pilgrimage*, M. Wendell Belew, 1989, p. 189-190

423. *USA Weekend*, April 24, 1992, p. 4

424. *Ministry Currents*, April-June 1993, p. 17; Bill Hybels, "Homosexuality," March 7, 1993

425. *Family Research Council Washington Watch*, Oct. 9, 1992, p. 2; *Parade*, Oct. 22, 1992, p. 20; "An Open Letter to the Clergy from Houston Mayor," Bob Lanier, Nov. 1992

426. *Leadership 1990*, p. 128

427. *Marriage Partnership*, Spring 1992, p. 84

428. *All Things Are Possible through Prayer*, Charles Allen, 1958, p. 16-17; 43

429. *Plus*, Dec. 1985, p. 28

430. *Stick a Geranium in Your Hat and Be Happy*, Barbara Johnson, 1990, p. 60-61

431. *Bits & Pieces*, Feb. 6, 1992, p. 15

432. *Houston Chronicle*, Jan. 30, 1993, p. 11A

433. *Church Management*, April 1984, p. 99

434. *Houston Chronicle*, Jan. 2, 1993, p. 11A

435. *Church Around the World*, Sept. 1994, p. 1

436. *Homemade*, Aug. 1991

437. *Houston Post*, July 21, 1991, p. A-2

438. *Leadership*, 1989

439. *PrimeTime Live*, Dec. 17, 1992

440. Author's files

441. *Baptist Standard*, March 25, 1992, p. 16

442. *Houston Chronicle*, March 13, 1992, p. 21A, 10D

443. *Moody*, Dec. 1992, p. 8

444. *Today in the Word*, March 1992, p. 35

445. "Behold, the What?" Charles Swindoll, Orlando Conference, 1992

446. *U.S. News & World Report*, Oct. 2, 1995, p. 88

447. "Successful and Unsuccessful Pastors: How Are They Different?" John Maxwell, Injoy, Oct. 1992

448. *Facts & Trends*, June 1991, p. 5

449. *Moody*, July/Aug. 1992, p. 26

450. *Houston Chronicle*, Sept. 13, 1992, p. 10A

451. *Preacher Talk*, Brian Harbor, Vol. 3 Tape 1, 1995; *Progress*, Dec. 1992, p. 43

452. *Houston Post*, Sept. 10, 1994, p. A-16

453. *Encyclopedia of 7700 Illustrations*, Paul Lee Tan, 1982, p. 669

454. *Vision*, March-April 1995, p. 2

455. *Dying for Change*, Leith Anderson, 1990, p. 109-110

456. *Decision*, Dec. 1992, p. 11

457. *Bits & Pieces*, Dec. 12, 1991, p. 4-6

458. *The Frog in the Kettle*, George Barna, 1990, p. 53-54

459. *Radically Committed*, Jim Burns, 1991

460. *Newsweek*, July 29, 1991, p. 13

461. *Leadership*, May 11, 1993, p. 24

462. Leighton Ford Evangelism Leadership Seminar, 1991

463. Author's files

464. *Navigator's Daily Walk*, July 25, 1991

465. *Commission*, March 1991

466. "Living in Little Communities," Bill Hybels, Seeds Tape Ministry, Sept. 10, 1995

467. *Houston Post*, March 18, 1992, p. A-10

468. *Handbook to the Baptist Hymnal*, Wesley L. Forbis, editor, 1992, p. 274

469. "Don't Worry, Be Happy," Rodrick Walters, Gulf Meadows Baptist Church, April 11, 1995

470. "Peace I Leave with You," Frank Pollard, *The Baptist Hour*, Dec. 24, 1992

471. *Houston Chronicle*, Feb. 29, 1993, p. 4A

472. *Houston Chronicle*, June 3, 1993, p. 16C

473. *Parables, etc.*, Oct. 1993, p. 5

474. *Proclaim*, July-Sept. 1994, p. 15

475. "Victory for Us," Earl Palmer, *Preaching Today*, Tape 127

476. "What Jesus Would Say to David Letterman," Lee Strobel, Seeds Tape Ministry, Aug. 21, 1994

477. *A Pastoral Letter*, Paul Powell, July 1993

478. *Houston Chronicle*, Dec. 4, 1992, p. 10B

479. "Reach Out and Grow," Institute for American Church Growth, 1974

480. *Jubilee*, Chuck Colson, April 1992, p. 7; *Houston Chronicle*, April 24, 1992, p. 2A

481. *Partnership*, Winter 1989

482. *Moody*, March 1993, p. 32

483. *Commission*, Sept. 1993, p. 4

484. *USA Weekend*, July 15, 1994, p. 5

485. *Reader's Digest*, Dec. 1990, p. 104

486. *Houston Chronicle*, July 2, 1995, p. 4G

487. "What Followers Expect from Leaders," John Maxwell, *Injoy Life*, Vol. 7 No. 4

488. *More of Paul Harvey's The Rest of the Story*, Paul Aurandt, 1981, p. 79-80

489. Author's files

490. "Seven Habits of Effective Church Leaders," Robert Clinton, *The Pastor's Update*, July 1991

491. Author's files

492. Author's files

493. Southeast Texas Home School Association Conference, Houston, Texas, June 19, 1993; *Focus on the Family*, June 1993, p. 1

494. *Baptist Program*, 1991

495. Author's files

496. *Full Armor*, July 1991, p. 21

497. Author's files

498. Author's files

499. "Changes that Change You," John Maxwell, July 1993

500. *U.S News & World Report*, April 10, 1995, p. 17

501. *Lead On!*, J. Haggai, 1986, p. 140

502. "Taking God Seriously," Rick Warren, *The Encouraging Word*, 1992

503. *Newsweek*, Nov.. 8, 1993, p. 42; *Houston Chronicle*, Feb. 5, 1993, p. 23A

504. Author's files

505. Adapted from Rick Warren, Saddleback Valley Community Church

506. *Houston Post*, July 18, 1994, p. A-9

507. *Progress*, Feb./March 1993, p. 40

508. *Christian Reader*, Nov./Dec. 1992, p. 72

509. *Guideposts*, Oct.1992, p. 28

510. *Leadership*, April 12, 1994, p. 16

511. *Leadership Journal*, Spring 1991, p. 114

512. "God's Outrageous Claims," Lee Strobel, Seeds Tape Ministry, July 22, 1990

513. "Honey, I Shrunk Our God," Lee Strobel, Seeds Tape Ministry, Nov. 8, 1992

514. *Saturday Evening Post*, Sept./Oct. 1992, p. 14

515. *Baptist Standard*, April 6, 1994, p. 6; United States Census Bureau, 1990

516. *Marriage Partnership*, Vol. 9 No. 4, 1992, p. 14

517. Author's files

518. *USA Today*, Jan. 9, 1992, p. 4D

519. *USA Weekend*, Aug. 30, 1991, p. 4-5

520. *Houston Post*, Dec. 10, 1993, p. C-9

521. *Christian Reader*, May/June 1992, p. 57

522. Author's files

523. *Rotarian*, May 1993, p. 64

524. *Our Daily Bread*, June 15, 1991

525. *Marriage Partnership*, Spring 1991, p. 42

526. *Progress*, Feb./March 1993, p. 19

527. *U.S. News & World Report*, Oct. 2, 1995, p. 88

528. *Good News Is for Sharing*, Leighton Ford, 1977, p. 16

529. Author's files

530. *Houston Post,* Nov. 30, 1992, p. A-2

531. *Christian Financial Concepts*, March 1, 1994

532. "The Sermon on the Amount," Heidi Husted, *Preaching Today*, Tape 122

533. "How to Get Commitment for Ministry," John Maxwell, *The Pastor's Update*, April 1991

534. "Saddleback's Core Values," Rick Warren, *Leadership Lifter* 49

535. *Peak Performers*, Charles Garfield, 1987, p. 160

536. *Our Daily Bread*, Special Edition, Day 26

537. *Baptist Standard,* Aug. 23, 1989

538. *Daily Study Bible Series: the Gospel of Luke*, William Barclay, 1975, p. 205

539. *Houston Post*, Oct. 21, 1994, p. A-20

540. *Thinking the Unthinkable*, John Wesley White, 1992, p. 7

541. Author's files

542. *Houston Post*, July 25, 1994, p. B-2

543. *Newsweek*, May 31, 1993, p. 17

544. *Crossroads*, Vol. 1 No. 7, p. 3-4

545. *Merriam Webster's Collegiate Dictionary*, Tenth Edition, 1993, p. 592

546. *Decision*, May 1990, p. 16-17

547. *Reader's Digest*, Dec. 1992, p. 28

548. *Our Daily Bread*, Aug. 26, 1993

549. *Kindred Spirit*, May-Aug. 1994, p. 11; *U.S. News & World Report*, June 27, 1994, p. 32

550. Author's files

551. *Homemade*, May 1992, p. 1; *Houston Chronicle,* April 15, 1992, p. 19A & May 27, 1992, p. 9A

552. *Houston Chronicle*, June 7, 1995, p. 2A

553. Monopoly Board Game, 1985; "The Game of Life," Lee Strobel, Seeds Tape Ministry, July 28, 1991

554. *Houston Post*, April 23, 1994, p. E-3

555. *The World Almanac*, 1993, p. 958

556. *Houston Chronicle*, Aug. 17, 1994

557. Guided tour of the Temple Complex in Salt Lake City, Utah

558. *Houston Chronicle*, May 5, 1990, Mini Page

559. *Focus on the Family*, Jan. 1992, p. 7

560. Author's files

561. *Focus on the Family*, May 1988, p. 3

562. *Family Research Council*, May 9, 1994, p. 4

563. "Small Group Ministry through the Sunday School," Josh Hunt, Innovative Church Growth Conference, 1994

564. *Newsweek*, Feb. 17, 1992, p. 50

565. *Houston Post*, June 26, 1994, p. A-25

566. *Partnership Challenge*, April 1993; *The NEWSLETTER Newsletter*, June 1993; *Christian Reader*, May/June 1993, p. 48

567. *Newsweek*, May 6, 1991, p. 21

568. *Houston Post*, April 25, 1994, p. A-6

569. *Words in Season*, Penelope Stokes, p. 22

570. *Baptist Program*, April 1992, p. 10

571. *Baptist Program*, Jan.1992, p. 5-9

572. *Reader's Digest*, May 1988, p. 105-109

573. Author's files

574. "How to Keep the Elephants Off Your Airhose," Howard Hendricks, Tape 2705D

575. *USA Weekend*, Jan. 31, 1992, p. 5

576. *U.S. News & World Report*, Oct. 24, 1994, p. 17

577. *The Phone's for You*, Norman Whan, 1988, Tape 1

578. *Paradigms*, Joel Barker Video

579. *Houston Chronicle*, May 20, 1991, p. 2A

580. *Communication Briefings*, Sept. 1993
581. Author's files
582. *Reader's Digest*, Oct. 1990
583. Author's files
584. *Executive Speechwriter Newsletter*, Vol. 8 No. 1
585. Author's files
586. *How to Make a New Start*, Norman Vincent Peale, 1989, p. 24-25
587. "Win or Lose? The Choice is Yours," John Maxwell, *Injoy*, March 1993
588. *Ministry Currents*, Jan.-March 1992, p. 10
589. *Proclaim*, Fall 1991, p. 13; *What Americans Believe*, George Barna, 1991, p. 274-276
590. "Special Message from Billy Graham on Global Mission," 1995; "How to Double Your Attendance," Elmer Towns, Church Growth Institute, 1995
591. *Church Administration*, Oct. 1995, p. 19
592. "How to Get Morale Up . . . In Down Times," John Maxwell, Injoy, Oct. 1993
593. *Why Teenagers Act the Way They Do*, G. Keith Olson, 1987, p. 66-67; *Focus on the Family*, Feb. 1992, p. 5; *Houston Chronicle*, Dec. 29, 1991, p. G-1
594. *Houston Chronicle*, Jan. 17, 1993, p. 2B
595. Author's files
596. *Homemade*, Aug. 1991
597. Author's files
598. *Straight Talk to Men and Their Wives*, James Dobson, 1980, p. 52-53
599. Author's files
600. *Focus on the Family*, "Crafting Your Child's Education," Jan. 1994, p. 1
601. *Houston Chronicle*, May 5, 1995, p. 1D
602. *Homemade*, March 1992, p. 1
603. Author's files
604. Author's files
605. *Houston Post*, date unknown
606. *Home Life*, Nov. 1993, p. 18
607. Author's files
608. *Baptist Beacon*, Oct. 1, 1992, p. 3
609. *Reader's Digest*, Feb. 1993, p. 17-18
610. "Growing with Your Church," Doug Murren, *The Pastor's Update*, Dec. 91
611. Charles E. Fuller Institute of Evangelism and Church Growth, 1991
612. *Have a Good Day*, May 1992, p. 2
613. *Today's Christian Woman*, May/June 1992, p. 36-37
614. Author's files
615. *Leadership*, Jan. 19, 1993, p. 3
616. *Living Above the Level of Mediocrity*, Charles Swindoll, 1987, p. 226-227
617. "Followership," Joseph Stowell, Seeds Tape Ministry, Aug. 25, 1993
618. *Homemade*, Sept.1992
619. *Positioning: the Battle for Your Mind*, Al Ries & Jack Trout, 1986, p. 65
620. *Inc.*, Nov. 1993, p. 11
621. *Sports Spectrum*, Nov./Dec.1992, p. 18
622. Charles Swindoll, Congress on Biblical Exposition, 1988
623. *San Antonio Express-News*, April 9, 1995, p. 1A
624. Author's files
625. *Bits & Pieces*, Houston Public Library Information Service; Dec. 9, 1993, p. 4-5
626. *Parenting Isn't for Cowards*, James Dobson, 1987, p. 114-115
627. "A Mind-Expanding Faith," John Ortberg, Preaching Today, Tape 126
628. *Houston Chronicle*, Dec. 26, 1992, p. 10B

629. *Pastor to Pastor*, H. B. London, Vol. 13

630. *Leadership Journal*, Winter 1994, p. 47

631. *Newsweek*, March 23, 1992, p. 21

632. *Parade*, Dec. 27, 1992, p. 5

633. *Stick a Geranium in Your Hat and Be Happy*, Barbara Johnson, 1990, p. 10

634. "The Greatest Sermon in History," Part 17, Bill Hybels, Seeds Tape Ministry, Jan. 16, 1994

635. *Newsweek*, Feb. 10, 1992, p. 50; *Houston Chronicle*, Feb. 3, 1992, p. C-1

636. Author's files

637. *Creative Suffering*, Paul Tournier, 1981, p. 51

638. *Where Is God When It Hurts?*, Philip Yancey, 1977, p. 180; *Reader's Digest*, Feb.1992, p. 91

639. *Houston Post*, Jan. 29, 1994, p. B-2

640. *The Myth of the Greener Grass*, J. Allen Petersen, 1983, p. 14

641. *Preacher Talk*, Brian Harbour, Vol. 1 Tape 1

642. *Reader's Digest*, Sept. 1992, p. 38

643. *Houston Chronicle*, Jan. 23, 1993, p. 2E

644. *HomeLife*, Feb. 1994, p. 42; *Houston Post*, Dec. 20, 1994, p. A-18

645. "The Day Willow Creek Community Church Told the Truth," Bill Hybels, Seeds Tape Ministry

646. *Fatal Addiction*, Jan. 23, 1989

647. "Successful and Unsuccessful Pastors: How Are They Different?" John Maxwell, *Injoy*, Oct. 1992

648. *The Sandwich Years,* Dennis & Ruth Gibson, 1991, p. 11

649. *Focus on the Family*, Jan. 1993, p. 2

650. Author's files

651. *Today in the Word*, Dec. 1992, p. 8

652. *Tracks of a Fellow Struggler*, John Claypool, 1976, p. 38-39

653. Author's files

654. *U.S. News & World Report*, Aug. 22, 1994, p. 10

655. *Power House: a Step by Step Guide to Building a Church that Prays,* Glen Martin & Dian Ginter, 1994, p. 1-2

656. *Illustrations for Biblical Preaching*, Michael Green, editor, 1989, p. 275

657. Author's files

658. *Today's Christian Woman*, May/June 1994, p. 33

659. *Peak Performers*, Charles Garfield, 1987, p. 294

660. "Do Something!" Emmanuel McCall, 1993

661. *Commission*, Dec. 1991, p. 4-5

662. *Deacon*, Winter 1995, p. 38

663. *SBC Life*, Jan. 1994, p .3; *Christian Reader*, Sept./Oct.1993, p. 46

664. *Guideposts*, Jan. 1993, p. 46

665. "How to Pray," R. C. Sproul, Ligonier Ministries, 1991

666. *Facts & Trends*, July/Aug. 1994, p. 10

667. Author's files

668. Author's files

669. Author's files

670. *A Hunger for Healing*, J. Keith Miller, 1991, p. 36

671. *Homemade*, Dec. 1991, p. 1

672. Author's files

673. Author's files

674. Author's files

675. Author's files

676. *Teaching to Change Lives*, Howard Hendricks, 1987, p. 60

677. "Solitaire," Gene Appel, Seeds Tape Ministry, July 24, 1994

678. *Christians in Pain*, B. W. Woods, 1974, p. 57

679. "The Human Side of Ministry," Rick Warren, *The Pastor's Update*, Feb. 1991

680. Author's files
681. *Houston Post*, Jan.. 7, 1995, p. A-16
682. *Our Daily Bread*, Aug. 2, 1992
683. Author's files
684. *Straight Talk*, James Dobson, 1991, p. 207-208
685. *Houston Post*, June 6, 1991, p. B-18
686. Ibid, March 28, 1995, p. A-2
687. *Pastor's Weekly Briefing*, Feb. 11, 1994, p. 1
688. *Executive Speechwriter Newsletter*, Vol. 8 No. 2
689. *Sermon Notes & Illustrations*, Sept. 1994, p. 22
690. Author's files
691. Author's files
692. *Houston Chronicle*, Oct. 9, 1995, p. 2D
693. "The Innovating Model," Leith Anderson, Innovative Church Growth Conference, 1994
694. Author's files
695. Author's files
696. *Pastor's Update*, Jan. 1992, p. 4
697. *Houston Post*, Jan. 15, 1995, p. A-26
698. *Odyssey*, John Sculley, 1987, p. 90
699. *Leadership*, Aug. 2, 1994, p. 1
700. "Yea God . . . for Being an Equal Opportunity Employer," John Ortberg, Seeds Tape Ministry, Feb. 5, 1995
701. "Our Modern Moral Trifecta: Racism," Bill Hybels, Seeds Tape Ministry, March 21, 1993; *ABC's of the Human Body*, 1987, p. 130
702. Author's files
703. "How to Stay Mentally Fit," Rick Warren, *Leadership Lifter*, No. 59; Preacher Talk, Vol. 3 Tape 1, 1995
704. *Today in the Word*, Nov. 1991, p. 8
705. *Homemade*, Jan. 1993, p. 1
706. "The Innovating Man," Sam Williams, Innovative Church Growth Conference, 1994
707. *Refiner*, Dec. 1993, p. 1
708. Rick Warren, *Leadership Lifters*, No. 54
709. Author's files
710. *Houston Post*, Oct. 5, 1994, p. D-6
711. *Proclaim*, Jan.-March 1989, p. 33
712. *Total Church Life*, Darrell Robinson, 1985; Leighton Ford, Leighton Ford Evangelism Leadership Seminar 1991; *Church Growth Newsletter*, Vol. 2 No.1, p. 1-3
713. *Houston Chronicle*, Dec. 5, 1991, p. 32A
714. *Leadership*, Summer 1991, p. 71
715. *Seven World's Publishing*, May/June 1991
716. *Preacher Talk*, Brian Harbor, Vol. 2 Tape 3
717. Barna Research Group, 1990
718. Author's files
719. "God Is First a Father," Peter Lord, Agape Ministries, Jan. 6, 1991
720. *Our Daily Bread*, March 19, 1992
721. *The Christian Persuader*, Leighton Ford, 1988, p. 10
722. *Leadership*, Nov. 1995, p. 2
723. *Proclaim,* Jan.-March 1993, p. 28
724. *The Psychology of Winning*, Denis Waitley, 1984, p. 56
725. *Houston Chronicle*, June 5, 1993, p. 1-B
726. Associated Press, May 14, 1992
727. *Today in the Word*, June 1991, p. 35
728. Ibid, Dec. 1993, p. 24
729. *The Psychology of Winning*, Denis Waitley, 1984, p. 111
730. *Houston Chronicle*, June 19, 1993, p. 10C; *Illustrations for Biblical Preaching*, Michael Green, editor, 1989, p .209
731. *Our Daily Bread*, Oct. 31, 1992
732. *Houston Post*, March 8, 1992, p. A-2
733. *Houston Chronicle*, May 20, 1993, p. 2A
734. *The Body*, Charles Colson, 1992
735. *Today in the Word*, Feb. 1991, p. 27

736. *Baptist Standard*, March 4, 1987 and Jan. 24, 1990; *Dallas Morning News*, Jan. 25, 1986

737. Author's files

738. *NEWSLETTER Newsletter*, May 1993

739. *USA Weekend*, Jan. 31, 1992, p. 18-20

740. "The Power of Love," Jack Graham, Prestonwood Baptist Church, June 11, 1995

741. *Focus on the Family Newsletter*, Feb. 1992, p. 2-5

742. *A Missions People: the Southern Baptist Pilgrimage*, M. Wendell Belew, 1989, p. 66

743. *Houston Post*, April 3, 1992, p. 2

744. *Pastor to Pastor*, H. B. London, Vol. 9 Tape 3

745. *Houston Post*, April 16, 1992, Front page

746. "What Jesus Would Say to Billy Graham," Lee Strobel, Seeds Tape Ministry, Aug. 28, 1994

747. *Leadership Journal*, Fall 1988, p. 33

748. *The Body*, Charles Colson, 1992, p. 318-327

749. *The Frog in the Kettle*, George Barna, 1990, p. 205

750. *Baptist Standard*, Sept. 16, 1992, p. 7-15

751. *When God Doesn't Make Sense*, James Dobson, 1993, p. 194-195

752. *Houston Chronicle*, Dec. 24, 1992, p. 8C

753. *Baptist Standard*, Jan. 6, 1993, p. 7

754. *Proclaim*, July-Sept. 1991, p. 29

755. *Houston Chronicle*, May 16, 1992

756. *Houston Post*, Nov. 1, 1993, p. A-12

757. Ibid, Oct. 10, 1993, p. B17-18

758. *Houston Chronicle*, Nov. 3, 1992, p. 11A

759. Ibid, Dec. 10, 1992, p. C-9

760. *The Golden Gate Bridge*, A&E Television Networks, 1994

761. *Parade*, Oct. 1, 1995, p. 35

762. "Love for the Least," Max Lucado, Seeds Tape Ministry, July 16, 1994

763. *Ministry Currents*, Spring 1993, p. 6

764. "Assimilation: Drawing Visitors into the Life of Your Church," Robert Logan, *The Pastor's Update*, Feb. 1991

765. *Houston Chronicle*, July 31, 1992, p. 13C

766. *Who Switched the Price Tags?*, Tony Campolo, 1986, p. 28-29

767. *Houston Post*, Oct. 29, 1993, p. A-6

768. Ibid, May 20, 1994, p. A-15

769. Author's files; *Reader's Digest*, July 1989, p. 8

770. *Guideposts*, May 1993, p. 5

771. *Saturday Evening Post*, Sept./Oct. 1992, p. 61

772. *LifeWalk*, May/June 1991, Compassion, p. 3

773. Author's files

774. Author's files

775. Author's files

776. Author's files

777. Author's files

778. "The Payoff for Sexual Purity," Jim Dethmer, Seeds Tape Ministry, Jan. 31, 1993

779. *Houston Post*, Jan. 10, 1994, p. A-10

780. *Facing Death and the Life After*, Billy Graham, 1987, p. 93-94

781. *Media Management Newsletter*, April 1994, p. 3

782. *Seven Worlds Publishing*

783. *Inc.*, Aug. 1991, p. 44

784. Author's files

785. *Newsweek*, Feb. 3, 1992, p. 44-51

786. *Bits & Pieces*, March May 92, p. 10

787. *Reader's Digest*, Dec. 1992, p. 18

788. *Leadership Journal*, Fall 1988

789. *Daily Walk*, June 19, 1991

790. *Seeds of Greatness*, Denis Waitley, 1983, p. 84

791. *Illustration Digest*, Sept.-Nov. 1992, p. 22

792. "What Jesus Would Say to Murphy Brown," Lee Strobel, Seeds Tape Ministry, July 19, 1992

793. *Better Families*, Aug. 1993, p. 1

794. *Communication Briefings*, Vol. 12 No. 6, p. 4

795. *American Bible Society Record*, March 1990

796. *Crossroads*, Issue 8, p. 21

797. *Leadership*, Jan. 22, 1992, p. 7-8

798. *Houston Post*, June 20, 1994, p. A-8

799. *Baptist Standard*, Dec. 22, 1993, p. 11

800. *Leadership*, Aug. 1994, p. 18

801. *Fresh Encounter Leader Manual*, Henry Blackaby & Claude King, 1993, p. 8

802. *Houston Chronicle*, Nov. 10, 1991, p. 33A

803. *Church Administration*, Oct. 1995, p. 17

804. *The Years Ahead*, Summer 1993

805. *Teaching to Change Lives*, Howard Hendricks, 1987, p. 66

806. *Houston Post*, April 14, 1995, p. A-22

807. Bob Reccord, Leighton Ford Evangelism Leadership Seminar, 1991

808. *Media Management Newsletter*, April 1994, p. 4

809. *Today in the Word*, May 1991, p. 33

810. *Kindred Spirit*, Vol. 16 No. 1, p. 6

811. *Pryor Report*, May 1993, p. 2

812. *The Seven Habits Report*, Fall 1991, p. 5

813. *Newsweek*, Jan. 6, 1992, p. 30-32

814. *Megatrends 2000*, John Naisbitt & Patricia Aburdene, p. 276, 294

815. *NEWSLETTER Newsletter*, Aug. 1994

816. *Baptist Standard*, May 12, 1993, p. 24; *Facts & Trends*, May 1988, p. 3

817. *Baptist Program*, Aug. 1991, p. 23

818. *Houston Chronicle*, June 18, 1995, p. 23A

819. Ibid, Sept. 7, 1992, p. 1A

820. *Houston Post,* July 26, 1992, p. C-1

821. *Reader's Digest*, Aug. 1987, p. 23-29

822. Author's files

823. *Houston Chronicle*, Nov. 7, 1989, p. 2D

824. "Panorama of Parenting," Howard Hendricks, Dallas Theological Seminary, T42PEY

825. *Laugh Again*, Charles Swindoll, 1992, p. 99

826. *Houston Post*, Oct. 20, 1994, p. A-10

827. *Baptist Standard*, July 22, 1992, p. 8

828. *Master Your Money Video Series*, Ron Blue, 1990

829. *Reader's Digest*, Aug. 1991, p. 163

830. Author's files

831. *Decision*, Feb. 1994, p. 12

832. *Path to Victory*, International Bible Society, 1993

833. "The Profit of Financial Integrity," Jim Dethmer, Seeds Tape Ministry, Feb. 21, 1993; *Baptist Standard,* June 30, 1993, p. 4

834. *Houston Post,* Jan. 2, 1995, p. C-4; *Ministry Currents,* Spring 1994, p. 14; *Houston Chronicle*, Jan. 5, 1992, p. 2G

835. Author's files

836. *Proclaim*, Jan.-March, 1989, p. 34

837. Author's files

838. *Inc.*, Jan. 1992, p. 11

839. Author's files

840. *Leadership*, Vol. B No. 2, 1991, p. 1

841. *Inc.*, Nov. 1992, p. 101-102

842. Author's files

843. Author's files

844. Author's files

845. Author's files

846. *Hope for the Sick and Hurting*, Linda Raney Wright, 1990, p. 156; *Facing Death and the Life After*, Billy Graham, 1987, p. 111-112

847. *Our Daily Bread*, May 5, 1992
848. *Baptist Standard*, Sept. 28, 1994, p. 7; *Houston Post*, Dec. 22, 1993, p. A-20
849. *Reminisce*, May/June 1995
850. *Sagemont Challenger*, Jan. 11, 1993, p. 1
851. *Houston Chronicle*, Jan. 24, 1993, p. 7G; *Parade*, Dec. 27, 1992, p. 5
852. *Lead On*, John Haggai, 1986, p. 50-51
853. *Houston Post*, April 13, 1994, p. B-2
854. *Mature Living*, April 1994, p. 46
855. *Wall Street Journal*, May 11, 1994, p. A-1
856. *Bits & Pieces*, April 2, 1992, p. 22
857. *Pryor Report*, Dec. 1992, p. 1
858. *Life and Work Lesson Plan*, Lucien Coleman, March 5, 1989, p. 1
859. Author's files
860. *Bits & Pieces,* Dec. 12, 1991, p. 14
861. *Today in the Word*, May 1991, p. 35
862. *Marriage Partnership*, Summer 1991, p. 87
863. *Rebuilding Your Broken World*, Gordan MacDonald, 1988, p. 53
864. *Houston Post*, Feb. 18, 1995, p. A-18
865. Author's files
866. *The Rebirth of America*, Nancy Leigh DeMoss, editor, 1986, p. 82
867. *Houston Post,* Nov. 5, 1991, p. D-7
868. *Your Pastor & You*, Richard DeHaan, 1992, p. 22-23
869. *Newsweek*, March 23, 1992, p. 24-31; *A Greek-English Lexicon of the New Testament and Other Early Christian Literature*, Arndt & Gingrich, p. 810-811
870. "Studying Adult Life and Work Lessons," Herschel Hobbs, Jan. 30, 1994, p. 47
871. *LifeWalk, Jesus the God-Man*, p. 4, May/June 1991
872. Author's files
873. Author's files
874. *Sermon Notes & Illustrations*, Sept. 1994, p. 17; *Houston Post*, Oct. 11, 1994, p. A-10
875. "Time Management for the Busy Pastor," Bob Logan
876. *Unleashing Connection*, Winter 1990, p. 3
877. *Pastor to Pastor*, H. B. London, Vol. 7
878. *Leadership Journal*, Spring 1988, p. 46
879. *Baptist Program*, Nov. 1992, p. 19
880. Contributed by Tim Wilkins
881. *Leadership*, Nov. 1993, p. 4
882. *Daily Walk*, Oct. 23, 1991
883. *TableTalk*, March 1991, p. 27
884. *Houston Chronicle*, Sept. 1989
885. *Proclaim*, April-June 1991, p. 35
886. Author's files
887. Author's files
888. *Houston Chronicle*, Feb. 20, 1993, p. 4E
889. *Houston Post*, March 7, 1994, p. A-12
890. *The World Almanac and Book of Facts 1993*, p. 639
891. *Newsweek*, Sept. 30, 1991, p. 48
892. "The Innovating Man," Tony Evans, Innovative Church Growth Conference, 1994
893. Ronnie Floyd, SBC Pastor's Conference, 1993
894. *Sagemont Challenger*, Feb. 18, 1991, p. 2
895. *Newsweek*, Oct. 14, 1991, p. 21
896. *Houston Post*, April 19, 1992, p. A-27
897. Author's files
898. *Have a Good Day*, May 1992, p. 4
899. Author's files
900. *Houston Chronicle,* Sept. 29, 1991, p. 7C; *Houston Post*, Sept. 29, 1991, p. A-24
901. *Ministry Currents*, Aug. 1991, p. 1
902. "The Sexual Side of Love," Lee Strobel, Seeds Tape Ministry, Oct. 30, 1994; *Focus on the Family*, Sept. 1995, p. 10

903. *Reminisce*, Nov./Dec. 1995, p. 19; Author's files
904. *Houston Post*, Oct. 3, 1994, p. A-5; *National Geographic*, Dec. 1986, p. 700
905. *Reader's Digest*, June 1988, p. 163-170
906. *Our Daily Bread*, Special Edition, Day 15
907. *New Life for Your Church*, Doyle L. Young, 1989, p. 63
908. *Discipleship Journal*, July/Aug. 1991, p. 55
909. Author's files
910. *Houston Chronicle*, June 7, 1995, p. 7A
911. *Living Obediently*, Brian Harbour, 1992, p. 98-99
912. Southern Baptist Sunday School Board statistics
913. *No Wonder They Call Him the Savior*, Max Lucado, 1986, p. 31-32
914. Author's files
915. "Taking Orange County By Storm," Rick Warren, *The Encouraging Word*, Tape 42; *Houston Post*, June 5, 1994, p. V-5
916. *Houston Post*, Oct. 19, 1994, p. A-10
917. *Inc.*, Sept. 1991, p. 69
918. *Houston Chronicle*, May 23, 1991, p. 9A
919. *Houston Post*, Sept. 18, 1992, p. A-2
920. *Newsweek*, Nov. 4, 1991, p. 43
921. Author's files
922. "The Foundation for a Strong Family," Rick Warren, *The Encouraging Word*, 1992
923. *Baptist Standard*, June 5, 1991, p. 12
924. *U.S. News & World Report*, Aug. 7, 1995, p. 45
925. Contributed by Al McHenry
926. *Houston Chronicle*, Feb. 5, 1993, p. 4C
927. Author's files
928. *Dallas Morning News*, April 1995, p. 2G
929. *Houston Post*, Sept. 25, 1992, p. B-1
930. *Leadership*, March 16, 1993, p. 1
931. *Houston Chronicle*, March 4, 1993, p. 8E
932. Ibid, April 26, 1992, p. 11A
933. *Proclaim,* July/Aug./Sept. 1991, p. 31; *Houston Chronicle*, Aug. 13, 1991, p. 2D; *Houston Post*, Dec. 3, 1994, p. C-1
934. *Houston Chronicle*, Oct. 31, 1993, p. 16B
935. Ibid, May 3, 1991, p. 1C
936. *Baptist Standard*, May 12, 1993, p. 8-10;
937. *Christian Behaviour*, C. S. Lewis, 1946, p. 51
938. "You Don't Have to Worry," Michael Dean, Baptist Hour, Feb. 5, 1993
939. *Lead the Field*, Earl Nightingale, 1990, p. 24
940. *LifeWalk*, May/June, 1991; *Worship*, p. 2
941. Author's files
942. Author's files
943. *Houston Post,* Jan. 31, 1993, Section A
944. *Merriam-Webster's Collegiate Dictionary,* Tenth Edition, 1993
945. Author's files
946. *NEWSLETTER Newsletter*, March 1994
947. *Teaching to Change Lives*, Howard Hendricks, 1987, p. 156
948. *The Best of Grandparents' Brag Board*, Judy Pregel & Robin Riley, 1993, p. 33
949. *Rotarian*, Oct. 1993, p. 72
950. *Baptist Beacon*, April 27, 1995, p. 5
951. *NEWSLETTER Newsletter*, Aug. 1994
952. Author's files
953. *Reader's Digest*, Feb. 1991, p. 58

954. Bill Thorn, Banquet at GMBC, Nov. 22, 1991
955. *NEWSLETTER Newsletter*, June 1995
956. Bill Thorn, Banquet at GMBC, Nov. 22, 1991
957. *Houston Post*, May 17, 1993, p. B-6
958. "How to Grow a Marriage," Howard Hendricks, Dallas Theological Seminary, Tape T42M1Y
959. *Mature Living*, April 1994, p. 49
960. *Curtis Vaughan*, SWBTS, 1991
961. *Mature Living*, March 1993, p. 48
962. *Reminisce*, July/Aug. 1994, p. 64
963. *Houston Post,* Oct. 20, 1990
964. *Reminisce*, Sept./Oct. 1992, p. 59
965. *Winning Walk*, Ed Young
966. *Houston Post*, Sept. 21, 1993, p. B-7
967. *Houston Chronicle*, Oct. 8, 1992, p. 8B
968. *Sesame Street Parents' Guide*, Nov. 1991, p. 74
969. *Illustration Digest*, Summer 1994, p. 11
970. *Children's Letters to God*, Stuart Hample & Eric Marshall, 1991, Letter 6
971. *Reader's Digest*, Sept. 1990, p. 44
972. "Panorama of Parenting," Howard Hendricks, Dallas Theological Seminary, T42PEY
973. *Houston Chronicle*, April 25, 1993, p. 23
974. *Newsweek*, March 16, 1992, p. 70
975. *Rotarian*, April 1993, p. 64
976. *Parade,* March 10, 1991, p. 11
977. *Reader's Digest*, Dec. 1992, p. 28
978. Ibid, Aug. 1989, p. 16
979. Ibid, Aug. 1991, p. 50
980. "A Hunger for Healing," Keith Miller, Seeds Tape Ministry, Jan. 19, 1992
981. *Reader's Digest*, Nov. 1992, p. 89
982. *Christian Reader*, Nov./Dec. 1994, p. 48
983. *Positive Living*, Sept./Oct. 1995, p. 39
984. *Houston Chronicle*, March 30, 1991
985. *The Happy Clergy*, Herb Walker, 1977, p. 7
986. *Reminisce*, July/Aug. 1993, p. 60
987. *Great Stories*, David Sylvester
988. *Reader's Digest*, Sept. 1992, p. 98
989. *Dying for Change*, Leith Anderson, 1990, p. 9-10
990. "Passages that Pump Me Up," John Ortberg, Seeds Tape Ministry, M9523
991. *Preacher Talk*, Vol. 3 Tape 2, 1995
992. *Houston Chronicle*, July 19, 1992
993. Author's files
994. *Houston Post*, Dec. 2, 1991, p. A-17
995. "Telling the Truth," Rick Warren, *The Encouraging Word*
996. *Positive Living*, Sept./Oct. 1995, p. 39
997. *Christian Parenting Today*, May/June 1991, p. 73
998. "Understanding the Times: the 90s," Lee Strobel, Seeds Tape Ministry, Oct. 4, 1992
999. *Christian Parenting Today*, March/April 1991, p. 59
1000. Contributed by Wayne Rouse
1001. *Mature Living*, Feb. 1994, p. 48
1002. *Houston Post*, Oct. 25, 1993, p. B-6
1003. *Reader's Digest*, Feb. 1992, p. 59
1004. "The Difference between Managers and Leaders," John Maxwell, *Injoy,* Jan. 1993
1005. *Rotarian*, Sept. 1993, p. 72
1006. *Saturday Evening Post*, Jan./Feb. 1993, p. 35
1007. *Saturday Evening Post*, March/April 1992, p. 28
1008. *Houston Chronicle*, June 14, 1995
1009. *American Health*, March 1992, p. 73

1010. *Mature Living*, May 1993, p. 46

1011. *Houston Post*, May 19, 1992, p. D-6

1012. "A Time for Extravagance," Jerry Clower, 1992

1013. Author's personal true story

1014. Contributed by Wayne Rouse

1015. *Christian Parenting*, July/Aug. 1991, p. 59

1016. Innovative Church Growth Conference, 1994

1017. *Reader's Digest*, Dec. 1991, p. 63

1018. *Illustration Digest*, March/April 1994, p. 7

1019. *Pastor's Update*, Feb. 1992, p. 3

1020. Author's files

1021. "A Time for Extravagance," Jerry Clower, 1992

1022. *Executive Speechwriter Newsletter*, Vol. 8 No. 4

1023. *Reader's Digest*, Feb. 1991, p. 58

1024. Author's files

1025. *Illustration Digest*, Fall 1993

1026. *Encouraging Word*, Rick Warren

1027. *Laugh*, Feb. 1994

1028. *The Happy Clergy*, Herb Walker, 1977, p. 14

1029. *Reader's Digest*, Oct. 1990, p. 90

1030. "Becoming a Contagious Christian: Authenticity," Bill Hybels, Seeds Tape Ministry

1031. *Parenting Isn't for Cowards*, James Dobson, 1987, p. 118-119

1032. *Watching the World Go By*, W. E. Thorn, p. 46

1033. *Houston Post*

1034. *Charles Lowery*, SBC Pastor's Conference, 1993

1035. *Rotarian*, Sept. 1993, p. 72

1036. *Reader's Digest*, Nov. 1992, p. 64

1037. *Saturday Evening Post*, Nov./Dec. 1992, p. 35

1038. *Reader's Digest*, Oct. 1992, p. 73

1039. Author's files

1040. *Reader's Digest*, Aug. 1992, p. 71

1041. Adapted from *The Happy Clergy*, Herb Walker, 1977, p. 16

1042. *Inc.*, Aug. 1994, p. 10

1043. *Reader's Digest*, Jan. 1993, p. 72

1044. *Houston Post*, Dec. 4, 1994, p. B-2

1045. *Reader's Digest*, Oct. 1990, p. 90

1046. *Rotarian*, May 1994, p. 64

1047. *The Happy Clergy*, Herb Walker, 1977, p. 12

1048. *The Best of Grandparents' Brag Board*, Judy Pregel & Robin Riley, 1993, p. 13

1049. *NEWSLETTER Newsletter*, Dec. 1995, p. 3

1050. *The Word*, Doug Jackson, April 18, 1990, p. 4

1051. *Reader's Digest*, Nov. 1992, p. 128

1052. Ibid, March 1991, p. 60

1053. *Bits & Pieces*, March 5, 1992, p. 21-22

1054. *Rotarian*, June 1993, p. 56

1055. *King's Treasury of Dynamic Humor*, King Duncan, 1990, p. 25

1056. *Bits & Pieces*, Dec. 9, 1993, p. 17

1057. *Houston Chronicle*, June 27, 1993, p. 16B

1058. "Love for the Least," Max Lucado, Seeds Tape Ministry, July 16, 1994

1059. *Leadership*, Feb. 15, 1994, p. 17

1060. *Your Church*, May/June 1994, p. 8

1061. *Reader's Digest*, July 1991, p. 43

1062. Author's files

1063. *Executive Speechwriter Newsletter*, "Religion & Philosophy," Vol. 1

1064. Author's files

1065. *Proclaim*, July-Sept. 1994, p. 39

1066. *Reminisce*, Jan./Feb. 1993, p. 59

1067. *Christian Parenting Today*, Nov./Dec. 1991, p. 93

1068. *Houston Post*, Sept. 11, 1992, p. E-14

1069. *Guideposts*, Oct. 1992, p. 13

1070. *Our Daily Bread*, Special Edition, Day 24

1071. *Mature Living*, June 1992, p. 49

1072. *Reminisce*, May/June 1995, p. 61

1073. *Houston Post*, May 12, 1994, p. D-6

1074. Colonel Chuck Scott, Kiwanis National Prayer Breakfast, 1992

1075. Author's files

1076. *Executive Speechwriter Newsletter*, Vol. 8 No. 2

1077. *Homemade*, May 1993, p. 2

1078. *Reader's Digest*, Nov. 1989, p. 11

1079. Author's files

1080. *Arizona Highways*, Oct. 1995, p. 48

1081. *Brian's Lines*, Aug. 1991

1082. *Houston Post*, Feb. 20, 1995, p. D-7

1083. *Reminisce*, Aug. 1994, p. 60

1084. *Leadership*, Vol. B No. 1, p. 23-24

1085. *Saturday Evening Post*, Jan./Feb. 1994, p. 32

1086. *Parade*, April 25, 1993, p. 14

1087. *Houston Post*, May 21, 1994, p. G-3

1088. Adapted from *Reader's Digest*, Sept. 1992, p. 126

1089. *Rotarian,* Oct. 1992, p. 64

1090. *Reader's Digest*, Oct. 1991, p. 86

1091. *Houston Post*, Dec. 31, 1992, p. D-11

1092. Ibid, Dec. 12, 1992, p. A-2

1093. *Reader's Digest*, Oct. 1991, p. 183

1094. *Laugh Again*, Charles Swindoll, 1992, p. 126

1095. *Reminisce*, Nov./Dec. 1994, p. 65

1096. *Houston Post*, Dec. 12, 1992, p. A-2

1097. Ike Reighard, SBC Pastor's Conference, 1993

1098. *Better Families*, June 1994, p. 2

1099. *Home Life*, Nov. 1992, p. 23

1100. *Baptist Beacon*, May 14, 1992, p. 4

1101. *Reminisce*, Jan./Feb. 1993, p. 58

1102. *Reader's Digest*, Oct. 1989, p. 75

1103. Ibid, Sept. 1990

1104. *Good Housekeeping*, June 1992, p. 214

1105. Author's files

1106. "Survival for the Pastor," Charles Swindoll, 1981

1107. Author's files

1108. *Houston Chronicle*, May 9, 1995, p. 9D

1109. *Houston Post*, Feb. 20, 1995, p. D-7

1110. *Bits & Pieces*, Feb. 4, 1993, p. 8

1111. *Mature Living*, Nov. 1992, p. 49

1112. Adapted from *Encyclopedia of 7700 Illustrations*, Paul Tan, p. 440

1113. *American Health*, March 1992, p. 79

1114. *Proclaim*, Spring 1991, p. 48

1115. *Houston Post*, Sept. 11, 1992, p. E-15

1116. *Leadership*, April 12, 1994, p. 23

1117. *Better Families*, Jan. 1994, p. 2

1118. *Mature Living*, April 1995, p. 7

1119. *Homemade*, April 1992, p. 3

1120. *Christian Reader*, Nov./Dec. 1994, p. 105

1121. *Saturday Evening Post*, March/April 1992, p. 30

1122. *Watching the World Go By*, W. E. Thorn, 1987, p. 26

1123. Author's files

1124. *Reader's Digest*, Jan. 1993, p. 50

1125. *Christian Parenting Today*, Sept./Oct. 1992, p. 83

1126. *Brian's Lines*, March/April 1995

1127. *Seven World's Publishing*, May/June 1991

1128. *Lockhorns*, Dec. 14, 1992

1129. Stuart Briscoe, *Preaching Today,* Tape 89

1130. "Secrets of a Successful Ministry," Rick Warren, *Leadership Lifters* Tape 68

1131. Author's personal true story

1132. *Rotarian*, Nov. 1991, p. 64

1133. *Houston Post*, June 25, 1994, p. F-13

1134. *Reader's Digest*, March 1992, p. 144

1135. *Sermons Illustrated*, Jan./Feb. 1993
1136. *Plains Crusader*, Date Unknown
1137. *Houston Post*, Oct. 17, 1994, p. C-7
1138. *NEWSLETTER Newsletter*, June 1994
1139. *Reminisce*, Jan./Feb. 1994, p. 61
1140. Ibid, Feb. 1995, p. 61
1141. Ibid, Jan./Feb. 1993, p. 58
1142. *The Happy Clergy*, Herb Walker, 1977, p. 12
1143. *Rotarian*, Dec. 1993, p. 64
1144. *The Treasury of Clean Church Jokes*, Tal Bonham, 1986 p. 26-27
1145. *Houston Post*, Nov. 16, 1991
1146. *Christian Parenting Today*, July/Aug. 1992, p. 67
1147. *Mule Eggs and Topknots*, King Duncan, 1987, p. 148
1148. *Rapha Report*, June 10, 1994, p. 1
1149. *Today in the Word*, May 1993, p. 27
1150. *King's Treasury of Dynamic Humor*, King Duncan, p. 56
1151. *Humorous Notes, Quotes, and Anecdotes*, Leslie & Bernice Flynn, 1973, p. 110
1152. *Mule Eggs and Topknots*, King Duncan, 1987, p. 155
1153. *Humorous Notes, Quotes, And Anecdotes*, Leslie & Bernice Flynn, 1973, p. 110
1154. *Mature Living*, Sept. 1991, p. 49
1155. *Kid's Corner*, July 1992, p. 1
1156. Author's files
1157. *Reader's Digest*, Dec. 1991, p. 66
1158. "What Leaders Expect From Followers," John Maxwell, Vol. 8 No. 10, 1993
1159. *Saturday Evening Post*, Nov./Dec. 1992, p. 34
1160. *Houston Post*, Dec. 31, 1991, p. D-9
1161. *Reminisce*, Jan./Feb. 1993, p. 59
1162. *Better Families*, Aug. 1993, p. 2
1163. *Leadership*, Dec. 23, 1993, p. 14
1164. *Southwestern News*, May/June 1992, p. 3
1165. *Bits & Pieces*, Nov. 12, 1992, p. 22
1166. *Baptist Program*, April 1992, p. 6
1167. "The Aftermath of Easter," Lee Strobel, Seeds Tape Ministry, April 14, 1992
1168. Author's files
1169. *Watching the World Go By*, W. E. Thorn, p. 14
1170. *Leadership*, July 5, 1994, p. 24
1171. *Executive Speechwriter Newsletter*, Vol. 8 No. 1
1172. *Leadership*, Winter 1990, p. 50
1173. *Houston Post*, Feb. 10, 1992, p. D-6
1174. *Houston Chronicle*, July 9, 1995, p. 12B
1175. *Rotarian*, Sept. 1993, p. 72
1176. *Reader's Digest*, Date Unknown
1177. *Baptist Beacon*, Feb. 20, 1992, p. 5
1178. *Houston Chronicle*, Oct. 1, 1995, p. 9D
1179. *Reader's Digest*, Jan. 1991, p. 113
1180. *Christian Reader*, Sept./Oct. 1993, p. 40-41
1181. *Sermon Notes and Illustrations*, May 1995
1182. *Homemade*, March 1993, p. 2
1183. *King's Treasury of Dynamic Humor*, King Duncan, 1990, p. 28
1184. "Power," Howard Hendricks, *Preaching Today*, Tape 119
1185. *Christian Parenting Today*, March/April 1991, p. 79
1186. *Have a Good Day*, Nov. 1993, p. 3
1187. *Houston Chronicle*, April 27, 1995, p. 17D
1188. Bob Reccord, Leighton Ford Evangelism Leadership Seminar, 1991
1189. *Christian Reader*, Sept./Oct. 1992, p. 40
1190. *King's Treasury of Dynamic Humor*, King Duncan, 1990, p. 19-20
1191. "How to Communicate to Change Lives," Rick Warren, 1992

1192. *Pastor's Professional Research Service*, Jan./Feb. 1994
1193. Author's files
1194. *USA Weekend*, May 1, 1992, p. 21
1195. *NEWSLETTER Newsletter*, Nov. 1992, p. 4
1196. "Solitaire," Gene Appel, Seeds Tape Ministry, July 24, 1994
1197. *Reader's Digest*, June 1991, p. 73
1198. John Paite, Innovative Church Growth Conference, 1994
1199. *Christian Reader*, July/Aug. 1991, p. 40
1200. Author's files
1201. *Parade*, Aug. 16, 1992
1202. *Reader's Digest*, July 1992, p. 62
1203. Ibid, date unknown
1204. Contributed by Will Passmore
1205. *Reader's Digest*, Jan. 1989, p. 50
1206. *Saturday Evening Post*, May 1993, p. 36
1207. Author's files
1208. Author's files
1209. "A Hunger for Healing," Keith Miller, Seeds Tape Ministry, Jan. 19, 1992
1210. *Reminisce*, March/April 1993, p. 60
1211. *Rotarian*, Jan. 1993, p. 72
1212. *Crossroads*, Vol. 1 No. 5, p. 3
1213. Contributed by Lauretta Reynolds
1214. *Reader's Digest*, May 1992, p. 72
1215. *Christian Parenting Today*, Nov./Dec. 1991, p. 106
1216. *Houston Post*, May 14, 1994, p. E-4
1217. *Houston Chronicle*, June 12, 1992
1218. Ibid, June 20, 1995, p. 6D
1219. *Family Circus*, March 6, 1993
1220. Author's files
1221. *Have a Good Day*, Oct. 1991
1222. "The Sermon on the Amount," Heidi Husted, *Preaching Today*, Tape 122
1223. *Executive Speechwriter Newsletter*, Vol. 8 No. 2
1224. *Christian Reader*, May/June 1992, p. 23
1225. *Houston Post*, May 2, 1991
1226. *The Purpose-Driven Church*, Rick Warren, Feb. 26, 1993
1227. Adapted from *Brian's Lines*, March/April 1994
1228. *Christian Parenting Today*, July/Aug. 1992, p. 67
1229. *Humorous Notes, Quotes, and Anecdotes*, Leslie & Bernice Flynn, 1973, p. 27
1230. Adapted from Leith Anderson, author of *Dying for Change*
1231. *Houston Chronicle*, Jan. 9, 1993, p. 10C
1232. Author's files
1233. *Saturday Evening Post*, Sept./Oct. 1992, p. 20
1234. *Reader's Digest*, May 1990
1235. Adapted from *Reader's Digest*, April 1991, p. 115
1236. James Merritt, Great Hills Men's Conference
1237. *Seven Worlds Publishing*
1238. *Houston Chronicle*, Sept. 25, 1995
1239. *Saturday Evening Post*, Jan./Feb. 1993, p. 100
1240. *Illustrations for Biblical Preaching*, Michael Green, ed., 1989, p. 57
1241. "Solitaire," Gene Appel, Seeds Tape Ministry, July 24, 1994
1242. *Our Daily Bread*, Feb. 6, 1992
1243. *Home Life*, Nov. 1991, p. 29
1244. *Bits & Pieces*, April 30, 1992, p. 19
1245. *Winning Walk*, Ed Young
1246. *Mature Living*, May 1992, p. 48
1247. *Injoy Life Club*, John Maxwell, March 1993
1248. *Reader's Digest*, June 1992, p. 102
1249. *Houston Chronicle*, July 16, 1995
1250. Ibid, April 27, 1995, p. 16D; *U.S. News & World Report*, March 7, 1994, p. 92
1251. *Reminisce*, March/April 1993, p. 60

1252. *Crossroads*, Vol. 1 No. 2, p. 6

1253. *Houston Chronicle*, Feb. 21, 1993

1254. *HomeLife*, Aug. 1994, p. 63

1255. *King's Treasury of Dynamic Humor*, King Duncan, 1990, p. 53

1256. "Behold the What?" Charles Swindoll, Orlando Conference 1992

1257. *The Phone's for You*, Norman Whan, 1988

1258. *Seven Worlds Publishing*, May/June 1991

1259. *Pastor's Professional Research Service*, Nov./Dec. 1991

1260. *Mature Living*, May 1992, p. 49

1261. *Reader's Digest*, Jan. 1989, p. 49

1262. *Rotarian*, Nov. 1992, p. 72

1263. *Houston Chronicle*, May 1 & 3, 1992

1264. Author's files

1265. *Baptist Standard*, June 7, 1995, p. 7

1266. *Reminisce*, Jan./Feb. 1994, p. 61

1267. *The Best of Grandparents' Brag Board*, Pregel & Riley, 1993, p. 47

1268. *Houston Chronicle*, Oct. 19, 1995, p. 8D

1269. *Mature Living*, April 1995, p. 7

1270. *Reader's Digest*, April 1991, p. 67

1271. *The Best of Grandparents Brag Board*, Judy Pregel & Robin Riley, 1993, p. 22

1272. *Reader's Digest*, Aug. 1992, p. 71

1273. *Watching the World Go By*, W. E. Thorn, 1987, p. 68

1274. *Inc.*, Sept. 1991, p. 13

1275. *Reminisce*, Premiere Issue, 1991, p. 46

1276. *Reminisce Extra,* Collector's Edition, p. 59

1277. *Herschel Hobbs Commentary*, July-Sept. 1995, p. 126

1278. *Houston Post*, March 17, 1992, p. D-7

1279. "The Lostness of Humankind," Ravi Zacharias, *Preaching Today*, Tape 118

# Summary Index
## *Motivational Stories*

| | |
|---|---|
| **Anxiety** | Physicians and ministers address adverse affects of anxiety. |
| **Apples of Gold** | Woman left unfinished suicide note: "They said . . ." |
| **Aptitude vs. Attitude** | Valedictorians aren't always successful. |
| **Arguing** | Hot-head wins argument with boss, never gets promotion. |
| **Armageddon** | Boxer knocked out in four seconds parallels Armageddon. |
| **Assumptions** | Lady eats man's cookies in airport, assuming they're hers. |
| **Atheistic Concession** | O'Hair concedes decline of atheism. |
| **Atonement** | Jesus' death proves we're not just "marginal offenders." |
| | Medical missionary injects self with disease to find a cure. |
| **Audio/Visual Faith** | A verbal witness that accompanies a Christian lifestyle. |
| **Authority** | Margaret Thatcher says you can't tell people you're powerful. |
| | Battleship captain ordered lighthouse to change its course. |
| **Availability** | Michelangelo didn't say, "I don't do ceilings." |
| **Awesome Victory** | Georgia Tech beat Cumberland football team 222–0. |
| **Backdoor Reminder** | Churches have trouble closing the back door. |
| **Backsliding** | Hymn writer mourns his backslidden condition. |
| **Bad Habits** | Bad habits are the unlocked door to failure. |
| **Baptism** | Woman takes picture of baptistry and calls it a "pool-pit." |
| **Baptisms** | Statistics on the world's population growth. |
| **Basketball with Purpose** | Sport invented with spiritual purpose. |
| **Behavioral Modification** | Natives chose death rather than change. |
| | Eighty percent require a relationship to change. |
| **Bible** | Kay Arthur founded "Precepts" after personal tragedy. |
| | Thomas Jefferson picked the Bible as a primary textbook. |
| **Bible Reading** | Terry Anderson found strength in the Bible while a hostage. |
| | To read the entire Bible takes twelve minutes a day for one year. |
| **Bible Shortage** | Bible funding is the greatest need of missionaries. |
| **Bible Study** | Hudson Taylor reads Bible for fortieth time. |
| **Biblical Apathy** | Mahatma Gandhi noted apathy of Christians toward Bible. |
| **Biblical Application** | Woman never hears a sermon that applies to her. |
| **Biblical Authority** | Bibles printed in Voltaire's home after his death. |
| **Biblical Illiteracy** | Church can't answer, "Who destroyed Jericho's wall?" |
| **Big Biblical Bang** | NASA satellite affirms biblical account of creation. |
| **Big Fish Story** | Deacon hooks $20,000 fish; sends pastor to mission field. |
| **Biggest Fears** | *U.S. News & World Report* reveals Americans biggest fears. |
| **Biodegradability** | Marilyn vos Savant: "Remember, we're all biodegradable." |
| **Birthdays** | Birthdays are nice, but too many of them will kill you! |
| **Bob** | "Bob" becomes a Christian and an international influence. |
| **Body of Death** | Term comes from sentence of carrying corpse until death. |
| **Born Against** | "Some people are born again, and some are born against!" |
| **Boundaries** | Research shows children play better with a fenced playground. |
| **Bowling Ball Booze** | Some party-goers drink from bowling balls. |
| **Brevity of Life** | Henry Kissinger is surprised by how quickly life passes. |
| **Brotherly Love** | Boy gives transfusion to his sister, thinks he will die. |
| **Bullet Hole Clothing** | Man sells clothes with bullet holes in them. |

| | |
|---|---|
| **Church Membership** | Eighty percent of "new" members come from another church. |
| **Church Purpose** | Peter Drucker says the church should not be "non-profit." |
| **Circumstances** | Life is 10 percent what happens, 90 percent how I react. |
| | Couple marries during 1992 Los Angeles riots. |
| | Woman wins $10.2 million the day after her divorce. |
| **Clean Hands** | Unclean hands and hearts are deadly. |
| **Clear Conscience** | John Wesley told friend he's ready for Christ's return. |
| | "There is no pillow as soft as a clear conscience." |
| **Cohabitation** | Living together before marriage leads to 50 percent higher divorce rate. |
| **Commercials** | Advertisers use strategy of Deuteronomy 6. |
| **Commitment** | Jimmy Johnson says victory comes when people do their best. |
| | Store in Salt Lake for Mormon missionaries. |
| | President Kennedy talks of tossing hat over the wall. |
| **Commitments** | When you say yes to one thing, you say no to another. |
| **Committees** | "If you see a snake, kill it. Don't appoint a committee on snakes." |
| **Common Sense** | Bill Moyers wished for "a sudden epidemic of common sense." |
| **Communication** | Divorce lawyers agree bad communication causes divorce. |
| | Dad unsuccessfully explains to son why apples turn brown. |
| | Never be afraid to state the obvious. |
| | Peter Drucker: "Hear what isn't being said." |
| | Ten Commands use 297 words, cabbage pricing uses 15,629. |
| | There are two kinds of people who don't say much. |
| **Communism** | Billy Graham said Russia did not obliterate religion. |
| **Comparing** | Comparison is the favorite indoor sport of Christians. |
| **Compassion** | Doctors advised to take acting classes. |
| | Alzheimer's victim asked spouse, "Do you want me?" |
| | Children disrupt subway until riders learn their mom just died. |
| | President Reagan: "I don't find compassion a bad precedent." |
| **Complaints** | Lady claims Daylight Savings Time burned up her lawn. |
| **Compliments** | Editor's compliment inspired Charles Dickens to write. |
| **Compromise** | Boy Scouts say their values aren't for sale. |
| **Con"fax"ion** | Italy's church fair offers confessional fax machine. |
| **Conflict Resolution** | Hot heads and cold hearts never solved anything. |
| | Angry man cut off his finger and mailed it to official. |
| **Conformity** | Farmer grew pumpkin to look like two-gallon jug. |
| **Conscience** | "Mommy tellin' you not to do somethin' but she isn't there." |
| | Boy defines conscience as "feeling bad when you kick girls." |
| **Consistency** | Inconsistent dieting more dangerous than being overweight. |
| **Constitution** | Contradictions of morality and legislation in America. |
| **Convenience** | Phone company earns two million by dialing for customers. |
| **Conviction** | Standing in the middle of the road is very dangerous. |
| **Cooperation** | It takes 300 muscles just to stand still. |
| | Southern Seminary financially supports Southwestern Seminary. |
| **Corporate Purpose** | Purpose statement of Chick-fil-A involves glorifying God. |

| | |
|---|---|
| **Discipleship** | Bank is robbed during crime prevention meeting. |
| | Ninety-seven percent of disciples are made, not born. |
| | Baseball player's motto: "Go hard or go home!" |
| | Children need two pats on the back. |
| **Disobedience** | At Houston zoo, people disobey signs and hurt alligators. |
| **Disposition** | Clergymen I knew looked and acted like undertakers. |
| **Distractions** | Deion Sanders left football game to fix his earring. |
| **Divine Protection** | Angels saved a missionary in the New Hebrides Islands. |
| **Divine Retraction** | Newspaper error says God "resigns" instead of reigns. |
| **Divorce** | Statistics prove children are the big losers in divorce. |
| | Eighty percent in America marry for life. |
| **Doctor's Orders** | More than half of all patients don't follow doctor's orders |
| **Domestic Violence** | During Vietnam war 54,000 women were murdered in U.S. |
| **Doubt** | John Wesley doubted his salvation. |
| **Dreams** | Some dream of accomplishment; others stay awake, do it. |
| **Drink Offering** | Missionaries poisoned to test validity of their message. |
| **Drug Prevention** | Parents who model Christ have fewer problems with kids. |
| **Drunken Driving** | In Malaysia spouse must also go to jail. |
| | One-quarter of auto insurance goes for drunk-driving claims. |
| **Dumpster Dining** | Video for homeless called *The Fine Art of Dumpster Dining.* |
| **Easter** | Church bells at Easter cause Napoleon to retreat. |
| **Easter Celebration** | Sangster mourns that he has no voice to shout, "He is risen!" |
| **Easter Eggs** | Terminally ill child shows empty egg has message of Easter. |
| **Easter Humor** | Church would tell jokes on day after Easter. |
| **Easter Lily** | Flower symbolizes trumpet heralding resurrection. |
| **Easy Street** | Dead-end street in Hawaii is named "Easy Street." |
| **Education** | Harvard was founded to train ministers. |
| **Effort** | There's no traffic jam on the second mile. |
| | Pathologist has never seen a worn out brain. |
| **Egotism** | At least egotists don't talk about other people. |
| **Emotions** | Plane crashed because pilot "felt" gauges were wrong. |
| | Child needs Snoopy band-aid for hurt feelings. |
| **Encouragement** | Solzhenitsyn strengthened by fellow prisoner drawing a cross. |
| | Lincoln died with a letter of praise in his pocket. |
| | Teacher helps misfit boy become a doctor. |
| | "Man doesn't live by bread alone, he needs buttering up." |
| | Leonard Bernstein's father didn't encourage him. |
| **Envy** | Envy: counting another's blessings instead of one's own! |
| **Eternal Life** | H. L. Hunt "traded the here, for the hereafter." |
| | Steve McQueen found hope in Christ before dying of cancer. |
| | Child quotes John 3:16 as, "live happily ever after." |
| **Eternal Rewards** | Widow's coins worth $4,800,000,000,000,000,000,000,000. |
| **Ethically Challenged** | New way to say "dishonest." |
| **Euthanasia** | Suicide manual becomes a best-seller. |
| **Evangelical Warning** | YMCA started with evangelistic zeal but later drifted. |

| | |
|---|---|
| **Family** | Ninety-six percent would take pay cut for more family time. |
| | Research yields six characteristics of strong families. |
| | The concepts of family were not human inventions. |
| | Gallup says Americans are feeling stronger about the family. |
| | No one at death said, "I wish I'd spent more time at the office." |
| **Family Feud** | Feud between Hatfields and McCoys originally about a hog. |
| **Family Rental** | In Japan, "rented" personnel visit relatives of busy people. |
| **Family Resemblance** | Picture of Alamo hero is actually portrait of his nephew. |
| **Fatalism** | James Dean: "Live fast, die young, leave a good-lookin' corpse." |
| **Father's Day** | Father's Day card says fatherhood is a lot like golf. |
| | A Father's Day poem. |
| | History of Father's Day. |
| **Father's Perspective** | Pictures of birthplace and cemetery keep perspective. |
| **Fatherhood** | Fatherlessness affects as many as three of four teen suicides. |
| | Boys argue over prestige of dads; one says, "My dad knows God!" |
| | One size of fathering does not fit all. |
| | The best thing fathers can spend on their children is time. |
| | Children need to see dad love mom. |
| | Fathers average thirty-seven seconds a day with their children. |
| **Fatherly Example** | "I didn't know what God looked like, so I drew my daddy." |
| **Fatherly Love** | Father and son die together on a fishing trip in Alaska. |
| **Fathers** | "You're better than just a father. You're a DADDY!" |
| | Over 20 percent of children live without a male figure. |
| | "Success is knowing which appointments to keep." |
| **Fear** | Remember that everyone you meet is afraid of something. |
| **Feast** | Olympic food supply compared to Heaven's wedding feast. |
| **Fighting** | Never fight with ugly people; they have nothing to lose. |
| **Financial Contentment** | Most want $8,000–$11,000 more per year. |
| **Financial Planning** | Willie Nelson: "It's more fun if we don't plan." |
| **Financial Woes** | Woman wins one million dollars but has cancer. |
| **Flexibility** | Edgar Bergen became a famous ventriloquist accidentally. |
| **Foreign Missions** | Proportionately, India sends more missionaries than U.S. |
| **Forgiveness** | Father writes daughter who he thinks is pregnant. |
| | Mechanic causes crash, pilot forgives him. |
| | Forgiveness a good idea until you have something to forgive. |
| | Israeli widow gives husband's heart to Palestinian. |
| | Freeway on-ramps provide a lesson in forgiveness. |
| | Japanese pilot who attacked Pearl Harbor became a Christian. |
| **Fornication** | Birth rate soars in high school with free condoms. |
| **Freedom** | Few prisoners would gamble with general's offer of freedom. |
| | Pope says freedom is "the right to do what we ought." |
| **Friends** | Thief wants valuables, victim gives his friends. |
| **Friendship** | Friendships require mutual patience. |
| **Fudging** | Term for deception comes from British Captain Fudge. |
| **Funeral Custom** | Black Muslim funeral custom of eating candy by casket. |

| | |
|---|---|
| Guilt | Some people are travel agents for guilt trips. |
| Guilty as Charged | Two criminals raise their hands in court to confess. |
| Guilty Conscience | Twelve men leave country after receiving "all is discovered." |
| Happiness | Happiness is not circumstances, but attitudes. |
| | Gallup: 6–10 percent of Americans are committed Christians. |
| | Vast difference between Mother Teresa and Madonna. |
| Healing Attitude | Doctor: "I look upon disease from the curative standpoint." |
| Health | "Godlessness may be harmful to your health." |
| Heaven | Little girl sees stars as "wrong side of heaven." |
| | Emerson: "We can get along without the world." |
| Heaven Can Wait | Man wants to know if we can "just mess around" in heaven. |
| Heavenly Father | Bus driver picks up his son in middle of the block. |
| Hell | "If we neglect bad news, some people won't listen to good." |
| | Billy Graham: "Would you fly on a plane with a 10 percent chance of crashing?" |
| | The safest road to hell is the gradual one. |
| Heritage | Patrick Henry's will bequeathed to his children faith in Christ. |
| Heroes | Gallup says majority of teenagers lack a role model. |
| Holiday Feasts | Each year Americans gain 1.1 billion pounds. |
| Holiness | Same steel makes cheap horseshoes or expensive watch springs. |
| Hollywood | Survey shows Hollywood's values. |
| Hollywood Morals | Examples show detachment from America's true values. |
| Holy Spirit | It is possible to operate our lives apart from his control. |
| | In *Ben Hur*, director makes sure actor wins chariot race. |
| | If the Holy Spirit left, 95 percent would go unchanged. |
| | Without Holy Spirit we may be spectacular, but not miraculous. |
| Home | Child says we have a home, just no house. |
| | Jonathan Edwards: "Every Christian family is a church." |
| | The most influential of all educational factors is the home. |
| Home Life | "If your Christianity doesn't work at home, don't export it." |
| Home Missions | Annie Armstrong responded to a sea of immigrants. |
| Homeless Help | Pre-teen uses Christmas money to buy socks for homeless. |
| Homosexuality | Monogamous homosexuals are one-tenth of 1 percent of American population. |
| | U.S. spends more tax dollars on AIDS than cancer. |
| Honesty | Chaplain finds student only attends chapel to meet women. |
| Honeymoon Tip | Tradition: why a man carries his bride across the threshold. |
| Hope | "When a man has lost God, ain't nothing to do but jump." |
| | Medical team agrees hope is essential. |
| | Boy waits for gum on escalator handrail to come back. |
| | Plans for a new dam caused town to stop maintenance. |
| Hopelessness | Man jumps off Golden Gate Bridge with daughter. |
| Hospitality | Most influential question to visitors: "Join us for dinner?" |
| Hostage Situation | Woman calls police thinking husband is hostage; just TV. |
| Housewife Comeback | Fastest-growing household includes stay-at-home mom. |

| | |
|---|---|
| **Judging** | Critic says Babe Ruth ruined career when he gave up pitching. |
| **Judgment** | Men will be born again, or wish they'd never been born at all. |
| **Justice** | Thieves sue innocent victims and win. |
| **Kissing Benefits** | Marital kissing has physical and financial benefits. |
| **Kneeling** | Joni Eareckson Tada looks to the day she can kneel. |
| **Koinonitis** | Disease: too much fellowship, not enough mission activity. |
| **Laughter** | Children laugh 400 times a day, adults just 15. |
| **Lawsuits** | Today, Adam and Eve would sue the snake. |
| | Inmate sues himself for five million dollars. |
| **Leadership** | Five syndromes that hinder energy and effectiveness. |
| | Doctor proves theory about anesthesia by operating on self. |
| | Survey shows leaders are out of step with followers' desires. |
| | Less than one in four Biblical leaders finished well. |
| | Best test of leadership: is anyone following? |
| **Learning** | The things worth learning, you learn after you know it all. |
| **Legacy** | Tombstone of James Dobson, Sr.: "He Prayed." |
| **Letters to God** | Israel post office receives letters addressed to God. |
| **Lies** | Half-right is not right at all. |
| | Iraqis were told Marines had to kill their own relatives. |
| | It is twice as hard to crush a half-truth as a whole lie. |
| **Life** | Don't fear your life will end; fear it will never begin. |
| | Emerson: "People always getting ready to live but never living." |
| **Life's Work** | Lincoln died just five days after the Civil War ended. |
| | "Be ashamed to die until you have won a victory for humanity." |
| **Lifestyle Evangelism** | Some reject Christ because they met a Christian. |
| **Light and Darkness** | Scientists show power of reflecting sunlight from space. |
| **Listening** | A poor listener seldom hears a good sermon. |
| | Three primary elements that get our attention. |
| | The inner ear demands the most bodily energy. |
| **Listening Skills** | Roosevelt told inattentive guests he killed his grandmother. |
| **Listening to God** | Lost watch in icehouse is found by being quiet. |
| **Living Water** | Sailors nearly died of thirst while surrounded by fresh water. |
| **Loneliness** | Orphan left note: "To whoever finds this—I love you!" |
| | Twenty-two percent of Americans eat dinner alone. |
| **Loopholes** | Near death, W. C. Fields looked in the Bible for "loopholes." |
| **Lord's Prayer** | "Our Father . . . in New Haven, how'd you know my name?" |
| **Lord's Supper** | Research shows grape juice can help the heart. |
| **Lotto Bucks** | Texans give more to lottery than they do to churches. |
| **Love** | "The greatest privilege of my life is taking care of your mother." |
| | The one who loves least controls the relationship. |
| **Lying** | Ninety-one percent of Americans lie routinely. |
| **Marathon Living** | Dying man becomes a marathon runner at ninety years old. |
| **Marital Responsibility** | In Russia, best man must guarantee marriage. |
| **Marriage** | "A good marriage is made up of two good forgivers." |
| | Ask yourself, "What is it like being married to me?" |

| | |
|---|---|
| **Mummy's Burial** | Corpse buried after sixty-six-year stay in mortician's closet. |
| **My Fair Lady** | Eliza Doolittle cries, "Don't tell me you love me, show me!" |
| **New Age** | Professor proposes we blow up the moon. |
| **New Name** | Teenager changed his name to "Trout Fishing In America." |
| **New Year's Resolution** | Turning over new leaf twice leaves you where you started. |
| **Nintendo** | U.S. missions gifts equal Nintendo purchases. |
| **Numbering Our Days** | A lifetime calculated into single-day equivalent. |
| **Obedience** | Man killed nineteen minutes after citation for no seat belt. |
| | The part of the Bible you truly believe is the part you obey. |
| | Some read from the Reversed Bible. |
| **Obstacles** | Gold medalist wore corrective shoes as a child. |
| **Occult** | Salem now has three thousand who practice witchcraft. |
| **Offering Applause** | Korea and Nigeria applaud before taking the offering. |
| **Open Minded** | Swiss lost watch industry market share because they rejected the quartz watch. |
| **Opinions** | Harry Reasoner predicted *60 Minutes* "wouldn't fly." |
| **Opportunistic** | Broken escalator sign: "This escalator temporarily a stairway." |
| **Opportunities** | A wise man makes more opportunities than he finds. |
| **Opportunity** | Bell's patent for the telephone came hours before another. |
| | Everyone can start now and have a new ending. |
| | Levi Strauss quit making tents and made jeans. |
| | When opportunity knocks many are out looking for four-leaf clovers. |
| **Optimism** | Harvard study shows healthy advantages of optimism. |
| **Others** | "Entire population, with one exception, composed of others." |
| **Outreach** | Of all new sales, 80 percent are closed on the fifth sales call. |
| | Fifty-four percent of American Christians aren't inviting people to church. |
| | Eighty-six percent find Jesus as a result of a friend or relative. |
| | Advertising strategy uses "six sticks." |
| **Overload** | "God put me on earth to do certain things . . . I'm so far behind I'll never die." |
| **Pace of Life** | Dobson gives new meaning to Maslow's Hierarchy of Needs. |
| **Paradigm Shift** | Little boy on Mickey Mantle: "Daddy, that's an old man." |
| **Parental Advice** | Enjoy your kids while they're on your side. |
| **Parental Encouragement** | Most teens have a good relationship with parents. |
| **Parenting** | When we realize our parents were right, our children think we're wrong. |
| | Dr. James Dobson fasts one day a week for his children. |
| | Live so your children see an example, not an object lesson. |
| | Parenting compared to being a general contractor. |
| | Expert notes impact of parenting one generation well. |
| | Socrates quote on work versus family. |
| | While providing our kids what we didn't have, we can neglect what we did have. |

| | |
|---|---|
| **Possessions** | Mother Teresa: "If it takes more than fifteen minutes to pack, you have too much." |
| **Potential** | Don't look too soon for what a child will later become. |
| | One of the greatest sins is not reaching the potential God placed in us. |
| | James Whistler said a blank canvas wasn't valuable—yet. |
| | Dead Sea potash could fertilize the earth for five years. |
| | We were created in God's image, and God is no weakling. |
| **Poverty** | U.S. has spent one billion dollars towards poverty reform. |
| **Prayer** | Study of heart patients shows prayer works. |
| | Church prays for tavern to close; denies responsibility when it burns down. |
| | Behind every work of God you will find a kneeling form. |
| | "While Americans are sleeping, many Koreans have prayed several hours." |
| | Apollo moon missions spent 90 percent of the time off course. |
| | Pioneer sends food and supplies to fire victims, calls it prayer. |
| | Weekly group meets in Uruguay to pray—against Christians. |
| | Woman hears prayer to Jesus for the first time. |
| | At Pentecost they prayed ten days, preached ten minutes; we reverse those proportions. |
| | "Prayer may not change things for you, but it sure changes you for things." |
| | "Prayer without action is hypocrisy." |
| | "The biggest non-biblical aspect of praying today is the lack of intercession." |
| | Prayer's power is in the one who hears it, not the one who prays. |
| | The three secrets to successful ministry are prayer, prayer, and more prayer. |
| | We will never have time for prayer; we must make time. |
| **Prayer Experiment** | Minister proposed a "Thirty-Day Prayer Experiment." |
| **Premarital Counseling** | "A wedding doesn't equip one for marriage." |
| **Preaching** | One of the best proofs for Biblical inspiration is preaching. |
| | Preaching without application is like shouting to a drowning man, "Swim!" |
| | The devil will let a preacher prepare a sermon. |
| | Use me not because it's the hour, but because I have a message. |
| | "What in the world are you trying to do to these people?" |
| **Prenuptial Agreement** | Defined as, "I love you almost as much as my money." |
| **Pride** | Modern parallel of Pharisee and Publican praying. |
| | Captain James Cook killed because he let islanders believe he was a god. |
| | Nothing so needs reforming as other people's habits. |
| | Thief tells store employees he'll return in thirty minutes. |
| | Romanian dictator's song: "I am good, righteous, and holy." |

| | |
|---|---|
| **Responsibility** | "Need a Statue of Responsibility to match Statue of Liberty." |
| | A tired Greyhound bus driver let a passenger drive for him. |
| | Bill Cosby exhorts graduates to, "Get a job." |
| | "Humpty Dumpty was pushed." |
| **Resurrection** | Translator says, "They're never going to believe this." |
| **Retirement** | "Just kicking back in retirement" leads to a funeral in four to seven years. |
| **Revenge** | Several wives get revenge for their husbands' betrayal. |
| **Righteousness** | Chinese character has "lamb" above the pronoun "I." |
| **Risks** | ABC rejected the Cosby Show, and NBC made millions. |
| **Role Model** | Willie Nelson: "Look at everything I do and do the opposite." |
| **Romanian Revolution** | Christians lead in toppling of Romanian government. |
| **Rumors** | Abraham Lincoln's coffin exhumed twice because of rumors. |
| | Christians still worry about a petition defeated in 1975. |
| **Russian Revival** | Large percentage of conversions from atheism. |
| **Sabbath** | Voltaire said Christianity can't be destroyed unless the Sabbath is destroyed. |
| **Sacrifice** | Nancy Kerrigan's family made big sacrifices for her skating. |
| **Sacrificial Love** | Tom Landry's daughter died to give birth. |
| **Safe Sex** | Advocates of condoms say they aren't really safe. |
| **Saint Patrick** | Patrick sent missionaries from Ireland. |
| **Saints and Sinners** | Jesse James was killed by a member of his own gang. |
| **Salt** | Spoiled meat is not the fault of the meat but lack of salt. |
| **Salvation** | Fisherman loses $21,786 because he didn't follow the rules. |
| | Even Billy Graham's works won't save him. |
| | In revival, murderer shouts, "Saved! Saved! Saved!" |
| | Priest died for another in Nazi concentration camp. |
| | Two-thirds accept Christ before age eighteen. |
| **Sandwich Generation** | Adults spend thirty-five years caring for children and parents. |
| **Satan** | Missionary shot huge snake; it destroyed house while dying. |
| | Man takes even chance snakes will bite his wooden leg. |
| **Savior** | Lenin's tomb declared, "He was the savior of the world." |
| **Schedules** | Bus drivers pass bus stops to stay on schedule. |
| **School Prayer** | As long as there are exams, there will be prayer in school. |
| **Scrooge** | The Puritans made it illegal to observe Christmas. |
| **Second Coming** | Greatest comeback in NFL resembles God's final victory. |
| | Pastor predicts end of world but makes future investments. |
| | World won't end for "at least another ten billion years." |
| **Security of Believers** | Net under Golden Gate Bridge prevented deaths. |
| **Selective Listening** | "Most of the stuff we hear is just audible junk mail." |
| **Self Image** | God does not remember us by our mistakes. |
| **Self-Sufficiency** | God drops importance to Americans as their income rises. |
| **Selfishness** | Many listen to WII FM: "What's In It For Me?" |
| **Senior Adults** | Gold medalist credits victory to seventy-six-year-old mentor. |
| **Senior Advice** | Ninety-year-olds tell how they would re-live their lives. |

| | |
|---|---|
| **Spiritual Growth** | Seventy-eight percent achieve success through hard work and determination. |
| | Unlike students, farmers can't cram; neither can Christians. |
| | Iacocca is at his best when climbing the mountain. |
| **Spiritual Hunger** | Corporations spend four billion on New Age Consultants. |
| **Spiritual Immunity** | Like a vaccine, small doses of God create an immunity. |
| **Spiritual Maturity** | "In our country there is spiritual chaos." |
| **Spiritual Needs** | Gallup reveals American's six basic spiritual needs. |
| **Spiritual Rejection** | Archaeologists find Bethsaida. |
| **Spiritual Significance** | Beautician ponders life after Hurricane Andrew. |
| **Spiritual Vacuum** | Dr. Spock sees "dearth of spiritual values." |
| **Spiritual Warfare** | Lightning bolts start from the ground and move upward. |
| | Many think this world is a playground, not a battleground. |
| **Spousal Concern** | Man quits smoking for the sake of his dog, not his wife. |
| **Spousal Responsibility** | "If she wasn't that way before, it's your fault." |
| **Statistics** | Chuck Swindoll gives a humorous look at statistics. |
| **Stealing** | Child dropped from high-rise because he wouldn't steal. |
| **Stepfamilies** | Over 1,300 new stepfamilies are created each day. |
| **Stewardship** | Modern concept for steward is that of a banker. |
| | George Burns: "It's easier to make a paying audience laugh." |
| | How much of God's money will I keep for myself? |
| | "It's the Lord's; I'm not smart enough to make that money." |
| **Strength** | Vietnam vet walked across America on his hands. |
| **Stress** | Like piano strings, people require balanced tension. |
| | Sixty-two percent of Americans experience a great deal of stress at least once a week. |
| | For fast-acting relief, try slowing down. |
| | Chlorine for swimming pool explodes under pressure. |
| **Submission** | Lord, I will receive what you give, lack what you withhold. |
| **Success** | Schwarzkopf says, "Don't repaint the flagpole." |
| | People who excelled only slightly over others in their field. |
| | "Doing your best is more important than being the best." |
| | Business survey shows 62 percent equate success with a happy family. |
| | Success is sweet, but usually has the scent of sweat about it. |
| | There is less to fear from outside competition than from inside inefficiency. |
| | Only place success comes before work is in the dictionary. |
| | Road to success is uphill all the way. |
| **Suffering** | Amy Carmichael: "Wise master never wastes servant's time." |
| | "Plimsoll Mark" shows the capacity a ship can bear. |
| **Suicide** | Most jumpers from Golden Gate bridge used city side. |
| **Superstition** | Rabbit's foot didn't help the rabbit. |
| **Support Groups** | Cancer patients lived twice as long with support groups. |
| **Sweepstakes Winners** | Dead man reached the third stage in sweepstakes. |

| | |
|---|---|
| **Tranquility** | In the ocean all is calm twenty-five feet below the surface. |
| **Transformation** | We should be more like a thermostat than a thermometer. |
| **Treasurer's Report** | Church treasurer deducted tithe from members' money. |
| **Trivializing Death** | Man gives dead mother a beer and a cigarette. |
| **Trust** | Atheists had sign reading, "In God We Trust. Not!" |
| **Truth** | Get your facts first, then distort them as you please. |
| | Smoker quits reading rather than quit smoking. |
| | The truth's not going to hurt you, unless it should. |
| | National Research Council proves subliminal tapes worthless. |
| **Truth Deficit** | In America 52 percent of Christians think truth is relative. |
| **TV Sex** | On TV, 93 percent of sex involves non-married people. |
| **'Twas the Night Before ...** | Second Coming adaptation of poem. |
| **Uncertainty of Life** | The *Titanic*'s Captain was to retire after maiden voyage. |
| **Unconditional Love** | Greg Louganis credits his success to mom's love. |
| **Unity** | Two horses can pull more together than each separately. |
| | Church splits over peg for pastor's hat. |
| **Universalism** | At Urbana, only 37 percent believe "a person who doesn't hear the gospel is lost." |
| | Unitarian minister boasts of openly atheistic members. |
| **Unwed Mothers** | Out-of-marriage births has risen 50 percent since 1980. |
| **Urgency** | "Why didn't you come sooner? My father died seeking truth." |
| **Vacation Bible School** | In 1991, 61,420 recorded professions of faith, etc. |
| **Values** | Thieves broke into a store and switched the price tags. |
| **Verbosity** | President Harrison died after delivering the longest inaugural speech. |
| **Victorious Spirit** | Military dictionary doesn't contain "surrender" or "retreat." |
| **Violence** | Small girl kicked and stoned to death by three-year-old boys. |
| **Vision** | Philip Knight started Nike from his station wagon. |
| **Visions** | Lady claims to see Jesus in Pizza Hut's spaghetti billboard. |
| **Voting** | Greater percentage of people in mental institutions vote than people in "normal" world. |
| **War** | Results of war-torn Cambodia, yesterday and today. |
| **Wealth** | Measured by the things you have for which you would not take money. |
| **Weddings** | Harvard study: spiritual commitment decreases divorce rate. |
| **Weekends** | National survey reveals American's use of weekends. |
| **Weight Loss** | Americans spend $30–$50 billion per year on weight-los. |
| **West Point Advice** | "Don't let what you can't do, interfere with what you can do." |
| **Winning** | Larry Bird: "I put on a uniform to win." |
| **Wisdom** | Every man is foolish at least five minutes a day; don't exceed the limit. |
| **Witnessing** | Cartoon artist shares his faith. |
| | Muhammad Ali is a zealous evangelist for Islam. |
| **Women's Rights** | Harry Truman's thoughts on a woman President. |
| **Word Association** | Child gets caught saying a "television word." |

## Motivational Humor

| | |
|---|---|
| **Bowling Words** | Child fears dad won't reach heaven due to "bowling words." |
| **Box Office Surprise** | Man complains of movie price; told they now have sound. |
| **Bragging Rights** | Farmer to bragging Texan: "I used to have a truck like that." |
| **Brain Dead** | "I don't know if I'll be an uncle or an aunt." |
| **Brains vs. Brawn** | Men dig holes, then fill them in because the tree planter is sick. |
| **Breaking Bad News** | "Two of our three children didn't break an arm today." |
| **Card Trick** | "Dad says you're not playing with a full deck." |
| **Christmas Presents** | Hub gives wife gift to make her look "sexy"—an exercise bike. |
| **Clowning Around** | Clown to drunk: "I get paid to be a fool; what's your excuse?" |
| **Coaching Fatigue** | "I left due to illness and fatigue: they were sick and tired of me." |
| **Codependency** | Other people's lives flash before dying woman. |
| **College Concerns** | "They just study, I don't know why they came to college." |
| **Commercial Cleaning** | Woman cleans house during TV commercials. |
| **Communication** | "My wife talks to herself, but she thinks I'm listening." |
| | "Sure we can talk, just don't block the T.V." |
| **Complaining** | Pastor spends two hours listening to health problems. |
| **Confidence** | Ty Cobb told reporter he could still bat .290 at age seventy. |
| **Conflict Resolution** | Churchill told lady he'd drink arsenic if she were his wife. |
| **Consequences** | "If David has to live with the consequences can I have his room?" |
| **Contemporary Preaching** | Pastor plans to take a church into the nineteenth century. |
| **Contentment** | Man with seven children is more content than man with seven million dollars. |
| **Cooperation** | "As long as I'm around ain't nothin gonna be unanimous." |
| **Couch Potato** | Wife notes life is a do-it-yourself deal. |
| **Couch Potatoes** | Children of couch potatoes are "tater-tots." |
| **Credit Cards** | "I'd like to pay off my Master Card. Do you take Visa?" |
| **Cuckoo Cover-Up** | Son cuckoos for dad after violating curfew. |
| **Daddy** | Kids think they're getting rid of Daddy, not hamster, Danny. |
| **Daily Devotions** | "Mommy, you forgot to ask Jesus to help you be nice today." |
| **Dangerous Crowd** | Boy thinks people in church killed Jesus. |
| **Dangerous Preacher** | Child thinks lapel mic is a leash. |
| **Death Bed Reflections** | Dying man realizes his wife is bad luck. |
| **Depravity** | "Mama, have I blown my cookies?" |
| **Desserts** | It's "stressed" spelled backwards. |
| **Disappointing Cure** | Psychiatric patient goes from being Joan of Arc to nobody. |
| **Discernment** | Coach looks for player who is knocking everybody down. |
| | Wife concedes men have better judgment because she picked him, but he picked her. |
| **Disgruntled Member** | It doesn't take much to make him happy or mad. |
| **Dishonest Gain** | Three friends asked to throw money in friend's grave. |
| **Disposition** | "He can be nice when he wants to. . . just never wants to!" |
| **Doctor's Orders** | Wife tells hub he'll die (she won't follow doctor's orders to pamper him). |
| | "Take one pill as often as you can afford it." |
| **Doctors** | Doc making house calls equals Ph.D. selling vacuum cleaners. |

| | |
|---|---|
| **Golf** | Golfer won't play with friend who cheats. |
| **Golfing Buddies** | Golfer with bad eyes plays with absent-minded spotter. |
| **Golfing Hiccups** | Golfer thrown off by caddie's hiccups. |
| **Golfing Widow** | Want ad: "Lost, golfing husband and dog. Reward for dog." |
| **Good Intentions** | Wrong passenger is thrown off the train. |
| **Good Losers** | "A good loser is a man playing golf with his boss." |
| **Good News/Bad News** | Sanctuary is so full, the Fire Marshall can't get in. |
| **Good Samaritan** | Man tells Peter good deed from forty seconds ago got him to heaven. |
| **Gossip Column** | Three ministers in support group: alcoholic, gambler, gossip. |
| **Grace** | Man dreams he's behind Mother Teresa at the Judgment. |
| **Grandparents** | Man thanks woman for not showing pictures of grandchildren. |
| **Grapevine Gossip** | Woman criticizes pastor; deacon says she just repeats others. |
| **Green Bananas** | Old-timer says, "At my age I don't even buy green bananas." |
| **Headache Remedy** | Child tells pastor his headache means his head is empty. |
| **Health Insurance** | "I am not sick, never was sick, and will never get sick." |
| **Healthy Self Esteem** | Boy tells mom, "I was thanking God for me!" |
| **Hearing Check** | Man asks wife if she can hear him; he can't hear her answer. |
| **Hearing Test** | Granddaddy passes all of car inspection except hearing test. |
| **Heaven** | Boy thinks he must miss heaven to get home on time. |
| **Heavenly Suggestion Box** | Some people aren't happy unless they complain. |
| **Heavenly Wedding** | Couple can't divorce because Heaven has no lawyers. |
| **Helping Zeke** | Boy says he's helping his brother "do nothing." |
| **Heroes** | Student lists football players as eleven greatest Americans. |
| **History Lesson** | Student thinks he's famous because teacher says he's history. |
| | Child claims her teacher attended the first thanksgiving. |
| **Holiday Spirit** | Teenager tells mom take the day off—do dishes tomorrow. |
| **Holiday Travel** | Little boys who lie fly half price. |
| **Hollow Threat** | "My dad can beat up your dad." "Big deal. So can my mom!" |
| **Home Improvement** | Man ties portable phone to the wall. |
| **Home Library** | Encyclopedias no longer needed, wife knows everything. |
| **Homesickness** | Only kids who have dogs at home are homesick at camp. |
| **Honest Confession** | "Why aren't you working?" "I didn't see you coming." |
| **Honest Workout** | Results from a new fitness program: aches and pains. |
| **Honesty** | Grandson notes wrinkle cream doesn't work. |
| **Honey-Do** | Minister is thankful all carpet cleaners are checked out. |
| **Honking Samaritan** | Woman asks rude driver to help start car while she honks. |
| **Hourly Wages** | Woman makes repairman rake to finish one-hour service call. |
| **House** | Parents overhear kids "play house" by fretting over the bills. |
| **Husband Swapping** | Little difference in husbands, so might as well keep first one. |
| **Hypocrite** | Hypocrite says there's too much sex and violence on his VCR. |
| **Ice Cream to Go** | Nervous woman sees Paul Newman, puts ice cream in purse. |
| **Impoverished Pastor** | "Daddy said you're the poorest preacher he's ever heard." |
| **Income Tax** | Einstein: "Most difficult thing to understand is income tax." |
| **Inerrancy** | Man badgers woman about literal story of Jonah. |

| | |
|---|---|
| **Ministerially Speaking** | What does a minister say when he hits his thumb with a hammer? |
| **Miracles** | Teenager changes details of miracles to make it believable. |
| **Mom and Rover** | Teenage son hugs dog but won't kiss mom. |
| **Mom's Favorite Book** | Child brings *TV Guide* for visiting pastor to read. |
| **Mom's Stress** | "She gets mad at little things . . . like children." |
| **Mommy Noises** | "Sheep goes baaa. Cow . . . mooo. Mama . . . no, no, no!" |
| **Money** | Jack Benny has to think about robber's threat, "Your money or your life." |
| **Monogamy** | "A man can only have one wife. That's called monotony." |
| **Motherhood** | Private waves to mother after sergeant orders him to stop. |
| | Mother would have children again, but not the same ones. |
| | Son promises to buy his mom an electric chair. |
| | The joy of motherhood: when all the children are in bed. |
| | Girl thinks her mother is a slave after dad tells a story. |
| **Mothers** | "Mothers! They're never around when you need them." |
| **Namesake** | "I'm glad my name is Ashley, because that's what everyone calls me." |
| **Narcissism** | Narcissist football player says, "My name's not John!" |
| **Nativity Seat** | "Here's baby Jesus in his car seat!" |
| **Negative Imaging** | Man convinces himself a farmer won't loan him a car jack. |
| **Nest Egg** | Nest egg vanished because the old hen got tired of sitting on it. |
| **New Year's Resolutions** | Couple thinks up resolutions for each other. |
| **Nice Comeback** | Rabbi promises to eat ham at priest's wedding. |
| **No Win Situation** | Wife asks husband, "Why'd you stop brushing your teeth?" |
| **Noah Syndrome** | Eating two helpings of everything. |
| **Obligatory Prayer** | GA says she's "supposed" to pray for seminary president. |
| **Old Age** | Inside every older person is a younger person wondering, "What happened?" |
| | Boy tells eighty-six-year-old, "You're old enough to be dead!" |
| | Man is so old, he knew the Dead Sea when it was just sick. |
| **Omnipresence** | Burglar is surprised by a Doberman named Jesus. |
| **Opposition** | Old man says he's seen lots of change; been against all of it. |
| **Optimism** | An optimist thinks the "E" on a gas gauge means "Enough." |
| **Optimist** | Pastor calls problems "opportunities;" deacon notes they have many "opportunities." |
| **Optimistic Hunters** | Hunters think they're rich when surrounded by wolves. |
| **Out-of-Body Experience** | Doctor sees why fat man had an out-of-body experience. |
| **Out of Shape** | "I have the body of a man half my age . . . he's in terrible shape." |
| **Out of Sight/Out of Mind** | Seated man closes his eyes while ladies stand on the bus. |
| **Over My Dead Body** | "I'm going to get a motorcycle as soon as my dad dies." |
| **Overpriced Church** | Child during the offering; "You mean we gotta pay for this?" |
| **Painful Diet** | "If you cheat on your diet you're only hurting yourself!" |
| **Paper Work** | Woman fills out paperwork just to visit a friend at hospital. |
| **Pardon Me** | Hospital patient curses before learning roommate's a preacher. |

| | |
|---|---|
| **Retirement** | "Twice as much husband and half as much money." |
| **Revival Fatigue** | Child tells long-winded evangelist, "I want to go home." |
| **Rock-a-Bye Baby** | New parents see who can pretend to be asleep the longest. |
| **Rolex Ripoff** | Yuppie loses his arm in a wreck; mourns the loss of his Rolex. |
| **Running on Empty** | Teenager out of gas:, "Will it hurt to drive it home like that?" |
| **Satisfaction Guaranteed** | "After the circus you'll never be satisfied with church." |
| **Scrooge** | "Now the church is trying to horn in on Christmas!" |
| **Season Tickets** | Crook breaks into car, leaves season tickets to losing team. |
| **Second Best** | John Madden tells ref he's second-best in the league. |
| **Second Opinion** | Doctor golfs ten strokes lower than patient's blood pressure. |
| **Self-Help** | "I got in touch with my inner self. She's as confused as I am." |
| **Self-Righteous Driving** | Slower drivers are idiots, faster ones are maniacs. |
| **Sermon Notes** | Pastor sees sermon notes; listener wrote, "Don't fall asleep." |
| **Sermonic Anesthesia** | God put Adam to sleep with a sermon. |
| **Sermons** | Paramedics try six church members before finding the dead one. |
| **Shopping** | "You told me to avoid sales, so I bought everything full price." |
| **Side Effects** | "Mad about the cost of your medicine? That's a side effect." |
| **Silent Night** | "Sleep in heavenly peas." |
| **Single Life** | Woman has "husbands to burn." |
| **Single-Hearted Devotion** | Soldier has final letter for several girls. |
| **Sleepless Nights** | Counselor gives couple No-Doz so they won't go to bed mad. |
| **Son-in-Law Mystery** | This idiot fathered the world's smartest grandchildren. |
| **Source of Love** | "We're both in love with the same person—you!" |
| **Spell Check** | Granddaughter goes to the liberry; Nana says library. |
| **Stress Relief** | Abused luggage handler sends rude man's bags to Brazil. |
| **Sunday Morning Rush** | Husband tells his wife she'd look better in the car. |
| **Sweepstakes** | Ed McMahon showed up only to ask directions to neighbor's. |
| **Taxes** | IRS wants to know why any money is left after taxes. |
| **Teenage Crowd Control** | Mother pits sons against each other to find culprit. |
| **Teenage Shopping** | "If my parents like this shirt, can I return it?" |
| **Teenagers** | The best of parenting is no match for ordinary teenagering! |
| **Telephone Etiquette** | "I don't know if he's home, hold on while I ask him." |
| **Ten Yellow Commandments** | Boy says they Commandments might be in the Yellow Pages. |
| **The Epistles** | "The Epistles aren't the Apostles' wives? Whose wives are they?" |
| **The Phone's for You** | Humorous responses to program, "The Phone's for You." |
| **Thunder** | "I'll sleep here with Daddy; you go in there with God." |
| **Tough Course** | After missing golfball four times, "This is a tough course!" |
| **Tricky Teeth** | "Grandma, when will my teeth come in and out like that?" |
| **Truck Driver** | Truck driver runs over motorcycles of discourteous bikers. |
| **TV vs. Books** | "How can you sit there and read with forty channels of TV?" |
| **Umbiblical Cord** | "Babies are connected to their mothers by a biblical cord." |
| **Unresolved Conflict** | Wife plans to live with sister after God kills her husband. |
| **Vacation Bible School** | Boy's enrollment card says, "Brace yourselves!" |
| **Vacation Fatigue** | "You can see the pictures when we get home." |
| **Value** | "Look, Grandma, I'm worthless!" |

# MASTER INDEX